Kickstart Unsupervised Machine Learning

Master Unsupervised Machine Learning Through Pattern Discovery, Clustering, and Dimensionality Reduction to Build Intelligent, Real-World Applications

Dr. Nimrita Koul

www.orangeava.com

First Published: December 2025

Published By: Orange Education Pvt Ltd, AVA®

Address: 9, Daryaganj, Delhi, 110002, India

275 New North Road Islington Suite 1314 London,

N1 7AA, United Kingdom

ISBN (PBK): 978-93-49887-43-5

ISBN (E-BOOK): 978-93-49887-83-1

Scan the QR code to explore our entire catalogue

www.orangeava.com

Dedicated To

Bhagwan Shri Ramana Maharshi

The Saint of Arunachala, Who Saved Me.

About the Author

Dr. Nimrita Koul is an Associate Professor of Computer Science and Engineering in Bengaluru, India's IT hub. She holds a PhD in Machine Learning, and graduated with gold medals in both her Bachelor of Engineering and Master of Technology degrees.

She is the principal investigator of three research projects in Machine Learning and Natural Language Processing funded by the Department of Science and Technology, Government of India. Dr. Koul has authored 35 research articles, four books, and holds a patent. She also consults deep-tech startups worldwide on AI solutions, and regularly contributes to open-source software forums and blogs.

Her work has been recognized with the IBM Generative AI Faculty Award (2024), the NVIDIA Research Accelerator Award (2022), and the NVIDIA Jetson Nano Grant (2020). She is also a Senior Member of IEEE and ACM.

Dr. Koul has actively participated in numerous international workshops and seminars on Machine Learning and Generative AI.

About the Technical Reviewer

Kaushal Singh is an accomplished Data Scientist and Artificial Intelligence (AI) researcher with five years of diverse professional experience. He currently serves as an Assistant Professor and Training and Placement Officer in the Department of Computer Science and Information Technology at the School of Engineering, P. P. Savani University, Surat, Gujarat. Driven by a passion for data and artificial intelligence, he has made significant contributions to the field through impactful research and strong technical expertise.

Throughout his career, he has explored the depths of Data Science and AI, developing advanced skills in Machine Learning, Deep Learning, and Data Analytics. His work includes building state-of-the-art AI models and applying data-driven approaches to solve complex, real-world problems. As both a practitioner and a dedicated researcher, he has authored 13 research papers, holds 5 patents (4 national and 1 international), and has contributed to 6 book chapters published in reputable journals and conferences, contributing meaningfully to the advancement of emerging AI technologies.

His expertise stands out in Natural Language Processing, Computer Vision, and Predictive Analytics. Beyond research, he is also a sought-after technical reviewer, known for his attention to detail and deep domain knowledge. His constructive feedback helps enhance the quality, credibility, and innovation of technical work in Data Science and AI.

With extensive hands-on experience and a relentless commitment to technological progress, Kaushal Singh continues to shape the landscape of Artificial Intelligence and Data Science, fostering innovation, excellence, and meaningful impact in the industry.

Acknowledgments

Authoring this book has been both a challenging and rewarding journey, and I am deeply grateful to many people who made it possible.

I thank my parents, Late Shri Chand Kishen Koul and Smt. Gudhi Dhar Koul, for believing in me. I am also grateful to my sister, Mrs. Amrita Koul Arora, for her constant encouragement; my brother-in-law, Mr. Tarun Arora; and my dearest nephew, Agastya Arora, for their patience and unwavering support throughout this journey. Their love, motivation, and belief in me have been the foundation upon which this book was built.

I also thank my students and colleagues whose curiosity and questions continually inspired me to simplify complex ideas in technical domains. Their feedback shaped much of the practical approach taken in this book.

I acknowledge the support of the Department of Science and Technology, Government of India, whose research grants enabled me to deepen my work in Machine Learning and Natural Language Processing.

I am thankful to my collaborators in academia and industry worldwide for their insightful discussions and encouragement. My gratitude also extends to the vibrant open-source community, whose tools and contributions made many of the examples in this book possible.

Finally, I express my sincere appreciation to the editorial team at Orange Education Pvt. Ltd. for their thoughtful reviews, suggestions and willingness to provide me the time I needed to write and publish this book..

Preface

Unsupervised machine learning is one of the most fascinating areas of artificial intelligence, yet often one of the least understood by beginners. Unlike supervised learning, where data is clearly labeled, unsupervised methods require us to find hidden patterns, clusters, and structures without guidance. This makes the field both challenging and rewarding–demanding not only technical skill but also creativity and intuition. The purpose of this book is to simplify these concepts and present them in a structured, hands-on manner that is accessible to students, researchers, and professionals, alike.

Over the past decade, I have had the opportunity to teach, research, and consult in the fields of Machine Learning and Natural Language Processing. Time and again, I observed that learners struggled most with unsupervised methods–not because the ideas were beyond reach, but because resources often explained them in abstract terms or skipped over the practical aspects. This book is my attempt to bridge that gap by blending theory with implementation, guiding readers from foundational algorithms to real-world applications across text, images, and anomaly detection.

This book is intended as both a learning companion and a practical reference. Each chapter introduces key concepts with clear explanations, follows them up with Python-based examples, and concludes with exercises to strengthen understanding. My goal is not only to help readers master unsupervised learning techniques but also to inspire them to apply these methods to their own domains and research problems. Hence, I hope this book equips the readers with the confidence to explore, experiment, and innovate with unsupervised machine learning.

The book is organized into 11 chapters, each building progressively on the concepts and applications of unsupervised machine learning.

Chapter 1 introduces the fundamentals of unsupervised learning, key differences from supervised approaches, and the types of problems, it solves. It provides an overview of clustering, dimensionality reduction, anomaly detection, and applications that set the foundation for later chapters.

Chapter 2 covers essential Python programming concepts and libraries such as NumPy, Pandas, Matplotlib, and Scikit-learn, and ensures readers build the coding foundation necessary to implement machine learning algorithms as well as work with real-world datasets.

Chapter 3 explores clustering algorithms including K-means, hierarchical clustering, and DBSCAN. It explains how these methods group unlabeled data into meaningful clusters, with practical coding examples and case studies.

Chapter 4 explains the need to simplify high-dimensional datasets. It covers techniques such as PCA, t-SNE, and so on, showing how they improve visualization, efficiency, and interpretability in machine learning workflows.

Chapter 5 focuses on methods for identifying rare or unusual data points. This chapter discusses statistical techniques, distance-based approaches, and machine learning models, commonly applied in fraud detection, cybersecurity, and quality control.

Chapter 6 introduces neural network–based methods such as autoencoders, Variational Auto Encoders (VAEs), and Generative Adversarial Networks (GANs). It demonstrates how deep learning extends from unsupervised methods to complex data like images and text.

Chapter 7 presents real-world scenarios where unsupervised learning is applied, from customer segmentation and recommender systems to medical diagnostics and industrial monitoring. It highlights cross-domain impact of these techniques.

Chapter 8 explains how unsupervised methods power NLP tasks such as topic modeling, word embeddings, and clustering of text documents. It includes hands-on demonstrations as well.

Chapter 9 discusses the unique challenges of evaluating models without labeled data. It covers internal and external evaluation metrics, cluster validation techniques, and visualization methods to assess model performance.

Chapter 10 provides a practical guide to taking models from experimentation to deployment. It covers pipelines, scalability, monitoring, and integration with applications in production environments.

Chapter 11 concludes with real-world case studies and lessons learned from research and industry projects. It summarizes best practices, pitfalls to avoid, and guidance for future exploration in unsupervised learning.

Get a Free eBook

We hope you are enjoying your recently purchased book! Your feedback is incredibly valuable to us, and to all other readers looking for great books.

If you found this book helpful or enjoyable, we would truly appreciate it, if you could take a moment to leave a short review with a 5 star rating on Amazon. It helps us grow, and lets other readers discover our books.

As a thank you, we would love to send you a free digital copy of this book, and a **30%** discount code on your next cart value on our official websites:

www.orangeava.com

www.orangeava.in (For Indian Subcontinent)

☑ **Here's how:**

Leave a review for the book on Amazon.

Take a screenshot of your review, and send an email to **info@orangeava.com** (it can be just the confirmation screen).

Once, we receive your screenshot, we will send you the digital file, within 24 hours.

Thank you so much for your support – it means a lot to us!

Downloading the code bundles and colored images

Please follow the links or scan the QR codes to download the ***Code Bundles and Images*** of the book:

https://github.com/ava-orange-education/Kickstart-Unsupervised-Machine-Learning

The code bundles and images of the book are also hosted on ***https://rebrand.ly/851315***

In case there's an update to the code, it will be updated on the existing GitHub repository.

Errata

We take immense pride in our work at **Orange Education Pvt Ltd,** and follow best practices to ensure the accuracy of our content to provide an indulging reading experience to our subscribers. Our readers are our mirrors, and we use their inputs to reflect and improve upon human errors, if any, that may have occurred during the publishing processes involved. To let us maintain the quality and help us reach out to any readers who might be having difficulties due to any unforeseen errors, please write to us at :

errata@orangeava.com

Your support, suggestions, and feedback are highly appreciated.

DID YOU KNOW

Did you know that Orange Education Pvt Ltd offers eBook versions of every book published, with PDF and ePub files available? You can upgrade to the eBook version at **www.orangeava.com** and as a print book customer, you are entitled to a discount on the eBook copy. Get in touch with us at: **info@orangeava.com** for more details.

At **www.orangeava.com**, you can also read a collection of free technical articles, sign up for a range of free newsletters, and receive exclusive discounts and offers on Print Books and eBooks.

PIRACY

If you come across any illegal copies of our works in any form on the internet, we would be grateful if you would provide us with the location address or website name. Please contact us at **info@orangeava.com** with a link to the material.

ARE YOU INTERESTED IN AUTHORING WITH US?

If there is a topic that you have expertise in, and you are interested in either writing or contributing to a book, please write to us at **business@orangeava.com**. We are on a journey to help developers and tech professionals to gain insights on the present technological advancements and innovations happening across the globe and build a community that believes Knowledge is best acquired by sharing and learning with others. Please reach out to us to learn what our audience demands and how you can be part of this educational reform. We also welcome ideas from tech experts and help them build learning and development content for their domains.

REVIEWS

Please leave a review. Once you have read and used this book, why not leave a review on the site that you purchased it from? Potential readers can then see and use your unbiased opinion to make purchase decisions. We at Orange Education would love to know what you think about our products, and our authors can learn from your feedback. Thank you!

For more information about Orange Education, please visit **www.orangeava.com**.

Table of Contents

Chapter 1
Understanding Unsupervised Learning

Introduction

This chapter introduces the foundational concepts of unsupervised learning. You will explore what is unsupervised learning, how it differs from supervised learning, and why it is crucial in today's data-driven world. The chapter will also cover the key types of problems that can be solved via unsupervised learning, such as clustering, anomaly detection, and dimensionality reduction. The focus will be on understanding the broad applications of unsupervised learning in diverse industries. By the end of this chapter, you will have a strong grasp of the foundational concepts covered in the subsequent chapters.

Structure

In this chapter, we will discuss the following topics:

- Introduction to Unsupervised Learning
  - Why Unsupervised Learning Matters
  - History of Unsupervised Learning
- Unsupervised versus Supervised Learning
- Mathematical Concepts in Unsupervised Learning
  - Linear Algebra
  - Probability and Statistics
  - Optimization and Convex Analysis in Unsupervised Learning
  - Graph Theory

- Manifold Learning and Nonlinear Dimensionality Reduction
  - Clustering Objective Functions
  - Prominent Distance Metrics
- Types of Unsupervised Learning Problems
  - Clustering
  - Dimensionality Reduction
  - Association Rule Learning
  - Anomaly Detection
  - Generative Modeling
- Real-World Applications of Unsupervised Learning

Introduction to Unsupervised Learning

The ability to uncover hidden patterns without human supervision is a powerful and essential capability for an algorithm to have in a world driven by data. Unsupervised learning, which is a key branch of machine learning, enables algorithms to analyze vast amounts of unlabeled data and identifies structures, clusters, and relationships that might go unnoticed otherwise.

Unlike supervised learning, which relies on predefined labels, unsupervised learning operates in an open-ended manner. This ability makes it invaluable for tasks like customer segmentation, anomaly detection, and representation learning. With advancements in machine learning, unsupervised techniques are taking up a larger role in fields ranging from natural language processing to computer vision. These techniques further push the boundaries of what AI can achieve without explicit guidance.

Importance of Unsupervised Learning Matters

The rapid growth of data in today's digital age presents both an opportunity and a challenge as a vast majority of generated text, images, videos, sensor logs remain unlabeled. Therefore, it is impractical to rely solely on supervised learning techniques that require human-annotated labels. Unsupervised learning bridges this gap by extracting meaningful insights from raw, unstructured data, thereby allowing systems to autonomously discover patterns and make sense of information without external supervision.

Consider the example of an e-commerce platform analyzing customer behavior. With millions of users interacting with products daily, manually categorizing each user's preferences is infeasible. However, with unsupervised learning, the system can automatically group customers based on their browsing patterns, thus helping businesses tailor recommendations and marketing strategies.

Unsupervised learning is also crucial in fields where labeled data is scarce or expensive to obtain. In medical research, for example, clustering techniques can help identify unknown disease subtypes based on genetic data, resulting in the development of more personalized treatments. Similarly, in the realm of cyber security, anomaly detection methods can identify fraudulent transactions or network intrusions without relying on predefined attack signatures.

History of Unsupervised Learning

Unsupervised learning has evolved over more than a century and has been driven by advancements in statistics, optimization, and computational power. It is rooted in **statistics, information theory,** and **cognitive science**, with key mathematical developments occurring over a century before computational implementations. Unsupervised learning originated from classical clustering and dimensionality reduction techniques, with the base later expanding to include probabilistic models, manifold learning, and deep unsupervised learning.

Let us have a look at the chronological milestones in the development of unsupervised learning:

Early Statistical Foundations in 1800s

The concept of grouping similar data points (also called cluster analysis) dates back to the late 1800s and was propounded by Francis Galton. In 1901, Karl Pearson went on to introduce a foundational dimensionality reduction technique called **Principal Component Analysis.**

Growth of Statistical and Information: Theoretic Ideas during 1900-1950

In the 1930s, **hierarchical clustering** was first used in taxonomy to classify organisms. It was during this period that ideas of agglomerative clustering began to appear in biological and social sciences. In 1948, early maximum-likelihood estimation techniques were developed but they were formalized in 1977. In 1948, Claude Shannon introduced the idea of entropy, which served as an influence on unsupervised methods for feature selection, clustering and dimensionality reduction.

Early Computational Unsupervised Learning during 1950 - 1970

This period saw the first computational implementations of clustering, dimensionality reduction, and early neural networks. The developments are mentioned chronologically as follows:

- **1950s: Early Clustering Algorithms**

- First computational k-means algorithm appeared in the 1950s and were attributed to Hugo Steinhaus (1956). These were later refined by Stuart Lloyd (1957, Lloyd, Stuart P. (1982), "Least squares quantization in PCM", IEEE *Transactions on Information Theory*, **28** (2): 129–137, doi:10.1109/TIT.1982.1056489).
- Hierarchical clustering techniques became more formalized during this period.

- **Self-Organizing Maps (SOMs): Kohonen (1970s)**
  - Early neural-based clustering approach emerged on the scene, paving the way for deep unsupervised methods.
- **Latent Semantic Analysis (LSA): 1960s**
  - LSA was introduced in Natural Language Processing (NLP) to discover latent structures in text.

Expansion with Machine Learning and Probabilistic Methods (1980s to 1990s)

By the 1980s and 1990s, unsupervised learning became a key part of machine learning research, influenced by neural networks and probabilistic models.

- **Gaussian Mixture Models (GMMs): 1980s**
  - Used EM algorithm for clustering and density estimation
- **Independent Component Analysis (ICA): 1990s**
  - Developed for separating mixed signals (for instance, blind source separation in audio processing)
- **Early Generative Models**
  - **Boltzmann Machines (1985)** and **Restricted Boltzmann Machines (RBMs, 1990s)** introduced energy-based unsupervised learning

Modern Unsupervised Learning (2000s–Present)

The 21st century saw an explosion of the following deep learning-based unsupervised techniques:

- **Deep Belief Networks (2006, Hinton et al.)**
  - Revived interest in deep learning for unsupervised feature learning
- **Autoencoders (2000s)**
  - Became widely used for feature learning, anomaly detection, and generative modeling
- **Generative Adversarial Networks (GANs, 2014)**
  - Revolutionized unsupervised learning by enabling high-quality data generation

- **Self-Supervised Learning (2020s)**
    - Methods such as SimCLR, BYOL, and DINO pushed unsupervised learning into vision, NLP, and multimodal AI

Unsupervised learning has evolved from early statistical methods (1900s) to neural and probabilistic models (1980s–2000s). Now, it also includes deep generative and self-supervised approaches (2010s–present). While modern computational implementations began in the 1950s, their roots stretch back over a century in statistics and probability theory.

Unsupervised versus Supervised Learning

Machine learning is broadly classified into **supervised** and **unsupervised** learning. This division depends on whether labeled data is available for training. Supervised learning is the more commonly used approach out of the two. It is where the algorithm learns from input-output pairs and makes predictions based on past examples. In contrast, unsupervised learning deals with raw, unlabeled data, uncovering hidden patterns without predefined outputs.

Supervised learning is ideal for tasks where historical data is available with clear labels, such as in fraud detection (fraudulent or non-fraudulent transactions), medical diagnosis (disease or no disease), and email filtering (spam or no spam). The goal is to minimize the difference between predicted and actual outcomes, using techniques like classification and regression.

Figure 1.1 highlights the difference between the supervised and the unsupervised machine learning. While supervised learning methods learn a decision boundary based on provided labels, unsupervised learning methods depend on the structural similarities inherent in the data.

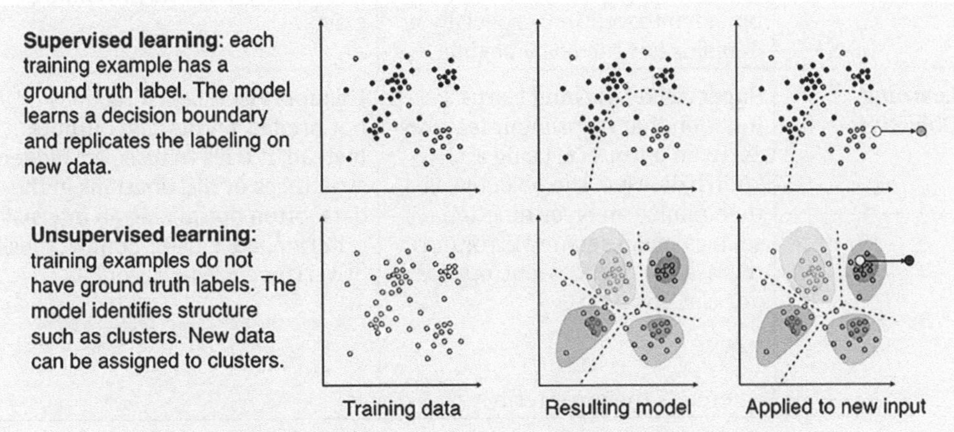

Figure 1.1: *Supervised Learning vs Unsupervised Learning Image (Source: https://commons.wikimedia.org/* CC-BY-4.0)

However, supervised learning has a major limitation–it requires a large labeled dataset, which is often expensive and time-consuming to create.

Unsupervised learning, on the other hand, works in scenarios where explicit labels are unavailable. Instead of predicting an outcome, it identifies patterns, structures, or anomalies within the data. Clustering techniques, such as K-Means and hierarchical clustering, group similar data points together, while dimensionality reduction methods such as PCA and t-SNE compress data into a lower-dimensional representation and retain essential information. Since unsupervised learning does not require labeled data, it is useful for exploratory data analysis, anomaly detection, and feature learning in complex datasets.

While supervised learning is highly accurate when sufficient labeled data is available, unsupervised learning is better suited to discover unknown relationships in large-scale unlabeled datasets. Many modern AI systems, particularly in deep learning, integrate both approaches by using unsupervised learning for feature extraction and supervised learning for predictive modeling.

Feature	**Supervised Learning**	**Unsupervised Learning**
Training Data	**Supervised Learning** requires a labeled dataset, where each input sample has a corresponding ground truth output.	**Unsupervised Learning** operates on unlabeled data, which means that the algorithm must infer structure without explicit labels. For example, clustering algorithms group similar images together without knowing their actual category.
Dependency on Labels	**Supervised Learning** requires labeled data, which is costly and time-consuming to obtain. Data labeling often requires human intervention, especially in domains like medical imaging.	**Unsupervised Learning** eliminates the need for manual labeling, making it scalable but challenging to evaluate since no ground truth exists.
Learning Objective	**Supervised Learning** learns a function that maps input features (X) to an output (Y) using a known dataset. The objective is to minimize an error function, such as mean squared error (for regression) or cross-entropy loss (for classification). $Y=f(X)+\epsilon$ where ϵ is the error term	**Unsupervised Learning** does not predict predefined outputs. Instead, it tries to discover hidden structures or distributions in the data, often optimizing an internal criterion like cluster compactness or variance preservation.

Tasks	**Regression** (for example, predicting house prices using linear regression) **Classification** (for example, detecting spam emails using logistic regression)	**Clustering** (for example, customer segmentation using K-Means) **Dimensionality Reduction** (for example, PCA for feature extraction)
Prominent Learning Algorithms	**Supervised Learning** algorithms optimize for loss functions like Mean Squared Error (MSE) or Binary Cross-Entropy: • Decision Trees, Random Forests • Support Vector Machines (SVM) • Neural Networks (CNNs, LSTMs)	**Unsupervised Learning** algorithms focus on finding patterns based on similarity metrics, probability distributions, or reconstruction loss: • K-Means, DBSCAN (density-based clustering) • Principal Component Analysis (PCA), t-SNE (for dimensionality reduction) • Variational Autoencoders (VAEs), GANs (Generative Models)
Evaluation Metrics	**Supervised Learning** is evaluated using standard metrics: • **Classification**: Accuracy, Precision, Recall, F1-score • **Regression**: RMSE, MAE, R^2 score	**Unsupervised Learning** lacks ground truth, making evaluation subjective: • **Clustering**: Silhouette Score, Davies–Bouldin Index • **Dimensionality Reduction**: Explained Variance Ratio • **Generative Models**: FID (Fréchet Inception Distance)
Accuracy	Typically, high when enough labeled data is available	Varies based on data complexity and algorithm
Interpretability	**Supervised Learning** models like Decision Trees provide human-readable rules, while deep models (e.g., CNNs) require techniques like SHAP for explainability.	**Unsupervised Learning** outputs often require post-processing, such as clustering visualization or latent space interpretation, to extract meaning.
Use Cases	**Supervised Learning** is best for applications where past data predicts future outcomes: • **Medical Diagnosis** (labeling X-rays as 'disease' or 'normal') • **Stock Market Prediction** (forecasting prices based on historical data)	**Unsupervised Learning** is ideal for exploratory tasks: • **Fraud Detection** (detecting anomalies in transactions) • **Recommender Systems** (collaborative filtering to suggest products)

***Table 1.1**: Differences between Supervised and Unsupervised Learning*

Mathematical Concepts in Unsupervised Learning

Unsupervised learning relies on several mathematical foundations that enable algorithms to identify patterns, group data, and reduce dimensionality. Some key mathematical concepts used in unsupervised learning include:

Linear Algebra

Linear algebra is the backbone of many unsupervised learning techniques, and is particularly useful for clustering, dimensionality reduction, and generative models. It provides the mathematical tools necessary for representing and manipulating data in high-dimensional spaces. Let us look at some of the important concepts in linear algebra that are useful in machine learning:

Vector Spaces

- A vector space is a collection of vectors that can be scaled and added together while still remaining within the space.
- In unsupervised learning, data points are represented as vectors in high-dimensional spaces where the relationships between these vectors are used for clustering, similarity measurement, and data transformation. For example, during document clustering, text documents are often represented as vectors in a high-dimensional space using the TF-IDF (Term Frequency-Inverse Document Frequency) representation.

Matrix Factorization

Matrix factorization techniques are used to decompose large datasets into simpler structures, and are useful for dimensionality reduction, clustering, and recommendation systems. It is used in techniques such as Principal Component Analysis (PCA) and Singular Value Decomposition (SVD) to reduce data dimensions while preserving variance.

- Singular Value Decomposition (SVD) is used to factorize a matrix A into three matrices:

$$A = U\Sigma V^T$$

  Where:

  U and **V** are orthogonal matrices

  Σ is a diagonal matrix containing singular values.

Singular value decomposition is used in PCA, Latent Semantic analysis (LSA) in Natural Language Processing and collaborative filtering for recommender systems.

- Non-Negative Matrix Factorization (NMF) factorizes a non-negative matrix into two lower-rank non-negative matrices. It is commonly used in topic modelling, bioinformatics and image processing.

Eigenvalues & Eigenvectors

Eigenvalues and eigenvectors are fundamental in many dimensionality reduction techniques.

Given a square matrix **A**, an eigenvector **v** is a vector that satisfies the equation:

$$Av = \lambda v$$

Where **λ** is the eigenvalue corresponding to the eigenvector **v**.

In Principal Component Analysis, the eigenvectors of the covariance matrix define the new feature space, while the eigenvalues represent the amount of variance captured by each eigenvector. The top-k eigenvectors with the largest eigenvalues are selected as principal components, reducing data dimensionality while preserving variance.

Norms and Distance Metrics

Linear algebra also plays an important part in the calculation of distance metrics and norms used for clustering of data points. Some common norms used in unsupervised learning are:

- **L1 norm (Manhattan distance):** Measures distance by summing absolute differences across dimensions
- **L2 norm (Euclidean distance):** Measures the straight-line distance, commonly used in clustering algorithms such as K-Means
- **Frobenius norm:** A matrix norm used in evaluating reconstruction error in matrix factorization techniques

Orthogonality and Projections

Dimensionality reduction methods often use orthogonality of vectors and vector projections to a lower-dimensional space to reduce the dimensionality of the data. Two vectors are considered orthogonal if their dot product is zero.

Low-Rank Approximations

Low-Rank approximations like Moore-Penrose Pseudoinverse are used to solve least squares problems in machine learning when an exact inverse does not exist and for understanding data complexity in dimensionality reduction.

Probability and Statistics

Probability and statistics play a crucial role in unsupervised learning, particularly in clustering, anomaly detection, dimensionality reduction, and generative modeling. Many unsupervised algorithms rely on probabilistic approaches to estimate distributions, measure similarity, and infer hidden structures from unlabeled data. Several unsupervised learning techniques assume that data follows a certain probability distribution. Understanding these distributions helps users in density estimation, clustering, and generative modeling.

Probability Distributions in Unsupervised Learning

The Gaussian (Normal) distribution is commonly used in clustering algorithms such as Gaussian Mixture Models (GMMs), where data is assumed to be generated from a mixture of Gaussian distributions. It is also a key assumption in Principal Component Analysis (PCA), which models data using a multivariate normal distribution. The Multivariate Gaussian distribution extends this concept to multiple dimensions and plays a central role in GMMs, where each cluster is represented by a different Gaussian distribution with distinct means and covariances.

Other important distributions include the Bernoulli and Categorical distributions, which are widely used in Latent Dirichlet Allocation (LDA) for topic modeling, where documents are treated as mixtures of topics following categorical distributions. The Exponential and Poisson distributions are applied in modeling event occurrence frequencies, such as in anomaly detection for network traffic. Additionally, the Dirichlet distribution serves as a prior in Bayesian clustering and topic modeling methods and helps in modeling uncertainty in cluster assignments. Understanding these distributions enhances the effectiveness of probabilistic unsupervised learning methods.

Expectation-Maximization (EM) Algorithm

The Expectation-Maximization (EM) Algorithm is a fundamental technique in unsupervised learning. It is used to estimate parameters of probabilistic models when direct computation is infeasible. The EM algorithm is widely used in Gaussian Mixture Models (GMMs) to iteratively refine cluster assignments by optimizing the likelihood of the observed data.

The algorithm alternates between two key steps: The Expectation (E-step), where it estimates the probability distributions of latent variables given the current parameter values, and the Maximization (M-step), where it updates the model parameters to maximize the expected likelihood. This iterative process continues until convergence, thus making EM a powerful approach to handle missing data and optimize complex probabilistic models.

Bayesian Methods in Unsupervised Learning

Bayesian statistics provide a powerful probabilistic framework for modeling uncertainty in unsupervised learning. At its core, **Bayes' Theorem** expresses the relationship between conditional probabilities, allowing models to update their beliefs based on new data. It is given by:

$$P(A \mid B) = \frac{P(B \mid A)P(A)}{P(B)}$$

This theorem is widely used in Gaussian Mixture Models (GMMs) for soft clustering, where data points are assigned probabilistic memberships to multiple clusters rather than belonging to a single one. It also plays a crucial role in Hidden Markov Models (HMMs), which are used for sequence modeling in applications such as speech recognition and natural language processing.

Another important Bayesian approach is Maximum A-Posteriori (MAP) Estimation, which extends Maximum Likelihood Estimation (MLE) by incorporating prior knowledge into parameter estimation, making it particularly useful when data is sparse or uncertain. Bayesian techniques enhance the adaptability and robustness of unsupervised learning models in handling real-world data.

Entropy and Information Theory

Entropy and information theory play a crucial role in unsupervised learning, particularly in feature selection, clustering, and dimensionality reduction. One of the key concepts is Shannon Entropy, which quantifies the uncertainty in a dataset and is defined as:

$$H(X) = -\sum p(x) \log p(x)$$

Entropy is widely used in feature selection for clustering, helping to determine optimal cluster sizes by measuring the amount of randomness in data distributions.

Another important concept is Kullback-Leibler (KL) Divergence, which measures the difference between two probability distributions. KL divergence is particularly useful in Variational Autoencoders (VAEs) and t-SNE, where it helps in dimensionality reduction by optimizing how data points are mapped in a lower-dimensional space.

Additionally, Mutual Information quantifies the amount of shared information between two variables and is often used in feature selection for clustering, ensuring that selected features retain the most relevant structure in the data. These information-theoretic measures enhance the effectiveness of unsupervised learning by guiding model decisions based on the statistical properties of data.

Statistical Distance and Similarity Measures

Distance metrics play a fundamental role in unsupervised learning as they provide a quantitative measure of similarity or dissimilarity between data points. Since unsupervised learning lacks labeled data, algorithms must rely on these metrics to discover patterns, structure, and relationships within datasets.

In clustering, distance metrics define how data points are grouped into clusters. For example, in K-Means, Hierarchical Clustering, and DBSCAN, the choice of distance metric impacts cluster formation. K-Means clustering algorithm minimizes the sum of squared Euclidean distances between points and cluster centroids to identify the data clusters.

In dimensionality reduction techniques like PCA and t-SNE, distance metrics are used to map high-dimensional data into lower dimensions while preserving meaningful relationships. t-SNE uses Euclidean distance in high-dimensional space to maintain local similarities in lower dimensions. During anomaly detection, outliers are detected by measuring how far a point is from others in the dataset. Mahalanobis distance is often used in anomaly detection because it accounts for correlations among features. DBSCAN uses a neighborhood-based distance threshold to identify anomalies.

Recommender Systems use distance metrics to find similar users or items in collaborative filtering, while Cosine Similarity is commonly used to measure the similarity between user preferences or product features. Distance measures help estimate the probability density function of data. Kernel Density Estimation (KDE) relies on distance functions to smooth distributions. Distance metrics define edge weights in graph-based clustering and spectral clustering. Graph Laplacian methods use similarity matrices derived from distance functions to partition data

Markov Chains and Stochastic Processes

Markov Chains and Stochastic Processes are essential mathematical tools in unsupervised learning, particularly for modeling sequential and probabilistic relationships in data.

Markov Chains form the foundation of Hidden Markov Models (HMMs), which are widely used for unsupervised sequence learning in applications such as speech recognition and part-of-speech tagging. A key property of Markov Chains is the Markov assumption, which states that the probability of transitioning to the next state depends only on the current state, making them useful for modeling time-series and sequential data.

In contrast, Gaussian Processes provide a non-parametric approach to modeling complex distributions in probabilistic clustering and regression. By defining a distribution over functions, Gaussian Processes allow models to make uncertainty-aware predictions, making them particularly valuable in scenarios where data is sparse or noisy.

Together, these stochastic methods bring about more flexible and robust unsupervised learning techniques.

Optimization and Convex Analysis in Unsupervised Learning

Optimization plays a crucial role in unsupervised learning, as many algorithms minimize or maximize objective functions to find meaningful patterns in data. Whether it is clustering, reducing dimensionality, or detecting anomalies, unsupervised learning methods often rely on convex and non-convex optimization techniques to improve performance and convergence. Convex analysis is particularly important because convex functions guarantee a global optimum, thus making optimization problems more stable and easier.

One of the most widely used optimization techniques in unsupervised learning is gradient descent, which is an iterative method that minimizes an objective function by following the direction of the steepest descent. Stochastic Gradient Descent (SGD), a variant that updates parameters using small, randomly selected batches of data, is especially useful in large-scale unsupervised learning applications, such as autoencoders, variational autoencoders (VAEs), and Generative Adversarial Networks (GANs).

Another key method, Expectation-Maximization (EM), is used in Gaussian Mixture Models (GMMs) to iteratively refine cluster assignments by maximizing the likelihood of data under a probabilistic model. EM is an example of an optimization approach where closed-form solutions are unavailable, necessitating an iterative approach to reach the best possible model parameters.

Dimensionality reduction techniques like Principal Component Analysis (PCA) also rely on convex optimization principles. PCA seeks to find the optimal projection of high-dimensional data onto a lower-dimensional space by solving an eigenvalue problem, which is a convex optimization task. Similarly, t-Distributed Stochastic Neighbor Embedding (t-SNE) and Uniform Manifold Approximation and Projection (UMAP) minimize a non-convex loss function to preserve local data structures, requiring advanced optimization techniques, such as adaptive learning rates and momentum-based optimizers.

Clustering algorithms like K-Means rely on optimization to minimize the sum of squared distances between data points and their assigned cluster centroids. Although K-Means optimization is non-convex, techniques such as Lloyd's algorithm ensure that each step reduces the objective function, leading to a locally optimal clustering. More sophisticated clustering methods, such as density-based clustering (DBSCAN) and spectral clustering, incorporate graph-based optimization techniques, where convexity is important in defining similarity measures and partitioning data.

Unsupervised learning models also benefit from regularization techniques, which add constraints to the optimization problem to prevent overfitting and improve generalization. For example, L1 (Lasso) and L2 (Ridge) regularization are commonly used in dimensionality reduction and clustering models to enforce sparsity and stability in feature selection. Convex optimization methods such as Lagrange multipliers help incorporate these constraints while ensuring that solutions remain computationally feasible.

Ultimately, optimization and convex analysis provide the mathematical foundation for solving complex unsupervised learning problems. While convex optimization ensures global convergence in models such as PCA and some clustering techniques, non-convex optimization methods like gradient descent and EM enable the training of more sophisticated models such as VAEs, GANs, and deep clustering frameworks. A solid understanding of these principles is essential for designing scalable and efficient unsupervised learning algorithms.

Graph Theory

Graph theory plays a fundamental role in many unsupervised learning techniques and provides a structured way to represent and analyze relationships between data points. In unsupervised learning, data is often represented as a graph, where nodes correspond to individual data points and edges define relationships based on similarity, distance, or connectivity. This graph-based representation is particularly useful for clustering, dimensionality reduction, and manifold learning, as it enables algorithms to capture complex structures that might not be apparent in traditional vector-based representations.

One of the most widely used applications of graph theory in unsupervised learning is spectral clustering, which leverages the eigenvalues of graph Laplacians to partition data into meaningful clusters. Unlike traditional methods such as K-Means, which rely on explicit distance metrics, spectral clustering operates on the graph representation of data, allowing it to detect clusters of arbitrary shapes and sizes. The method constructs a similarity graph using techniques like k-nearest neighbors (k-NN) or fully connected graphs, then computes the Laplacian matrix, whose eigenvectors help identify optimal cluster assignments. This makes spectral clustering particularly effective in cases where data exhibits non-convex structures, such as social network analysis or image segmentation.

Another major application of graph theory in unsupervised learning is manifold learning, a technique used for dimensionality reduction. High-dimensional data often lies on a lower-dimensional manifold, meaning that the true structure of the data can be captured using a reduced number of meaningful dimensions. Methods such as Isomap (Isometric Mapping), Locally Linear Embedding (LLE), and Laplacian Eigenmaps construct graphs to model local neighborhood relationships between data points. By preserving these local structures, manifold learning techniques provide more accurate low-dimensional representations compared to traditional methods like PCA, making them valuable for tasks such as data visualization, feature extraction, and preprocessing for clustering.

Graph-based approaches also play a significant role in density-based clustering algorithms, such as DBSCAN (Density-Based Spatial Clustering of Applications with Noise) and HDBSCAN (Hierarchical DBSCAN). These methods use graph connectivity properties to identify dense regions of data while distinguishing noise or outliers. Unlike K-Means, which requires a predefined number of clusters, DBSCAN defines clusters as groups of connected points exceeding a certain density threshold, allowing it to discover arbitrarily shaped clusters without prior knowledge of cluster count.

In recommender systems and link prediction, graph-based unsupervised learning is used to infer hidden patterns and relationships. Graph-based clustering techniques, such as community detection in social networks, rely on algorithms like Louvain modularity optimization and spectral partitioning to identify groups of similar entities. Similarly, random walk-based methods like PageRank and Personalized PageRank enable unsupervised learning systems to rank and recommend items based on user interactions.

Recent advances in Graph Neural Networks (GNNs) and self-supervised learning on graphs have further expanded the application of graph theory in unsupervised learning. Methods like DeepWalk and GraphSAGE use graph structures to learn meaningful representations of nodes without requiring labeled data, thus enabling users to perform tasks like node classification, community detection, and anomaly detection in large-scale networks.

Thus, graph theory provides a powerful framework for modeling complex relationships in unsupervised learning. By leveraging graphs to represent data structures, algorithms can uncover hidden patterns, improve clustering accuracy, and enhance dimensionality reduction. As data continues to grow in complexity, graph-based unsupervised learning techniques will play an increasingly critical role in extracting meaningful insights from unstructured and high-dimensional datasets.

Manifold Learning and Nonlinear Dimensionality Reduction

High-dimensional data often contains inherent structure that lies on a lower-dimensional manifold, which is a smooth, continuous surface embedded within a higher-dimensional space. Manifold learning is an essential unsupervised learning technique that seeks to uncover these underlying low-dimensional representations, while preserving essential geometric and topological properties.

Unlike traditional linear dimensionality reduction methods like Principal Component Analysis (PCA), which assume that data can be represented as a linear combination of basis vectors, manifold learning focuses on nonlinear relationships, making it particularly effective for datasets with complex structures.

One of the most widely used manifold learning techniques is Isometric Mapping (Isomap), which extends classical Multidimensional Scaling (MDS) by preserving geodesic distances rather than simple Euclidean distances. Isomap constructs a weighted graph where data points are connected to their nearest neighbors, and distances along the manifold are computed using shortest paths. This approach allows Isomap to capture the intrinsic structure of curved manifolds, making it useful in image processing, robotics, and bioinformatics.

Another key technique is Locally Linear Embedding (LLE), which assumes that each data point and its nearest neighbors lie on a locally linear patch of the manifold. LLE reconstructs each data point as a linear combination of its neighbors and finds a lower-dimensional embedding that best preserves these local relationships. Unlike PCA, which focuses on maximizing variance, LLE focuses on preserving local neighborhood structures, making it well-suited for high-dimensional visualization and feature learning.

Laplacian Eigenmaps, which is another popular manifold learning approach, constructs a graph representation of data and applies spectral decomposition to find an embedding that preserves local affinities between points. By leveraging the graph Laplacian, this method excels in tasks where preserving local neighborhood information is crucial, such as semi-supervised learning and spectral clustering.

A more recent and widely adopted nonlinear dimensionality reduction method is t-Distributed Stochastic Neighbor Embedding (t-SNE), which maps high-dimensional data into a lower-dimensional space by preserving pairwise similarities between points. Unlike Isomap and LLE, which focus on global or local geometric structure, t-SNE is specifically designed for visualization and is ideal for exploring high-dimensional datasets such as word embeddings, genomic data, and deep learning activations. However, t-SNE is computationally expensive and less effective for general-purpose feature extraction.

Another powerful approach is Uniform Manifold Approximation and Projection (UMAP), which builds upon principles of topology and Riemannian geometry to create more flexible and scalable embeddings. Compared to t-SNE, UMAP is faster, better preserves global structures, and works well for both visualization and downstream machine learning tasks. It has now become particularly popular in bioinformatics, image recognition, and natural language processing.

Manifold learning techniques have significantly advanced the field of nonlinear dimensionality reduction, allowing for better understanding and processing of complex, high-dimensional data. By preserving geometric relationships rather than relying on simple linear projections, these methods enable more interpretable feature representations, enhancing clustering, visualization, and anomaly detection in unsupervised learning. As datasets continue to grow in complexity, manifold learning will remain a crucial tool to extract meaningful insights from structured and unstructured data.

Clustering Objective Functions

The performance of clustering algorithms is driven by objective functions, which define how well the clusters are formed by optimizing a specific criterion. Different clustering methods use different objective functions, depending on whether they focus on compactness, separation, density, or probabilistic likelihood. These objective functions guide the algorithm in assigning data points to clusters in a way that maximizes coherence within clusters, while maintaining meaningful distinctions between them.

One of the most widely used objective functions is the Sum of Squared Errors (SSE), also known as inertia, which is used in K-Means clustering. It measures the total squared Euclidean distance between each data point and its assigned cluster centroid. Its objective is to minimize this intra-cluster variance, ensuring that data points within a cluster are as close to each other as possible. However, SSE-based clustering assumes spherical clusters and is sensitive to outliers, which can significantly distort cluster assignments.

For density-based clustering algorithms like Density-Based Spatial Clustering of Applications with Noise (DBSCAN), the objective function focuses on identifying high-density regions of data, while distinguishing noise and outliers. Instead of minimizing an explicit distance metric, DBSCAN uses a density reachability criterion, where points within a predefined distance (epsilon) must contain at least a minimum number of neighbors to form a dense cluster. This allows it to discover clusters of arbitrary shapes, unlike centroid-based methods like K-Means.

In hierarchical clustering, objective functions are based on linkage criteria, which determine how distances between clusters are computed. The most common linkage methods include single linkage (minimizing the minimum distance between points in different clusters), complete linkage (minimizing the maximum distance), and average linkage (minimizing the mean distance). These methods define how clusters merge or split in a dendrogram-based hierarchical structure.

Another critical objective function in clustering is silhouette score, which evaluates the quality of cluster assignments by measuring how similar a point is to its own cluster compared to other clusters. Given a data point, the silhouette score is defined as:

$$s = \frac{b - a}{\max(a, b)}$$

Where **a** is the average intra-cluster distance (how close the point is to others in the same cluster), and **b** is the average nearest-cluster distance (how far the point is from the closest other cluster). A high silhouette score (closer to 1) indicates well-defined clusters, while lower values suggest poor clustering.

For probabilistic clustering methods, such as Gaussian Mixture Models (GMMs), the objective function is based on Maximum Likelihood Estimation (MLE). Instead of assigning data points to fixed clusters, GMMs model data as a mixture of Gaussian distributions and seek to maximize the likelihood that the observed data was generated from these distributions. This is done using the Expectation-Maximization (EM) algorithm, which iteratively refines cluster assignments by optimizing the probability of data points belonging to different Gaussian components.

Other important objective functions include the Davies-Bouldin Index (DBI), which measures the ratio of within-cluster scatter to between-cluster separation; and the Dunn Index, which evaluates the compactness and separation of clusters. These metrics assess clustering performance and selecting the optimal number of clusters.

Clustering objective functions are essential in guiding algorithms toward meaningful data segmentation. While centroid-based methods optimize intra-cluster variance, density-based approaches maximize data density cohesion, and probabilistic models maximize likelihood estimates. Understanding these objective functions helps in selecting the most suitable clustering technique based on the dataset characteristics and application requirements.

Prominent Distance Metrics

Some prominent distance metrics used in clustering are:

- **Euclidean Distance (L2 Norm)**: This measures the straight-line distance between two points in n-dimensional space and is the most common metric for measuring similarity in clustering (such as K-Means). The formula for calculating Euclidean distance between two n-dimensional data points x and y is given by:

$$d(x, y) = \sqrt{\sum_{i=1}^{n} (x_i - y_i)^2}$$

Where,

- **x, y** are two data points (vectors) in n-dimensional space
- x_i, y_i is the *i*th component of vectors x and y
- *n* is the number of dimensions in vectors x and y
- *d(x,y)* is the Euclidean distance between x and y

Let us see an example of calculation of Euclidean distance between two vectors A and B:

A = (2,3,5)

B = (6,8,10)

The resultant Euclidean distance formula is mentioned as follows:

$$d(A, B) = \sqrt{(x2 - x1)^2 + (y2 - y1)^2 + (z2 - z1)^2}$$

$$= \sqrt{(6 - 2)^2 + (8 - 3)^2 + (10 - 5)^2}$$

$$= \sqrt{4^2 + 5^2 + 5^2}$$

$$= \sqrt{66}$$

$$= 8.12$$

- **Manhattan Distance (L1 Norm/Taxicab Distance):** Manhattan distance measures the sum of absolute differences between corresponding coordinates of two data points in n-dimensional space. It is given by the following formula:

$$d(x, y) = \sum_{i=1}^{n} |x_i - y_i|$$

Where,

- *x,y* are two data points in n-dimensional space
- x_i, y_i is the *i*th component of vectors x and y
- *n* = Number of dimensions
- *d(x,y)* is the Manhattan distance between x and y

- **Cosine Similarity**: Cosine similarity measures the cosine of the angle between two vectors. It is used in high-dimensional data, such as text analysis and document clustering, where angles between vectors matter more than magnitude. Cosine similarity between two vectors x and y is given by:

$$\cos \Theta = \frac{x.y}{||x|| \, ||y||}$$

Where,

- x, y are two data vectors
- $x \cdot y$ is the dot product of x and y
- $||x||$ is the magnitude of vector x
- $||y||$ is the magnitude of vector y
- $\cos(\theta)$ is the similarity score in the range [−1,1] where 1 means identical and -1 means completely opposite

- **Mahalanobis Distance:** This distance metric accounts for correlations in data, and considers the data distribution. It is often used in anomaly detection and clustering algorithms. Mahalanobis distance between two n-dimensional vectors x and y is given by:

$$d(x, y) = \sqrt{(x - y)^T S^{-1}(x - y)}$$

Where,

- x, y are two n-dimensional vectors
- $(x-y)$ is the difference vector between the x and y
- S is the covariance matrix of the dataset
- S^{-1} is the inverse of the covariance matrix
- $(x-y)^T$ is the transpose of the difference vector
- $d(x,y)$ is the Mahalanobis distance between x and y

- **Jaccard Similarity:** This metric measures the similarity between two sets A and B. It is measured by the formula:

$$J(A, B) = \frac{|A \cap B|}{|A \cup B|}$$

Where,

- A, B are two sets
- $|A \cap B|$ is the set intersection between A and B
- $|A \cap B|$ is the set union between A and B
- $J(A. B)$ is the Jaccard similarity score. The range of Jaccard similarity is [0, 1]

- **Hamming Distance** This distance metric counts the number of differing elements between two binary or categorical sequences. It is given by the following formula:

$$d(x,y) = \sum_{i=1}^{n} 1(x_i \neq y_i)$$

Where,

- x, y are two sequences of length n
- x_i, y_i is the ith element of x and y
- $1(x_i \neq y_i)$ is the indicator function (its values is 1 if $1(x_i \neq y_i)$, it is 0 otherwise)
- $d(x,y)$ is Hamming distance

Types of Unsupervised Learning Problems

Unsupervised learning encompasses a range of problem types, with each designed to extract meaningful patterns from unlabeled data. Unlike supervised learning, which relies on predefined labels, unsupervised methods autonomously uncover structures and relationships within data. The major types of unsupervised learning problems include clustering, dimensionality reduction, association rule learning, anomaly detection, and generative modeling. These techniques are widely used across various domains, including customer segmentation, fraud detection, recommender systems, and scientific research.

Clustering

Clustering involves grouping similar data points into clusters based on inherent structures in the dataset. It is widely used in customer segmentation, image classification, bioinformatics, and social network analysis. Clustering algorithms detect patterns by grouping data points based on similarity measures, such as Euclidean distance, cosine similarity, or probabilistic distributions. Clusters can be hard (where each point belongs to one cluster) or soft (where each point has a probability of belonging to multiple clusters).

Common Clustering Algorithms

Clustering algorithms identify groups of similar data points based on defined similarity metrics. The choice of the clustering algorithm depends on the dataset's characteristics, such as cluster shape, density, and scale. We have mentioned some widely used clustering algorithms, along with their working principles, advantages, and limitations in the following sections:

K-Means Clustering

K-Means is one of the most commonly used centroid-based clustering algorithms. It partitions data into K clusters by minimizing intra-cluster variance, ensuring that data points within a cluster are as close as possible to their cluster centroid.

Working:

1. Randomly initialize K centroids within the dataset.
2. Assign each data point to the closest centroid based on Euclidean distance.
3. Recalculate the centroids as the mean of all assigned points in each cluster.
4. Repeat steps 2 and 3 until centroids no longer change or a predefined iteration limit is reached.

Advantages:

- Efficient and scalable for large datasets
- Easy to interpret and implement
- Works well for spherical, well-separated clusters

Limitations:

- Requires predefining the number of clusters K, which is not always known
- Sensitive to outliers and initialization of centroids, leading to local minima
- Struggles with non-spherical clusters or varying cluster densities

Hierarchical Clustering

Hierarchical clustering creates a hierarchy of clusters that can be represented as a dendrogram (tree structure). It does not require predefining the number of clusters, which is why it is useful for exploratory data analysis.

Types of Hierarchical Clustering:

- **Agglomerative (Bottom-Up):** Starts with each data point as a singleton cluster and iteratively merges the two closest clusters until a single cluster remains
- **Divisive (Top-Down):** Starts with all data points in a single cluster and recursively splits them into smaller clusters

Linkage Criteria (used to measure inter-cluster similarity):

- **Single Linkage:** Distance between the closest points of two clusters
- **Complete Linkage:** Distance between the farthest points of two clusters

- **Average Linkage:** Average distance between all points in two clusters

Advantages:

- Does not require predefining K
- Captures hierarchical relationships in data
- Works well for datasets where nested cluster structures exist

Limitations:

- Computationally expensive ($O(n^2 \log n)$ complexity), making it unsuitable for large datasets
- Sensitive to noisy data and outliers, which may impact cluster formation
- Cannot easily reassign points once merged or split

Hierarchical clustering is used in genomic classification, image segmentation, and social network analysis.

3. DBSCAN (Density-Based Spatial Clustering of Applications with Noise)

DBSCAN is a density-based clustering algorithm that groups together points that are densely packed while marking points in low-density regions as outliers or noise. Unlike K-Means and hierarchical clustering, DBSCAN does not require the number of clusters to be specified beforehand and is robust to clusters of arbitrary shapes.

Working:

1. Select an arbitrary point and retrieve all points within a specified radius ε (epsilon).
2. If there are at least MinPts points within ε, it is considered a core point, and a new cluster is formed.
3. Expand the cluster by iterating through all directly and indirectly density-reachable points.
4. If a point is within ε but does not have enough neighbors, it is classified as noise.
5. Repeat the process until all points are visited.

Advantages:

- Does not require specifying K (automatically finds the number of clusters)
- Handles clusters of arbitrary shapes (such as elongated or curved clusters)
- Robust to outliers, marking them as noise instead of forcing them into clusters

Limitations:

- Requires careful tuning of ε (epsilon) and MinPts, which significantly affect performance.
- Struggles with clusters of varying densities, as it assumes a uniform density for all clusters.
- Performance degrades with high-dimensional data due to the curse of dimensionality.

Density based clustering is often used in geospatial analysis, anomaly detection, and customer segmentation.

Gaussian Mixture Models (GMMs)

GMM is a probabilistic model which assumes that data is generated from a mixture of several Gaussian distributions. Unlike K-Means, which assigns points strictly to a single cluster, GMM assigns soft cluster memberships, meaning each data point has a probabilistic likelihood of belonging to multiple clusters.

Working:

1. Assume data follows a mixture of K Gaussian distributions, each characterized by:
    a. **Mean (μ):** Cluster center
    b. **Covariance matrix (Σ):** Shape and orientation of the distribution
    c. **Mixing coefficient (π):** Weight of each Gaussian component
2. Use the Expectation-Maximization (EM) algorithm to iteratively refine the following parameters:
    a. **Expectation (E-step):** Compute probabilities of each data point belonging to each Gaussian component
    b. **Maximization (M-step):** Update Gaussian parameters (μ, Σ, π) to maximize the likelihood
3. Iterate until convergence and assign each point to the Gaussian component with the highest probability.

Advantages:

- Soft clustering allows uncertainty in cluster assignments
- Can model elliptical clusters rather than just spherical clusters (like K-Means)
- Probabilistic interpretation makes it useful for applications requiring uncertainty estimation

Limitations:

- Computationally expensive, especially for high-dimensional data
- Requires specifying K beforehand
- Sensitive to poor initialization, often requiring multiple runs with different starting conditions

Gaussian mixture models are often used in speaker diarization (identifying speakers in an audio stream), image segmentation, and financial risk modeling.

Choosing the right clustering algorithm

The choice of clustering algorithm depends on the dataset's properties. For datasets with spherical clusters, K-Means is a simple and effective choice. When hierarchical relationships matter, hierarchical clustering is preferred. If the dataset contains arbitrarily shaped clusters with noise, DBSCAN is more effective. Finally, GMM is ideal when clusters exhibit soft membership and Gaussian-like distributions.

Each algorithm has trade-offs, and hybrid approaches (like using K-Means to initialize GMMs or using DBSCAN for preprocessing) can further enhance performance. Understanding these differences is crucial to apply clustering effectively in real-world scenarios (*Figure 1.2*).

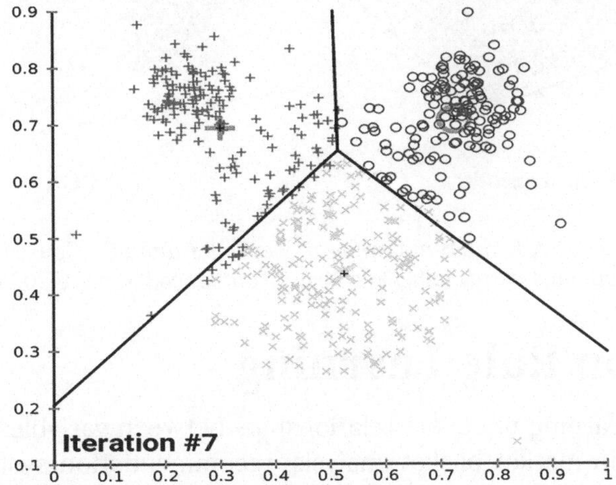

Figure 1.2: *Clustering of data Data Based on Inherent Similarity*
(*Source Credits: https://commons.wikimedia.org/* CC-BY-4.0)

Dimensionality Reduction

Dimensionality reduction techniques transform high-dimensional data into a lower-dimensional representation while preserving essential structures. They are useful for data visualization, noise reduction, and feature extraction.

Dimensionality reduction reduces computational complexity and storage requirements. It helps overcome the curse of dimensionality in high-dimensional datasets and is often used before applying clustering or classification algorithms.

Common Dimensionality Reduction Algorithms:

- **Principal Component Analysis (PCA)**: Projects data onto orthogonal axes of maximum variance
- **t-Distributed Stochastic Neighbor Embedding (t-SNE)**: Preserves local relationships for visualization
- **Autoencoders**: Neural networks that learn compact representations of data
- **Independent Component Analysis (ICA)**: Separates mixed signals into independent sources

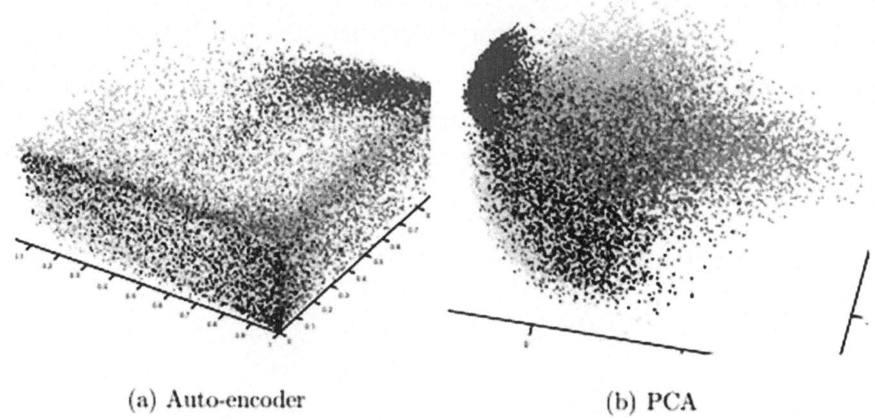

***Figure 1.3**: Dimensionality Reduction Using Auto-encoder and PCA Source: https://commons.wikimedia.org/wiki/File:Pca-vs-autoencoder.png CC0 1.0*

Association Rule Learning

Association rule learning uncovers relationships between variables in large datasets. It is widely used in market basket analysis, recommendation systems, and medical diagnosis.

Association rule mining Identifies frequent patterns, correlations, and dependencies. It produces rules in the form "*If* X, *then* Y" (for example, "*If a customer buys milk, they are likely to buy bread*") and is evaluated using support, confidence, and lift metrics (*Figure 1.4*).

Common Association Rule Algorithms

- **Apriori Algorithm**: Identifies frequent itemsets and derives association rules

- **FP-Growth:** More efficient alternative to Apriori, avoiding candidate generation
- **Eclat Algorithm:** Uses depth-first search for frequent itemset mining

Example Rule:

- `{Milk, Bread} → {Butter}` (Customers who buy milk and bread often buy butter)

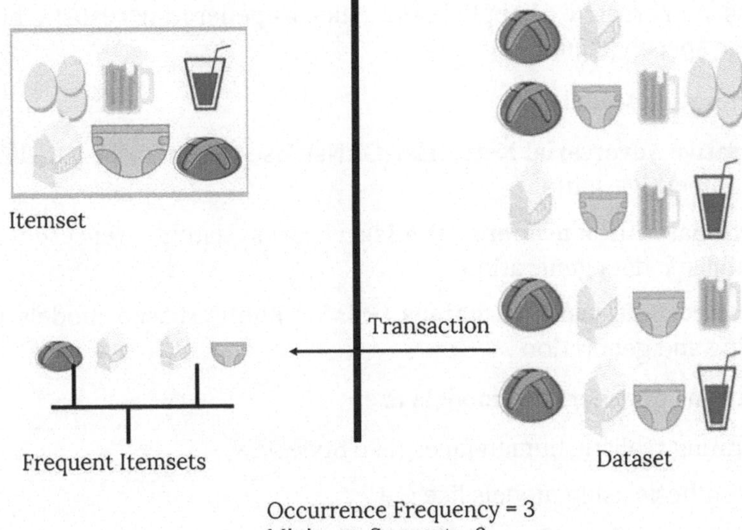

Figure 1.4: *Association Rule Mining in Market Basket Analysis Source Credits: https://commons.wikimedia.org/wiki/File:AffinityAnalysis.png* CC0 1.0 Universal Public Domain Dedication

Anomaly Detection

Anomaly detection identifies rare or unusual data points that deviate from normal patterns. It is critical in fraud detection, cybersecurity, and fault diagnosis.

Anomaly detection identifies outliers which may represent errors, fraud, or novel discoveries. It requires defining what constitutes "*normal*" behavior in a dataset. Anomaly detection works well with both structured and unstructured data.

Common Anomaly Detection Algorithms

- **Isolation Forest:** Isolates anomalies by recursively partitioning data
- **One-Class SVM:** Learns a boundary around normal data to identify outliers
- **Local Outlier Factor (LOF):** Detects outliers based on local density
- **Autoencoders:** Neural networks that reconstruct normal patterns and detect deviations

Generative Modeling

Generative models aim to learn the underlying probability distribution of data, thus enabling them to generate new samples. These models are widely used in image generation, text synthesis, and data augmentation.

Generative Modeling learns complex data distributions instead of just finding patterns. It can generate completely new data points similar to training examples. Generative modeling is used in creative AI applications, such as generating realistic human faces or synthesizing speech (*Figure* 1.5).

Common Generative Models

- **Generative Adversarial Networks (GANs):** Uses a generator and discriminator in a competitive setup
- **Variational Autoencoders (VAEs):** Learns latent representations for probabilistic data generation
- **Restricted Boltzmann Machines (RBMs):** Energy-based models for feature learning and generation

Some applications of generative models are:

- Generating realistic human faces (like StyleGAN)
- Text synthesis using models like GPT
- Drug discovery by generating molecular structures

Unsupervised learning encompasses a diverse set of problem types, each serving a distinct purpose. Clustering groups similar data points, dimensionality reduction simplifies complex datasets, association rule learning uncovers hidden correlations, anomaly detection identifies rare patterns, while generative models create new synthetic data. Choosing a method depends on the problem domain, data properties, and computational constraints.

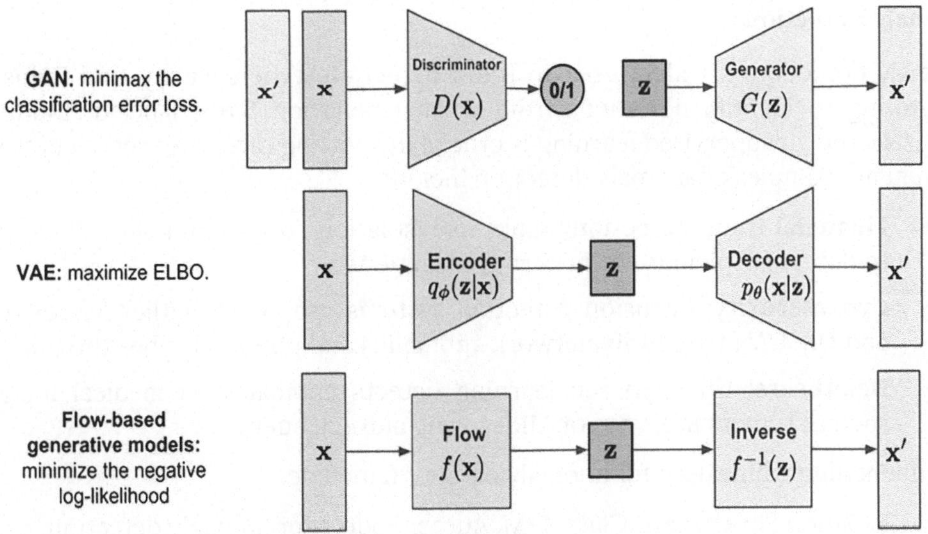

Figure 1.5: *Generative Modelling (Source Credits: https://commons.wikimedia.org/wiki/File:-Three-generative-models.png* CC-BY-SA-4.0)

Real-World Applications of Unsupervised Learning

The versatility of unsupervised learning makes it a fundamental tool across industries, enabling data-driven decision-making without the need for labeled datasets. By uncovering hidden structures in data, unsupervised learning helps businesses and researchers improve efficiency, personalize experiences, and make scientific discoveries. Let us discuss some important real-world applications of unsupervised learning:

Customer Segmentation

Retail and marketing industries rely on clustering techniques to segment customers based on purchasing behavior, demographics, and preferences. By grouping similar customers, businesses can tailor personalized recommendations, targeted advertising campaigns, and pricing strategies. E-commerce platforms (like Amazon) use K-Means clustering to group users with similar shopping behaviors, optimizing product recommendations. Telecom companies analyze customer data to identify churn risks and provide personalized retention offers. Banks segment customers based on transaction history to offer customized financial products. Some prominent algorithms used in customer segmentation are:

- K-Means, DBSCAN, Gaussian Mixture Models (GMMs) for customer grouping.
- Association Rule Learning to identify frequently purchased item combinations.

Anomaly Detection

Anomaly detection is widely used in fraud detection, cybersecurity, and industrial monitoring to identify deviations from normal behavior. Since labeled fraudulent data is scarce, unsupervised learning is crucial in spotting rare, unexpected patterns. Prominent examples of anomaly detection include:

- **Financial fraud detection:** Banks use Isolation Forests and One-Class SVMs to detect suspicious credit card transactions.
- **Cybersecurity:** Intrusion detection systems use Local Outlier Factor (LOF) and DBSCAN to identify network anomalies and potential cyber threats.
- **Healthcare:** Unsupervised learning detects anomalies in medical imaging, such as tumors in X-rays or MRIs, using autoencoders.

Prominent algorithms used for anomaly detection include:

- Isolation Forest, One-Class SVM, Autoencoders for anomaly detection
- Density-based clustering (DBSCAN) to detect unusual behavior

Recommendation Systems

Streaming platforms and online marketplaces use unsupervised learning to recommend products, music, and movies by identifying hidden patterns in user preferences. Instead of relying on explicit labels, these systems cluster users with similar behaviors and generate personalized recommendations. Prominent examples of recommendation systems include:

- Netflix and YouTube use collaborative filtering and latent factor models to recommend content based on users with similar viewing habits.
- Spotify and Apple Music employ clustering and word embeddings to recommend songs based on listening patterns.
- E-commerce sites (like Amazon, eBay) suggest items using association rule learning and dimensionality reduction techniques.

Prominent algorithms for recommendation systems include:

- Matrix Factorization (SVD, NMF) to learn latent user preferences
- K-Means, DBSCAN for grouping users with similar interests
- Association Rule Learning (Apriori, FP-Growth) for identifying frequently bought items together

Medical and Biological Research

In medicine and biotechnology, unsupervised learning enables breakthroughs by analyzing genetic sequences, classifying diseases, and uncovering hidden patterns in medical data. Since medical data is vast and often lacks labeled diagnoses, clustering and dimensionality reduction techniques are crucial. Prominent examples of the use of unsupervised learning in medical and biological research include:

- **Genomics:** Researchers use hierarchical clustering to classify gene expression profiles, helping to identify subtypes of diseases like cancer.
- **Drug discovery:** Pharmaceutical companies use Generative Adversarial Networks (GANs) and Variational Autoencoders (VAEs) to generate potential drug molecules.
- **Medical Imaging:** Autoencoders help detect abnormalities in medical scans by learning normal patterns and flagging deviations as potential anomalies.

Prominent algorithms used for this research are:

- Hierarchical Clustering, PCA, t-SNE for analyzing genomic data
- Autoencoders, GANs, VAEs for medical image generation and enhancement

Natural Language Processing (NLP)

Unsupervised learning plays a crucial role in understanding, organizing, and generating text without labeled datasets. Techniques like word embeddings, topic modeling, and document clustering allow AI models to process massive volumes of unstructured text efficiently. A few important examples of the use of unsupervised learning in NLP are:

- Search Engines (Google, Bing) use word embeddings (such as, Word2Vec and GloVe) to improve search relevance by clustering similar words together
- News Aggregators (Google News, Flipboard) use topic modeling (LDA, NMF) to categorize articles into different themes
- Chatbots and Virtual Assistants apply self-supervised learning to understand text structure and generate human-like responses

Important unsupervised learning algorithms used in NLP are:

- Word Embeddings (Word2Vec, GloVe, FastText) for text representation
- Topic Modeling (Latent Dirichlet Allocation, Non-Negative Matrix Factorization) for document classification
- Hierarchical Clustering and DBSCAN for grouping similar text documents

Supply Chain and Logistics Optimization

Unsupervised learning optimizes supply chain networks, inventory management, and delivery logistics by analyzing patterns in demand, transportation routes, and warehouse efficiency.

Some important examples of the use of unsupervised learning in supply chain and logistics optimization are as follows:

- Retailers like Walmart and Amazon use clustering to optimize warehouse distribution based on customer demand.
- Delivery companies (FedEx, UPS, and DHL) use anomaly detection to spot inefficiencies in supply chain operations.
- Traffic and route optimization systems use density-based clustering (DBSCAN) to analyze congestion patterns and improve fleet management.

Important algorithms used in supply chain and logistics optimization are:

- K-Means, Hierarchical Clustering for demand forecasting and supplier segmentation
- DBSCAN, Isolation Forest for detecting inefficiencies in logistics

Social Network and Community Detection

Unsupervised learning helps identify communities, influencers, and trends within social networks by analyzing interactions between users.

The following are important examples demonstrating the application of unsupervised learning in social network analysis:

- Facebook and Twitter use graph-based clustering (Louvain method, Spectral Clustering) to detect online communities.
- LinkedIn and Instagram analyze user behavior to recommend connections and suggest relevant content.
- Social media monitoring tools use unsupervised NLP techniques to detect trends, sentiment, and fake news.

Important algorithms used in in social network analysis are:

- Spectral Clustering, Louvain Algorithm for community detection
- t-SNE, PCA for visualizing relationships in high-dimensional social data

Conclusion

Unsupervised learning is revolutionizing industries by uncovering hidden patterns, improving decision-making, and enhancing automation. From customer segmentation and fraud detection to medical research and NLP, these techniques allow organizations to extract valuable insights from vast amounts of unlabeled data. As unsupervised learning methods continue to evolve, they will play an increasingly crucial role in AI-driven innovation and large-scale data analysis.

In this chapter, we familiarized ourselves with the fundamentals of unsupervised learning. In the next chapter, we will learn Python programming basics required to implement the concepts we learn throughout this book.

Key Terms

- **Unsupervised Learning:** A type of machine learning where the model learns patterns and structures from unlabeled data
- **Clustering:** A technique used to group similar data points together based on their inherent characteristics
- **Dimensionality Reduction:** The process of reducing the number of input variables while retaining essential information
- **Principal Component Analysis (PCA):** A technique for reducing dimensionality by transforming data into a set of orthogonal components
- **K-Means Clustering:** A centroid-based clustering algorithm that partitions data into K groups by minimizing intra-cluster variance
- **DBSCAN (Density-Based Spatial Clustering of Applications with Noise):** A density-based clustering algorithm that identifies clusters of varying shapes and detects outliers
- **Autoencoder:** A type of neural network used for learning efficient data representations, often for dimensionality reduction or anomaly detection
- **Generative Adversarial Networks (GANs):** A framework where two neural networks, a generator and a discriminator, compete to generate realistic synthetic data
- **t-SNE (t-Distributed Stochastic Neighbor Embedding):** A visualization technique that maps high-dimensional data into a lower-dimensional space while preserving local structure
- **Anomaly Detection:** The identification of rare or unusual data points that differ significantly from the majority of the dataset

Questions

1. Define unsupervised learning. How does it differ from supervised learning? Provide an example of each.
2. Explain the significance of clustering in unsupervised learning. What are some real-world applications of clustering algorithms?
3. What is dimensionality reduction, and why is it important in machine learning? Discuss how Principal Component Analysis (PCA) helps in reducing dimensionality.

4. Compare and contrast K-Means clustering and DBSCAN. When would you prefer DBSCAN over K-Means?
5. Describe the working principle of an autoencoder. How is it used for anomaly detection and feature learning?
6. What are Generative Adversarial Networks (GANs), and how do they work? Explain the roles of the generator and discriminator.
7. How does t-SNE help in visualizing high-dimensional data? What are its advantages and limitations?
8. What is the role of density-based clustering methods in unsupervised learning? Discuss how DBSCAN identifies noise and outliers.
9. Explain how unsupervised learning can be used for anomaly detection. Provide an example where it is useful.
10. Discuss the main challenges in unsupervised learning. Why is evaluating the performance of unsupervised algorithms more difficult than supervised ones?

Multiple Choice Questions

1. What is the primary characteristic of unsupervised learning?
   a. It uses labeled data for training.
   b. It learns patterns from unlabeled data.
   c. It requires human supervision for every step.
   d. It is primarily used for classification tasks.
2. Which of the following is NOT a common unsupervised learning task?
   a. Clustering
   b. Dimensionality reduction
   c. Classification
   d. Anomaly detection
3. What determines the number of clusters in K-Means clustering?
   a. The algorithm automatically decides the optimal number
   b. A predefined parameter kkk set by the user
   c. The size of the dataset
   d. The distance metric used

4. What is the main purpose of PCA (Principal Component Analysis)?
    a. To cluster data into meaningful groups
    b. To reduce the number of features while preserving variance
    c. To generate synthetic data
    d. To classify labeled data
5. How does DBSCAN (Density-Based Spatial Clustering) differ from K-Means?
    a. DBSCAN requires specifying the number of clusters in advance.
    b. DBSCAN works well with arbitrary-shaped clusters and noise.
    c. DBSCAN only works on high-dimensional data.
    d. DBSCAN is a type of supervised learning algorithm.
6. Which of the following best describes autoencoders?
    a. They are used to classify images into different categories.
    b. They reconstruct input data by learning a compressed representation.
    c. They generate completely new data from scratch.
    d. They are only used for clustering.
7. What is the primary purpose of Generative Adversarial Networks (GANs)?
    a. To classify data into predefined categories
    b. To generate new data similar to the training data
    c. To group similar data points together
    d. To reduce dimensionality
8. Which algorithm is the most suitable for detecting rare fraudulent transactions?
    a. K-Means Clustering
    b. One-Class SVM
    c. t-SNE
    d. GANs

9. Why is t-SNE commonly used in data visualization?
    a. It reduces dimensionality while preserving local relationships.
    b. It clusters data into predefined groups.
    c. It identifies anomalies in high-dimensional data.
    d. It generates new synthetic samples.
10. Which statement about unsupervised learning is TRUE?
    a. It requires labeled data to function.
    b. It is mainly used for supervised tasks like regression.
    c. It helps find hidden patterns and structures in data.
    d. It cannot be used for real-world applications.

Answers

1. b
2. c
3. b
4. b
5. b
6. b
7. b
8. b
9. a
10. c

CHAPTER 2
Python Basics for Machine Learning

Introduction

This chapter is a quick refresher on essential Python programming concepts, libraries, and tools used in machine learning. You will learn how to use NumPy for numerical computing, Pandas for data manipulation, and Matplotlib for visualizing data, Scikit-learn for machine learning. The chapter also includes hands-on examples and exercises that will get you up to speed with Python's powerful capabilities for data preprocessing and visualization. It is designed for those who may not be fully familiar with these Python libraries and ensures that you are ready for the upcoming chapters. However, familiarity with general Python syntax such as loops, conditionals, and functions is a prerequisite.

Structure

The chapter addresses the following topics:

- Python for Machine Learning
- Setting up Python
- Core Python Skills for ML
    - NumPy
    - Pandas
    - Matplotlib
    - Seaborn for Advanced Data Visualization in Python
- Introduction to Scikit-learn
- Jupyter Notebooks

Python for Machine Learning

Python is the most preferred programming language for Machine Learning (ML). The choice of programming language can significantly impact your productivity, the quality of your models, and your ability to iterate quickly. Among the many options available, Python has emerged as the de facto standard for machine learning. Its versatility, simplicity, and rich ecosystem of libraries make it an ideal choice for both beginners and seasoned data scientists tackling complex real-world problems. In this section, we will explore why Python stands out as the language of choice for machine learning.

A Language Built for Readability and Rapid Prototyping

Python's syntax is clean and intuitive. Its readability lowers the barrier to entry for newcomers and allows experienced developers to focus on solving ML problems rather than getting stuck with complex syntax. Python lets you write, test, and refine code quickly. For example, implementing a K-means clustering model in Python with Scikit-learn takes just a few lines of code, compared to the verbose boilerplate required in languages such as C++ or Java.

A Thriving Ecosystem of Machine Learning Libraries

Python's dominance in ML is also because of its vast ecosystem of open-source libraries, which provide pre-built tools for most of the tasks. For unsupervised learning, libraries such as Scikit-learn, NumPy, and Pandas form the backbone of data manipulation, preprocessing, and algorithm implementation. Scikit-learn, in particular, offers a unified interface for clustering (such as, K-means, DBSCAN), dimensionality reduction (such as, PCA, t-SNE), and anomaly detection. Meanwhile, TensorFlow and PyTorch enable users to employ advanced techniques such as autoencoders and Generative Adversarial Networks (GANs). These libraries are not only powerful but also well-documented and supported by a global community, which ensures that you get enough support whenever required.

Python integrates seamlessly with visualization libraries such as Matplotlib and Seaborn, which are essential for interpreting the results of ML models. Since unsupervised learning lacks labeled data to guide evaluation, visualizing clusters, dimension reduction, and anomalies become very important.

Community and Industry Adoption

Python has a vibrant community of users and widespread adoption in industry and academia. As of March 2025, Python consistently ranks at the top of programming language indices, such as TIOBE and PYPL, that reflect its dominance in data science and ML. This popularity means that you can accelerate your learning and problem-solving via many resources such as tutorials, forums, and open-source projects. Major tech companies such as Google, Facebook, and Netflix rely on Python for ML tasks, often open sourcing their tools (like TensorFlow from Google), which further enriches their ecosystem. For unsupervised learning, Python's adoption in fields (such as natural language processing) and anomaly detection ensures that you can directly apply these skills to cutting-edge applications.

Flexibility for Research and Production

Python is used for both research and deployment. Its flexibility allows researchers to prototype ideas quickly by leveraging tools such as Jupyter Notebooks for interactive development. At the same time, Python's integration with production-ready frameworks, such as Flask, FastAPI, or cloud platforms such as AWS and GCP, makes it a practical choice for deploying models.

Alternative Programming Languages

There are other alternatives such as R, Julia, or C++. While each has strengths–R for statistical analysis, Julia for performance, C++ for speed–none of them can match Python's balance of simplicity, ecosystem, and community support. R is excellent for statistics but lacks Python's general-purpose flexibility and production-ready tools. Julia, though fast and promising, has a smaller ecosystem and steeper learning curve. C++ offers unparalleled performance but demands significant effort for rapid prototyping, which can be better spent refining your unsupervised models. Python strikes a sweet spot and is the ideal vehicle for our journey through unsupervised learning.

Throughout this book, we will use Python to explore clustering, dimensionality reduction, anomaly detection, and beyond, starting with the foundational skills in this chapter. Whether you are segmenting customers, compressing data, or generating synthetic images, Python will be your trusted companion. Let us dive into the practicalities of setting it up and putting it to work.

Setting up Python

Before we start coding unsupervised machine learning models, we need to set up a robust and efficient Python environment. In this section, we will walk through installing Python, managing dependencies with Anaconda, and setting up Jupyter Notebooks, which is a powerful tool for interactive development. By the end, you will have everything you need to follow along with the examples in this chapter and beyond.

Step 1: Installing Python with Anaconda

While Python can be installed directly from python.org, we recommend using **Anaconda**, a distribution tailored for data science and machine learning. Anaconda simplifies package management, includes essential libraries out of the box, and ensures compatibility across platforms (Windows, macOS, Linux). As of March 2025, Anaconda remains a go-to choice for ML practitioners. Follow these steps to install Python with Anaconda:

1. **Download and Install**: Visit anaconda.com and download the latest Anaconda Individual Edition (such as, Python 3.11 or newer). Follow the installer's

instructions, accept the defaults unless you have specific needs. Check out the official installation page of Anaconda **(https://www.anaconda.com/docs/getting-started/anaconda/install)** for available releases based on your system configuration.

2. **Verify Installation**: Open a terminal (or Anaconda Prompt on Windows) and type the following commands to check the version of the conda and python installed on your computer (*Figure 2.1*).

```
conda --version
python --version
```

You should see outputs, such as conda 23.x.x and Python 3.11.x. If not, revisit the installation steps.

Anaconda is preloaded with tools, such as NumPy, Pandas, and Scikit-learn, which we will use extensively. It also includes **conda**, a package manager we will leverage in the next section.

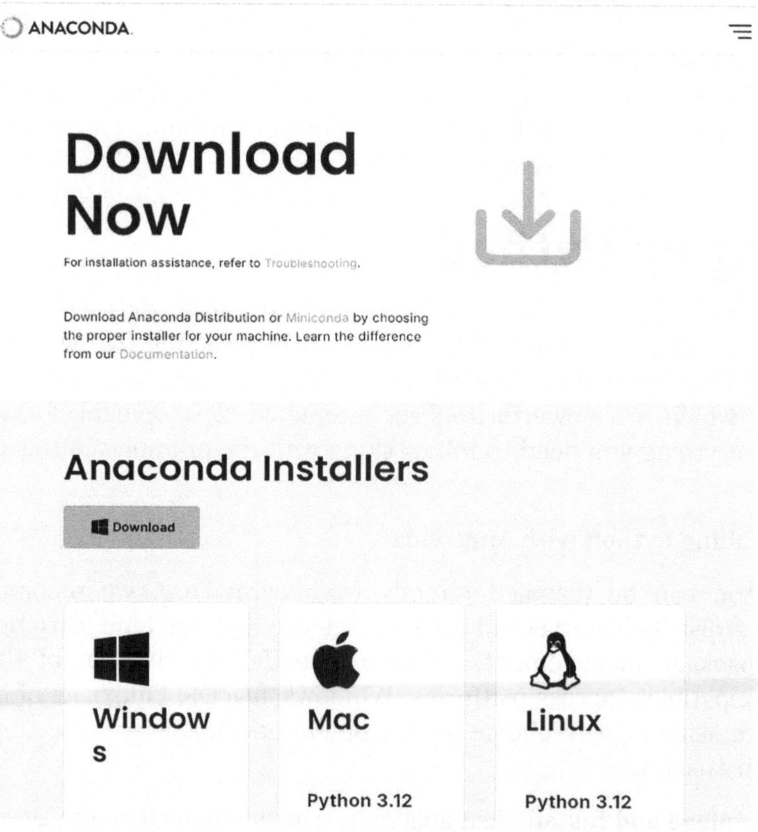

Figure 2.1: *Install Anaconda Distribution from www.anaconda.com*

Step 2: Creating a Virtual Environment

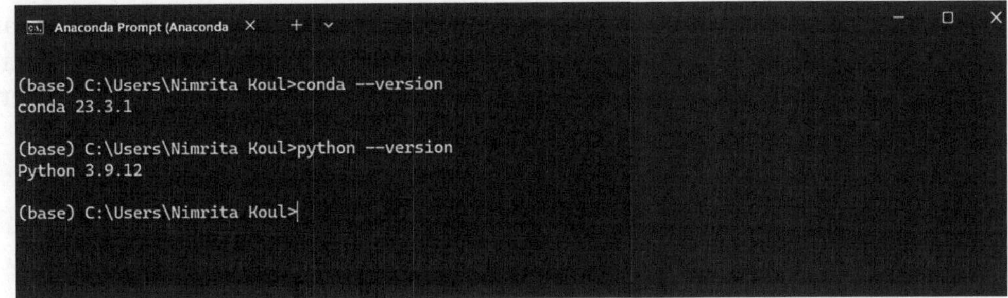

Figure 2.2: *Verify Your installation*

To keep your projects organized and avoid dependency conflicts, create a dedicated virtual environment for this book's examples:

Run the following command in your Anaconda Prompt (terminal) to create a new environment. The name of this environment is "**`ml-unsupervised`**" and Python 3.11 will be installed in this environment as demonstrated:

```
conda create -n ml-unsupervised python=3.11
```

The preceding command creates an environment named **`ml-unsupervised`** with Python 3.11.

Next, we need to activate the newly created environment:

```
conda activate ml-unsupervised
```

Your terminal prompt should now show (**`ml-unsupervised`**).

Virtual environments let you experiment freely without risking your system-wide setup.

Step 3: Installing Key Libraries

With your environment active, install the core libraries for unsupervised learning:

```
conda install numpy pandas matplotlib seaborn scikit-learn jupyter
```

- **`NumPy`:** For numerical operations such as array manipulation
- **`Pandas`:** For data handling and preprocessing
- **`Matplotlib/Seaborn`:** For visualizing results (such as, clusters or reduced dimensions)
- **`Scikit-learn`:** For implementing unsupervised algorithms
- **`Jupyter`:** For interactive coding

Verify installations by running **`python -c "import sklearn; print(sklearn.__version__)"`** you should see a version number (such as, 1.4.x).

Step 4: Setting Up Jupyter Notebooks

Jupyter Notebooks are an ideal environment for ML experimentation. They can blend code, visualizations, and explanations in one place. They are especially useful for unsupervised learning, where iterating on visualizations or tweaking parameters is common.

Launch Jupyter from your terminal using the following:

```
jupyter notebook
```

A browser window will open with the Jupyter interface.

- Create a new notebook: Click "**New**" > "**Python 3**." You will see a cell where you can type and execute code.
- Test it. Enter and run:

```
import numpy as np
print(np.__version__)
```

If a version prints, you are ready!

Save notebooks in a dedicated folder (such as, **book_projects/**) to stay organized.

You can also launch Jupyter Notebook from your start menu.

Troubleshooting Tips:

- **Command Not Found:** Ensure conda is in your PATH. On Windows, use Anaconda Prompt; on macOS/Linux, restart your terminal after installation.
- **Internet Issues:** If downloads fail, check your connection or use pip as a fallback (such as, pip install numpy).
- **Version Conflicts:** Stick to conda for consistency, as it resolves dependencies better than pip.

Core Python Skills for ML

Python libraries–**NumPy** for numerical computation, **Pandas** for data manipulation, and **Matplotlib** paired with **Seaborn** for visualization–are powerful tools that make Python useful for machine learning. In this section, we will explore these libraries and their core functionalities.

NumPy: The Backbone of Numerical Operations

NumPy (Numerical Python) provides fast array operations that are critical for handling datasets and performing mathematical computations. It provides support for large multi-dimensional arrays and matrices, along with mathematical functions to operate on these data structures efficiently. In unsupervised learning, you will use NumPy to manage feature matrices, compute distances, and preprocess data.

Installing NumPy

All prominent libraries that are used for machine learning and data science tasks are already installed on your computer in the base environment when you install Anaconda Distribution of Python. However, if for some reason, you have not installed NumPy, you can do it via:

```
pip install numpy
```

Importing NumPy

Use the following Python code to import numpy into your Python script or notebook:

```
import numpy as np
```

NumPy Data Structures

NumPy's primary data structure is the **ndarray** (N-dimensional array). It is more efficient than Python lists in terms of speed and memory. The **ndarray** is a powerful, flexible, and highly optimized tool for handling large datasets, making it indispensable for tasks such as clustering, dimensionality reduction, and matrix operations.

ndarray has several important features, such as multidimensionality, homogeneous data type, attributes, efficient memory layout, broadcasting, element-wise operations, indexing and slicing, and universal functions.

- **Multidimensionality:** The **ndarray** supports multiple dimensions, allowing it to represent scalars (0D), vectors (1D), matrices (2D), or higher-dimensional arrays (such as 3D tensors).
- **Homogeneous Data Type:** All elements in an **ndarray** must share the same data type (such as **int32**, **float64**), enforced by NumPy's type system. This homogeneity enables optimized memory usage and fast computation, as opposed to Python's native lists, which allow mixed types but incur performance overhead.
- **Shape and Size:** The shape attribute of an **ndarray** defines its dimensions (such as, (3, 4) for a 3-row, 4-column matrix), while the size attribute gives the total number of elements. These properties allow for dynamic reshaping, a common operation in unsupervised learning, like flattening a matrix into a vector for input into algorithms such as k-means clustering.
- **Efficient Memory Layout:** Unlike Python lists, that store pointers to objects, **ndarray** uses a contiguous block of memory. This layout minimizes overhead and enables vectorized operations via low-level optimizations. For instance, computing pairwise distances in a dataset, which is a frequent step in clustering, benefits immensely from this efficiency.

- **Indexing and Slicing:** Advanced indexing and slicing allow for efficient access to subsets of data. For example, **`array[0, :]`** retrieves the first row of a 2D array, while Boolean indexing (such as, **`array[array > 0]`**) extracts elements that meet a condition. These operations are essential for preprocessing tasks, such as filtering outliers or selecting features in unsupervised learning pipelines.
- **Broadcasting:** NumPy's broadcasting allows the user to perform operations on arrays of different shapes without explicit looping. For example, adding a scalar to every element of an **`ndarray`**, or multiplying a matrix by a vector is handled seamlessly. This feature simplifies code and accelerates computations in algorithms, such as Principal Component Analysis (PCA), where normalization or scaling of features is required.
- **Vectorization:** Vectorization leverages the **`ndarray`**'s contiguous memory layout and NumPy's optimized, low-level implementations to execute operations in bulk. Instead of iterating over array elements with a Python for loop (which is slow due to Python's interpreted nature), vectorized operations delegate the heavy lifting to precompiled C code. This results in significant speedups, making it ideal for the computationally intensive tasks. As datasets grow in size, vectorized operations scale efficiently. The ndarray enables vectorization through the mechanisms like – element wise operations, broadcasting, universal functions (ufuncs).
- **Element-Wise Operations:** The **`ndarray`** supports element-wise arithmetic, logical, and mathematical operations (such as, **`+`**, **`*`**, **`sin`**, **`exp`**).
- **Universal Functions (`ufuncs`):** NumPy provides a suite of universal functions optimized for ndarray operations, such as **`np.mean`**, **`np.std`**, and **`np.dot`**. These functions are both fast and expressive and enable concise implementations of mathematical operations.

Creating a NumPy Array

In *Figure* 2.3, we have created a basic NumPy array using **`array()`** function:

```
import numpy as np
arr = np.array([1, 2, 3, 4, 5])
print(arr)  # Output: [1 2 3 4 5]
print(type(arr))

```

```
[1 2 3 4 5]
<class 'numpy.ndarray'>
```

Figure 2.3: *Creating a 1-Dimensional NumPy Array*

Let us print and check the attributes of the array created as in *Figure 2.4*:

```
print(arr.shape)    # Shape of the array
print(arr.ndim)     # Number of dimensions
print(arr.dtype)    # Data type of elements
print(arr.size)     # Number of elements

```

```
(5,)
1
int32
5
```

Figure 2.4: *Checking Array Attributes*

We can create an array using other functions as well, like in *Figure 2.5*, we have used the **`arrange()`** function to create an array:

```
arr2 = np.arange(1, 10, 2)  # Start=1, Stop=10, Step=2
print(arr2)  # Output: [1 3 5 7 9]

```

```
[1 3 5 7 9]
```

Figure 2.5: ***`arange()`*** *Function to Create an ndarray*

We can also use **`linspace()`** function to generate an array of n evenly spaced values between a given range of values as shown in *Figure 2.6*:

```
arr3 = np.linspace(0, 1, 5)  # 5 points between 0 and 1
print(arr3)  # Output: [0.   0.25 0.5  0.75 1.  ]

```

```
[0.   0.25 0.5  0.75 1.  ]
```

Figure 2.6: ***`linspace()`*** *Function to Create an ndarray*

In *Figure 2.7*, we use the function **`zeros()`** and **`ones()`** to create an **`ndarray`**:

```
zeros_array = np.zeros((3, 3))  # 3x3 array of zeros
ones_array = np.ones((2, 4))
print(zeros_array)
print(ones_array)
```

```
[[0. 0. 0.]
 [0. 0. 0.]
 [0. 0. 0.]]
[[1. 1. 1. 1.]
 [1. 1. 1. 1.]]
```

Figure 2.7: *Using* ***`zeros()`*** *and* ***`ones()`*** *to Create an ndarray*

To create an array containing random values, we can use the random module of NumPy as shown in *Figure* 2.8.

```
rand_arr = np.random.rand(3, 3)# 3x3 random values between 0 and 1
rand_ints = np.random.randint(1, 10, (2, 2)) # 2x2 random ints from 1 to 9
print(rand_arr)
print(rand_ints)
```

```
[[0.55976757 0.64035114 0.60312024]
 [0.3112788  0.10806105 0.86359397]
 [0.7668379  0.96794757 0.13472177]]
[[5 8]
 [1 6]]
```

Figure 2.8: *Using NumPy's random Module to Create ndarrays with Random Values*

NumPy Array Operations

NumPy offers different categories of operations on ndarrays. Let us explore these one by one:

Arithmetic Operations

NumPy arrays support element-wise arithmetic operations as shown in *Figure* 2.9.

```
# Arithmetic Operations
import numpy as np

a = np.array([1, 2, 3])
b = np.array([4, 5, 6])

print(a + b)  # Output: [5 7 9]
print(a - b)  # Output: [-3 -3 -3]
print(a * b)  # Output: [4 10 18]
print(a / b)  # Output: [0.25 0.4  0.5 ]
```

```
[5 7 9]
[-3 -3 -3]
[ 4 10 18]
[0.25 0.4  0.5 ]
```

Figure 2.9: *ndarray Arithmetic Operations*

NumPy allows broadcasting to carry out operations between arrays of different shapes as shown in *Figure* 2.10:

```
# Broadcasting
import numpy as np
arr = np.array([1, 2, 3])

scalar = 2
print(arr * scalar)  # Output: [2 4 6]

```

```
[2 4 6]
```

Figure 2.10: Broadcasting

NumPy arrays support indexing and slicing

Indexing on a numpy array is shown in *Figure* 2.11 and *Figure* 2.12:

```
#Indexing
arr = np.array([10, 20, 30, 40])
print(arr[1])   # Output: 20

```

```
20
```

Figure 2.11: Array Indexing

Indexing in Multi-Dimensional Arrays

```
#Indexing in Multi-Dimensional Arrays
import numpy as np
mat = np.array([[10, 20, 30], [40, 50, 60], [70, 80, 90]])
print(mat[1, 2])  # Access element at row 1, column 2 -> Output: 60
print(mat[:, 1])  # All rows, second column -> Output: [20 50 80]
print(mat[1, :])  # Second row

```

```
60
[20 50 80]
[40 50 60]
```

Figure 2.12: Creating and Indexing Multidimensional Arrays

Slicing

You can slice a NumPy array as shown in *Figure* 2.13:

```
#Slicing
import numpy as np
arr = np.array([0, 1, 2, 3, 4, 5])
print(arr[1:4])  # Output: [1 2 3]
print(arr[:3])   # First 3 elements
print(arr[3:])   # Elements from index 3 onwards
print(arr[::-1]) # Reverse array
```

```
[1 2 3]
[0 1 2]
[3 4 5]
[5 4 3 2 1 0]
```

Figure 2.13: *Slicing an ndarray*

Reshaping and Manipulating Arrays

Reshaping an array changes its dimensions, which is demonstrated in *Figure* 2.14:

```
#Reshaping and Manipulating Arrays
#Reshaping
import numpy as np
arr = np.array([1, 2, 3, 4, 5, 6])
reshaped = arr.reshape(2, 3)
print(reshaped)
```

```
[[1 2 3]
 [4 5 6]]
```

Figure 2.14: *Reshaping an ndarray*

Transposing an array interchanges the elements in rows and columns, which is shown in *Figure* 2.15:

```
#Transposing
import numpy as np
arr = np.array([[1, 2, 3], [4, 5, 6]])
print(arr.T)
```

```
[[1 4]
 [2 5]
 [3 6]]
```

Figure 2.15: *Transposing an ndarray*

Concatenation and Stacking

Concatenation means to combine elements of an array horizontally, while stacking means to combine the elements vertically. These operations are shown in *Figure 2.16*:

```
#Concatenation and Stacking
import numpy as np
a = np.array([1, 2, 3])
b = np.array([4, 5, 6])

print(np.concatenate((a, b)))  # Output: [1 2 3 4 5 6]
print(np.vstack((a, b)))  # Vertical stack
print(np.hstack((a, b)))  # Horizontal stack

```

```
[1 2 3 4 5 6]
[[1 2 3]
 [4 5 6]]
[1 2 3 4 5 6]
```

Figure 2.16: *Concatenation and Stacking*

Linear Algebra in NumPy

NumPy includes linear algebra functions such as matrix multiplication, inverse, and determinant as shown in *Figure 2.17*:

```
import numpy as np
A = np.array([[1, 2], [3, 4]])
B = np.array([[5, 6], [7, 8]])

# Matrix Multiplication
print(np.dot(A, B))

# Inverse of a Matrix
print(np.linalg.inv(A))

# Determinant
print(np.linalg.det(A))

```

```
[[19 22]
 [43 50]]
[[-2.   1. ]
 [ 1.5 -0.5]]
-2.0000000000000004
```

Figure 2.17: *Linear Algebra Operations*

NumPy supports Statistical and Mathematical Functions as shown in *Figure* 2.18:

```
#Statistical and Mathematical Functions
import numpy as np
arr = np.array([1, 2, 3, 4, 5])
print(np.mean(arr))    # Mean
print(np.median(arr)) # Median
print(np.std(arr))     # Standard deviation
print(np.min(arr))     # Minimum value
print(np.max(arr))     # Maximum value
print(np.sum(arr))     # Sum of elements
print(np.cumsum(arr)) # Cumulative sum
```

```
3.0
3.0
1.4142135623730951
1
5
15
[ 1  3  6 10 15]
```

Figure 2.18: *Statistical and Mathematical Operations*

Saving and Loading NumPy Arrays

You can save a NumPy array to a file on your local disk, with the extension of these files being '**.npy**'. You can also load these files into a Python program. The save and load operation is shown in *Figure* 2.19. *Figure* 2.20 demonstrates how to save data to a CSV file and load it from a CSV file:

```
#Saving and Loading NumPy Arrays
import numpy as np
arr = np.array([1, 2, 3, 4])
np.save("array.npy", arr)  # Save to file
loaded_arr = np.load("array.npy")  # Load from file
print(loaded_arr)
```

```
[1 2 3 4]
```

Figure 2.19: *Saving and Loading Numpy Arrays*

Reading and Writing CSV

Use the following code snippet to write data from a pandas dataframe to a csv file and read data from a csv file into a pandas dataframe:

```
#Reading and Writing CSV
import numpy as np
import pandas as pd
data = np.array([[1, 2, 3], [4, 5, 6]])
df = pd.DataFrame(data, columns=["A", "B", "C"])
df.to_csv("data.csv", index=False)  # Save to CSV
df_read = pd.read_csv("data.csv")   # Read from CSV
print(df_read)

```

```
   A  B  C
0  1  2  3
1  4  5  6
```

Figure 2.20: *Reading and Writing Data to a CSV File*

NumPy is a fundamental library for numerical computing in Python, which provides fast and efficient data structures, mathematical operations, and array manipulations. Understanding its core features helps in optimizing performance for machine learning and data science applications.

Pandas Library

Pandas is a powerful Python library, that is built on top of NumPy for data analysis and manipulation. It consists of flexible data structures and functions for handling structured data, that make it essential for machine learning and data science workflows. Pandas simplifies working with structured data, such as datasets in CSV files or tables.

Installing Pandas

In case you have not installed Pandas, you can install it using the following command at your Anaconda Prompt:

```
pip install pandas
```

Importing Pandas

Use the following code to import Pandas into your Python code:

```
import pandas as pd
import numpy as np
```

Pandas Data Structures

Pandas provides two core data structures:

- **Series:** One-dimensional labeled array
- **DataFrame:** Two-dimensional labeled table

Series: One-Dimensional Data Structure

A Series data structure in Pandas is a one-dimensional NumPy ndarray paired with an index, which labels each element of the series. For example, a Series might store ages **`[25, 30, 35]`** with an index **`[0, 1, 2]`** or custom labels such as **`['Alice', 'Bob', 'Charlie']`**. This labeled structure distinguishes it from a raw ndarray. A Series is like a column in a spreadsheet, with an index.

The index enables data access by label rather than just position. For instance, **`series['Alice']`** retrieves Alice's age, while **`series[0]`** uses positional indexing.

Like an ndarray, a Series enforces a uniform data type for its elements (such as, **`int64`**, **`float64`**, object for strings). The Series supports handling of missing values (NaN), with methods such as **`series.dropna()`** to remove them or **`series.fillna(value)`** to impute them.

When performing operations between two Series objects, Pandas aligns them by their indices, and automatically handles mismatches. For example, adding two Series with overlapping but non-identical indices results in NaN where alignment fails. This can be useful for comparing feature transformations or merging results.

Creating a Series

Figure 2.21 demonstrates the creation of a series object using Pandas:

```
# Creating a Series
import pandas as pd
import numpy as np
data = [10, 20, 30, 40]
series = pd.Series(data)
print(series)

```

```
0    10
1    20
2    30
3    40
dtype: int64
```

Figure 2.21: *Creating a Series Object*

You can also create a series with a customized index as shown in *Figure* 2.22:

```
# Creating a Series with a custom index
import pandas as pd
import numpy as np
data = [10, 20, 30, 40]
series = pd.Series(data, index=['a', 'b', 'c', 'd'])
print(series)
```

```
a    10
b    20
c    30
d    40
dtype: int64
```

Figure 2.22: *Creating a Series Object with a Custom Index*

Accessing Elements in a Series

Accessing elements in a Series object is simple. You can access using index values as shown in *Figure* 2.23:

```
# Accessing series elements
import pandas as pd
import numpy as np
data = [10, 20, 30, 40]
series = pd.Series(data, index=['a', 'b', 'c', 'd'])
print(series['b'])  # Output: 20
print(series[1])    # Output: 20
```

```
20
20
```

Figure 2.23: *Creating a Series Object with a Custom Index*

Let us create a series object called "**incomes**", normalize the values in this series, and handle missing values, if any, as shown in *Figure* 2.24:

```
## Data cleaning in a series object
import pandas as pd

# Create a Series
incomes = pd.Series([50000, 60000, 65000,70000],
                    index=['cust1', 'cust2', 'cust3', 'cust4'])
print("Original Incomes", incomes)

# Normalize the Series
normalized_incomes = (incomes - incomes.mean()) / incomes.std()
print("Normalized Incomes",normalized_incomes)

# Handle missing data (if any)
incomes_cleaned = incomes.fillna(incomes.median())
print("Cleaned Incomes",incomes_cleaned)
```

```
Original Incomes cust1    50000
cust2    60000
cust3    65000
cust4    70000
dtype: int64
Normalized Incomes cust1   -1.317465
cust2   -0.146385
cust3    0.439155
cust4    1.024695
dtype: float64
Cleaned Incomes cust1    50000
cust2    60000
cust3    65000
cust4    70000
dtype: int64
```

Figure 2.24: *Data Cleaning in a Series Object*

DataFrame: Two-Dimensional Data Structure

Real-world machine learning often involves dealing with heterogeneous, structured data. Pandas introduces the DataFrame object. A DataFrame is a two-dimensional data structure similar to an Excel table or SQL table. It can be thought of as a collection of labeled columns, where each column is a Pandas Series (a one-dimensional array-like object) and all columns share a common index.

Unlike the ndarray, which enforces a single data type, a DataFrame supports heterogeneous types across columns. For example, one column might store integers (such as, int64 for cluster labels), another floats (such as, float64 for feature values), and yet another strings (such as, categorical variables such as "`region`").

The DataFrame's rows and columns are labeled with index and column names, respectively. This labeling provides intuitive access to data, such as, **`df['age']`** to select the "**age**" column or **`df.loc[0]`** to retrieve the first row.

Similar to an ndarray, a DataFrame has a shape attribute (such as, (100, 5) for 100 rows and 5 columns) and a size equal to the total number of elements. However, its tabular nature makes it more suited for dataset manipulation than raw matrix operations. You can easily add or drop columns **`(df.drop('column', axis=1))`** or rows, adapting the data to the needs of algorithms such as PCA or k-means.

The DataFrame object has built-in methods to handle missing values (represented as NaN). Methods such as **`df.dropna()`** remove rows with missing data, while **`df.fillna(0)`** imputes values–both common preprocessing steps in unsupervised learning to ensure algorithms can process the data without errors.

DataFrame columns inherit NumPy's vectorization capabilities. Operations such as **`df['feature'] = df['feature'] / df['feature'].std()`** normalize a column efficiently. Additionally, Pandas supports broadcasting and alignment based on indices, ensuring operations respect the labeled structure. This is particularly useful for feature scaling or computing pairwise correlations **`(df.corr())`** in preparation for dimensionality reduction.

The DataFrame's groupby functionality allows data to be split, aggregated, and summarized–a powerful feature for exploratory data analysis in unsupervised learning. For instance, **`df.groupby('cluster_label').mean()`** computes feature averages per cluster after running a clustering algorithm, aiding in the interpretation of results.

Let us creating a DataFrame from a Dictionary as shown in *Figure 2.24*:

```
# Creating a DataFrame from a Dictionary
import pandas as pd

data = {
    "Name": ["Alice", "Bob", "Charlie"],
    "Age": [25, 30, 35],
    "Salary": [50000, 60000, 70000]
}
df = pd.DataFrame(data)
print(df)

```

```
      Name  Age  Salary
0    Alice   25   50000
1      Bob   30   60000
2  Charlie   35   70000
```

Figure 2.25: *Creating a DataFrame from a Dictionary*

Reading and Writing Data

Pandas provides several methods for reading data from different types of files and writing data to them:

Reading CSV Files

You can use pandas function **read_csv()** to read the contents of a CSV file into a dataframe and the function **to_csv()** to write the contents of a dataframe to a CSV file as shown in *Figure* 2.26 and *Figure* 2.27 respectively. You can also read from and write to a Microsoft Excel file using functions **read_excel()** and **to_excel()**, as shown in *Figure* 2.28.

```
import pandas as pd
df = pd.read_csv("data.csv") #create a dataframe 'df' with the contents of file
print(df.head())  # Display first 5 rows of the data.csv file

```

Figure 2.26: *Reading a CSV File into a DataFrame*

Writing to a CSV File

```
df.to_csv("output.csv", index=False)  # Save without index column
```

Figure 2.27: *Save your DataFrame to a CSV File without an Index Column*

Reading and Writing Excel Files

```
df = pd.read_excel("data.xlsx", sheet_name="Sheet1")
df.to_excel("output.xlsx", sheet_name="Results", index=False)
```

Figure 2.28: *Read Data from an Excel File to a DataFrame and Write back to an Excel File*

Data Exploration and Summary

Pandas provides built in functions that help you explore your data and summarize it. Some of these functions are shown in *Figure* 2.29:

```
print(df.info())  # Column data types and memory usage
print(df.describe())  # Summary statistics
print(df.head(3))  # First 3 rows
print(df.tail(3))  # Last 3 rows
print(df.isnull().sum())  # Count missing values in each column
```

Figure 2.29: *Describe Data in the DataFrame*

Selecting and Filtering Data

You can use indexing to select and filter data. In addition to this, Pandas provides the **`loc()`** and **`iloc()`** methods to access data from rows and columns in a dataframe, as shown in *Figure 2.30*:

```
#Selecting Columns

print(df["Name"])  # Select single column whose column name is 'Name'
print(df[["Name", "Age"]])  # Select multiple columns

#Selecting Rows by Index
print(df.iloc[1])  # Select row by integer index
print(df.loc[1])   # Select row by label

#Filtering Rows
print(df[df["Age"] > 28])  # Filter rows where Age > 28

Using Multiple Conditions
filtered_df = df[(df["Age"] > 25) & (df["Salary"] > 50000)]
```

Figure 2.30: *Data Filtering*

Modifying Data

It is very easy to modify the data in a Pandas dataframe. You have many built in functions to delete rows and columns or to update the values in selected rows and columns, as shown in *Figure 2.31*:

```
#Adding a New Column
df["Bonus"] = df["Salary"] * 0.1

#Updating Column Values
df["Age"] = df["Age"] + 1

#Renaming Columns
df.rename(columns={"Salary": "Annual_Salary"}, inplace=True)

#Removing Columns and Rows
df.drop(columns=["Bonus"], inplace=True)  # Remove column
df.drop(index=0, inplace=True)  # Remove first row
```

Figure 2.31: *Data Updating*

Handling Missing Data

Pandas provides functions such as **dropna()**, **fillna()** to handle missing values in a dataframe, as shown in *Figure 2.32*:

```
#Filling Missing Values
df.fillna(0, inplace=True)  # Replace NaN with 0
df["Age"].fillna(df["Age"].mean(), inplace=True)  # Fill NaN with column mean
#Dropping Missing Values
df.dropna(inplace=True)  # Remove rows with NaN
```

Figure 2.32: *Handling Missing Values in a DataFrame*

Sorting and Grouping Data

Pandas has built-in functions for data sorting and grouping of data that are based on conditions, as shown in *Figure 2.33*:

```
#Sorting Data
df_sorted = df.sort_values(by="Age", ascending=False)

#Grouping Data
grouped = df.groupby("Age")["Salary"].mean()
print(grouped)

#Merging and Joining Data
#Merging DataFrames
df1 = pd.DataFrame({"ID": [1, 2], "Name": ["Alice", "Bob"]})
df2 = pd.DataFrame({"ID": [1, 2], "Salary": [50000, 60000]})
merged_df = pd.merge(df1, df2, on="ID")

#Concatenating DataFrames
df_concat = pd.concat([df1, df2], axis=1)
```

Figure 2.33: *Sorting and Grouping Data*

Applying Functions

The **apply()** and **map()** functions allow you to apply custom functions to entire dataframe or a subset of it, as shown in *Figure 2.34*:

```
#Using apply()
df["New_Column"] = df["Salary"].apply(lambda x: x * 1.1)

#Using map() for Element-Wise Operations
df["Age"] = df["Age"].map(lambda x: x + 1)

```

Figure 2.34: *Applying Functions*

Time Series Data in Pandas

Pandas supports working with time series data as well. Using **`to_datetime()`** function you can transform values in any column into a data time object.

```
df["Date"] = pd.to_datetime(df["Date"])
df.set_index("Date", inplace=True)
df.resample("M").mean()  # Resample by month
```

Figure 2.35: *Time Series Data Handling with Pandas*

Matplotlib

Matplotlib is a versatile and widely used Python library used for creating high-quality plots and charts. Built to integrate seamlessly with NumPy and Pandas, Matplotlib enables practitioners to transform raw data, such as ndarrays, DataFrames, or Series, into visual representations such as scatter plots, histograms, and heatmaps.

Installing Matplotlib

Though Matplotlib, such as numpy and pandas comes pre-installed with Anaconda Distribution, you can still install it via the following pip command:

```
pip install matplotlib
```

Importing Matplotlib

Use the following code snippet to import matplotlib into your code:

```
import matplotlib.pyplot as plt
import numpy as np
```

Basic Plotting with Matplotlib

Let us create a simple Line Plot as shown in *Figure* 2.36:

```
import matplotlib.pyplot as plt
import numpy as np
x = np.linspace(0, 10, 100)  # Generate 100 points between 0 and 10
y = np.sin(x)

plt.plot(x, y)
plt.title("Simple Line Plot")
plt.xlabel("X-axis")
plt.ylabel("Y-axis")
plt.show()

```

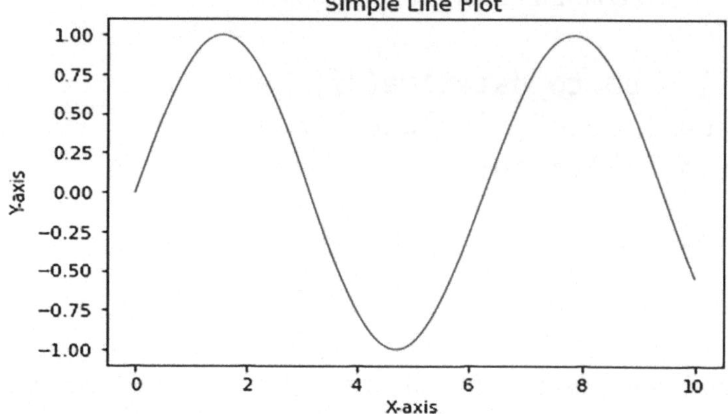

Figure 2.36: *Creating a Basic Line Plot*

Let us customize our Plots by changing line style as shown in *Figure* 2.37:

```
#Customizing Plots
#Adding Labels, Titles, and Legends

import matplotlib.pyplot as plt
import numpy as np
x = np.linspace(0, 10, 100)  # Generate 100 points between 0 and 10
y = np.sin(x)
plt.plot(x, y, label="Sine Wave", color="red", linestyle="--", linewidth=2)
plt.title("Customized Line Plot")
plt.xlabel("X-axis")
plt.ylabel("Y-axis")
plt.legend()
plt.grid(True)
plt.show()

```

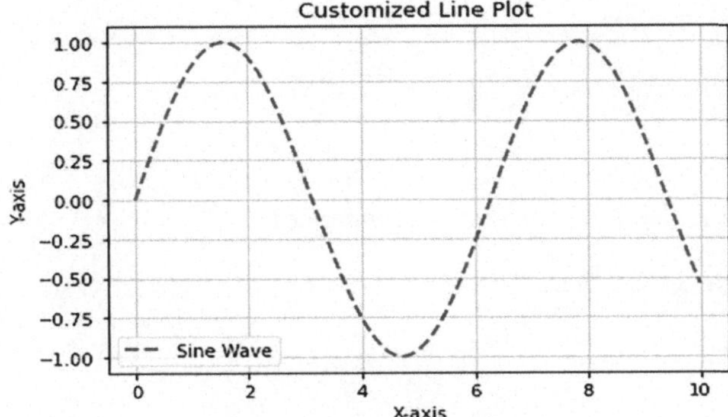

Figure 2.37: *Adding Labels, Titles and Legends to the Basic Plot*

Let us make more changes to Line Styles, Colors, and Markers as shown in *Figure* 2.38:

```
#Changing Line Styles, Colors, and Markers
import matplotlib.pyplot as plt
import numpy as np
x = np.linspace(0, 10, 100)  # Generate 100 points between 0 and 10
y = np.sin(x)
plt.plot(x, y, "g--o", label="Green Dashed Line with Circles")  # Green dashed line with circle m
plt.legend()
plt.show()

```

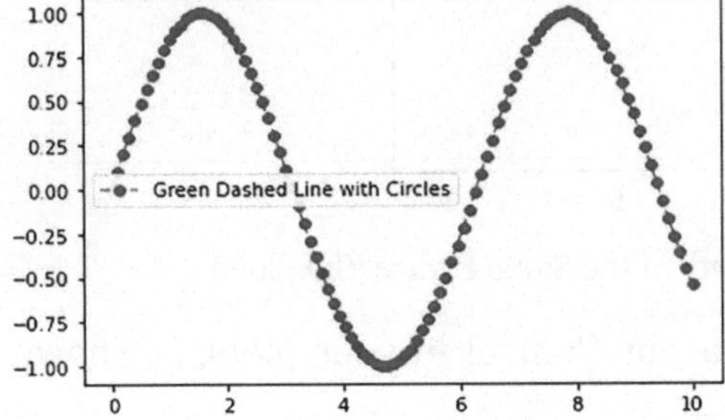

Figure 2.38: *Changing Plot Style*

Subplots: Multiple Plots in One Figure

You can create multiple plots in a single Matplotlib figure using **`subplot()`** function, as shown in *Figure 2.39*:

```
#Creating Multiple Plots Using subplot()
import matplotlib.pyplot as plt
import numpy as np


x = np.linspace(0, 10, 10)  # Generate 10 points between 0 and 10
y1 = np.power(x,2)
y2 = np.power(x,0.5)

plt.subplot(2, 1, 1)  # 2 rows, 1 column, first plot
plt.plot(x, y1, "r")
plt.title("x Squared")

plt.subplot(2, 1, 2)  # 2 rows, 1 column, second plot
plt.plot(x, y2, "b")
plt.title("Square Root of x")

plt.tight_layout()
plt.show()

```

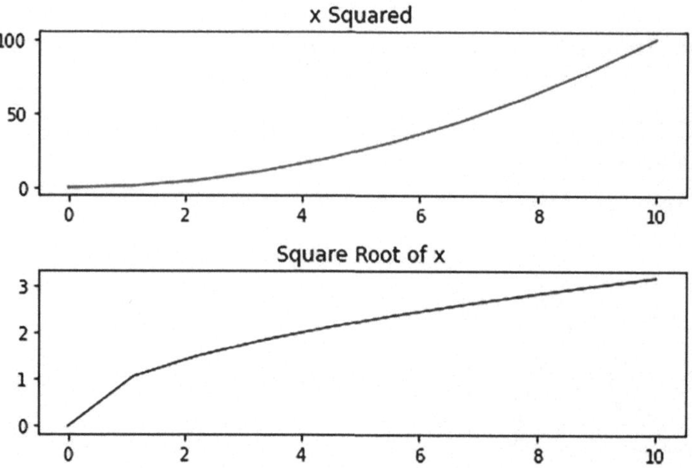

Figure 2.39: *Creating Multiple Plots in the Same Figure (Subplots)*

You can use **`plt.subplots()`** for better Layout Control in your plots, as shown in *Figure 2.40*:

```
#Using plt.subplots() for Better Layout Control
import matplotlib.pyplot as plt
import numpy as np

x = np.linspace(0, 10, 10)  # Generate 10 points between 0 and 10
y1 = np.power(x,2)
y2 = np.power(x,0.5)
y3 = np.power(x,3)
y4 = np.power(x,0.33)

fig, axes = plt.subplots(2, 2, figsize=(8, 6))  # 2x2 grid of subplots
axes[0, 0].plot(x, y1, "r")
axes[0, 0].set_title("x Squared")

axes[0, 1].plot(x, y2, "b")
axes[0, 1].set_title("Square Root of x")

axes[1, 0].plot(x, y3, "g")
axes[1, 0].set_title("X Cubed")

axes[1, 1].plot(x, y4, "k")
axes[1, 1].set_title("Cube Root of x")

plt.tight_layout()
plt.show()
```

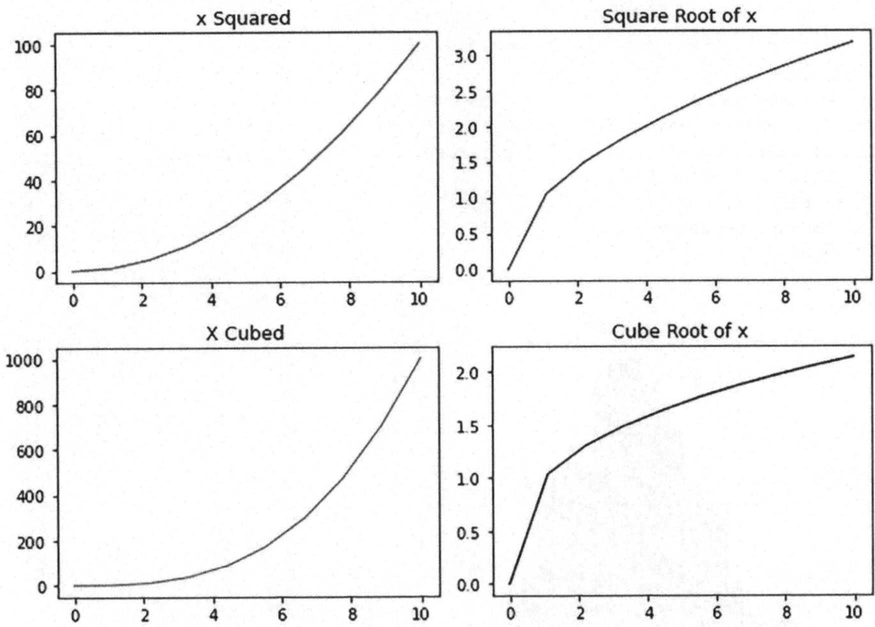

Figure 2.40: *Creating Multiple Plots in the Same Figure (Subplots)*

Matplotlib supports several types of Plots including line plots, bar plots, scatter plots, pie plots and so on, as shown in *Figure 2.41*:

```
#Scatter Plot
import numpy as np
x = np.random.rand(50)
y = np.random.rand(50)

plt.scatter(x, y, color="red", marker="o")
plt.title("Scatter Plot Example")
plt.xlabel("X-axis")
plt.ylabel("Y-axis")
plt.show()
```

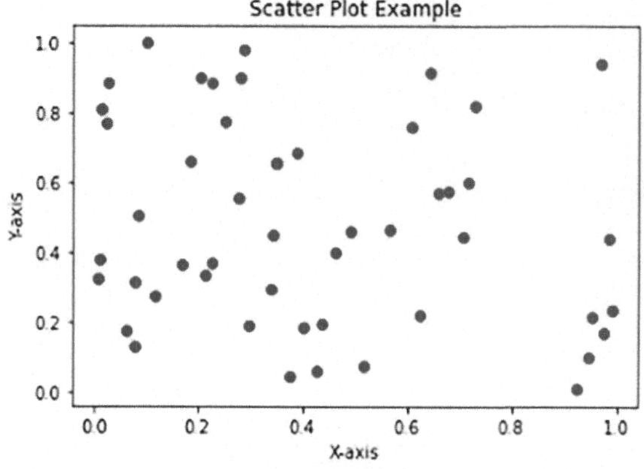


```
#Histogram
import numpy as np
data = np.random.randn(1000)  # 1000 random numbers from normal distribution
plt.hist(data, bins=30, color="blue", edgecolor="black", alpha=0.7)
plt.title("Histogram Example")
plt.xlabel("Value")
plt.ylabel("Frequency")
plt.show()
```

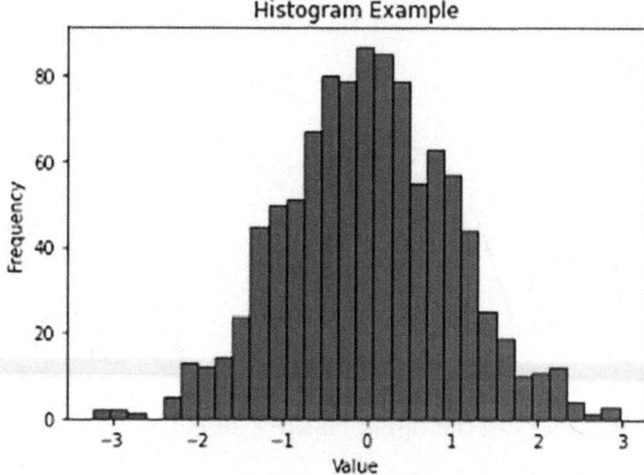

Figure 2.41: Scatter Plot and Histogram

Adding Annotations to a plot is easy with Matplotlib as shown in *Figure* 2.42:

```
#Adding Annotations
import numpy as np
x = np.linspace(0, 10, 100)
y = np.sin(x)

plt.plot(x, y, label="Sine Wave")
plt.annotate("Peak", xy=(np.pi/2, 1), xytext=(2, 1.5),
             arrowprops=dict(facecolor="black", arrowstyle="->"))
plt.legend()
plt.show()
```

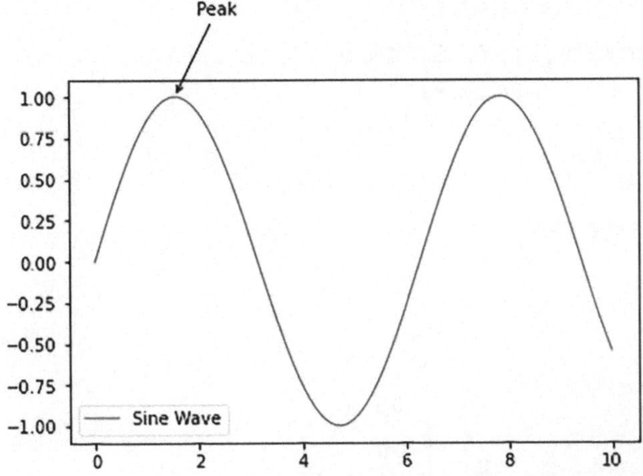

Figure 2.42: *Annotating Your Plot*

Saving Plots to a File

You can easily save a plot in various image formats using **savefig()** function, as shown in *Figure* 2.43:

```
# Saving a plot to your hard drive
plt.plot(x, y)
plt.title("Saved Plot")
plt.savefig("plot.png", dpi=300, bbox_inches="tight")  # Save as PNG with high resolution
plt.show()
```

Figure 2.43: *savefig() to Save a Plot to Hard Drive*

3D Plotting with Matplotlib

You can also create 3D plots using Matplotlib, as shown in *Figure 2.44*:

```
from mpl_toolkits.mplot3d import Axes3D
fig = plt.figure()
ax = fig.add_subplot(111, projection="3d")

x = np.linspace(-5, 5, 100)
y = np.linspace(-5, 5, 100)
X, Y = np.meshgrid(x, y)
Z = np.sin(np.sqrt(X**2 + Y**2))

ax.plot_surface(X, Y, Z, cmap="viridis")
plt.title("3D Surface Plot")
plt.show()
```

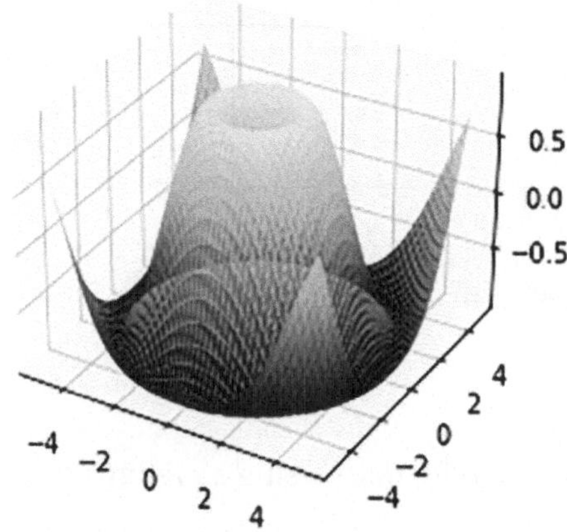

Figure 2.44: 3D Plotting Using Matplotlib

Seaborn for Advanced Data Visualization in Python

Seaborn is a powerful Python visualization library built on top of Matplotlib. It provides a high-level interface to draw attractive and informative statistical graphics. Seaborn simplifies the creation of complex visualizations, such as pair plots, violin plots, and correlation heatmaps, with minimal code. It is designed to work effortlessly with Pandas DataFrames and Series and enhances exploratory data analysis by automatically handling tasks like aggregating data and applying visually-pleasing defaults. Let us see the steps required to install and import Seaborn into your Python code.

Installing Seaborn

Use the following command to install Seaborn if you do not already have it installed:

```
pip install seaborn
```

Importing Seaborn

Once installed, you can import seaborn into your Python code as follows:

```
import seaborn as sns
```

Seaborn's Built-in Datasets

Seaborn provides several built-in datasets that can be loaded using the **load_dataset()** function. *Figure* 2.45 shows the first 5 rows of tips dataset that are built into Seaborn:

```
import seaborn as sns
tips = sns.load_dataset('tips')
tips.head()
```

	total_bill	tip	sex	smoker	day	time	size
0	16.99	1.01	Female	No	Sun	Dinner	2
1	10.34	1.66	Male	No	Sun	Dinner	3
2	21.01	3.50	Male	No	Sun	Dinner	3
3	23.68	3.31	Male	No	Sun	Dinner	2
4	24.59	3.61	Female	No	Sun	Dinner	4

Figure 2.45: *Tips Dataset in One of the Built-in Datasets in Seaborn*

Basic Plotting with Seaborn

Seaborn provides many different types of plots for data visualization like scatter plot, line plot, hist plot, kde plot, regression plot, and so on. *Figure* 2.46 shows the creation of a regression plot and a residual plot created with Seaborn:

```
# Regression Plot
import seaborn as sns
# Load dataset
tips = sns.load_dataset("tips")
sns.regplot(x="total_bill", y="tip", data=tips)
plt.title("Regression Plot of Tip vs. Total Bill")
plt.show()
```

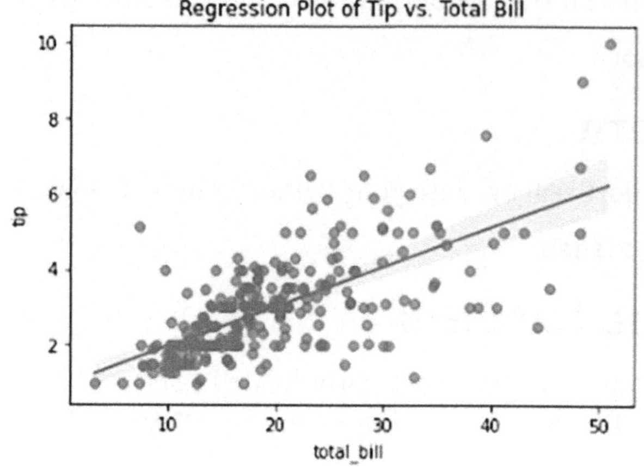


```
# Residual Plot
import seaborn as sns
# Load dataset
tips = sns.load_dataset("tips")
sns.residplot(x="total_bill", y="tip", data=tips)
plt.title("Residual Plot of Tip vs. Total Bill")
plt.show()
```

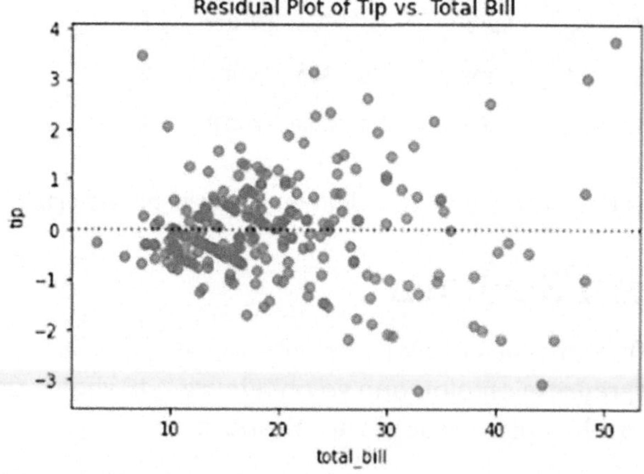

Figure 2.46: *Regression Plot and Residual Plot in Seaborn*

Introduction to Scikit-learn

Scikit-learn (sklearn) is an open-source library for implementing ML algorithms. It offers a consistent interface, robust tools, and extensive documentation, along with simple and efficient tools for tasks like data preprocessing, supervised and unsupervised learning, model evaluation and selection, and feature engineering. Scikit-learn provides seamless integration with Pandas and Matplotlib, which makes it the most popular library for machine learning and data science tasks.

In addition to almost all supervised learning algorithms, data pre-processing methods feature selection and extraction methods, Scikit-learn offers a wide array of unsupervised learning methods, including:

- **Clustering:** Algorithms such as KMeans, DBSCAN, group data points based on similarity, which are essential for tasks like customer segmentation or anomaly detection.
- **Dimensionality Reduction:** Techniques like Principal Component Analysis (PCA), tSNE, and UMAP reduce high-dimensional data into lower-dimensional representations, aiding visualization and computation efficiency.
- **Density Estimation:** Tools such as KernelDensity model the underlying distribution of data, which is useful for outlier detection or generative tasks.

A particularly important feature of scikit-learn is its uniform interface. Every algorithm follows a fit, transform or `fit_transform` paradigm.

Scikit-learn's API is intuitive because of the following features:

- **Instantiate:** Create a model object with parameters
- **Fit:** Train the model on data using `fit()`
- **Transform or Predict:** Apply the model to data with `transform ()` (for preprocessing or decomposition), or `predict ()` (for clustering labels)

This consistency reduces the learning curve and streamlines experimentation across different methods.

Scikit-learn operates seamlessly with NumPy ndarrays and Pandas DataFrames and Series. You can pass a preprocessed DataFrame directly to an algorithm (such as, `kmeans.fit(df.to_numpy())`), or use the resulting labels as a Series for further analysis for a smooth transition from data preparation to modeling.

Scikit-learn provides the following tools to prepare data for unsupervised learning:

- **Scaling:** StandardScaler or MinMaxScaler normalize features, that are critical for distance-based algorithms such as k-means.
- **Encoding:** LabelEncoder or OneHotEncoder handles categorical variables, allowing the user to process mixed datasets.

- **Imputation:** SimpleImputer fills missing values, ensuring that datasets are algorithm-ready.

Scikit-learn is optimized with Cython and it leverages NumPy's vectorization, which makes it efficient to handle moderate-sized datasets. For larger datasets, it includes scalable variants such as MiniBatchKMeans, or interfaces with external libraries (such as, IncrementalPCA), balancing performance with practicality. Let us Python commands to install and import Scikit-learn.

Installing Scikit-Learn

Use this code to install Scikit-Learn if it is not already installed on your machine:

```
pip install scikit-learn
```

Importing Scikit-Learn

We can import the Scikit-Learn library as:

```
import sklearn
```

However, we might also need many other libraries besides Scikit-Learn in a data science or machine learning project.

```
import numpy as np
import pandas as pd
import matplotlib.pyplot as plt
import seaborn as sns
from sklearn import datasets
from sklearn.model_selection import train_test_split
from sklearn.preprocessing import StandardScaler
from sklearn.linear_model import LinearRegression,
LogisticRegression
from sklearn.ensemble import RandomForestClassifier
from sklearn.metrics import accuracy_score, classification_report,
mean_squared_error
```

Exploring Built-in Datasets

Scikit-learn provides many built-in datasets to practice with, like the following:

- **Iris Dataset**: 150 samples of flowers with 4 features (sepal/petal length/width)
- **Digits Dataset**: 1,797 handwritten digits with 64-pixel features

Let us load and inspect the Iris dataset, as shown in *Figure* 2.47:

```
#Exploring built in dataset iris in sklearn
from sklearn.datasets import load_iris
import pandas as pd

iris = load_iris()
X = iris.data  # Features as NumPy array
print(X.shape)  # Output: (150, 4)
print(iris.feature_names)  # ['sepal length (cm)', ...]

# Convert to DataFrame for exploration
df = pd.DataFrame(X, columns=iris.feature_names)
df.head()

```

```
(150, 4)
['sepal length (cm)', 'sepal width (cm)', 'petal length (cm)', 'petal width (cm)']
```

	sepal length (cm)	sepal width (cm)	petal length (cm)	petal width (cm)
0	5.1	3.5	1.4	0.2
1	4.9	3.0	1.4	0.2
2	4.7	3.2	1.3	0.2
3	4.6	3.1	1.5	0.2
4	5.0	3.6	1.4	0.2

Figure 2.47: *Exploring Iris Dataset in Sklearn*

Data Preprocessing with Scikit-learn

Scikit-learn's **`sklearn.preprocessing`** module allows us to perform data preprocessing easily.

Figure 2.48 shows the code for applying normalization to data columns in a dataframe via the StandardScaler preprocessing module of sklearn and converting categorical labels to numerical values using **`LabelEncoder`** module.

```
# Feature Scaling
from sklearn.datasets import load_iris
from sklearn.preprocessing import StandardScaler
import pandas as pd
iris = load_iris()
df = pd.DataFrame(iris.data, columns=iris.feature_names)
df['target'] = iris.target

scaler = StandardScaler()
df_scaled = pd.DataFrame(scaler.fit_transform(df.iloc[:, :-1]), columns=df.columns[:-1])

df_scaled.head()
```

	sepal length (cm)	sepal width (cm)	petal length (cm)	petal width (cm)
0	-0.900681	1.019004	-1.340227	-1.315444
1	-1.143017	-0.131979	-1.340227	-1.315444
2	-1.385353	0.328414	-1.397064	-1.315444
3	-1.506521	0.098217	-1.283389	-1.315444
4	-1.021849	1.249201	-1.340227	-1.315444

```
# Encoding Categorical Variables
from sklearn.preprocessing import StandardScaler
from sklearn.preprocessing import LabelEncoder
import pandas as pd
from sklearn.datasets import load_iris
iris = load_iris()
df = pd.DataFrame(iris.data, columns=iris.feature_names)
df['target'] = iris.target

encoder = LabelEncoder()
df["target"] = encoder.fit_transform(df["target"])

df.head()
```

	sepal length (cm)	sepal width (cm)	petal length (cm)	petal width (cm)	target
0	5.1	3.5	1.4	0.2	0
1	4.9	3.0	1.4	0.2	0
2	4.7	3.2	1.3	0.2	0
3	4.6	3.1	1.5	0.2	0
4	5.0	3.6	1.4	0.2	0

Figure 2.48: *Label Encoding to Convert Categorical Labels to Numbers*

Fitting Machine Learning Models Using Sklearn

Fitting a machine learning model follows data preprocessing and data preparation steps. Then the cleaned dataset is split into train and test portions for training a model. *Figure* 2.49 demonstrates the code for applying LinearRegression ad well as KMeans clustering to a dataset.

```
# Splitting data into train and test sets
from sklearn.datasets import load_iris
from sklearn.model_selection import train_test_split
import pandas as pd
iris = load_iris()
df = pd.DataFrame(iris.data, columns=iris.feature_names)
df['target'] = iris.target

X = df.iloc[:, :-1]
y = df["target"]

X_train, X_test, y_train, y_test = train_test_split(X, y, test_size=0.2, random_state=42)
```

```
#Linear Regression
from sklearn.linear_model import LinearRegression
from sklearn.metrics import mean_squared_error
lr = LinearRegression()
lr.fit(X_train, y_train)

y_pred = lr.predict(X_test)
mse = mean_squared_error(y_test, y_pred)

print(f"Mean Squared Error: {mse}")
```

```
Mean Squared Error: 0.03711379440797686
```

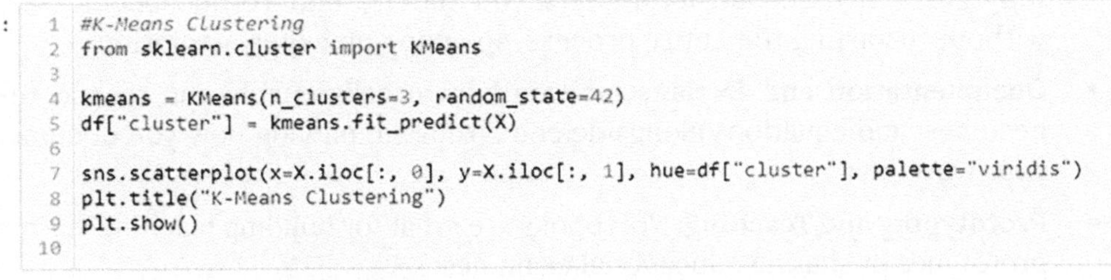

```
#K-Means Clustering
from sklearn.cluster import KMeans

kmeans = KMeans(n_clusters=3, random_state=42)
df["cluster"] = kmeans.fit_predict(X)

sns.scatterplot(x=X.iloc[:, 0], y=X.iloc[:, 1], hue=df["cluster"], palette="viridis")
plt.title("K-Means Clustering")
plt.show()
```

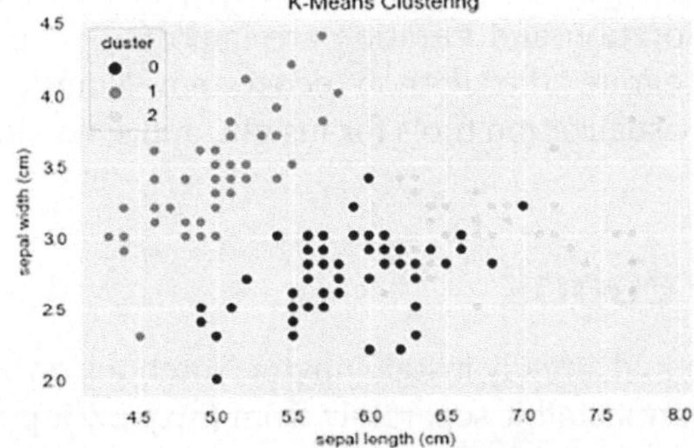

Figure 2.49: *Implementing ML Algorithms with Sklearn*

Jupyter Notebooks

Jupyter Notebook is an open-source, web-based interactive computing environment that allows users to create and share documents containing live code, equations, visualizations, and narrative text. Originally developed as part of the

IPython project, it supports multiple programming languages (with Python being the most common).

Each notebook is a single file with the extension "**.ipynb**" (Interactive Python Notebook), that can be saved, versioned, and shared, making it a versatile platform for experimentation and documentation. A notebook runs in a browser and consists of two main types of cells – code cells and markdown cells.

Some core features of Jupyter Notebooks that make it useful for machine learning are:

- **Interactive Code Execution:** Users can write and run code in small, manageable cells, seeing immediate outputs. For example, you can preprocess a dataset with a Pandas DataFrame in one cell, apply KMeans clustering in the next, and inspect results instantly.
- **Visualization Integration:** It seamlessly integrates with Matplotlib and Seaborn, allowing the use to display plots inline.
- **Iterative Development:** Machine learning often involves trial and error–tuning parameters, tweaking preprocessing, or comparing algorithms. Jupyter's cell-based structure lets you modify and rerun specific steps without restarting the entire process, speeding up experimentation.
- **Documentation and Explanation:** Markdown cells enable you to add text, headings, and equations alongside code, thus simplifying how you document your workflow.
- **Prototyping and Teaching:** Notebooks are great for building machine learning prototypes or sharing educational examples.

For machine learning tasks where exploration and iteration are important, Jupyter Notebook provides a sandbox to integrate the Python ecosystem–NumPy for computation, Pandas for data handling, visualization tools for insight, and scikit-learn for modeling.

Installing Jupyter Notebook

With your Anaconda distribution, you should already install Jupyter Notebook on your computer. If you haven't done so, you can install it separately from **(https://jupyter.org/)** or using pip:

```
pip install notebook
```

Launching Jupyter Notebook

To start Jupyter Notebook, run the following command at your Anaconda Prompt:

```
jupyter notebook
```

This will open a web-based interface at `http://localhost:8888/`.

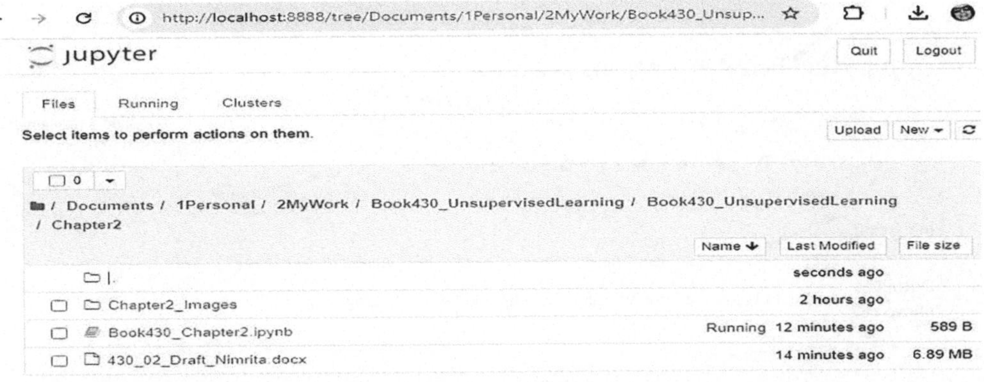

Figure 2.50: *Jupyter Notebook Dashboard (Home Page)*

When you open Jupyter Notebook, you will see the landing page of Jupyter Server, as shown in *Figure* 2.50:

The landing page shows:

- **Dashboard:** Lists all available notebooks and files
- **New Button:** Create a new notebook or terminal
- **Kernel:** Manages execution of the notebook (Python, R, and so on)
- **Cells:** Where you write and execute code or text

Prominent cell types in a Jupyter Notebook:

- **Code Cells:** Execute Python code
- **Markdown Cells:** Write formatted text using Markdown
- **Raw Cells:** Store unformatted text

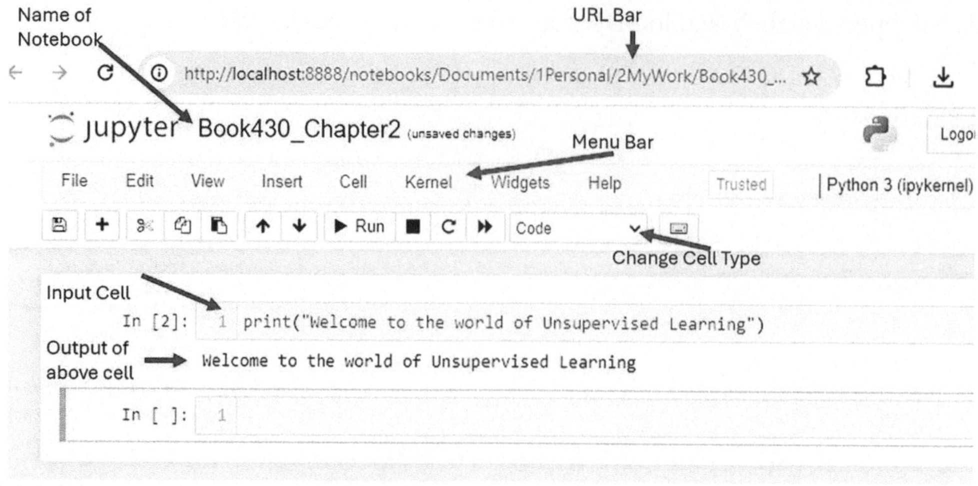

Figure 2.51: *A Jupyter Notebook*

Magic Commands

Jupyter supports special commands called **magic functions** for better efficiency.

Line Magic Commands (%)

```
%timeit sum(range(100))  # Measure execution time
%ls  # List directory contents
%pwd  # Print current working directory
```

Cell Magic Commands (%%)

```
%%time
for i in range(1000000):
    pass
```

Running Shell Commands in Jupyter

You can run terminal commands directly in Jupyter Notebook by prefixing "!" to them.

```
!ls  # List files (Linux/macOS)
!dir  # List files (Windows)
!pip install numpy  # Install Python package
```

Jupyter Notebook is a powerful tool for interactive programming, data analysis, and visualization. It allows you to write and execute Python code interactively, document your work with Markdown, visualize data via Matplotlib and Seaborn, run shell commands, and use magic functions.

Conclusion

In this chapter, we discussed the tools required to successfully implement unsupervised learning. These include libraries like NumPy, Pandas, Matplotlib, Seaborn, Scikit-learn. Scikit-learn provides a robust, unified framework for applying unsupervised learning. Together, these tools create a cohesive pipeline of data preparation, exploration, modeling, and interpretation, which empowers practitioners to uncover the latent stories within their data.

In the following chapters, we will explore different tasks in unsupervised learning and learn about different clustering techniques.

Key Terms

- **Unsupervised Learning:** A type of machine learning where the model learns patterns and structures from unlabeled data
- **Clustering:** A technique used to group similar data points together based on their inherent characteristics
- **ndarray:** NumPy's multidimensional array structure that stores homogeneous data efficiently for numerical computations
- **Vectorization:** The process of applying operations to entire arrays in NumPy without explicit loops, enhancing performance
- **DataFrame:** A two-dimensional, tabular data structure in Pandas with labeled rows and columns, supporting heterogeneous data types
- **Series:** A one-dimensional, labeled array in Pandas that holds a single column or sequence of data with an index
- **Matplotlib:** A Python library for creating customizable visualizations, such as scatter plots and histograms, to explore data
- **Seaborn:** A statistical visualization library built on Matplotlib, offering a high-level interface for attractive, data-driven plots
- **scikit-learn:** A Python library providing tools and algorithms, such as clustering and PCA, for machine learning tasks with a consistent API
- **Broadcasting:** A NumPy feature that automatically adjusts array shapes for compatible operations, simplifying computations
- **Principal Component Analysis (PCA):** A dimensionality reduction technique that transforms data into a lower-dimensional space while preserving variance

Questions

1. What is the main purpose of NumPy's ndarray in unsupervised machine learning?
2. Name three types of visualizations that Matplotlib can create to explore data in unsupervised machine learning.
3. Explain what vectorization means in the context of NumPy, and why it is faster than using loops.
4. Describe the difference between a Pandas DataFrame and a Pandas Series in simple terms.
5. How does Seaborn make plotting easier compared to Matplotlib, and what is one type of plot it can create?
6. Explain why handling missing data is important in unsupervised machine learning and name one Pandas method to deal with it.
7. Describe how you would use Matplotlib to create a scatter plot of cluster labels after running k-means with scikit-learn on a dataset.
8. Describe what broadcasting does in NumPy and give a simple example of how it could be used in an unsupervised learning task.
9. Explain why scikit-learn's StandardScaler is useful before running a clustering algorithm such as k-means, and what it does to the data.
10. Explain how the labeled index in a Pandas Series makes it different from a plain NumPy array and why this might be useful in data analysis.

Multiple Choice Questions

1. What is a key feature of NumPy's ndarray that enhances computational efficiency?
    a. It supports heterogeneous data types within a single array.
    b. It uses a contiguous block of memory.
    c. It requires explicit loops for operations.
    d. It cannot handle multidimensional data.
2. How does vectorization in NumPy benefit unsupervised machine learning?
    a. It increases memory usage without improving speed.
    b. It allows operations on entire arrays without explicit loops.

   c. It limits operations to one-dimensional arrays.
   d. It only works with Pandas DataFrames.
3. What distinguishes a Pandas DataFrame from a NumPy ndarray?
   a. It enforces a single data type across all elements.
   b. It supports labeled axes and heterogeneous column types.
   c. It is less efficient for numerical computations.
   d. It cannot be converted to a NumPy array.
4. What is the primary role of a Pandas Series in a machine learning workflow?
   a. It represents a two-dimensional table of data.
   b. It handles multidimensional numerical computations.
   c. It manages a single labeled column or sequence of data.
   d. It visualizes data distributions automatically.
5. What is the main purpose of Matplotlib in unsupervised machine learning?
   a. To preprocess data by scaling features
   b. To create visualizations such as scatter plots and histograms
   c. To implement clustering algorithms
   d. To handle missing data in datasets
6. How does Seaborn differ from Matplotlib in functionality?
   a. It provides a lower-level interface for plotting.
   b. It focuses on statistical graphics with a high-level interface.
   c. It cannot integrate with Pandas DataFrames.
   d. It is primarily used for numerical computations.
7. Which scikit-learn feature ensures the ease of use across its algorithms?
   a. A consistent API with fit and transform methods
   b. The requirement of manual parameter tuning for every model
   c. Limited support for NumPy arrays
   d. A focus solely on supervised learning tasks

8. What advantage does broadcasting provide when working with NumPy's ndarray?

    a. It allows operations on arrays of different shapes without explicit resizing.

    b. It ensures all arrays have the same data type.

    c. It limits computations to a single dimension.

    d. It requires manual alignment of array indices.

9. Which Pandas DataFrame method is most useful for removing missing values?

    a. `dropna()`

    b. `groupby()`

    c. `to_numpy()`

    d. `fillna()`

10. What is a key benefit of using Seaborn's pairplot in the context of unsupervised machine learning?

    a. It automatically performs clustering on the data.

    b. It visualizes pairwise relationships between features for exploratory analysis.

    c. It scales features to a common range.

    d. It computes the covariance matrix for dimensionality reduction.

Answers

1. b
2. b
3. b
4. c
5. b
6. b
7. a
8. a
9. a
10. b

Chapter 3

Clustering Techniques

Introduction

Clustering is one of the most widely used techniques in unsupervised learning. In this chapter, we will explore popular clustering algorithms: K-Means, Density-Based Spatial Clustering of Applications with Noise (DBSCAN), Hierarchical Clustering, and Gaussian Mixture Models (GMM). You will learn how each of these algorithms works, their strengths and weaknesses, and when you should apply them.

Structure

In this chapter, we will discuss the following topics:

- Introduction to Clustering
    - Cluster Characteristics: Cohesion and Separation
- Common Applications of Clustering
- Data Preparation for Effective Clustering
    - Exploratory Data Analysis
    - Normalization
    - Binning or Discretization
    - Handling Missing Data
    - Dimensionality Reduction
    - Removing Outliers
- Clustering Algorithms
    - Centroid Based Clustering
    - Density Based Clustering
    - Distribution Based Clustering
    - Hierarchical Clustering

- Clustering Techniques Using Deep Neural Networks
    - Deep Embedded Clustering
    - Variational Deep Embedding
    - DeepCluster
    - Contrastive Clustering Methods
- Biclustering

Introduction to Clustering

Clustering is the process of organizing a set of data points into groups, or clusters, where data points within the same cluster are more similar to each other, than to those in different clusters. Unlike supervised learning, where models are trained on labeled data, clustering falls under unsupervised learning, which means that it does not rely on predefined categories or labels. Instead, it identifies natural patterns and structures in data.

Thus, clustering is the process of discovering meaningful subgroups in data. The groups can be based on shared characteristics, similarities in numerical values, or proximity in multi-dimensional space. Clustering enables us to extract insights from raw, unstructured datasets and is widely used across various industries and scientific fields.

Figure 3.1 shows two plots, the plot on the left side contains unlabeled data points, while the plot on the right shows the same points organized in three clusters indicated by different colors. This clustering demonstrates the categorization of patients based on their blood pressure and cholesterol levels.

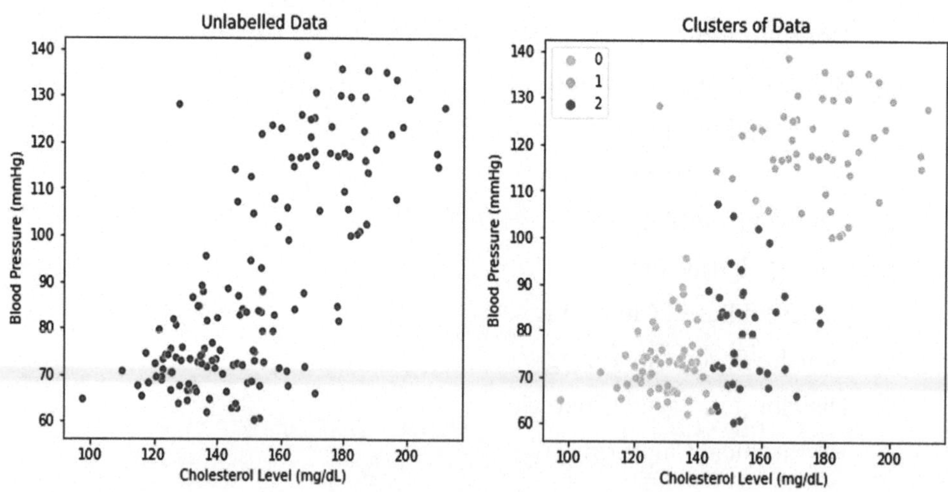

Figure 3.1: *Data Clustering*

Clustering relies on measuring similarity or dissimilarity between data points, and distance metrics play a crucial role in defining these relationships. Since clustering algorithms group similar data points together, the choice of distance metric directly impacts their formation, shape, and effectiveness.

In *Chapter 1*, we introduced various distance metrics used in unsupervised machine learning, including:

- **Euclidean Distance:** Measures straight-line distance between points in multi-dimensional space; is commonly used in the K-Means clustering algorithm
- **Manhattan Distance:** Measures distance along axes; is useful when movements are constrained (such as, city block distance).
- **Minkowski Distance:** Is a generalized form that includes both Euclidean and Manhattan as special cases
- **Cosine Similarity:** Measures the angle between vectors; useful in text clustering and high-dimensional spaces
- **Jaccard Similarity:** Measures set similarity; often used in document clustering

It is important to choose the distance metric carefully because the choice of a distance metric influences the following:

- **Cluster Shape and Structure:** Some metrics (like Euclidean distance) favor spherical clusters, while others (like cosine similarity) work better for non-geometric data.
- **Algorithm Behavior:** K-Means clustering relies on Euclidean distance, while DBSCAN and hierarchical clustering can use various distance metrics based on data characteristics.
- **Scalability and Efficiency:** The computational complexity of these distance metrics varies. Euclidean distance is simple to compute but may struggle in high dimensions, while cosine similarity though complex to compute handles sparse data better.
- **Handling Outliers:** Some metrics, such as Manhattan distance, are more robust to outliers as compared to Euclidean distance.

Cluster Characteristics: Cohesion and Separation

Effective clustering relies on two properties of the clusters formed: **cohesion** (how well data points within a cluster are grouped together) and **separation** (how distinct clusters are from one another). These properties assess the quality of clustering results and ensure that clusters represent meaningful patterns in data.

Cohesion: Intra-Cluster Similarity

Cohesion measures how closely related the data points within a single cluster are. A well-formed cluster should contain points that are highly similar to each other based on the chosen distance metric.

A cohesive cluster has the following properties:

- **Lower Internal Variance:** A good cluster has data points that are tightly packed together. If points within a cluster are too spread out, the cluster might not be well-defined.
- **Minimized Intra-Cluster Distance:** The distance between data points within the same cluster should be small, ensuring strong internal similarity.
- **Dependence on Distance Metric:** The measure of similarity (such as, Euclidean, cosine, Jaccard) affects how cohesion is evaluated.

For example, in customer segmentation, if a cluster represents "budget-conscious shoppers," strong cohesion means that all customers in this group exhibit similar purchasing behaviors, such as preferring discounts and avoiding premium products.

One common way to measure cohesion is the **sum of squared distances from the cluster centroid** (used in K-Means clustering), represented via the following formula:

Where:

$$\sum_{i \in C} d(x_i, \mu_C)^2$$

C is the cluster,

x are data points in the cluster,

μ is the centroid,

(x_i, μ_C) is the distance metric (such as Euclidean Distance).

Lower values of the sum of squared distances from the cluster centroid indicate higher cohesion, implying that the data points are well-grouped.

Separation: Inter-Cluster Dissimilarity

The separation between the clusters ensures that clusters are distinct from one another, meaning that the data points in different clusters should be as dissimilar as possible. Poor separation can result in overlapping or indistinct clusters, making interpretation difficult.

Well-separated clusters have the following properties:

- **Maximized Inter-Cluster Distance**: The greater the distance between clusters, the better defined they are.
- **Avoiding Cluster Overlap**: If clusters overlap significantly, their boundaries become unclear, reducing the effectiveness of the clustering model.
- **Influence of Clustering Algorithm**: Some methods (such as K-Means) aim for compact clusters, while others (like DBSCAN) separate clusters based on density.

For example, in fraud detection, a well-separated fraudulent transaction cluster would be distinct from normal transactions, thereby ensuring clear identification of suspicious activity.

Separation is often measured by the distance between cluster centroids or the nearest points between clusters:

$$\min d(C_i, C_j)$$

Where C_i and C_j are two different clusters.

Another method to measure the separation between clusters is the Silhouette Score, which balances cohesion and separation. It is demonstrated in the following formula:

$$S = \frac{b - a}{\max(a, b)}$$

Where,

a is the average intra-cluster distance (cohesion),

b is the average nearest-cluster distance (separation).

Silhouette score values close to 1 indicate well-formed clusters, while values close to 0 indicate poorly separated clusters.

A good clustering algorithm should balance or optimize both cohesion and separation. The following scenarios of cohesion and separation are possible:

- **High Cohesion and High Separation:** This is ideal clustering, where points within a cluster are tightly packed and well-separated from others.
- **High Cohesion and Low Separation:** This means that the clusters are distinct, but might be too small or too similar.
- **Low Cohesion and High Separation:** This means that the clusters are far apart but internally dispersed, leading to poor grouping.

- **Low Cohesion and Low Separation:** This is poor clustering, with unclear and overlapping groups.

Cohesion and separation are critical for evaluating clustering performance. A clustering method that finds well-cohesive and well-separated clusters will provide meaningful insights into the data. In the next section, we will explore popular clustering techniques and see how they balance these two properties to create effective clusters.

Common Applications of Clustering

The ability to find patterns without prior knowledge or labelled data makes clustering invaluable for exploring complex datasets. Some common use cases for clustering are:

- **Customer Segmentation:** Businesses categorize customers based on purchasing habits, demographics, or online behavior. This enables the execution of personalized marketing campaigns, recommendation systems, and customer retention strategies. For example, an e-commerce company like Amazon can cluster users based on shopping behavior to offer personalized discounts and recommendations, thus increasing sales and customer retention.
- **Image Compression:** Pixels in an image can be grouped based on color similarity, thereby reducing storage requirements without significant loss of quality. Used in formats like JPEG, where clustering simplifies color representation.
- **Anomaly Detection:** Unusual data points (fraudulent transactions, network intrusions, manufacturing defects) often stand apart from clusters of normal behavior. This aids fraud detection, strengthens cybersecurity, and fortifies predictive maintenance.
- **Medical and Bioinformatics Applications:** Clustering helps group similar genes based on expression levels, aiding in genetic research and disease prediction. This is used in identifying cancer subtypes by analyzing patient data and molecular profiles.
- **Search Engines and Recommendation Systems**: Search engines cluster similar web pages to improve retrieval efficiency. Streaming platforms (Netflix and Spotify) use clustering to group users with similar preferences for better recommendations.
- **Social Network Analysis:** Communities and friend groups on social media platforms can be identified using clustering. This is used for detecting fake profiles or bot networks.

Despite its usefulness, clustering has several inherent challenges like:

- **Choosing the Right Number of Clusters:** Many algorithms (for example,

K-Means) require specifying the number of clusters beforehand, which might not always be clear. K-Means struggles with choosing the right number of clusters, but methods like the Elbow Method or Silhouette Score can estimate the optimal number.

- **Handling High-Dimensional Data:** As the number of features grows, clustering effectiveness can decline due to the "curse of dimensionality." High-dimensional data can be tackled using dimensionality reduction techniques, such as PCA or t-SNE before clustering.
- **Dealing with Noise and Outliers:** Some clustering methods (such as, K-Means) are sensitive to anomalies, while others (such as, DBSCAN) are more robust.
- **Interpreting Results:** Unlike classification, where outputs have clear meanings, clustering results often require domain expertise for interpretation.

Data Preparation for Effective Clustering

Data preparation and preprocessing are important steps in all machine learning projects. In clustering, data preprocessing significantly impacts the quality and accuracy of the results. Raw data often contains inconsistencies, varying scales, and irrelevant features that can distort clustering outcomes. By applying appropriate data preprocessing techniques, we can ensure that clustering algorithms work as intended and produce meaningful groupings.

Before a Machine Learning (ML) algorithm can process your input data, you must represent the raw data in the form of trainable values in the feature vectors. The process of transforming raw data into feature vectors that can be ingested by ML algorithms is known as **feature engineering**.

In this section, we will discuss important data preprocessing steps that influence clustering, with a focus on normalization, feature scaling, handling missing values, and dimensionality reduction.

Exploratory Data Analysis

Exploratory Data Analysis (EDA) involves exploring your raw data before transforming it into feature vectors. EDA can be done using visualization through plots and graphs. Plots like scatter plots and histograms help you identify obvious patterns or outliers in your data. EDA can also be carried out statistically by computing statistics like mean, median, mode, range, variance, standard deviation, quantiles, and so on, on your data. This also helps in identifying the data distribution and outliers.

An outlier is a data value that is significantly different from most of the other data points in your data. For example, in a class of students pursuing undergraduate courses in Engineering, the most common age group is 17 to 25 years, an age of 70 years in this class will be an extreme value or an outlier; similarly an age of 5 years in such a class will be an outlier at another extreme.

Figure 3.2 shows the outliers, the values which are outside the 1.5x Interquartile Range of the data. Normal data points are shown in blue, while outliers are shown in red.

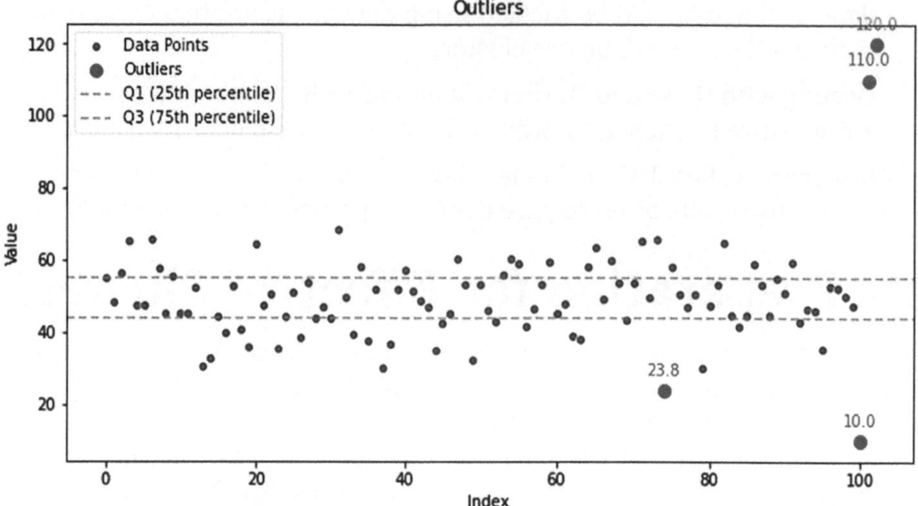

Figure 3.2: *Exploratory Data Analysis Helps in Identifying Outliers*

Next, we will look at some of the important data preparation and pre-processing techniques used to prepare your data before you feed it into a machine learning algorithm.

Normalization

Normalization is the process of transforming feature values in a way that they are on a similar scale.

For example, consider two features—**`years_of_experience`** and **`annual_salary`** in an employee dataset:

- **`years_of_experience`** will range normally from 0 to 50 years
- **`annual_salary`** will range normally from 400,000 to 10,000,000 Rupees

Therefore, as we see, these two features will have hugely different ranges (scales).

Clustering algorithms often rely on distance-based similarity measures, such as Euclidean distance or Manhattan distance. However, if features in the dataset have vastly different scales, clustering can be biased towards features with larger numerical values.

Therefore, normalization is applied to the feature values so that they range between a minimum and maximum value (usually 0 to 1).

Importance of Normalization

Normalization is an important step in machine learning because:

- Many clustering algorithms, such as K-Means, assume that all features contribute equally to similarity computations. If one feature has a much larger range (such as, annual income in thousands versus age in years), it might dominate distance calculations.
- Features with different measurement units (such as, "height in cm" and "weight in kg") need to be scaled to a common range to avoid misleading clusters.
- Normalization helps quickly converge ML model training and improves model predictions.

Common Normalization Techniques

There are several ways to normalize data before clustering such as:

- **Min-Max Scaling or Linear Scaling (Normalization):** Min-Max Scaling transforms all feature values into a fixed range, typically [0,1] or [-1,1]:

The formula used to scale the given value 'x' of a feature is:

$$x' = \frac{x - \min(x)}{\max(x) - \min(x)}$$

Where,

x is the original value of the feature,

x` is the scaled value,

x_{min} is the minimum value in the dataset of this feature,

x_{max} is the maximum value in the dataset of this feature.

Consider the feature `years_of_experience` with a range of 0 to 50 years; that is the minimum experience of employees in this dataset is 0 years and the maximum is 50 years. Then for an employee with an experience of 19 years, the linear scaling will transform the `years_of_experience` as follows:

- **`years_of_experience``** = (19 – 0) / (50- 0) = 0.38
- **Minimum years of experience** = (0-0)/(50-0) = 0
- **Maximum years of experience** = (50-0)/(50-0) = 1

Similarly, min-max scaling of the feature **`annual_salary`** will transform the values so that they lie between 0 and 1.

The Min-Max scaling is sensitive to outliers as extreme values affect the scaling range. It works well for features with a uniform distribution.

- **Standardization (Z-Score Normalization):** Z-score is the value in a column of a dataset (feature) is the number of standard deviations that value is away from the mean of the values in that column. For example, if a value has a Z-score of 2 then it is two standard deviations greater than the mean value in its column, if it has a Z-score of -2, then it is two standard deviations less than the mean value in its column in the dataset.

  Z-Score normalization rescales the data such that it has a mean of 0 and a standard deviation of 1. The formula for computing Z-score normalization is:

$$x' = \frac{x - \mu}{\sigma}$$

Where μ is the mean of the feature values and σ is the standard deviation of the feature values.

Z-Score normalization or Standardization is useful when features follow a normal distribution. It works well for hierarchical clustering and Gaussian Mixture Models (GMMs). Standardization is less sensitive to outliers compared to Min-Max scaling.

- **Log Transformation:** Log transformation or log scaling computes the natural log of a raw feature value. This transformation is useful if the data has a power law distribution, such as, Amazon product ratings data. In general, when features have a skewed distribution (such as, income or population size), applying a logarithmic transformation can help. The formula for applying log transformation is:

$$x' = \log(x + 1)$$

Where x is the original value of the feature and x` is its transformed value.

Log transformation reduces the influence of outliers, making the clusters seem more balanced. It is useful for data with exponential growth patterns, such as market trends or biological measurements.

Clipping: Clipping limits the value of outliers to specific minimum and maximum values. The formula used is:

If x > max, then x` = max

Else if x < min, then x` = min

Else x`= x

Where x is the original feature value, max is the maximum value that the feature can take, min is the minimum value that the feature can take, and x` is the clipped value.

Choosing the Right Scaling Method

- Use Min-Max Scaling when working with distance-based clustering algorithms, such as K-Means.
- Use Standardization when the data contains normally distributed features or outliers.
- Use Log Transformation for data with heavy skewness.

Binning or Discretization

Binning, also known as discretization, is the process of converting continuous numerical variables into categorical bins or intervals or buckets. Binning thus refers to the process of grouping different numerical values into bins or buckets. This is like assigning grade letters such as A, B, C, D, E, and F based on the percentage of marks obtained by students.

Advantages of Binning in Clustering

- **Noise Reduction:** Continuous data may contain minor fluctuations or outliers that are not meaningful. Binning smoothes these variations, reducing noise and making the underlying structure of the data more apparent to clustering algorithms.
- **Feature Transformation:** Some clustering techniques, especially those based on distance metrics such as k-means can be sensitive to the scale and distribution of input features. Binning transforms skewed distribution into more uniform categories, bringing about balance across dimensions.
- **Improved Interpretability:** Binned features can make cluster results more interpretable. For example, age bins like "<20", "20–40", "40–60", and ">60" are easier to relate to than raw numerical ages.
- **Categorical Data Support:** Algorithms such as k-modes and hierarchical clustering (using similarity metrics) can work directly with categorical variables. Binning allows continuous variables to be incorporated into such frameworks.
- **Dimensionality Reduction Aid:** When used alongside feature selection, binning can reduce the resolution of a feature, sometimes allowing for less informative dimensions to be dropped altogether without significant loss in performance.

Types of Binning

- **Equal-Width Binning:** Divides the range of values into intervals of equal size. This is a simple approach to binning but may lead to unbalanced bin counts.
- **Equal-Frequency Binning:** This binning ensures that each bin has roughly the same number of data points. It is useful for maintaining statistical balance.
- **Custom Binning:** Uses domain knowledge or specific thresholds relevant to the problem domain (such as, medical risk scores or financial credit tiers).

Binning can lead to information loss if not done carefully, especially when meaningful numerical granularity is removed. It is generally **not recommended** for algorithms that rely on preserving numeric relationships, such as DBSCAN or Gaussian Mixture Models. Inappropriate binning may distort clustering results by introducing artificial boundaries or misleading similarity structures.

Handling Missing Data

Missing data is a common issue in real-world datasets that can significantly impact the performance and validity of clustering algorithms. Missing values can distort clustering results, especially for distance-based algorithms. If missing values are ignored or replaced poorly, they can result in misleading clusters. Unlike supervised learning, clustering has no target variable to guide decisions, making proper handling of missing values even more critical.

Importance of Handling Missing Data

- **Distance Metric Sensitivity:** Many clustering algorithms, such as k-means, DBSCAN, and hierarchical clustering, rely on distance or similarity measures. Missing values can distort these calculations, leading to inaccurate clusters or algorithm failure.
- **Bias and Data Loss:** Simply dropping rows with missing values can reduce the dataset size and introduce bias if the missing values are not randomly distributed in the dataset.
- **Model Assumptions:** Some algorithms assume complete data matrices. For example, k-means cannot handle missing values directly and will throw errors unless the data is pre-processed.

Methods for Handling Missing Data

- **Removing Incomplete Rows:** If only a few rows have missing values, they can be dropped. However, this is not ideal for large datasets with many missing values.
- **Mean/Median Imputation:** Replace missing values with the feature's mean or median. This is simple but may reduce variability in the dataset.

- **K-Nearest Neighbors (KNN) Imputation:** Predict missing values using the most similar observations. This is more robust but computationally expensive. Regression or other machine learning models can also be used to predict missing values.
- **Multiple Imputation:** Uses probabilistic models such as Gaussian Mixture Models to estimate missing values, preserving data variability.

Poor handling of missing values can distort cluster assignments. A thoughtful imputation strategy ensures that missing values do not introduce bias in distance calculations.

Dimensionality Reduction

Many datasets contain a large number of features, some of which may be irrelevant. Dimensionality reduction is the process of transforming high-dimensional data into a lower-dimensional space while retaining as much relevant information as possible. In clustering, it plays a pivotal role in improving performance, efficiency, and interpretability.

High-dimensional data can make clustering ineffective due to the curse of dimensionality. In high-dimensional spaces, data points become sparse, and distances lose their discriminative power. Clustering algorithms, such as **k-means** and **DBSCAN,** struggle to identify meaningful patterns in high-dimensional data. Many features may be redundant or irrelevant for clustering. Dimensionality reduction helps eliminate such noise, enhancing the signal-to-noise ratio and improving cluster separability. Reducing data to 2 or 3 dimensions enables visualization of clusters. Tools such as **t-SNE** and **UMAP** are popular for visual cluster analysis and validation. Clustering algorithms often scale poorly with the number of features. Dimensionality reduction leads to more efficient computation, especially for large datasets.

Techniques for Reducing Dimensionality

- **Principal Component Analysis (PCA):** PCA reduces the dataset to a smaller number of uncorrelated components and preserves variance. It does so by projecting data onto directions of maximum variance while maintaining linear structure and global relationships in data. PCA is commonly used before applying clustering algorithms such as k-means or hierarchical clustering. It is often used for reducing the dimensionality while clustering text, genetic, and image data with many correlated features.
- **t-Distributed Stochastic Neighbor Embedding (t-SNE):** t-SNE is a nonlinear technique that maps high-dimensional data into a lower-dimensional space. It preserves local structure but may distort global relationships. It is useful for visualizing clusters in complex datasets. T-SNE is often used for exploring high-dimensional data before applying clustering.

- **Uniform Manifold Approximation and Projection (UMAP):** UMAP preserves both the local and global structure of data better than t-SNE. It is suitable for both visualization as well as pre-processing of data.
- **Autoencoders:** Autoencoder is a neural network architecture that learns compact feature representations of input data. It is useful for non-linear dimensionality reduction of high-dimensional complex data.
- **Feature Selection:** While feature extraction involves transforming features, feature selection involves directly removing the irrelevant or redundant features from the input dataset. Feature selection can use correlation and mutual information between the features to select relevant features. This can be done using:
  - **Correlation Analysis:** Remove features that are highly correlated with each other.
  - **Mutual Information:** Select features that provide the most information about the dataset.
  - **Domain Knowledge:** Experts can manually select the most relevant features.

Feature selection reduces the dimensionality of input data and thus improves computational efficiency and avoids overfitting, thereby leading to better-defined clusters. Feature selection is often used with other techniques of dimensionality reduction to build a robust clustering pipeline.

Removing Outliers

Outliers are data points that deviate significantly from the general distribution of the dataset. In clustering, outliers can distort the results, mislead cluster formation, and degrade the quality of the insights derived. Therefore, identifying and handling outliers is a critical preprocessing step in many clustering workflows.

Importance of handling outliers in Clustering

- **Distorted Cluster Centroids:** In centroid-based algorithms such as k-means, even a few outliers can skew the centroids, leading to inaccurate cluster assignments.
- **False Cluster Creation:** Outliers may be treated as separate clusters in density-based methods such as DBSCAN, which can misrepresent the underlying data distribution.
- **Poor Distance Metrics:** Outliers can inflate distances between data points, reducing the effectiveness of algorithms that rely on similarity or distance computations.
- **Reduced Interpretability:** Outliers can obscure true patterns and relationships, leading to confusing or misleading clustering results.

Methods to Handle Outliers

- **Statistical Methods** use thresholds based on standard deviation or interquartile range (IQR) to identify outliers. For example, points outside 1.5 x IQY in a feature are treated as outliers. Similarly, the Z-Score Method treats values beyond 3 standard deviations from the mean as outliers.
- **Distance-based Methods** identify points far from their neighbors using Euclidean or Mahalanobis distance. These methods are suitable for low-dimensional numerical data.
- **Density-based Methods** such as Local Outlier Factor (LOF) detect points in sparse regions of the data space. They are often used before clustering with DBSCAN or OPTICS.
- **Model-based Methods** use simple models such as one-class SVM or isolation forests to detect anomalous patterns. These are useful when data is high dimensional or complex.

Outlier removal ensures that clusters are not skewed by a few extreme data points. However, context is important when removing outliers. In some use cases (such as, fraud detection), outliers themselves may be of interest and should be analyzed separately, not removed. Removing too many points can eliminate rare but valid data. Always combine outlier detection with domain knowledge or visual inspection. In some cases, clustering itself can help detect outliers. Points that do not belong to any cluster or are very distant from centroids may be flagged.

Data preprocessing and preparation is an essential step that directly influences clustering outcomes. Applying the right scaling, missing data handling, dimensionality reduction, and outlier detection techniques ensure that clustering algorithms produce meaningful and interpretable results.

In the next section, we will explore specific clustering algorithms and how they work with pre-processed data.

Clustering Algorithms

In the literature, there are multiple approaches to clustering of data. Traditional clustering algorithms can be categorized into the following nine types (A *Comprehensive Survey of Clustering Algorithms*, Xu, D. & Tian, Y. Ann. Data. Sci. (2015) 2: 165.):

- **Algorithms based on Centroids or Partition**: For example, K-means and K-medoids
- **Algorithms based on Hierarchy**: For example, BIRCH, CURE, ROCK, Chameleon
- **Algorithms based on Fuzzy Theory**: For example, FCM, FCS, MM
- **Algorithms based on Distribution**: DBCLASD, GMM
- **Algorithms based on Density**: DBSCAN, OPTICS, Mean-shift

- **Algorithms based on Graph Theory**: CLICK, MST-based clustering
- **Algorithms based on Grid**: STING, CLIQUE
- **Algorithms based on Fractal Theory**: FC
- **Algorithms based on Model**: COBWEB, GMM (Statistical Models), SOM, ART (Neural Network Models)

Modern clustering algorithms are divided into 10 categories:

- **Algorithms based on Kernel:** Kernel K-means, kernel SOM, kernel FCM, SVC
- **Algorithms based on Ensemble**: CSPA, HGPA, MCLA, VM, HCE, LAC, WPCK
- **Algorithms based on Swarm Intelligence**: ACO_based(LF), PSO_based
- **Algorithms based on Quantum Theory**: QC, DQC
- **Algorithms based on Spectral Graph Theory**: SM, NJW
- **Algorithms based on Affinity Propagation**: AP
- **Algorithms based on Density and Distance**: DD
- **Algorithms based on Spatial Data**: DBSCAN, STING, Wavecluster, CLARANS
- **Algorithms based on Stream**: STREAM, CluStream, HPStream, DenStream
- **Algorithms based on Large-Scale Data:** K-Means, BIRCH, CLARA, DBSCAN, Wavecluster

However, there are four prominent clustering techniques that are most commonly used—centroid-based clustering, density-based clustering, distribution-based clustering, and hierarchical clustering.

Centroid Based Clustering

The centroid of a dataset is the arithmetic mean (average) of all the data points in the dataset. For a cluster containing many data points, the centroid is the datapoint whose values are the arithmetic mean of the values of all other points in the cluster.

For example, consider a cluster C containing five 3-dimensional data points as follows:

```
C = {x1, x2, x3, x4, x5}
X1 = [1.1, 1.5, 2.6]
X2 = [3.4,  5.3,  3.2]
X3 = [5.1,  6.4,  1.1]
X4 = [2.1,  4.7,  8.7]
X5 = [9.1, 1.2, 4.3]
```

Then centroid of this cluster can be calculated by computing the arithmetic mean of all dimensions of other data points separately:

```
Centroid = [(1.1+3.4+5.1+2.1+.1)/5 ,  (1.5+5.3+6.4+4.7+1.2)/5,
(2.6+3.2+1.1+8.7+4.3)/5]
= [2.36, 3.81, 3,97]
```

Centroid-based clustering algorithms are sensitive to outliers and the number of clusters. The clusters formed by the centroid-based clustering methods are non-hierarchical. K-means is the most prominent centroid-based clustering algorithm.

K-Means Clustering Algorithm

The steps in the K-means clustering algorithm are:

1. **Initialize Centroids**: Select k random points as initial centroids.
2. **Assign Data Points**: Each point is assigned to the nearest centroid.
3. **Update Centroids**: Recalculate centroids as the mean of assigned points.
4. **Repeat Until Convergence**: The process continues until centroids no longer change significantly.

Figure 3.3 shows the Python code to implement the K-means algorithm from the sklearn library:

```
#K-means
import numpy as np
import matplotlib.pyplot as plt
from sklearn.datasets import make_blobs
from sklearn.cluster import KMeans

# Generate a synthetic dataset with 3 clusters
X, _ = make_blobs(n_samples=300, centers=3, cluster_std=1.0,
                  random_state=42)

# Apply K-Means clustering with 3 clusters
kmeans = KMeans(n_clusters=3, random_state=42, n_init=10)  # Define number of clusters
labels = kmeans.fit_predict(X)  # Assign cluster labels to each data point
centroids = kmeans.cluster_centers_  # Get the cluster centers

# Plot the clustered data points
plt.figure(figsize=(8, 6))  # Set figure size

# Plot each cluster with a unique color
unique_labels = set(labels)
for label in unique_labels:
    plt.scatter(X[labels == label, 0], X[labels == label, 1],
                label=f"Cluster {label}", alpha=0.6)

# Plot centroids as larger red dots
plt.scatter(centroids[:, 0], centroids[:, 1],
            c="red", marker="X", s=200, label="Centroids")

# Set axis labels and title
plt.xlabel("Feature 1")  # Label x-axis
plt.ylabel("Feature 2")  # Label y-axis
plt.title("K-Means Clustering on Synthetic Dataset")  # Add plot title
plt.legend(loc="lower right")  # Place legend at bottom right
plt.show()  # Display the plot
```

Figure 3.3: *Python Implementation of K-means Algorithm*

The clusters obtained using the preceding code are shown in *Figure* 3.4:

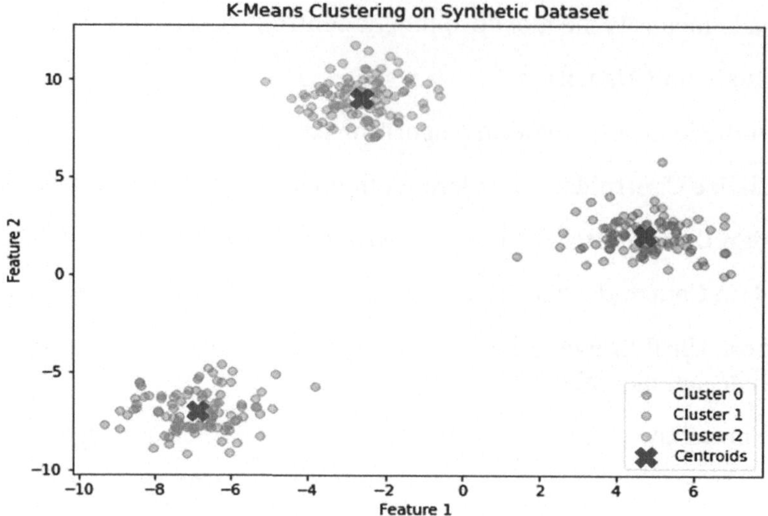

Figure 3.4: *Clusters Obtained Using K-means Clustering Algorithm*

Advantages of K-Means Algorithm:

- It is fast and scalable and works well for large datasets.
- It is simple and interpretable; it is easy to understand and implement.

Limitations:

- The user needs to define the number of centroids in the beginning.
- The algorithm is sensitive to initialization. Poor starting centroids can lead to incorrect clusters.
- It works well when the clusters are of similar size and density. And struggles with non-spherical clusters.

Applications:

- **Customer Segmentation:** Categorizing users based on shopping behavior
- **Image Compression:** Reducing colors in an image by clustering similar shades
- **Anomaly Detection:** Identifying unusual patterns in financial transactions

Despite its limitations, centroid-based clustering is a powerful and widely used clustering technique.

Density-Based Clustering

Density-based clustering groups data points based on how closely they are packed together. Instead of assuming clusters have a fixed shape, this method finds **dense**

areas in the data and separates them from **sparse regions**. It is useful when clusters are irregularly shaped or when there is noise in the data.

The most common density-based clustering algorithm is **Density-Based Spatial Clustering of Applications with Noise (DBSCAN)**.

DBSCAN Algorithm:

The steps in the DBSCAN algorithm are as follows:

1. **Pick a point**: Start with a random data point.
2. **Find nearby points**: Check how many other points are within a certain distance, called epsilon.
3. **Classify the point**:
    a. If a point has enough neighbors, at least a minimum number of points, it is a core point and forms a cluster.
    b. If a point is close to a core point but does not have enough neighbors itself, it is a border point.
    c. If a point does not fit into any cluster, it is labeled as noise or an outlier.
4. **Expand the cluster**: Repeat the process for each core point's neighbors.

Figure 3.5 shows the Python implementation of the DBSCAN algorithm from the sklearn library. The dataset is created using the `make_moons` module of sklearn datasets. It helps create non-spherical data.

```
#DBSCAN on make_moons dataset
import numpy as np
import matplotlib.pyplot as plt
from sklearn.datasets import make_moons
from sklearn.cluster import DBSCAN

# Generate synthetic dataset with two interleaving half-moon shapes
X, _ = make_moons(n_samples=300, noise=0.1, random_state=42)  # 300 points, some noise added

# Apply DBSCAN clustering
dbscan = DBSCAN(eps=0.2, min_samples=5)  # Set neighborhood radius (eps) and min cluster size
labels = dbscan.fit_predict(X)  # Perform clustering and get cluster labels

# Identify core points (points that form dense regions)
core_samples_mask = np.zeros_like(labels, dtype=bool)  # Create a mask for core points
core_samples_mask[dbscan.core_sample_indices_] = True  # Mark core points in the mask

# Plot the results
plt.figure(figsize=(8, 6))  # Set figure size
unique_labels = set(labels)  # Get unique cluster labels

for label in unique_labels:
    if label == -1:  # Noise points are labeled as -1 in DBSCAN
        color, marker, size = "red", "x", 100  # Noise points are marked with red 'x'
        label_name = "Noise"
    else:  # For valid clusters
        color, marker, size = plt.cm.viridis(label / len(unique_labels)), "o", 50
        label_name = f"Cluster {label}"  # Assign label names

    # Select points belonging to the current cluster
    class_member_mask = labels == label

    # Plot core points (high-density points)
    plt.scatter(X[class_member_mask & core_samples_mask, 0],
                X[class_member_mask & core_samples_mask, 1],
                c=[color], marker=marker, s=size, edgecolors="k", label=label_name)

    # Plot border points (points near dense regions)
    plt.scatter(X[class_member_mask & ~core_samples_mask, 0],
                X[class_member_mask & ~core_samples_mask, 1],
                c=[color], marker=marker, s=size/2, edgecolors="k")

# Set axis labels and title
plt.xlabel("Feature 1")  # Label x-axis
plt.ylabel("Feature 2")  # Label y-axis
plt.title("DBSCAN Clustering on make_moons Dataset")  # Add plot title
plt.legend(loc="upper right")  # Place legend in upper right
plt.show()  # Display the plot
```

Figure 3.5: *Python Implementation of DBSCAN Algorithm*

The output of the preceding DBSCAN implementation is shown in *Figure* 3.6. The clusters are non-spherical in shape.

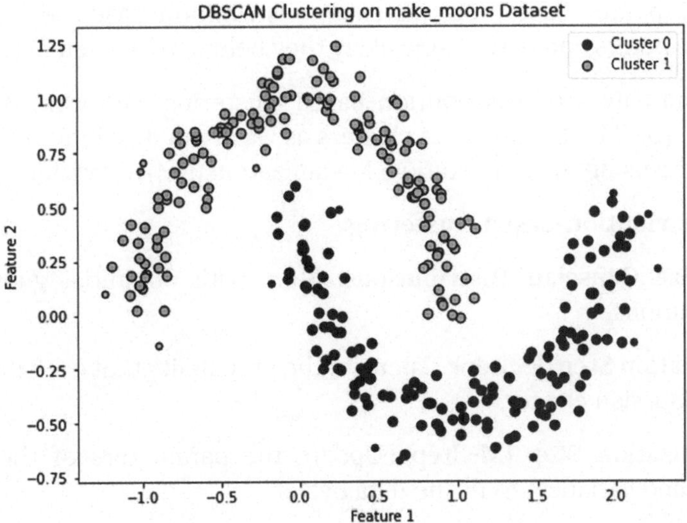

Figure 3.6: *Non-Spherical Clusters Formed Using DBSCAN Algorithm*

Advantages of Density-Based Clustering

Density-based clustering finds clusters of different shapes, unlike K-Means, which assumes clusters are round. It does not require specifying the number of clusters beforehand and can identify noise and outliers.

Challenges of Density-Based Clustering

Choosing the right values for epsilon and the minimum number of points is important. If set incorrectly, DBSCAN may miss clusters or merge too many points together. It also struggles when clusters have vastly different densities.

Applications of Density-Based Clustering

Density-based clustering is used in fraud detection to identify unusual banking transactions, in geospatial analysis to find high-density areas like crime hotspots, and in customer behavior analysis to group shoppers based on their activity.

This method is useful while working with complex datasets that have irregular shapes and outliers. It is widely used in areas where data is not evenly spread and predefined cluster shapes do not work well.

Distribution-Based Clustering

Distribution-based clustering models data as belonging to different probability distributions. These algorithms assume that clusters follow a specific statistical distribution, often Gaussian (normal distribution). Unlike centroid-based clustering, which groups points based on distance, distribution-based clustering assigns probabilities to points, indicating how likely they belong to a given cluster.

The most commonly used distribution-based clustering algorithm is the Gaussian Mixture Model (GMM). It represents clusters as Gaussian distributions and estimates their parameters using the Expectation-Maximization (EM) algorithm.

Working of distribution-based clustering

1. **Initialize Gaussian Distributions:** Start with an initial guess for cluster distributions.
2. **Expectation Step (E-Step):** Calculate the probability that each point belongs to each Gaussian cluster.
3. **Maximization Step (M-Step):** Update the parameters of the distributions (mean and variance) to fit the data better.
4. **Repeat Until Convergence:** Continue until changes in cluster assignments are minimal.

Advantages of Distribution-Based Clustering

- Distribution-based clustering works well when the clusters overlap or have soft boundaries.
- This clustering is more flexible than K-Means and can model clusters of different shapes and sizes.

Limitations of Distribution-Based Clustering

- This clustering approach requires that the user must specify the number of distributions or the number of clusters similar to K-Means where the user must specify the number of centroids.
- It is sensitive to initialization; poor initialization may lead to incorrect clustering.

Applications of Distribution Based Clustering

- **Anomaly Detection:** Identifying fraudulent transactions in finance
- **Image Segmentation:** Differentiating objects in an image based on pixel intensity
- **Genomics:** Grouping genes with similar expression patterns

Distribution-based clustering is useful when data naturally follows probabilistic patterns and when soft clustering (assigning probabilities instead of hard labels) is beneficial.

Let us see the Python Code for Gaussian Mixture Model-based clustering to the Iris dataset from sklearn datasets. The code is shown in *Figure 3.7*:

```
#Distribution based clustering: GMM Clustering on iris dataset
import numpy as np
import matplotlib.pyplot as plt
import seaborn as sns
from sklearn import datasets
from sklearn.mixture import GaussianMixture
from sklearn.preprocessing import StandardScaler

# Load the Iris dataset
iris = datasets.load_iris()
X = iris.data[:, :2]  # Select the first two features for visualization

# Standardize the features for better clustering
scaler = StandardScaler()
X_scaled = scaler.fit_transform(X)

# Apply Gaussian Mixture Model (GMM) clustering
gmm = GaussianMixture(n_components=3, random_state=42)  # Define 3 Gaussian components
labels = gmm.fit_predict(X_scaled)  # Assign probabilities and get cluster labels
centroids = gmm.means_  # Get estimated cluster centers (in scaled space)

# Transform centroids back to original scale
centroids_original = scaler.inverse_transform(centroids)

# Plot the clustered data points
plt.figure(figsize=(8, 6))
sns.scatterplot(x=X[:, 0], y=X[:, 1], hue=labels, palette="Set1", alpha=0.6, edgecolor="k")

# Plot centroids as larger red 'X' markers
plt.scatter(centroids_original[:, 0], centroids_original[:, 1],
            c="red", marker="X", s=200, label="Centroids")

# Set axis labels and title
plt.xlabel("Sepal Length")
plt.ylabel("Sepal Width")
plt.title("GMM Clustering on Iris Dataset")
plt.legend(loc="lower right")
plt.show()
```

Figure 3.7: GMM Clustering on Iris Dataset

The output of the preceding code is shown in *Figure 3.8*:

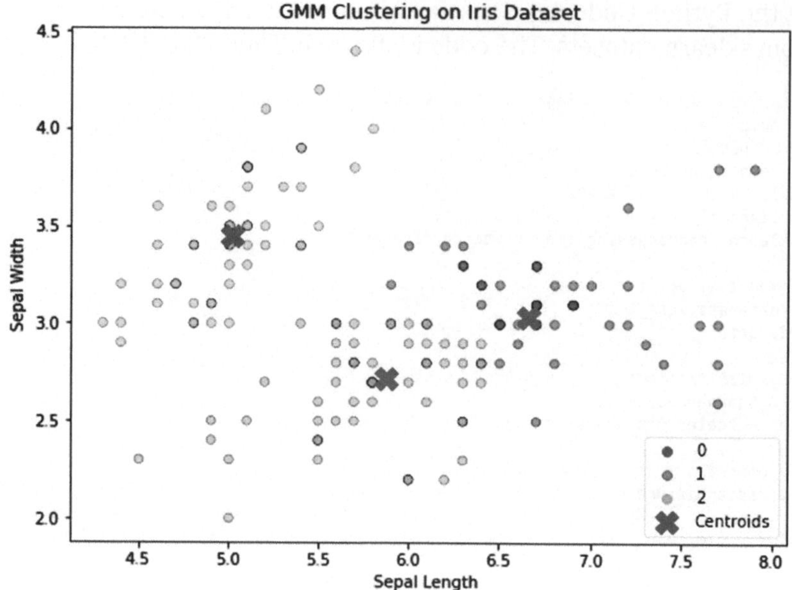

Figure 3.8: *GMM Clustering on Iris Dataset*

Hierarchical Clustering

Hierarchical clustering is a method that builds a hierarchy of clusters by either **merging smaller clusters** (agglomerative) or **splitting larger clusters** (divisive). Unlike centroid-based clustering, hierarchical methods do not require the number of clusters to be predefined, which makes them useful when the structure of the data is unknown.

Types of Hierarchical Clustering

Clustering algorithms are categorized as agglomerative and hierarchical clustering:

- **Agglomerative Hierarchical Clustering (Bottom-Up)**
  - Starts with each data point as an individual cluster
  - Merges the closest clusters iteratively until only one cluster remains
  - The process can be visualized using a dendrogram, a tree-like diagram

Working of Agglomerative Clustering

1. Compute the distance between every pair of points.
2. Merge the two closest clusters.
3. Update the distance matrix to reflect the new cluster.
4. Repeat until all points belong to a single cluster.

Let us see the Python implementation of Hierarchical Agglomerative Clustering on the Iris dataset from sklearn datasets in *Figure* 3.9:

```
## Hierarchical Clustering
import numpy as np
import matplotlib.pyplot as plt
import seaborn as sns
from sklearn import datasets
from sklearn.cluster import AgglomerativeClustering
from scipy.cluster.hierarchy import dendrogram, linkage
from sklearn.preprocessing import StandardScaler

# Load the Iris dataset
iris = datasets.load_iris()
X = iris.data[:, :2]  # Select only the first two features (Sepal Length and Sepal Width) for visualization

# Standardize the features for better clustering performance
scaler = StandardScaler()
X_scaled = scaler.fit_transform(X)

# Compute the hierarchical clustering linkage matrix
# 'ward' minimizes variance within clusters for optimal grouping
linkage_matrix = linkage(X_scaled, method="ward")

# Plot the dendrogram to visualize hierarchical clustering
plt.figure(figsize=(15, 8))
dendrogram(linkage_matrix, truncate_mode="level", p=10)  # Show only top 10 levels to simplify visualization
plt.xlabel("Data Points")  # Label x-axis
plt.ylabel("Cluster Distance")  # Label y-axis
plt.title("Hierarchical Clustering Dendrogram (Iris Dataset)")  # Add title
plt.show()

# Apply Agglomerative Clustering with 3 clusters (as Iris has 3 classes)
agg_clustering = AgglomerativeClustering(n_clusters=3, linkage="ward")
labels = agg_clustering.fit_predict(X_scaled)  # Assign cluster labels to each data point

# Plot the clustered data points with colors representing different clusters
plt.figure(figsize=(15, 8))
sns.scatterplot(x=X[:, 0], y=X[:, 1], hue=labels, palette="Set1", alpha=0.7, edgecolor="k")

# Set axis labels and title
plt.xlabel("Sepal Length")  # X-axis label
plt.ylabel("Sepal Width")  # Y-axis label
plt.title("Hierarchical Clustering on Iris Dataset")  # Plot title

# Add legend to show the clusters
plt.legend(title="Cluster", loc="lower right")
plt.show()
```

Figure 3.9: *Agglomerative Clustering on Iris Dataset*

The output of the preceding clustering is shown in *Figure* 3.10:

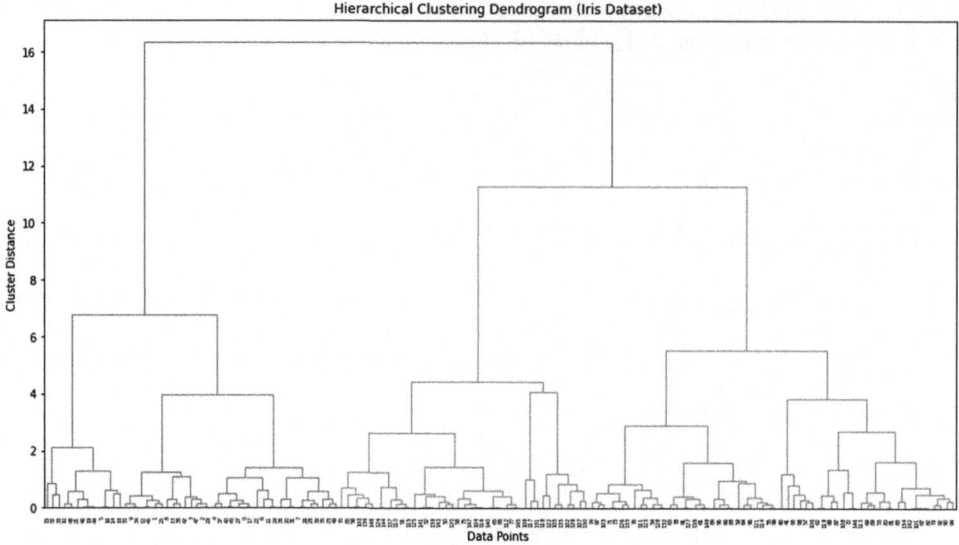

Figure 3.10: *Agglomerative Clustering on Iris Dataset*

- **Divisive Hierarchical Clustering (Top-Down Clustering)**

  Working of divisive hierarchical clustering:

  - Starts with a single large cluster containing all points
  - Splits the cluster iteratively into smaller clusters until each point is its own cluster

Divisive clustering is less commonly used than agglomerative clustering.

Linkage Methods in Hierarchical Clustering

The purpose of linkage methods in hierarchical clustering is to determine how the distance between two clusters is measured when deciding which clusters to merge at each step of the algorithm. Specifically, linkage methods help to define the inter-cluster distance based on the pairwise distances between their members. At each step, the algorithm merges the two clusters with the smallest inter-cluster distance as defined by the linkage methods. Linkage methods influence the types of clusters formed such as, compact, elongated, balanced, and so on.

Hierarchical clustering uses different linkage methods, the prominent ones being:

- **Single Linkage (Minimum Linkage):** Uses the shortest distance between any two points in two clusters to combine clusters. It tends to form elongated chain-like clusters. Single linkage is sensitive to noise and outliers.
- **Complete Linkage (Maximum Linkage):** It measures the longest distance between any two points in two clusters. It produces compact, spherical clusters and is less affected by outliers than single linkage.

- **Average Linkage (Unweighted Pair Group Method with Arithmetic Mean):** It computes the average distance between all pairs of points from the two clusters. This linkage method is a balance between single and complete linkage and often results in clusters of moderate compactness and separation.
- **Ward's Method:** This linkage method merges clusters that minimize the increase in total within-cluster variance. In other words, it minimizes variance within clusters, often producing balanced and compact clusters. It works best with Euclidean distance.

Advantages of Hierarchical Clustering

- There is no need to predefine the number of clusters.
- It works well with small to medium-sized datasets.
- The dendrogram provides insight into the data structure.

Limitations of Hierarchical Clustering

- It is computationally expensive for large datasets.
- It is sensitive to noise and outliers.
- Merging decisions is irreversible (cannot undo incorrect merges).

Applications of Hierarchical Clustering

- **Genetics:** Grouping similar DNA sequences
- **Social Network Analysis:** Identifying communities of users
- **Market Segmentation:** Finding customer groups with similar buying patterns

Hierarchical clustering is widely used when understanding relationships between data points is important. The dendrogram allows users to explore different cluster formations and offers flexibility in selecting the final clusters.

Clustering Techniques Using Deep Neural Networks

Traditional clustering algorithms such as K-Means, DBSCAN, and hierarchical clustering rely on fixed feature representations of data. However, in high-dimensional or unstructured data domains, such as images, text, or speech, these fixed features often fail to capture meaningful structure within data. Deep neural networks address this limitation by learning data representations (embeddings) that make the underlying clusters more separable.

In this subsection, we will explore the important deep learning-based clustering methods that combine representation learning with clustering objectives.

Deep Embedded Clustering

Deep Embedded Clustering (DEC) is a deep learning approach that combines representation learning with clustering. It first learns a compressed representation of data using an autoencoder (a type of deep neural network architecture), and then it fine-tunes these representations specifically to improve clustering.

An autoencoder is a neural network consisting of two component neural networks:

- **Encoder:** An encoder neural network compresses the input data into a lower-dimensional vector. This lower dimensional feature space learned by the encoder is known as latent space. Latent variables are not directly observed but inferred from the data for example the cluster membership is inferred from data.
- **Decoder:** A decoder neural network reconstructs the original input from this compressed vector.

KL Divergence is used as a statistical measure to fine-tune the clustering assignment by comparing predicted cluster distributions with a target distribution.

Working of DEC

1. Train an autoencoder on the data to learn compact representations of data.
2. Discard the decoder, and retain the encoder.
3. Add a clustering layer that assigns each point to a cluster using a soft probability distribution.
4. Optimize the encoder and clustering layer jointly to improve cluster purity.

DEC learns meaningful, task-specific representations that lead to better clustering, especially on high-dimensional data like images.

Variational Deep Embedding

Variational Deep Embedding (VaDE) is a deep clustering method that uses a Variational Autoencoder (VAE) and assumes that the latent space follows a Gaussian Mixture Model. That is, the data is assumed to come from a mixture of multiple Gaussian distributions. VaDE can be used for both clustering of data as well as generative modelling. It means that VaDE can be used as a clustering technique and to generate new data samples from each cluster. It is especially useful in applications requiring synthetic data generation for example anomaly detection or simulation.

Variational Autoencoder (VAE) is a generative model that learns to encode data into a latent space and reconstruct it. Unlike regular autoencoders, VAEs impose a probabilistic structure on the latent space.

Working of Variational Deep Embedding

1. Uses a variational autoencoder to learn a latent representation of the data
2. Models the latent space as a mixture of Gaussian, each representing a cluster
3. Optimizes both the VAE and the GMM together to improve clustering and reconstruction

DeepCluster

DeepCluster is a method for clustering image data using a Convolutional Neural Network (CNN). It alternates between learning image features and assigning pseudo-labels through clustering. Pseudo-labels are artificial labels assigned to data points during training. These pseudo-labels are not ground-truth labels but are generated by the algorithm itself. DeepCluster follows iterative learning where clustering and feature learning are alternated over several rounds.

Working of DeepCluster

1. Uses a CNN to extract features from raw images
2. Applies K-Means clustering on these features to generate pseudo-labels
3. Uses pseudo-labels to retrain the CNN, refining the feature extraction
4. Repeat the process to gradually improve clustering quality.

DeepCluster improves image representations without using any labelled data. It has been widely used for self-supervised learning in computer vision.

Contrastive Clustering Methods

Contrastive clustering methods integrate contrastive learning with clustering. Contrastive learning is a self-supervised approach that learns by comparing data pairs. Positive pairs (similar samples) are brought closer; negative pairs (dissimilar samples) are pushed apart. In clustering, a prototype is a representative feature vector (like a centroid) for a group of similar data points. Consistency ensures that similar inputs yield similar output, even under perturbations or different views of input data.

Working of Contrastive Clustering Methods:

1. Uses a neural network such as CNN or Transformer to extract features from data
2. Define contrastive loss function to learn representations of data such that similar samples cluster together

3. Based on learned representations, group the samples into clusters
4. If required, update cluster prototypes during training

These methods are highly effective in computer vision and natural language processing, where labelled data is scarce but contrastive pairs can be generated automatically, such as different views of the same image or augmented sentences.

Method	Neural Network	Clustering Type	Strengths	Use Cases
DEC	Autoencoder	Soft K-Means (Probabilistic K-Means)	Learns task-specific representations	General tabular/image data
VaDE	VAE	GMM-based	Probabilistic clustering and generation	Generative Applications
DeepCluster	CNN	K-Means + Iteration	Self-supervised feature learning	Large-scale image clustering
Contrastive	CNN/ Transformer	Cluster + Contrastive Learning	Robust, unsupervised representation learning	Vision and Natural Language Processing.

Table 3.1: *Summary of Deep Neural Network-Based Clustering Methods*

Biclustering

Biclustering is the simultaneous clustering of the rows and columns of a dataset. The clusters of rows and columns are called biclusters. Each bicluster determines a submatrix of the original data matrix with specific desired properties.

In traditional clustering techniques, the goal is to group similar data points, typically the rows of a dataset, based on their similarity across the entire set of features. This approach works well when the relevant patterns span all columns, or when all features contribute uniformly to the cluster formation. However, many real-world datasets, particularly those in domains such as bioinformatics, recommendation systems, and text mining, exhibit local patterns rather than global ones. In such cases, clustering either rows or columns alone can miss important structural relationships. Biclustering, also known as co-clustering or two-way clustering, addresses this by simultaneously clustering rows and columns, thereby uncovering submatrices within the data that represent coherent patterns.

The core idea of biclustering is to identify subsets of rows that exhibit similar behavior across subsets of columns. Unlike traditional clustering, where each data point belongs to one cluster based on the full feature set, biclustering allows the same row or column to participate in multiple biclusters if it demonstrates similarity in different contexts.

Common Algorithms for Defining Biclusters

Biclustering algorithms differ based on the kinds of patterns they search for in the data matrix. The most common types focus on constant patterns, extreme values, low variance, or correlations.

Some algorithms look for constant values, where all the elements in a bicluster are nearly equal. Others identify constant rows or constant columns, where either each row or each column has a fixed value pattern across a subset of the matrix. These are simple but powerful for spotting regular, repeated structures.

Another class of algorithms detects unusually high or low values. These biclusters highlight entries that stand out significantly from the rest and are useful in tasks such as anomaly detection, where rare or extreme behaviors are of interest.

Biclusters with low variance contain values that vary only slightly around a central trend. These are useful when you are interested in groups of data points that behave similarly but not identically. A popular example is the Cheng and Church algorithm, which minimizes a measure called the mean squared residue to find such patterns.

Finally, some algorithms aim to find correlated rows or columns, which are groups that rise and fall together even if their absolute values differ. These methods use statistical measures such as Pearson correlation to capture the overall similarity in trends.

Each type of biclustering algorithm is suited for specific data patterns. The best choice depends on what kind of structure you are trying to uncover. Thus, the biclusters are constructed using one of the following:

- Constant values, constant rows, or constant columns
- Unusually high or low values
- Submatrices with low variances
- Correlated rows or columns.

The flexibility makes biclustering particularly powerful in high-dimensional and noisy data, where meaningful structures may only be visible when viewed through specific, localized slices of the dataset.

An example use case of biclustering is in gene expression analysis, where rows represent genes and columns represent experimental conditions or tissue types. A traditional clustering algorithm might group together genes with similar expression patterns across all conditions. In contrast, biclustering can identify a subset of genes that are co-expressed only under a specific subset of conditions–providing more biologically relevant insights. Such a pattern may be invisible to global clustering methods that average overall conditions.

Biclustering optimizes a criterion that evaluates the homogeneity of values in the discovered submatrix or submatrices. Depending on the algorithm, this could involve minimizing variance within the submatrix, maximizing correlation among entries, or satisfying other statistical properties that define coherence. One of the earliest and most influential biclustering algorithms is the Cheng and Church algorithm, that searches for submatrices with low mean squared residue score, which is a measure of how much the elements deviate from the mean pattern in both rows and columns. Other approaches include spectral biclustering, which uses singular value decomposition to detect checkerboard patterns in the data matrix, and Bayesian biclustering, which employs probabilistic models to infer bicluster memberships with a degree of uncertainty.

Biclustering is also applicable to other use cases. In recommender systems, for instance, rows may correspond to users and columns to items. Biclustering can identify latent communities where a subset of users shows similar preferences for a subset of items, thus enabling more personalized recommendations. In text mining, biclustering can reveal sets of documents that use similar groups of terms, which is instrumental in topic discovery and document categorization.

Spectral Biclustering

Spectral biclustering is a specific method of performing biclustering via linear algebra and matrix factorization to detect hidden patterns in data. Rather than explicitly defining what a bicluster should look like (such as having low variance or high correlation), spectral biclustering implicitly uncovers structure by transforming the data into a spectral (eigen-vector-based) space and then applying clustering techniques to it. It is especially suited for data with a checkerboard structure.

A checkerboard structure refers to a specific pattern in a data matrix where certain groups of rows exhibit similar behaviors across certain groups of columns. This pattern repeats across the matrix in a block-like fashion, resembling the alternating dark and light squares of a checkerboard.

In a data matrix with a checkerboard structure:

- You can partition the matrix into submatrices (biclusters), where each submatrix (or block) shows a consistent internal pattern–such as high values, low values, or correlated values.
- These blocks are not necessarily adjacent but form a block-diagonal or tiled pattern.
- The structure reflects interdependence between subsets of rows and subsets of columns.

Figure 3.11 shows a checkerboard structure in the data matrix:

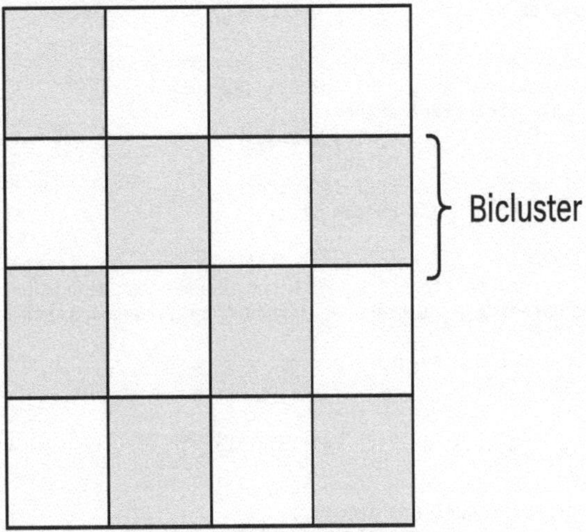

Figure 3.11: *Checkerboard Structure*

For example, for a gene expression dataset, consider the corresponding gene expression matrix in which: rows represent genes, columns represent different conditions or patients, and values represent expression levels of genes.

A checkerboard structure might reveal that genes 1 to 10 behave similarly (highly expressed) under conditions A to C and genes 11 to 20 behave similarly (low expression) under conditions D to F and so on. This creates a block-like pattern of similar values, with the "checkerboard" referring to these distinct, meaningful regions within the matrix.

Algorithms such as spectral biclustering are designed specifically to detect this kind of structure. They aim to rearrange the matrix so that these blocks become apparent and then identify the corresponding row-column groupings.

Figure 3.12 shows the implementation of Spectral Biclustering using the sklearn library in Python:

```
#Spectral Biclustering
import numpy as np
from sklearn.datasets import make_biclusters
from sklearn.cluster import SpectralBiclustering
import matplotlib.pyplot as plt

# Generate synthetic data with an embedded bicluster structure
# This creates a 50x50 matrix with 4 biclusters and some noise
data, rows, cols = make_biclusters(shape=(50, 50),
                                  n_clusters=4,
                                  noise=5,
                                  shuffle=False,
                                  random_state=0)

# Initialize the Spectral Biclustering model with 4 row-column cluster pairs
# The 'log' method is used to stabilize variance (useful for gene expression-like data)
model = SpectralBiclustering(n_clusters=4, method='log', random_state=0)

# Fit the model to the data to identify bicluster structure
model.fit(data)

# Rearrange the original matrix so that rows and columns are
# grouped by bicluster labels
# This makes the bicluster structure visually apparent
fit_data = data[np.argsort(model.row_labels_)]
fit_data = fit_data[:, np.argsort(model.column_labels_)]

# Plot the original matrix
fig, axes = plt.subplots(1, 2, figsize=(12, 5))
axes[0].imshow(data, aspect='auto', cmap='viridis')
axes[0].set_title("Original Data")

# Plot the matrix after biclustering to show grouped structure
axes[1].imshow(fit_data, aspect='auto', cmap='viridis')
axes[1].set_title("After Spectral Biclustering")

# Adjust spacing and display both plots
plt.tight_layout()
plt.show()
```

Figure 3.12: *Python Code for Spectral Biclustering on Synthetic Data*

Figure 3.13 shows the original dataset and the biclusters created out of this dataset using Spectral Biclustering.

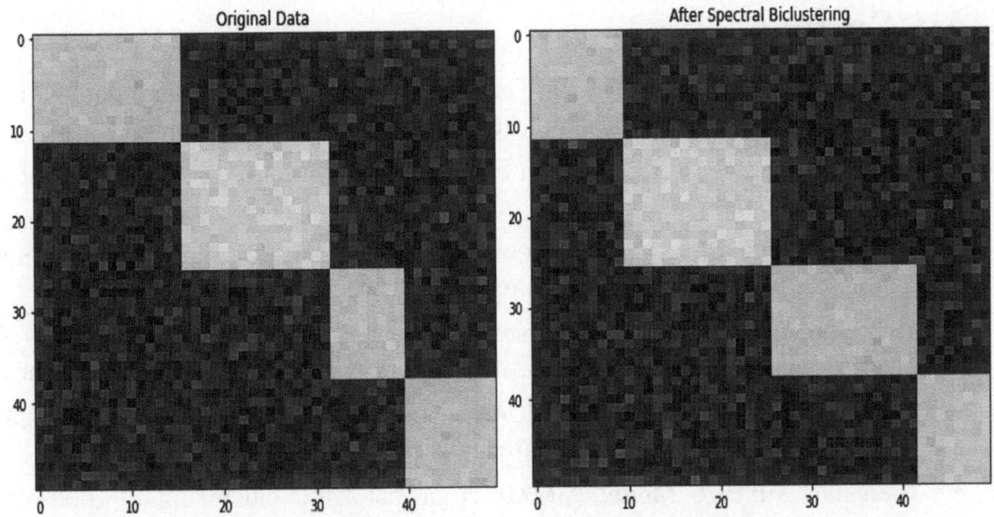

Figure 3.13: *Original and Biclustered Dataset Visualization*

While biclustering is not as widely used as traditional clustering methods, it is a powerful technique in situations where local structures are more meaningful than global ones. By capturing interactions between subsets of rows and columns, biclustering offers a better approach to pattern discovery in complex datasets.

Conclusion

Clustering is an important task in unsupervised learning, as it enables the discovery of inherent structure within data without predefined labels. This chapter presented important clustering techniques, ranging from classical methods such as k-means and hierarchical clustering to more advanced approaches such as DBSCAN and spectral clustering. We also explored biclustering, which identifies simultaneous patterns in both rows and columns of a matrix and is particularly useful in fields like bioinformatics and text mining.

Each method offers unique strengths depending on the data characteristics, such as shape, density, or dimensionality. Understanding these algorithms, their assumptions and appropriate use cases equips practitioners to select and apply the right technique. As real-world datasets become more complex and high-dimensional, clustering remains an essential tool for exploratory data analysis and knowledge discovery.

In the next chapter, we will explore dimensionality reduction techniques, which are an important category of unsupervised machine learning and often complement clustering by simplifying data representation while preserving the structure.

Key Terms

- **Clustering:** A machine learning technique that groups similar data points together based on specific similarity measures
- **Centroid:** The central point of a cluster, often computed as the mean of all points within the cluster
- **K-Means Algorithm:** A popular clustering algorithm that partitions data into *k*- clusters by minimizing intra-cluster variance
- **Hierarchical Clustering:** A clustering method that builds a hierarchy of clusters using agglomerative (bottom-up) or divisive (top-down) approaches
- **Density-Based Clustering (DBSCAN):** A clustering technique that identifies dense regions of data and separates noise or outliers
- **Gaussian Mixture Model (GMM):** A probabilistic clustering method that assumes data is generated from a mixture of Gaussian distributions
- **Silhouette Score:** A metric for evaluating clustering performance by measuring how similar a data point is to its own cluster compared to other clusters
- **Elbow Method:** A technique for determining the optimal number of clusters in K-Means by analyzing the inertia curve
- **Dendrogram:** A tree-like diagram used in hierarchical clustering to visualize the arrangement of clusters at different levels of granularity
- **Cluster Validity Index:** A quantitative measure (for example, Dunn Index, Davies-Bouldin Index) used to assess the quality of clustering results

Questions

1. Explain the concept of clustering in unsupervised learning. How does it differ from classification?
2. Describe the working mechanism of the K-Means algorithm. What are its advantages and limitations?
3. Discuss hierarchical clustering. Compare and contrast agglomerative and divisive clustering approaches.
4. What is the role of distance metrics (such as, Euclidean, Manhattan, Cosine) in clustering algorithms? How do they affect clustering results?
5. Explain the DBSCAN algorithm. How does it handle noise and detect clusters of arbitrary shape?
6. Describe the Gaussian Mixture Model (GMM) for clustering. How does it differ from K-Means, and when should it be used?

7. What are cluster validity indices? Discuss at least two commonly used metrics for evaluating clustering performance.
8. Explain the Elbow Method and Silhouette Score. How are they used to determine the optimal number of clusters?
9. What are the challenges in clustering high-dimensional data, and how can techniques such as PCA help in improving clustering performance?
10. Discuss real-world applications of clustering techniques in domains such as healthcare, finance, and customer segmentation.

Multiple Choice Questions

1. Which of the following best describes clustering in machine learning?
   a. A supervised learning technique for predicting labels
   b. A method to group similar data points together without predefined labels
   c. A technique used only for anomaly detection
   d. A method for feature selection in regression
2. In the K-Means clustering algorithm, what does 'K' represent?
   a. The number of features in the dataset
   b. The number of clusters to form
   c. The number of iterations for convergence
   d. The distance metric used
3. Which of the following is a key disadvantage of K-Means clustering?
   a. It is computationally expensive for small datasets.
   b. It cannot handle non-spherical clusters well.
   c. It does not require the number of clusters to be specified.
   d. It always finds the global optimum solution.
4. In hierarchical clustering, which approach starts with individual data points as separate clusters and merges them iteratively?
   a. Divisive clustering
   b. Agglomerative clustering

   c. K-Means clustering
   d. DBSCAN

5. Which clustering technique is best suited for detecting clusters of arbitrary shapes and filtering out noise?
   a. K-Means
   b. Hierarchical Clustering
   c. DBSCAN
   d. Gaussian Mixture Model

6. What does the Gaussian Mixture Model (GMM) assume about the distribution of data?
   a. Data points are uniformly distributed.
   b. Data is clustered in hyperspheres.
   c. Data is generated from a mixture of multiple Gaussian distributions.
   d. Data points belong to only one cluster with certainty.

7. Which of the following methods is commonly used to determine the optimal number of clusters in K-Means?
   a. Mean Squared Error (MSE)
   b. Principal Component Analysis (PCA)
   c. The Elbow Metho
   d. Least Squares Regression

8. What does the Silhouette Score measure in clustering evaluation?
   a. The compactness of each cluster and separation between clusters
   b. The computational efficiency of the clustering algorithm
   c. The number of clusters chosen by the model
   d. The standard deviation of distances within clusters

9. In hierarchical clustering, what is a dendrogram?
   a. A type of distance metric used in clustering
   b. A graphical representation of how clusters are merged at different levels

   c. A method for optimizing K-Means clustering

   d. A clustering algorithm used for large datasets

10. Which clustering algorithm does NOT require the number of clusters to be specified beforehand?

   a. K-Means

   b. DBSCAN

   c. Gaussian Mixture Model

   d. K-Medoids

Answers

1. b
2. b
3. b
4. b
5. c
6. c
7. c
8. a
9. b
10. b

CHAPTER 4
Dimensionality Reduction

Introduction

Dimensionality reduction techniques are used to reduce the number of features in large datasets while preserving important information. This chapter covers three widely used methods: Principal Component Analysis (PCA), t-SNE, and UMAP. You will learn about the theory behind each method and how each of them can be used to make high-dimensional data more manageable for visualization, analysis, and clustering. The chapter also emphasizes on the usefulness of these techniques in real-world applications like exploratory data analysis and feature engineering.

Structure

This chapter will address the following topics:

- Introduction to Dimensionality Reduction
    - The Curse of Dimensionality
    - Feature Selection vs Feature Extraction
- Linear Methods for Dimensionality Reduction: PCA, SVD
- Non-Linear Methods for Dimensionality Reduction
    - Manifold Learning
    - Isomap
    - t-SNE
    - UMAP
    - LLE
    - Advanced Methods

Introduction to Dimensionality Reduction

In any dataset, we typically deal with two components:

- **Observations/Samples/Data Points:** There are the individual items/entries in a tabular dataset. Each row in a dataset usually corresponds to one observation.
- **Features/Variables/Attributes:** These are the measurable properties/ features/characteristics of each observation. Each column typically represents one feature.

For example, consider the following patient dataset of a hospital:

Patient ID	Age	Blood Pressure	Cholesterol	Heart Rate
P001	45	120	180	72
P002	58	140	200	76
...	...	...	...	...

Figure 4.1: *A Sample Dataset*

In *Figure* 4.1, **patient dataset**, each **row** corresponds to a patient (an observation) and each **column** (excluding the ID) corresponds to a feature (such as, age, blood pressure, cholesterol, and heart rate). A **feature vector** is a list (or array) of feature values representing a single observation in the dataset. So, for **Patient P001**, the feature vector is **`[45, 120, 180, 72]`**.

The following vector represents the information that for the patient with ID P001:

- Age = 45
- Blood Pressure = 120
- Cholesterol = 180
- Heart Rate = 72

In general, if your dataset has n features, then each feature vector is an n-dimensional vector:

```
x=[x1, x2, x3,..., xn].
```

In machine learning, we usually exclude non-numeric identifiers (like Patient ID) and use only the **numerical or encoded features** as the feature vector. These vectors are then used as inputs for algorithms such as clustering, classification, or dimensionality reduction.

Since the feature vector here contains 4 values, it is said to be four-dimensional or to lie in a 4D vector space. A feature vector containing 20 values will be twenty-dimensional and lie in that vector space. Thus, the dimensionality of a dataset is the number of features it contains. A high dimensional vector is one containing many features. For example, a dataset with 1000 features (such as, gene expression levels or word frequencies in a document) lies in a **1000-dimensional** space.

High-dimensional data is common in fields such as genomics, text analysis, image processing, and sensor data. While such data is rich in information, it often introduces the following **challenges**:

- Increased computational cost
- Difficulty in visualization
- Risk of overfitting
- Sparse data distributions

This is where **dimensionality reduction** techniques come into play. They aim to reduce the number of features and preserve the essential structure of the data.

The Curse of Dimensionality

The curse of dimensionality refers to the various problems that arise when working with data in high-dimensional spaces. These problems include:

- **Data Sparsity:** In high dimensions, data points tend to be far apart from each other, which makes it harder to detect meaningful patterns or clusters.
- **Distance Degradation:** Many machine learning algorithms rely on distance metrics (like Euclidean distance). In high-dimensional space, the distance between any two points becomes nearly the same, thereby reducing the effectiveness of such algorithms.
- **Exponential Growth of Volume:** As dimensionality increases, the volume of the space increases exponentially. To maintain the same data density, the number of required data points also grows exponentially. This is practically infeasible.
- **Overfitting Risk:** With many features and limited data, models can easily fit noise rather than underlying patterns, leading to poor generalization.

Let us understand the curse of dimensionality with the following example:

Imagine trying to cover a line segment (1D) of length 1 with small intervals of length 0.1. You will need **10** such intervals to do so. Now try to cover a square (2D) of area 1 with small squares of side 0.1, for which you will need **100** such squares. In 3D, you would need **1,000** cubes of size 0.1. As the dimensions grow, the number of points needed to maintain the same granularity will also grow **exponentially**.

Table 4.1 shows how quickly the requirement for data points grows (to obtain the same level of information granularity) as dimensionality increases:

Dimensionality	**Number of 0.1-sized Units**
1	10
2	100
3	1000
10	10,000,000,000

Table 4.1: *Number of Data Points Required to Maintain Same Granularity of Information as Dimensionality Increases*

Importance of Dimensionality Reduction for Unsupervised Learning

In supervised learning, labels can sometimes guide models to ignore irrelevant features. However, in **unsupervised learning**, especially clustering and density estimation, we do not have labels. The algorithm relies entirely on distances, densities, and similarities, which are exactly the aspects distorted by high dimensionality. That is why **dimensionality reduction** is an important pre-processing step in unsupervised learning.

By reducing the number of dimensions, we aim to achieve the following goals:

- Remove noise
- Preserve essential structure
- Improve algorithm performance
- Enable visualization

Feature Selection vs Feature Extraction

Dimensionality reduction techniques generally fall into two broad categories: **feature selection** and **feature extraction**. While both aim to reduce the number of input features used in modeling, they do so in fundamentally different ways.

Feature Selection

Feature selection involves identifying and retaining a subset of the original features that are most relevant or informative, while discarding the rest.

- No transformation is applied; selected features retain their original meaning.
- The reduced dataset contains only a smaller number of original columns.

Common feature selection methods include filter methods, wrapper methods and embedded methods.

- **Filter Methods:** Use statistical measures like variance, correlation, or mutual information
- **Wrapper Methods:** Use a machine learning model to evaluate feature subsets (such as, recursive feature elimination)
- **Embedded Methods:** Perform feature selection during model training (such as, Lasso regression)

For instance, you might select only 3 features from a patient dataset with 10 health metrics–say, *blood pressure*, *cholesterol*, and *heart rate*–based on their predictive power.

Feature Extraction

Feature extraction involves creating new features by transforming or combining the original features in a way that retains essential information.

- The new features may not have a direct human-interpretable meaning.
- The transformation aims to represent the data in a more compact form.

Common Methods for Feature Extraction

- Principal Component Analysis (PCA)
- t-SNE
- UMAP
- Autoencoders

For instance, in PCA, a set of possibly correlated features is transformed into a set of linearly uncorrelated components (principal components). The first few components often capture most of the data's variance.

Let us summarize the difference between feature selection and feature extractions in *Table 4.2*:

Aspect	**Feature Selection**	**Feature Extraction**
Approach	Retains a most informative subset of original features, discarding the rest	Create new features by applying transformations to original features
Interpretability	High	Low
Purpose	Retain most informative features	New features capture essential structure or information in data
Techniques	Filter methods, wrapper methods and embedded methods	PCA, t-SNE, UMAP, Autoencoders

Table 4.2: *Comparison of Feature Selection and Feature Extraction Techniques*

Feature selection and feature extraction are often used as complementary approaches. **Feature selection** is simpler and more interpretable, while **feature extraction** is more powerful in uncovering latent structures, especially in unsupervised learning.

Linear Methods for Dimensionality Reduction

Linear methods apply linear transforms to high dimensional data to transform it into a lower dimensional space while retaining as much of the original structure or variance in data as possible. The goal is to reduce the complexity of the data to simplify visualization and analysis, while preventing significant loss of information. Often the data is represented as a matrix of numerical values and the linear transformations are represented as matrices, such that the linear transformations are the matrix multiplication operations.

Let us assume we have a dataset with two features (columns)–Height and Weight, and three observations or data points (rows) as shown in *Table* 4.3:

Data Point	Feature 1 (Height)	Feature 2 (Weight)
1	5.5	150
2	6.0	160
3	5.8	155

***Table* 4.3:** A *Sample Dataset*

In this dataset:

- **Feature 1** represents the height of individuals.
- **Feature 2** represents the weight of individuals.
- We have 3 data points (1, 2, 3) for which we have recorded height and weight.

To represent this dataset as a matrix, each row will correspond to a data point, and each column will correspond to a feature. The matrix X would look like this:

$$X = \begin{bmatrix} 5.5 & 150 \\ 6.0 & 160 \\ 5.8 & 155 \end{bmatrix}$$

Matrix X is the data matrix that represents our dataset in *Table* 4.3.

Some of the most common linear methods of dimensionality reduction are—Principal Component Analysis (PCA), Factor Analysis, Linear Discriminant Analysis (LDA), and Independent Component Analysis (ICA), Singular Value Decomposition (SVD).

These linear methods involve:

- **Maximizing Variance:** Linear methods like PCA focus on finding new axes (or directions) in the data space that maximize the variance, which typically corresponds to the most important features of the data. By doing so, these methods ensure that the reduced dimensions can still capture the primary sources of variability in the data.
- **Linear Transformation:** In contrast to non-linear methods (like t-SNE or UMAP), that may involve complex transformations, linear methods apply simple mathematical operations such as matrix multiplication and eigenvalue decomposition. This makes them computationally efficient and easy to implement in many applications.
- **Simplification and Interpretability:** By projecting high-dimensional data onto fewer dimensions (typically those that explain the most variance), linear methods make it easier to visualize and interpret the data. This is especially important in domains like machine learning and data analysis, where dimensionality reduction is used to enhance model performance or interpretability.
- **Capturing Global Structure:** Linear methods assume that the data lies in a linear subspace, meaning that the relationships between features can be described using straight lines or hyperplanes. While this assumption might not hold in all cases, linear methods can still effectively reduce dimensions when the data approximately follows a linear structure.
- **Computational Efficiency:** Linear methods tend to scale well with large datasets. PCA and SVD, for example, have efficient algorithms (such as, eigen-decomposition, singular value decomposition) that work well even with very large data matrices.

By reducing dimensions, we can eliminate irrelevant or redundant features, focusing on the most significant patterns and structures in the data. This makes the data easier to analyze but also and improves the effectiveness of machine learning models by removing noise and focusing on the core information, leading to better generalization and interpretability.

Principal Component Analysis (PCA)

Principal Component Analysis (PCA) is a statistical technique used to identify the directions, also known as principal components, that maximize the variance in high-dimensional data. The goal of PCA is to transform the original features into a new set of uncorrelated variables, called principal components, which capture the most significant patterns in the data. The first principal component captures the direction of maximum variance, the second component captures the next largest variance, and so on, with each subsequent component being orthogonal to the previous ones. This transformation reduces the dimensionality of the data while retaining as much of the original variance as possible.

To understand PCA mathematically, we need to understand the concepts of covariance, eigenvalues, and eigenvectors, that are used by PCA to identify the principal components in a data matrix.

Covariance Matrix

The covariance matrix is a square matrix that describes the covariance (a measure of how much two variables change together) between different features in the data. It captures how the features of the data are related to each other. For a dataset with `n` features, the covariance matrix will be an `n×n` matrix, where each element `cov(Xi,Xj)` represents the covariance between features `Xi` and `Xj`.

The covariance matrix is important for PCA because PCA identifies the directions (principal components) in which the data varies the most. If two features are highly correlated, their covariance will be large, indicating that they vary together. The covariance matrix is calculated as:

$$\Sigma = \frac{1}{m-1} X^T X$$

Where `X` is the matrix of centered data (data with the mean subtracted from each feature) and `m` is the number of data points.

Eigenvalues and Eigenvectors

The next step in PCA involves performing an eigenvalue decomposition on the covariance matrix. The eigenvalues and eigenvectors provide the important information about the principal components and magnitude of the variance in the data.

- **Eigenvalues:** An eigenvalue indicates how much variance there is along the corresponding eigenvector. In PCA, the larger the eigenvalue, the more variance is captured along that principal component. The eigenvalues represent the "importance" of each principal component.
- **Eigenvectors:** Eigenvectors define the directions in the feature space along which the data has the most variance. These directions are the principal components. Each eigenvector is associated with an eigenvalue, which indicates the amount of variance explained by that eigenvector.

The eigenvalue decomposition of the covariance matrix **Σ** is given by the equation:

$$\Sigma v = \lambda v$$

where **λ** is the eigenvalue and **v** is the eigenvector. This equation implies that when the covariance matrix is multiplied by an eigenvector, the result is the eigenvalue multiplied by that eigenvector.

PCA Process

Once the covariance matrix is computed, PCA involves solving the eigenvalue problem to find the eigenvalues and eigenvectors of the covariance matrix. The steps are mentioned as follows:

- **Step 1:** Center the data (subtract the mean of each feature from the corresponding values). Before applying PCA, it is important to standardize the data, especially when features have different units or scales. Standardization ensures that each feature contributes equally to the analysis. For each feature:

  $$x_{standardized} = (x - \mu)/\sigma$$

  Where:

  μ is the mean of the feature

  σ is the standard deviation of the feature

  After this step, all features will have mean 0 and standard deviation 1.

- **Step 2:** Calculate the covariance matrix of the centered data.
- **Step 3:** Perform eigenvalue decomposition on the covariance matrix to find the eigenvalues and eigenvectors. For a **nxn** covariance matrix, we will get **n** eigenvectors and corresponding eigenvalues.
- **Step 4:** Sort the eigenvectors by their corresponding eigenvalues in descending order. The eigenvectors with the largest eigenvalues represent the most significant directions in the data.
- **Step 5:** Select the top *k* eigenvectors (corresponding to the largest eigenvalues) to form a new feature space with reduced dimensions. These eigenvectors form the new basis for the reduced feature space. The associated eigenvalues indicate how much variance each principal component explains.
- **Step 6:** Project the data onto the Principal Components:

  $$X_{reduced} = X.W$$

  Where:

  W is the matrix of selected k eigenvectors (each column is an eigenvector)

  $\mathbf{X}_{reduced}$ is the transformed data in the reduced k-dimensional space

Geometric Interpretation

The eigenvectors provide the directions of maximum variance in the data, and the eigenvalues tell us how much variance there is along each of these directions. Geometrically, PCA transforms the original feature space into a new space where the axes (principal components) correspond to the directions of maximum variance, making the data easier to understand and work with.

In summary, PCA relies on the covariance matrix to capture the relationships between features and then uses eigenvalues and eigenvectors to identify the directions (principal components) along which the data varies the most. These components are then used to reduce the dimensionality of the data while retaining the most significant information.

Choosing the Number of Components

An important step in PCA is deciding how many principal components to keep. The goal is to reduce dimensionality while retaining as much useful information (variance) as possible.

Explained Variance

Each principal component captures a portion of the total variance in the data. The explained variance tells us how much information (or variability) is preserved by each component. It is directly related to the eigenvalue of the component:

$$\text{Explained Variance Ratio} = \frac{\lambda_i}{\sum_{j=1}^{n} \lambda_j}$$

Where:

- λ_i is the eigenvalue of the ith principal component
- The denominator is the sum of all eigenvalues

This ratio indicates the proportion of total variance captured by that component.

To decide how many components to retain, we often look at the cumulative explained variance–the total variance captured by the first k components

$$\text{Cumulative Explained Variance} = \sum_{i=1}^{k} \frac{\lambda_i}{\sum_{j=1}^{n} \lambda_j}$$

By plotting the cumulative explained variance against the number of components, we can identify the point where adding more components offers diminishing returns. This is often referred to as the **elbow point** in the plot.

There are three methods to choose the number of Components for your PCA

- **Threshold Method:** Choose the smallest number of components that explain a desired amount of variance (such as, 95%). This ensures most of the important information is retained.
- **Scree Plot (Elbow Method):** Plot the eigenvalues or cumulative variance and look for the "elbow", which is the point where the increase in explained variance becomes less significant.
- **Domain Knowledge:** In some cases, the number of components is selected on the basis of practical constraints or interpretability needs.

For example, if the first 3 components explain 95% of the variance, and the remaining components explain only 5%, then reducing the data to these 3 components achieves dimensionality reduction with minimal information loss.

Applications of PCA

Principal Component Analysis (PCA) is widely used in machine learning, data analysis, and signal processing. Let us look at the most common applications:

- **Data Visualization:** PCA is commonly used to reduce high-dimensional data to 2 or 3 dimensions for visualization. This helps analysts and researchers explore patterns, detect clusters, or spot outliers that are hard to observe in higher dimensions.
- **Noise Reduction:** By keeping only the components that capture the most variance, PCA can remove noise and irrelevant variability from the data. This improves the signal-to-noise ratio, especially in image/sensor data.
- **Preprocessing for Machine Learning:** PCA is often used as a preprocessing step to reduce dimensionality before applying machine learning algorithms. This can speed up training, reduce overfitting, and improve model performance for algorithms sensitive to the curse of dimensionality.
- **Feature Extraction and Engineering:** In cases where original features are highly correlated, PCA helps generate new, uncorrelated features (principal components) that capture the underlying structure of the data in a better way. These features can then be used in supervised or unsupervised learning tasks.
- **Image Compression:** PCA is used in image processing to compress images by representing them with fewer components, reducing storage requirements while preserving essential visual details. This is especially effective for grayscale and facial images.
- **Anomaly Detection:** By projecting data onto the principal components and reconstructing it, PCA can help identify data points that differ significantly from the norm, making it useful in anomaly or fraud detection.

- **Genomics and Bioinformatics:** In genetics, PCA helps analyze gene expression or DNA microarray data by identifying patterns, removing redundancies, and grouping similar samples based on genetic profiles.
- **Finance and Economics:** PCA is used to reduce the dimensionality of financial indicators or asset prices, allowing analysts to detect major trends, market factors, or to construct low-dimensional risk models.

Therefore, PCA is a powerful tool for simplifying data, enhancing interpretability, and improving the performance of downstream analysis across a wide range of domains.

Implementation of PCA Using Sklearn Library:

In this code example, we will implement face recognition. We will use the dataset **Labelled Faces in the Wild (LFW)** (https://scikit-learn.org/0.19/datasets/labeled_faces.html), which is built into the sklearn library. LFW dataset contains a total of 13,233 JPEG images of faces of 5,749 famous personalities collected from the web. Each original image has 2,914 features (pixels per image) when it is flattened. However, in this example, we will load only those image with a minimum of 100 features of a person and resize each image to 40% of its original size. After loading the images and their true labels, we will split the dataset into train and test portions. Standardize the images in both train and test portions. Then we will apply PCA to the train and test images. This identifies the principal components from each image. We will then train a Logistic Regression classifier to classify the images using Principal Components. The evaluation of the classifier shows that it has an accuracy of about 84% in predicting the true class of an image using Principal Components.

In *Figure* 4.1, we load the required Python libraries and the Images from the dataset:

```
# Step 1: Import required libraries
import numpy as np
import matplotlib.pyplot as plt
from sklearn.datasets import fetch_lfw_people
from sklearn.decomposition import PCA
from sklearn.model_selection import train_test_split
from sklearn.linear_model import LogisticRegression
from sklearn.preprocessing import StandardScaler
from sklearn.metrics import classification_report, confusion_matrix

# Step 2: Load the Labelled Faced in the Wild (LFW) dataset built into skleard datasets
# https://scikit-learn.org/0.19/datasets/labeled_faces.html
# LFW dataset contains a total of 13233 JPEG images of faces of 5749 famous persons collected
# from the web. Each original image has 2914 features (pixels per image)


# In this example, we will load only those image which have a minimum of
# 100 images of a person and resize each image to 40% of its original size
lfw = fetch_lfw_people(min_faces_per_person=100, resize=0.4)

X = lfw.data                        # Take Flattened face images in X
y = lfw.target                      # Class labels in y for each image in X
target_names = lfw.target_names     # Names of people in target_names
h, w = lfw.images[0].shape          # Dimensions (height and width) of each Image

print("Total number of images loaded", X.shape[0])
print(f"Height and Width of Each Reduced Size Image: {h}, {w}")
print("Number of pixels per image (after size reduction)", X.shape[1])
print("Names of Persons whose Images are Loaded (Target Names)", target_names)
```

```
Total number of images loaded 1140
Height and Width of Each Reduced Size Image: 50, 37
Number of pixels per image (after size reduction) 1850
Names of Persons whose Images are Loaded (Target Names) ['Colin Powell' 'Donald Rumsfeld' 'George W B
ush' 'Gerhard Schroeder'
 'Tony Blair']
```

Figure 4.2: *Import Libraries and Load the Image Data*

In *Figure* 4.2, we split the loaded dataset into train and test portions, apply standardization to the data, compute the 200 principal components from each image, and train a logistic regression classifier on the principal components. Then, we will print the classification report and the confusion matrix to evaluate the classifier.

```
# Step 2: Split into train/test sets
X_train, X_test, y_train, y_test = train_test_split(X, y, test_size=0.30, random_state=42)

#Step 3: Apply Standardization to Data
scaler = StandardScaler()
X_train = scaler.fit_transform(X_train)
X_test = scaler.transform(X_test)

# Step 4: Apply PCA for dimensionality reduction
# We will find 200 principal components of each image
n_components = 200
pca = PCA(n_components=n_components, svd_solver='randomized', whiten=True)
X_train_pca = pca.fit_transform(X_train)
X_test_pca = pca.transform(X_test)

# Step 5: Train a Logistic Regression classifier on Principal Components
clf = LogisticRegression(max_iter=1000, solver='lbfgs', multi_class='multinomial')
clf.fit(X_train_pca, y_train)

# Step 6: Evaluate the model
y_pred = clf.predict(X_test_pca)

print("Classification Report:\n")
print(classification_report(y_test, y_pred, target_names=target_names))
print("Confusion Matrix:\n")
print(confusion_matrix(y_test, y_pred))
```

```
Classification Report:

                   precision    recall  f1-score   support

     Colin Powell       0.86      0.87      0.87        78
  Donald Rumsfeld       0.70      0.68      0.69        38
    George W Bush       0.87      0.87      0.87       159
Gerhard Schroeder       0.81      0.87      0.84        30
       Tony Blair       0.80      0.76      0.78        37

         accuracy                           0.84       342
        macro avg       0.81      0.81      0.81       342
     weighted avg       0.84      0.84      0.84       342

Confusion Matrix:

[[ 68   3   5   1   1]
 [  2  26   7   1   2]
 [  8   7 139   2   3]
 [  0   0   3  26   1]
 [  1   1   5   2  28]]
```

Figure 4.3: *Applying PCA to the Images*

In *Figure* 4.3, we plot the images along with the true names and predicted names of the persons, the image belongs to:

```
# Step 7: Plot test images with predictions
def image_title(y_pred, y_true, target_names, i):
    pred_name = target_names[y_pred[i]]
    true_name = target_names[y_true[i]]
    return f'Pred: {pred_name}\nTrue: {true_name}'

def plot_gallery(images, titles, h, w, n_row=3, n_col=5):
    plt.figure(figsize=(1.8 * n_col, 2.4 * n_row))
    for i in range(n_row * n_col):
        plt.subplot(n_row, n_col, i + 1)
        plt.imshow(images[i].reshape((h, w)), cmap=plt.cm.gray)
        plt.title(titles[i], size=10)
        plt.xticks(()), plt.yticks(())
    plt.tight_layout()
    plt.show()

titles = [image_title(y_pred, y_test, target_names, i) for i in range(len(y_pred))]
plot_gallery(X_test, titles, h, w)
```

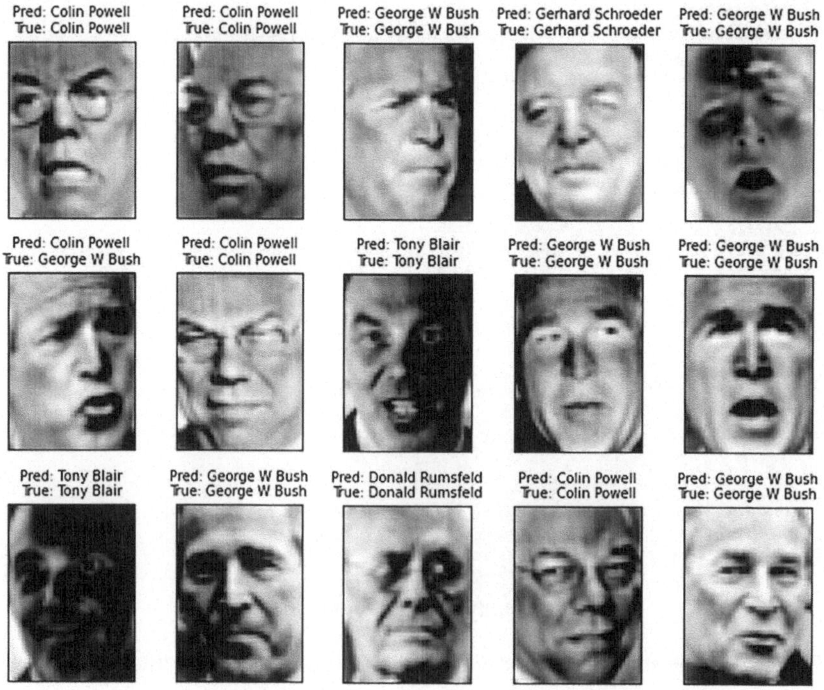

Pred: Colin Powell
True: Colin Powell
Pred: Colin Powell
True: Colin Powell
Pred: George W Bush
True: George W Bush
Pred: Gerhard Schroeder
True: Gerhard Schroeder
Pred: George W Bush
True: George W Bush
Pred: Colin Powell
True: George W Bush
Pred: Colin Powell
True: Colin Powell
Pred: Tony Blair
True: Tony Blair
Pred: George W Bush
True: George W Bush
Pred: George W Bush
True: George W Bush
Pred: Tony Blair
True: Tony Blair
Pred: George W Bush
True: George W Bush
Pred: Donald Rumsfeld
True: Donald Rumsfeld
Pred: Colin Powell
True: Colin Powell
Pred: George W Bush
True: George W Bush

Figure 4.4: *Images of Faces with True and Predicted Person Names*

Figure 4.4 shows the plots of eigenfaces of each of the face images in *Figure* 4.3:

```
# Step 8: Visualize eigenfaces
# Let us reshape principal components into h*w size for visualization as two dimensional image
# pca.components_ is a NumPy array of shape (n_components, n_features)
# Each row of this array is a principal component.
# Each component is a flattened image vector of length n_features = h × w.
# reshape((n_components, h, w)) converts these flat vectors back into 2D image shapes:
# So now eigenfaces is an array of shape (n_components, h, w).
# We can visualize them as grayscale images using matplotlib

eigenfaces = pca.components_.reshape((n_components, h, w))

def plot_eigenfaces(eigenfaces, h, w, n_row=3, n_col=5):
    plt.figure(figsize=(1.8 * n_col, 2.4 * n_row))
    for i in range(n_row * n_col):
        plt.subplot(n_row, n_col, i + 1)
        plt.imshow(eigenfaces[i], cmap=plt.cm.gray)
        plt.title(f"PC {i+1}", size=10)
        plt.xticks(()), plt.yticks(())
    plt.suptitle("Top Eigenfaces (Principal Components)", size=14)
    plt.tight_layout()
    plt.show()

plot_eigenfaces(eigenfaces, h, w)
```

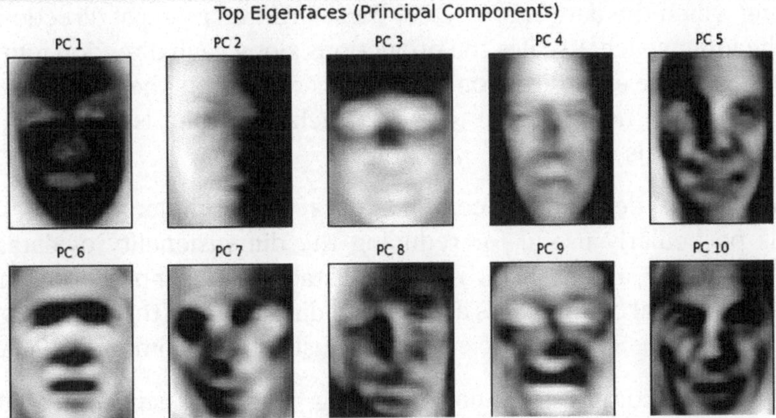

Figure 4.5: *Shows the Plots of Eigenfaces of Each of the Face Images*

Singular Value Decomposition (SVD)

Now that we have understood the basics of PCA, let us learn about Singular Value Decomposition (SVD). SVD is a fundamental matrix factorization technique derived from linear algebra. Given any real-valued matrix X of shape **m×n**, SVD factorizes it into three matrices:

$$X = U\Sigma V^T$$

Where,

U is an m*m orthogonal matrix containing the left singular vectors

Σ is an m*n diagonal matrix of non-negative singular values

$\mathbf{V}^T$ is the transpose of an n*n orthogonal matrix containing the right singular vectors.

SVD allows dimensionality reduction by truncating the smaller singular values and associated vectors. We keep only the top k singular values (and corresponding vectors) to approximate the original matrix:

$$A_k = U_k \Sigma_k V_k^T$$

This reduced representation retains most of the important information while reducing data dimensionality.

Geometric Interpretation of SVD:

In SVD, the matrices U and V are orthogonal. V represents the directions in the original feature space along which the data is projected, these are the principal directions or basis vectors of the input space. Σ scales the projections along each direction found in V. It tells how much variance each direction captures. U represents the coordinates of the transformed data in the new space. It tells how each data point is expressed as a combination of the new basis vectors.

SVD provides a way to decompose complex data into simpler, interpretable components. It is particularly useful for reducing the dimensionality of datasets, uncovering latent structure, and ensuring numerical stability in computations. In the context of PCA, the principal components are derived directly from the right singular vectors in V, thereby making SVD an efficient and robust tool for computing PCA.

SVD can be used for data compression, noise filtering, and latent semantic analysis (LSA) in natural language processing.

Implementation of SVD using sklearn library

Sklearn library offers TruncatedSVD (https://scikit-learn.org/stable/modules/generated/sklearn.decomposition.TruncatedSVD.html) algorithm that implements a variant of SVD. TruncatedSVD only computes the k largest singular values, where the user specifies the parameter k. TruncatedSVD differs from PCA, in that the input data matrix X does not need to be centered before computing the SVD. Therefore, SVD can work well for sparse matrices as well.

The succeeding code demonstrated the application of Truncated Singular Value Decomposition (TruncatedSVD) for dimensionality reduction in a face recognition task using the Labeled Faces in the Wild (LFW) dataset. Just like the code we used for PCA, we will load only those individuals who have at least 100 face images in the dataset. The images are flattened into 1D vectors and stored in the variable X, while their corresponding identity labels are stored in y. The data is then split into training and testing sets, followed by standardization to normalize feature scales. TruncatedSVD is applied to reduce the dimensionality of the input data to 150 components, capturing the most significant features while reducing computational cost. A logistic regression classifier is then trained on the reduced data and evaluated using a classification report and confusion matrix, which shows how well the model can recognize and classify faces based on the extracted features.

```
# Step 1: Import libraries
import numpy as np
import matplotlib.pyplot as plt
from sklearn.datasets import fetch_lfw_people
from sklearn.decomposition import TruncatedSVD
from sklearn.model_selection import train_test_split
from sklearn.linear_model import LogisticRegression
from sklearn.preprocessing import StandardScaler
from sklearn.metrics import classification_report, confusion_matrix

# Step 2: Load LFW dataset
lfw = fetch_lfw_people(min_faces_per_person=100, resize=0.4)
X = lfw.data
y = lfw.target
target_names = lfw.target_names
h, w = lfw.images[0].shape

# Step 3: Train-test split
X_train, X_test, y_train, y_test = train_test_split(X, y, test_size=0.3, random_state=42)

# Step 4: Standardize the data
scaler = StandardScaler()
X_train_scaled = scaler.fit_transform(X_train)
X_test_scaled = scaler.transform(X_test)

# Step 5: Apply Truncated SVD
n_components = 150
svd = TruncatedSVD(n_components=n_components, random_state=42)
X_train_svd = svd.fit_transform(X_train_scaled)
X_test_svd = svd.transform(X_test_scaled)

# Step 6: Train a classifier
clf = LogisticRegression(max_iter=1000, solver='lbfgs', multi_class='multinomial')
clf.fit(X_train_svd, y_train)

# Step 7: Evaluate model
y_pred = clf.predict(X_test_svd)
print("Classification Report:\n")
print(classification_report(y_test, y_pred, target_names=target_names))
print("Confusion Matrix:\n")
print(confusion_matrix(y_test, y_pred))
```

Figure 4.6: *Implementation of TruncatedSVD on LFW Dataset*

Figure 4.7 shows the classification report of the above code. We can see that when the dimensions are reduced using TruncatedSVD, we obtain a classification accuracy of 85% for face recognition.

```
Classification Report:

                   precision    recall  f1-score   support

      Colin Powell       0.90      0.85      0.87        78
   Donald Rumsfeld       0.71      0.76      0.73        38
     George W Bush       0.89      0.90      0.89       159
Gerhard Schroeder       0.79      0.77      0.78        30
       Tony Blair       0.76      0.78      0.77        37

         accuracy                           0.85       342
        macro avg       0.81      0.81      0.81       342
     weighted avg       0.85      0.85      0.85       342

Confusion Matrix:

[[ 66   5   5   1   1]
 [  0  29   6   2   1]
 [  4   7 143   1   4]
 [  2   0   2  23   3]
 [  1   0   5   2  29]]
```

Figure 4.7: *Classification Report and Confusion Matrix for TruncatedSVD Implementation*

Non-Linear Methods for Dimensionality Reduction

High-dimensional data often does not reside in a linear subspace. Instead, it can lie on or near a non-linear manifold. Linear methods, such as PCA, are limited in capturing these complex, non-linear relationships.

Limitations of Linear Methods

- **Linear Subspaces:** Linear methods assume that the data lies in a straight line or a flat subspace, which fails to capture the complexity of curved or folded manifolds.
- **Topological Complexity:** They are ineffective when the data has complex topologies, such as the well-known Swiss roll example, which cannot be captured by linear projections.

Non-linear dimensionality reduction methods, often referred to as manifold learning techniques, uncover these non-linear structures by preserving the relationships between data points in the high-dimensional space. These methods are particularly effective when data exhibits complex patterns, such as in images, text, or biological data where local or global neighborhood relationships are more meaningful than global linear projections.

Manifold Learning

A manifold is a topological or mathematical space which can be complex and curved in its high dimensional form but behaves like a flat (Euclidean) space when viewed locally. An n-dimensional manifold has the property that each point in it has a neighborhood that is homeomorphic to an open subset of n-dimensional Euclidean space. It is just like the surface of the Earth. That is, globally the Earth is a 3D sphere, but when looked locally over a small area, it appears to be a flat 2D plane.

In the context of dimensionality reduction, even though a dataset might be very high dimensional (for example, it might have 1000 features), the data points in this dataset lie on a much lower dimensional structure (manifold) within its high dimensional space. Manifold learning is a class of non-linear dimensionality reduction techniques that uncover the low-dimensional structure in high dimensional data. These methods work by preserving certain geometric or topological properties of the data, which are either local relationships or global structures (overall shape and paths of the data manifold). Manifold learning algorithms such as Isomap, LLE, t-SNE and UMAP effectively reduce the dimensionality, while maintaining the meaningful structure of the original data.

In *Figure* 4.8, on the left side we see a 3D Swiss Roll, a non-linear manifold representation of the original dataset, on the right side we see the unrolled 2D Swiss Roll (Isomap) representation of the same dataset which preserves the manifold's structure in lower dimensions. The Swiss Roll or rotating head images lie on curved surfaces in high-dimensional space; Isomap algorithm "unfolds" these manifolds into meaningful low-dimensional coordinates.

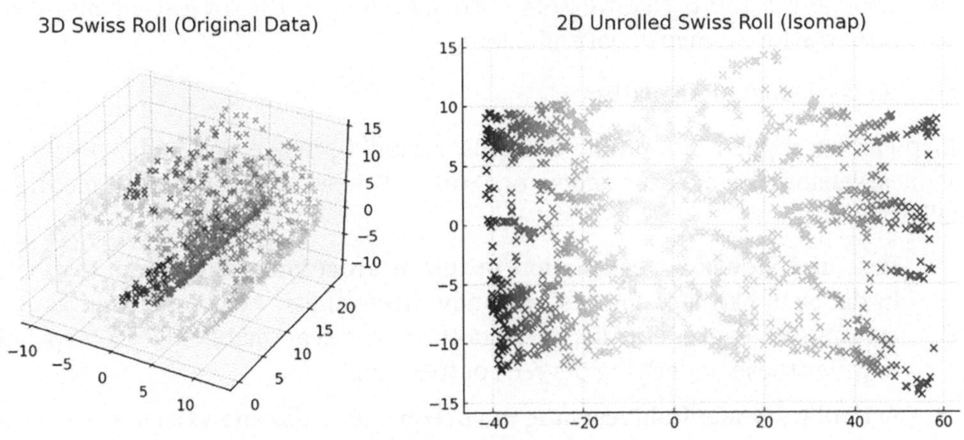

Figure 4.8: *Learning 2D Representation of a 3D Dataset Using Manifold Learning*

Next, we will learn about the algorithms for manifold learning including Isometric Mapping (Isomap), Locally Linear Embedding (LLE), t-SNE (t-Distributed Stochastic Neighbor Embedding) and Uniform Manifold Approximation and Projection (UMAP).

Isometric Mapping (ISOMAP)

Isometric Mapping (Isomap) is a global manifold learning technique that preserves the intrinsic geometry of data by approximating geodesic distances, or the shortest paths along the manifold surface. It learns the low dimensional representations of data lying on curved or folded manifolds.

Mathematical Foundations

Let {x1, x2, ...,xn} $\subset R^D$ represent a high dimensional data points. The Isomap algorithm will involve exercising the following steps on the datapoints:

1. Compute pairwise distances between data points and construct a neighborhood graph: Construct a weighted graph G = (V, E), where each vertex corresponds to a data point. Edges connect points that are nearest neighbors using k-nearest neighbors or a fixed-radius ε – neighborhood.
2. Estimate geodesic distance between all pairs of points as the shortest path distances in the graph G.
3. Perform eigenvalue decomposition on the geodesic distance matrix. This includes applying Multidimensional Scaling to the geodesic distance matrix to embed the data into a lower-dimensional space while preserving the pairwise distances between the data points.
4. Choose the top d eigenvectors corresponding to the largest eigenvalues to form the low-dimensional embedding.

Applications of Isomap Algorithm

Isomap can be applied in multiple domains, including image and audio processing, genomics, sensor data analysis and so on. Some of these applications are mentioned as follows:

- **Pose and viewpoint estimation in image processing and computer vision:** In datasets like face images or handwritten digits, variations such as pose, lighting, or expression lie on smooth, non-linear manifolds. Isomap helps uncover these underlying degrees of freedom.
- **Articulatory manifold learning in speech and audio analysis:** In speech data, different phonemes or vocal configurations vary smoothly. Isomap can capture these transitions, revealing low-dimensional structures related to vocal tract movements. For audio segments and chord progressions, Isomap helps map

complex relationships into low-dimensional timelines or embeddings that preserve temporal or harmonic structure.

- **Capturing gene expression patterns in genomics and bioinformatics:** High-dimensional gene expression data often resides on low-dimensional manifolds corresponding to biological states (such as, disease progression or cell differentiation). Isomap can reveal these trajectories. In developmental biology, it can help map single-cell RNA-seq data to visualize developmental pathways or lineage trajectories.
- **Localization and environment mapping in sensor networks and robotics:** When sensors or robots move in a physical space, Isomap can recover the spatial layout from pairwise signal similarities or distances. In robotics, non-linear dimensionality reduction like Isomap helps map high-dimensional sensor inputs (such as, LIDAR, sonar) to spatial representations.
- **Scientific data visualization for molecular simulations and climate modelling:** In chemistry or physics, Isomap can reduce the dimensionality of configuration spaces (such as, protein folding pathways) to visualize and analyze potential energy surfaces. For high-dimensional temporal-spatial data (such as, ocean temperatures), Isomap helps identify dominant global patterns.
- **Market state visualization in finance and economics:** Isomap can reveal non-linear structures in asset price movements or correlation patterns, helping detect market regimes or anomalies.

Isomap algorithm is the most effective when a dataset has an underlying smooth global structure and when preserving geodesic distances is essential for understanding or interpreting the data.

Implementation of Isomap Using Sklearn Library

The code in *Figure* 4.9 demonstrates a comparative visualization of linear versus non-linear dimensionality reduction techniques—PCA and Isomap—on the digits dataset from scikit-learn, which contains 1,797 grayscale images of handwritten digits (0–9), each represented as a 64-dimensional feature vector. PCA projects the high-dimensional data into a 2D space by preserving maximum variance in a linear sense, while Isomap reduces dimensions by preserving geodesic distances, capturing the non-linear manifold structure. The resulting scatter plots show how digit clusters are organized in 2D. While PCA might produce overlapping groups due to its linear nature, Isomap can achieve better separation of digit classes, revealing the underlying non-linear structure in the image space. The comparative plots in the output of this code illustrate the strength of Isomap in visualizing complex data, where global linear methods like PCA fall short.

```
#Isomap
import matplotlib.pyplot as plt
from sklearn.datasets import load_digits
from sklearn.manifold import Isomap
from sklearn.decomposition import PCA

# Load the digits dataset
digits = load_digits()
X = digits.data
y = digits.target

# Apply PCA
pca = PCA(n_components=2)
X_pca = pca.fit_transform(X)

# Apply Isomap
isomap = Isomap(n_neighbors=10, n_components=2)
X_isomap = isomap.fit_transform(X)

# Create plots with constrained layout
fig, axs = plt.subplots(1, 2, figsize=(14, 6), constrained_layout=True)

# PCA plot
sc1 = axs[0].scatter(X_pca[:, 0], X_pca[:, 1], c=y, cmap=plt.cm.tab10, s=15)
axs[0].set_title("PCA (Linear)")
axs[0].set_xlabel("Component 1")
axs[0].set_ylabel("Component 2")

# Isomap plot
sc2 = axs[1].scatter(X_isomap[:, 0], X_isomap[:, 1], c=y, cmap=plt.cm.tab10, s=15)
axs[1].set_title("Isomap (Non-Linear)")
axs[1].set_xlabel("Component 1")
axs[1].set_ylabel("Component 2")

# Shared colorbar
fig.colorbar(sc2, ax=axs, orientation='horizontal', fraction=0.05, pad=0.1, label='Digit Label')

# Super title
plt.suptitle("Isomap vs PCA on Handwritten Digits")
plt.show()
```

Figure 4.9: *Isomap and PCA to Visualize the Digit Clusters*

Figure 4.10 shows the corresponding plots for PCA and Isomap. We can see a clear separation between clusters that have been obtained using Isomap.

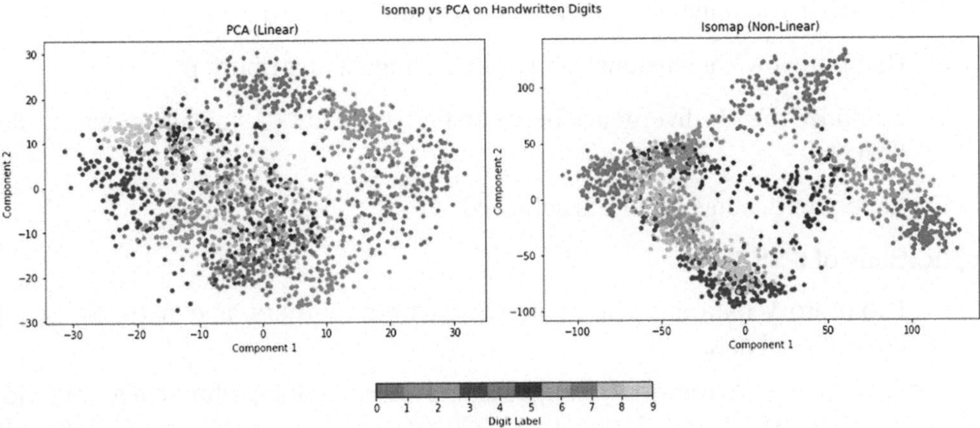

***Figure 4.10:** Visualization of Digit Clusters after PCA and Isomap*

t-SNE (t-distributed Stochastic Neighbor Embedding)

t-SNE focuses on preserving local neighborhood structure in data, rather than the global geometry. It is thus especially effective at revealing clusters or groupings in high-dimensional data. Unlike Isomap, t-SNE does not attempt to preserve global geometry; it maps similar points in high dimensions to nearby points in low dimensions. t-SNE constructs a probabilistic distribution over the pairwise similarities (distances) between data points based on how likely it is for one point to pick another as its neighbor. In the low-dimensional embedding, t-SNE creates a similar distribution and minimizes the difference between the two using Kullback - Liebler Divergence (KL-divergence) cost function.

Working of t-SNE

In high dimensional data, t-SNE uses a Gaussian distribution centered at each point to compute pairwise similarities between the data points. In low dimensions, it uses Student t-distribution with one degree of freedom. Student t-distribution with heavier tails avoids the crowding problem by allowing moderate dissimilarities in high dimensionality to be placed further apart in low dimensionality.

Parameters used in t-SNE calculation are perplexity, learning rate and random seed. Perplexity controls the balance between local and global aspects of the data. Its typical value lies between 5 and 50. Learning rate affects the convergence behaviour of the optimization. Random seed controls the stochastic nature of the algorithm over different runs. Steps in working of t-SNE are:

1. Compute pairwise similarities between high-dimensional points using a Gaussian-based distribution.

2. Initialize low-dimensional embeddings randomly.
3. Compute low-dimensional similarities using a t-distribution.
4. Minimize the KL-divergence between high- and low-D similarities via gradient descent.
5. Repeat until convergence is achieved.

Applications of t-SNE

- Exploratory data analysis to reveal clusters, outliers, and patterns in high dimensional data
- To visualize activations, latent features or embeddings for image and video analysis using convolutional neural networks or word embeddings from Word2Vec, GloVe, BERT, and so on
- Analysis of genomic data and medical diagnostics
- Outlier or anomaly detection for security
- Visualization of customer segmentation and risk profiles in finance and market analysis

Though t-SNE is not suitable for tasks such as classification or large-scale embedding, it is very powerful for visualizing complex, high-dimensional data where local structure is important. It is an important method in the unsupervised learning and helps build interpretability into your machine learning models.

Implementation Using Sklearn Library

The code in *Figure* 4.11 shows non-linear dimensionality reduction using t-SNE on the digits dataset from scikit-learn. The digits dataset contains 1,797 samples of handwritten digits (0–9), each represented as a 64-dimensional vector (8×8 grayscale images). It applies the t-SNE algorithm to reduce the data from 64 dimensions to 2 dimensions for visualization. The key parameters used are **`perplexity=30`** (balancing local vs. global structure), **`learning_rate=200`**, and **`init='pca'`** for a more stable initialization.

The resultant 2D scatter plot color-codes each point by its true digit label. The visualization in the output plot shows distinct clusters corresponding to different digits, which indicates that t-SNE effectively captures the underlying structure of the data while preserving local neighborhoods.

```
#t-SNE
import matplotlib.pyplot as plt
from sklearn.datasets import load_digits
from sklearn.manifold import TSNE

# Load digits data
digits = load_digits()
X = digits.data
y = digits.target

# Apply t-SNE
#tsne = TSNE(n_components=2, perplexity=30, learning_rate=200, random_state=42)
tsne = TSNE(n_components=2, perplexity=30, learning_rate=200, init='pca', random_state=42)

X_tsne = tsne.fit_transform(X)

# Plot
plt.figure(figsize=(10, 6))
scatter = plt.scatter(X_tsne[:, 0], X_tsne[:, 1], c=y, cmap=plt.cm.tab10, s=15)
plt.colorbar(scatter, ticks=range(10), label='Digit Label')
plt.title("t-SNE Embedding of Handwritten Digits")
plt.xlabel("Component 1")
plt.ylabel("Component 2")
plt.grid(True)
plt.show()
```

```
:\Anaconda3\lib\site-packages\sklearn\manifold\_t_sne.py:982: FutureWarning: The PCA initializ
 the standard deviation of PC1 equal to 1e-4 in 1.2. This will ensure better convergence.
  warnings.warn(
```

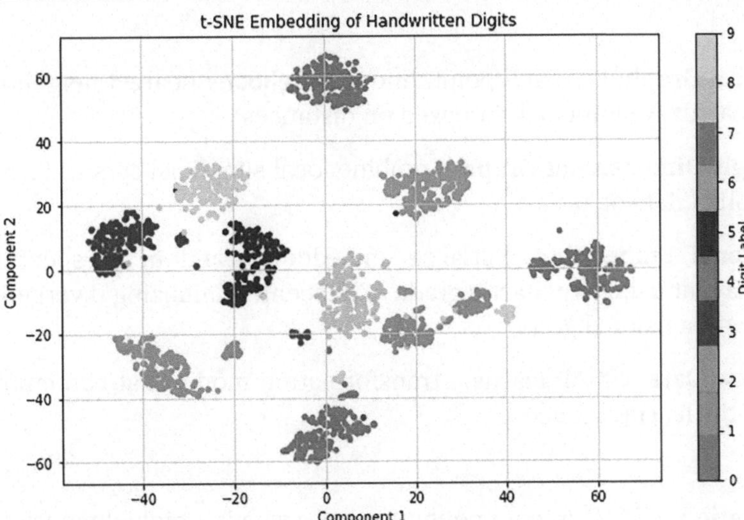

Figure 4.11: t-SNE *Applied to the Digits Dataset*

Uniform Manifold Approximation and Projection (UMAP)

Uniform Manifold Approximation and Projection (UMAP) preserves both local and global structure of high-dimensional data in the lower dimensional embedding.

Just like t-SNE, UMAP is useful to reduce the dimensionality of data for better data visualization. In addition, it supports transformation of new data and so can be used for broader machine learning workflows. It is based on manifold learning and topological data analysis and is often faster and more scalable than t-SNE.

UMAP is based on Riemannian geometry and algebraic topology and uses the following concepts:

- **Manifold Assumption:** The data is assumed to be uniformly distributed on a Riemannian manifold and local neighborhoods approximate Euclidean geometry.
- The Reimannian metric is locally constant or can be approximated as such.
- The manifold is locally connected.
- **Topological Representation:** UMAP constructs a fuzzy simplical complex representation of the high-dimensional topology of the data.
- **Optimization Objective:** The algorithm minimizes the cross-entropy between high-dimensional and low-dimensional fuzzy simplical sets.
- The cost function used in UMAP encourages preservation of local distances, and its structure retains global relationships better than t-SNE.

Working of UMAP

1. **Construct Local Graph**: For each point, find `n_neighbors` nearest neighbors. Compute a local fuzzy simplicial set based on distances.
2. **Construct High-Dimensional Graph**: Combine local simplicial sets to form a weighted graph of data structure.
3. **Low-Dimensional Embedding**: Initialize embedding (random or spectral). Optimize the layout using stochastic gradient descent, minimizing divergence from the high-dimensional graph.
4. **Transform New Data**: UMAP learns a transformation model that can embed new data into the learned space.

Applications

- **Data Visualization**: UMAP is commonly used to visualize high-dimensional data in 2D or 3D. It reveals clusters, outliers, and intrinsic structures in datasets such as: Images (such as, MNIST, CIFAR), Text embeddings (such as, BERT, TF-IDF), Biological data (such as, gene expression, single-cell RNA-seq).
- **Clustering Preprocessing**: UMAP can reduce dimensionality before applying clustering algorithms like K-means, DBSCAN, or HDBSCAN, thus improving their performance by removing noise and preserving meaningful relationships.

- **Classification Pipeline Optimization**: It is used as a feature reduction step before classification, particularly when dealing with high-dimensional input. This can improve classifier speed and accuracy.
- **Anomaly Detection**: By projecting data into a lower-dimensional space, UMAP helps isolate anomalous patterns that deviate from the main data structure, making it useful for fraud detection, system monitoring, and quality control.
- **Neural Network Embedding Analysis**: UMAP is used to explore and visualize the latent spaces of neural networks (such as, autoencoders or CNNs), helping users interpret learned representations.
- **Natural Language Processing**: In NLP, UMAP is applied to word embeddings or document vectors (such as, Word2Vec, BERT) for visualizing semantic relationships or preparing data for clustering or classification.
- **Genomics and Bioinformatics**: UMAP is heavily used to analyze gene expression data, especially in single-cell transcriptomics, where it reveals cell type clusters, developmental trajectories, and gene activity patterns.

As UMAP can transform new data after training, it is especially suitable for real-time inference pipelines that give it an advantage over t-SNE. UMAP is a standard tool used in modern unsupervised learning workflows.

Implementation of UMAP using Python libraries – Scanpy and Umap-learn

In the following code, we will apply UMAP to a digits dataset from sklearn. Umap-learn (https://pypi.org/project/umap-learn/) is a Python library that implements UMAP non-linear dimensionality reduction algorithm. Umap-learn depends on scikit-learn, numpy, and scipy, and additionally requires the numba library.

You can create a new Python environment in your computer and install the required libraries as follows:

```
pip install umap-learn
```

Once you have installed the requirements, you can run the code shown in *Figure 4.12* to implement the UMAP algorithm:

```
import umap
from sklearn.datasets import load_digits
import matplotlib.pyplot as plt
# Load sample data
digits = load_digits()
X = digits.data
y = digits.target
# Apply UMAP (sklearn-style API)
reducer = umap.UMAP(n_neighbors=15, min_dist=0.1, n_components=2)
X_umap = reducer.fit_transform(X)
# Plot the result
plt.figure(figsize=(8, 4))
scatter = plt.scatter(X_umap[:, 0], X_umap[:, 1], c=y, cmap=plt.cm.tab10, s=10)
plt.colorbar(scatter, label='Digit Label', ticks=range(10))
plt.title("UMAP Projection of the Digits Dataset")
plt.grid(True)
plt.show()
```

```
/usr/local/lib/python3.11/dist-packages/sklearn/utils/deprecation.py:151: FutureWarning: 'force_a
  warnings.warn(
```

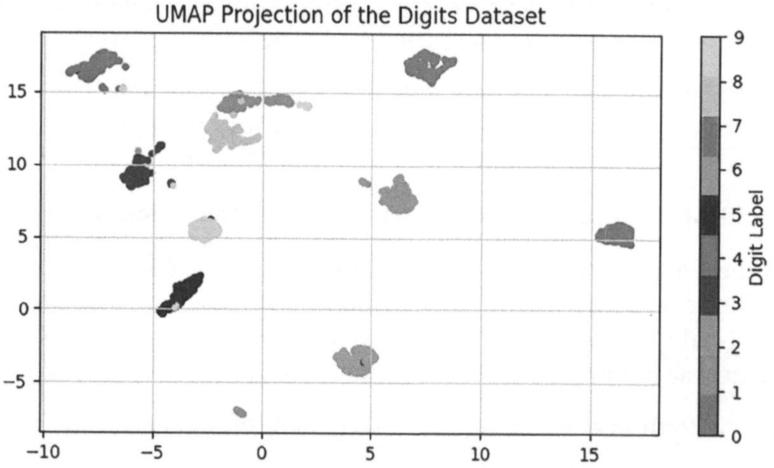

Figure 4.12: *Implementation of UMAP Algorithm on Digits Dataset*

Locally Linear Embedding (LLE)

Locally Linear Embedding (LLE) is a non-linear dimensionality reduction technique that assumes high-dimensional data lies on a smooth, lower-dimensional manifold. Unlike global methods such as Isomap, LLE focuses on preserving local relationships by reconstructing each data point using its nearest neighbors. The core assumption is that each point and its neighbors lie on or near a locally linear patch of the manifold.

LLE operates in three main steps:

1. **Neigborhood Selection**: For each data point x_i, it identifies its k-nearest neighbors using the Euclidean distance.
2. **Linear Reconstruction Weights**: Then it computes weights w_{ij} that best reconstruct each point x_i as a linear combination of its neighbors, such that:

$$x_i \approx \sum_j w_{ij} x_j$$

   The weights are computed to minimize the reconstruction error subject to the constraints that the weights "`wij`" sum to 1.

3. **Embedding**: Finally, it finds a low-dimensional representation y_i of each point that preserves these weights:

$$y_i \approx \sum_j w_{ij} y_j$$

   This equation is solved using an eigenvalue decomposition problem.

It is important that reconstruction weights capture the local geometry of the data, and the low-dimensional embedding is computed to preserve this geometry. Unlike Isomap, LLE does not need to compute global geodesic distances and is more suitable for data with locally linear structure.

Applications

Locally Linear Embedding (LLE) is a versatile technique that can be applied across many domains, such as computer vision and speech recognition, biomedical research, finance and market analysis, robotics and 3D shape recognition, natural language processing.

Implementation of LLE Using Sklearn Library

The code shown in *Figure* 4.13 demonstrates the application of LLE on the Swiss Roll dataset. It is a synthetic dataset often used in manifold learning examples. The dataset consists of 1,500 data points that lie on a two-dimensional surface (a "rolled" sheet) embedded in three-dimensional space, with added noise. LLE is applied with 12 nearest neighbors to reduce the data from 3D to 2D, while preserving the local geometric structure. The first subplot in the output visualizes the original 3D Swiss Roll colored by the intrinsic position along the roll, while the second subplot shows the

2D embedding produced by LLE. This embedding successfully "unrolls" the manifold, demonstrating LLE's strength in capturing and flattening non-linear structures when the data lies on a locally linear manifold.

```
import matplotlib.pyplot as plt
from sklearn.datasets import make_swiss_roll
from sklearn.manifold import LocallyLinearEmbedding

# Generate the Swiss Roll dataset
X, color = make_swiss_roll(n_samples=1500, noise=0.05)

# Apply LLE
lle = LocallyLinearEmbedding(n_neighbors=12, n_components=2, method='standard',
                             random_state=42)
X_lle = lle.fit_transform(X)

# Plot original 3D Swiss Roll
fig = plt.figure(figsize=(10, 4))

ax = fig.add_subplot(1, 2, 1, projection='3d')
ax.scatter(X[:, 0], X[:, 1], X[:, 2], c=color, cmap=plt.cm.Spectral)
ax.set_title("Original Swiss Roll (3D)")

# Plot 2D LLE embedding
ax2 = fig.add_subplot(1, 2, 2)
scatter = ax2.scatter(X_lle[:, 0], X_lle[:, 1], c=color, cmap=plt.cm.Spectral)
ax2.set_title("LLE Embedding (2D)")
ax2.set_xlabel("Component 1")
ax2.set_ylabel("Component 2")
plt.tight_layout()
plt.show()
```

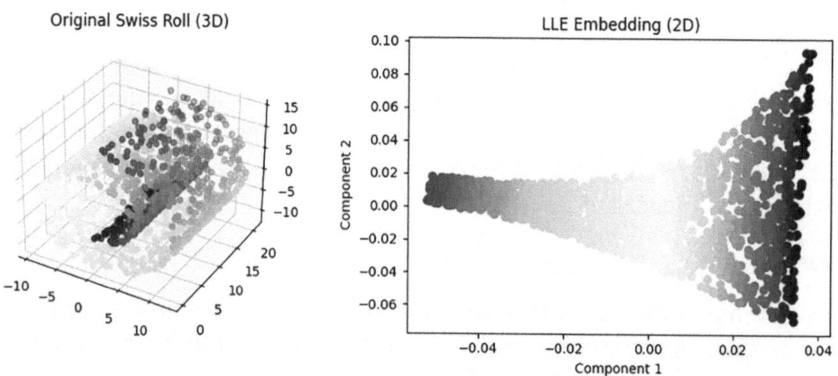

Figure 4.13: *Implementation of LLE on Swiss Roll Dataset*

Table 4.4 shows the comparison of prominent non-linear methods for dimensionality reduction:

Aspect	Isomap	t-SNE	UMAP	LLE
Approach	Captures global non-linearity	Focuses on local non-linear relationships	Captures local and global non-linearity	Captures local non-linearity via linear approximations of neighborhoods

Computational Complexity	High	Moderate	Moderate	Low
Scalability	Low	Low	High	High

Table 4.4: *Comparison of Non-Linear Dimensionality Reduction Methods*

Advanced Non-Linear Methods for Dimensionality Reduction

Up till now, we have discussed the core non-linear dimensionality reduction methods like Isomap, t-SNE, UMAP, and LLE. Besides these methods, there are more specialized non-linear approaches, such as Diffusion Maps, Kernel PCA, and Autoencoders, which are used for dimensionality reduction. These methods include Diffusion Maps, Kernel-PCA, and Autoencoders. Unlike t-SNE and UMAP, which prioritize preserving local or global geometric relationships, Diffusion Maps model the data manifold using Markov chains and diffusion processes, thus making them well-suited for capturing smooth transitions and temporal dynamics. Kernel PCA extends traditional PCA into a non-linear regime by using kernel functions to implicitly project data into a higher-dimensional space where linear separation is possible. This bridges linear and non-linear approaches. Autoencoders use neural networks to learn compact, non-linear representations by training an encoder–decoder architecture, offering scalability and flexibility for complex datasets. These methods are suitable for different types of data and use cases.

Diffusion Maps

Diffusion Maps leverages the idea of "diffusion" to capture the underlying structure of data. The main idea is to model how information or data "flows" (or diffuses) across the data manifold. Instead of just looking at direct distances between points (like in PCA or t-SNE), Diffusion Maps consider how data points are connected through a series of short, local paths, and how data "spreads" out when moving through those paths. The intuition is that points that are close in a manifold should have a more similar diffusion behavior, even if they are not close in Euclidean space. This helps capture the **intrinsic geometry** of the data, especially in cases where the data lies on a complex, non-linear manifold. It uses the idea of random walks over the data graph to uncover manifold structure, thereby making it effective for reducing the dimensionality of highly non-linear datasets.

Kernel PCA

Kernel PCA is an extension of the classic Principal Component Analysis (PCA) that allows for non-linear dimensionality reduction. While PCA enables linear dimensionality reduction, Kernel PCA can capture non-linear patterns in the data by transforming it into a higher-dimensional space. Kernel PCA applies the kernel trick, which allows for non-linear projections of data. Instead of directly computing the covariance matrix in this high-dimensional space, Kernel PCA uses a kernel function K(x,y), which computes the inner product of the data points in the higher-dimensional space without explicitly computing the transformation $\phi(x)$. Common kernel functions include polynomial kernel, radial basis function, Sigmoid kernel and so on. The kernel matrix K is computed, where each entry Kij is the kernel value between the data points x_i and x_j. The kernel matrix replaces the traditional covariance matrix in standard PCA. Eigenvalue decomposition is then performed on the kernel matrix K or its centered form. The top eigenvectors correspond to the principal components in the feature space, even though the original data never explicitly enters this space. Once the eigenvectors are found, the data is projected onto these components resulting in the lower dimensional representation.

Autoencoders

Autoencoders are a class of artificial neural networks used for unsupervised learning, typically for tasks such as dimensionality reduction, feature extraction, and anomaly detection. They are particularly effective for non-linear dimensionality reduction, offering a way to map high-dimensional data to a lower-dimensional space, preserving the most important features.

Unlike linear methods like PCA, autoencoders are capable of capturing complex, non-linear relationships in the data. Autoencoders are trained to compress data into a smaller representation and then reconstruct the data back to its original form as accurately as possible.

An autoencoder consists of three main components that are mentioned as follows:

- **Encoder:** The encoder network maps the input data to a lower-dimensional space (called the latent space or bottleneck). It learns to compress the input data by extracting the most important features.
- **Latent Space:** This is the bottleneck of the autoencoder. The compressed representation of the data lies in this space. It is typically smaller than the input data and captures the underlying structure or patterns in the data.
- **Decoder:** The decoder network takes the lower-dimensional representation and reconstructs the input data. The goal is to reconstruct the data as accurately as possible to minimize the reconstruction error.

The training objective is to minimize the difference between the original data and the reconstructed data (reconstruction loss).

Working of Autoencoders for Dimensionality Reduction

1. **Input Data:** The process starts with high-dimensional data being fed into the encoder.

2. **Compression (Encoder):** The encoder part of the network learns to reduce the dimensions by extracting the most meaningful patterns or features from the input data. It compresses the data into a lower-dimensional representation, typically using activation functions like ReLU, Sigmoid, or tanh.
3. **Latent Representation:** The encoder produces a compressed representation, which is the latent space of the data.
4. **Reconstruction (Decoder):** The decoder attempts to reconstruct the input data from the compressed representation. If the compression has been done effectively, the decoder will be able to approximate the original data accurately.
5. **Optimization:** The network is trained using a loss function (such as, Mean Squared Error or Cross-Entropy) to minimize the reconstruction error, ensuring that the latent representation retains the most crucial features of the input data while discarding less relevant ones.

Autoencoders reduce dimensionality by learning a compressed representation of the data that captures its most important aspects, while reconstructing the original input as closely as possible.

Implementation of Autoencoders Using Keras Library and MNIST Dataset from Sklearn

Figure 4.14 demonstrates the use of a vanilla autoencoder to perform dimensionality reduction on the MNIST dataset, which consists of 28x28 grayscale images of handwritten digits (0–9).

The dataset is first pre-processed by normalizing the pixel values to the range [0, 1] and flattening the images into 784-dimensional vectors. The autoencoder consists of two main parts: the encoder, which compresses the input into a lower-dimensional representation (32 dimensions), and the decoder, which reconstructs the original 784-dimensional input from the encoded representation. The model is trained to minimize the reconstruction loss (binary cross-entropy) between the original and reconstructed images.

After training, the code visualizes the original and reconstructed images side by side to evaluate how well the autoencoder has learned to compress and reconstruct the data. The output demonstrates how the model effectively reduces the dimensionality of the images, while maintaining their key features.

```
from keras.layers import Input, Dense
from keras.models import Model
from keras.datasets import mnist
import numpy as np
import matplotlib.pyplot as plt
# Load the MNIST dataset
(x_train, _), (x_test, _) = mnist.load_data()
x_train = x_train.astype('float32') / 255.
x_test = x_test.astype('float32') / 255.
x_train = x_train.reshape((len(x_train), np.prod(x_train.shape[1:])))
x_test = x_test.reshape((len(x_test), np.prod(x_test.shape[1:])))
# Define the size of the encoding
encoding_dim = 32
# Define the input layer
input_img = Input(shape=(784,))
# Define the encoded representation of the input
encoded = Dense(encoding_dim, activation='relu')(input_img)
# Define the decoded layer
decoded = Dense(784, activation='sigmoid')(encoded)
# Build the autoencoder model
autoencoder = Model(input_img, decoded)
# Build the encoder model
encoder = Model(input_img, encoded)
# Build the decoder model
encoded_input = Input(shape=(encoding_dim,))
decoder_layer = autoencoder.layers[-1]
decoder = Model(encoded_input, decoder_layer(encoded_input))
# Compile the autoencoder
autoencoder.compile(optimizer='adam', loss='binary_crossentropy')
# Train the autoencoder
autoencoder.fit(x_train, x_train, epochs=50, batch_size=256, shuffle=True, validation_data=(x_test, x_test))
# Use the encoder to get the reduced representation of the test data
encoded_imgs = encoder.predict(x_test)
# Visualize the original and the reconstructed images
decoded_imgs = decoder.predict(encoded_imgs)
n = 10  # Display first 10 images
plt.figure(figsize=(20, 4))
for i in range(n):
    ax = plt.subplot(2, n, i + 1)
    plt.imshow(x_test[i].reshape(28, 28))
    plt.gray()
    ax.get_xaxis().set_visible(False)
    ax.get_yaxis().set_visible(False)

    ax = plt.subplot(2, n, i + 1 + n)
    plt.imshow(decoded_imgs[i].reshape(28, 28))
    plt.gray()
    ax.get_xaxis().set_visible(False)
    ax.get_yaxis().set_visible(False)
plt.show()
```

Figure 4.14: *Implementation of Autoencoder for Dimensionality Reduction on an MNIST Dataset*

Figure 4.15 shows a subset of original digits and their reconstructed representations using preceding code (*Figure* 4.14):

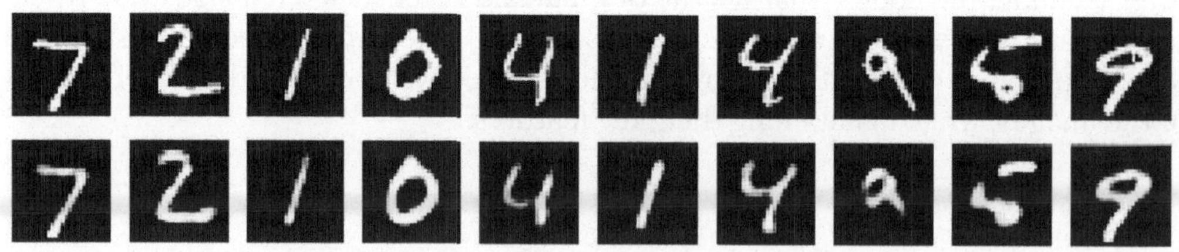

Figure 4.15: *Original Digits from MNIST Dataset and Their Reconstructed Representations Using Autoencoder.*

Conclusion

In this chapter, we explored various non-linear dimensionality reduction techniques, including t-SNE, UMAP, Locally Linear Embedding (LLE), Isomap, Diffusion Maps, Kernel PCA, and Autoencoders. These methods are powerful tools for uncovering complex structures in high-dimensional data that linear methods like PCA fail to capture. We examined their mathematical foundations, working principles, and key applications, providing practical Python implementations for each. While each method has its strengths and weaknesses, the choice of technique largely depends on the specific characteristics of the data and the task at hand. Hence, by understanding and applying these techniques, practitioners can visualize, interpret, and model high-dimensional data in a much better way, thus opening up new possibilities in fields ranging from machine learning to genomics.

In the next chapter, we will explore anomaly and outlier detection techniques in detail.

Key Terms

- **Manifold Learning**: A class of techniques in machine learning that assumes high-dimensional data lies on a lower-dimensional manifold and seeks to reduce the data to a simpler representation while preserving its geometric properties
- **t-SNE (t-Distributed Stochastic Neighbor Embedding)**: A non-linear dimensionality reduction technique that focuses on preserving local structure in high-dimensional data by minimizing the divergence between probability distributions representing pair-wise similarities in the original and reduced space
- **UMAP (Uniform Manifold Approximation and Projection)**: A non-linear dimensionality reduction method that aims to preserve both local and some global structure in data, often used for visualization and embeddings in machine learning tasks
- **Isomap**: A non-linear dimensionality reduction method that extends classical Multi-Dimensional Scaling (MDS) by incorporating geodesic distances, allowing it to preserve global manifold structure
- **Locally Linear Embedding (LLE)**: A non-linear dimensionality reduction technique that seeks to preserve local neighborhood structure by assuming each data point can be reconstructed from its neighbors using linear combinations
- **Geodesic Distance**: The shortest path between two points on a curved manifold; often used in methods like Isomap to capture global structure in high-dimensional data

- **Kernel PCA (Kernel Principal Component Analysis)**: A non-linear extension of PCA that uses kernel functions to map data into higher-dimensional spaces, enabling the capture of non-linear relationships in the data
- **Autoencoder**: A type of artificial neural network used for unsupervised learning that learns an efficient representation of data by encoding it into a lower-dimensional space and then decoding it back to the original space
- **Perplexity**: A hyperparameter in t-SNE that controls the balance between local and global aspects of the data's distribution. It defines the number of nearest neighbors considered when calculating pair-wise similarities
- **Diffusion Maps**: A dimensionality reduction method based on diffusion processes and Markov chains that capture the intrinsic geometry of data by modeling random walks on a graph; often useful for data with smooth transitions

Questions

1. Explain the concept of manifold learning and its significance in dimensionality reduction. How does it differ from linear methods like PCA?
2. Describe the working of t-SNE for dimensionality reduction. How does it preserve local structure in the data, and what are the challenges associated with using t-SNE?
3. What is the key difference between UMAP and t-SNE? In which situations would UMAP be preferred over t-SNE, and why?
4. Explain the Isomap algorithm and its approach to dimensionality reduction. How does Isomap handle the concept of geodesic distances and how is it different from other methods like PCA and t-SNE?
5. What is Locally Linear Embedding (LLE), and how does it use local linearity to achieve dimensionality reduction? Discuss the advantages and limitations of using LLE.
6. What are Diffusion Maps, and how do they utilize the concept of random walks on graphs to capture the geometry of data? Describe a scenario where Diffusion Maps would be particularly useful.
7. How does Kernel PCA extend the traditional PCA method to handle non-linear relationships in data? Explain the role of kernels in Kernel PCA and give an example of its application.
8. Describe the architecture and working principle of an autoencoder. How can autoencoders be used for non-linear dimensionality reduction? How do they compare to traditional linear methods like PCA.

9. What are the primary challenges when applying non-linear dimensionality reduction techniques like t-SNE or UMAP to real-world datasets? How do factors like perplexity, initialization, and scale affect the results?
10. Discuss the concept of global and local structure in the context of dimensionality reduction. Which methods are designed to preserve local structure and which are more focused on capturing global relationships? Provide examples for each case.

Multiple Choice Questions

1. Which of the following methods is primarily used to reduce dimensionality by preserving local relationships in the data?
   a. PCA
   b. t-SNE
   c. Isomap
   d. Autoencoders
2. What is the primary disadvantage of linear dimensionality reduction methods like PCA?
   a. They require labeled data.
   b. They cannot capture non-linear relationships in high-dimensional data.
   c. They are computationally expensive.
   d. They overfit the data.
3. Which non-linear dimensionality reduction method focuses on preserving global structure using geodesic distances?
   a. UMAP
   b. Isomap
   c. t-SNE
   d. LLE
4. Which of the following statements is true about t-SNE?
   a. It is good for preserving global structure, but poor for local relationships.
   b. It is mainly used for supervised learning tasks.

   c. It works well for high-dimensional, complex data visualizations.

   d. It cannot be used for visualizing data in 2D.

5. UMAP is most similar to which other dimensionality reduction method in terms of its approach to preserving local and global structures?

   a. PCA

   b. t-SNE

   c. LLE

   d. Isomap

6. In which scenario is Locally Linear Embedding (LLE) most effective?

   a. When the data lies on a linear manifold

   b. When data contains complex global structures

   c. When local structures are preserved, and global structures are not essential

   d. When data is sparse and high-dimensional

7. What does Kernel PCA do that standard PCA does not?

   a. It reduces data dimensionality using linear transformations only.

   b. It uses kernels to map data into a higher-dimensional space to capture non-linear relationships.

   c. It requires data to be labeled.

   d. It only works with small datasets.

8. What does the term "manifold learning" refer to in the context of dimensionality reduction?

   a. Reducing data to the lowest possible number of dimensions

   b. Learning a representation of data that preserves its topological structure

   c. A method of transforming non-linearly separable data into linearly separable form

   d. A process used to select the most important features for a model

9. Which of the following methods is best suited for reducing dimensionality in data with a complex, non-linear structure, such as images or speech?
   a. PCA
   b. Autoencoders
   c. LDA
   d. Naïve Bayes
10. What is the main advantage of using autoencoders for dimensionality reduction compared to traditional methods such as PCA or t-SNE?
    a. They can only handle linearly separable data.
    b. They require no labeled data.
    c. They can capture non-linear relationships and can be easily integrated into deep learning models.
    d. They work faster than all other methods for large datasets.

Answers

1. b
2. b
3. b
4. c
5. b
6. c
7. b
8. b
9. b
10. c

Chapter 5
Anomaly and Outlier Detection

Introduction

Anomalies and outliers are data points that deviate significantly from the majority of observations. While outliers are identified based on statistical deviation, anomalies are context-specific and often indicate meaningful irregularities such as fraud or faults. In unsupervised learning, detecting such points is challenging due to the absence of labels. This chapter will explain the key concepts of anomaly and outlier detection and presents commonly used statistical and machine learning methods for identifying unusual patterns in data.

Structure

In this chapter, we will discuss the following topics:

- Introduction to Anomaly and Outlier Detection
- Algorithms and Techniques for Anomaly and Outlier Detection
    - Statistical Methods
    - Distance-Based Methods
    - Density Based Methods
    - Clustering Based Methods
    - Isolation Based Methods
    - One-Class Classification
    - Neural Network Based Methods
- Evaluation of Anomaly Detection Methods
- Real-World Applications and Case Studies
- Best Practices and Pitfalls

Introduction to Anomaly and Outlier Detection

The terms outlier and anomaly are often used interchangeably in the context of data analysis and machine learning, but there are subtle distinctions in their meaning and usage, particularly in anomaly detection.

An Outlier

An outlier is a data point that deviates significantly from the rest of the dataset based on statistical or geometric properties. It is typically used in a statistical context to describe observations that lie outside the expected range or distribution of the data (for example, far from the mean in a Gaussian distribution or a Z-score > 3 or points beyond 1.5 * IQR in a boxplot). The term is more common in statistical analysis, data cleaning, or exploratory data analysis, where the focus is on identifying data points that skew results or violate assumptions of statistical models. They may or may not have practical importance. Detection of outliers often relies on statistical methods (for example, Z-score, IQR, or distance-based metrics) or visualization (for example, scatter plots, box plots) to identify points that are numerically distant from the majority.

Figure 5.1 shows an outlier in red, which is far away from most of the points in the dataset shown in blue:

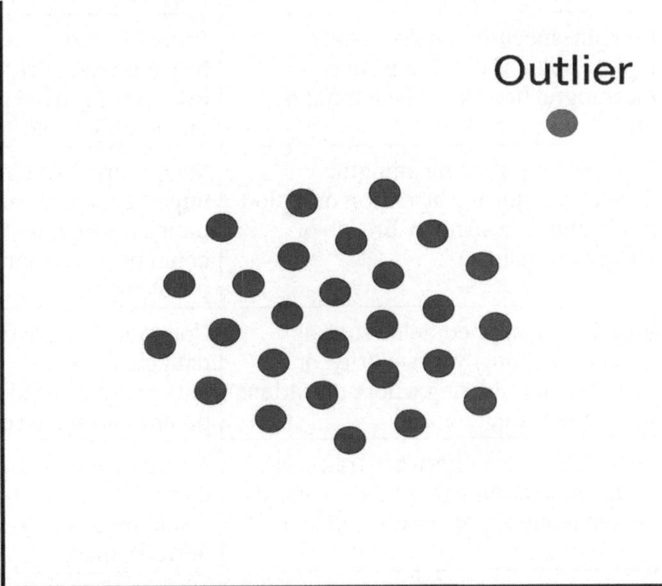

Figure 5.1: *An Outlier*

An Anomaly

An anomaly is a data point or pattern that does not conform to expected behavior and often carries practical significance, such as indicating an error, fraud, or rare event. Anomalies are context-dependent and may require domain knowledge to interpret. Anomalies typically imply a meaningful deviation that warrants attention or action, such as a security breach or equipment failure. Anomalies are often outliers, but not all outliers are anomalies. For instance, a legitimate large purchase might be an outlier in transaction data but not an anomaly if it aligns with expected behavior (for example, a customer buying an expensive item). The term is prevalent in applied fields such as fraud detection, cybersecurity, or industrial monitoring, where deviations have operational or business implications. Anomalies are often tied to specific use cases or domain-specific definitions of "normal" behavior. Detection of anomalies may involve more sophisticated techniques, including unsupervised learning (for example, Isolation Forest, Local Outlier Factor) or domain-specific rules, as anomalies must be interpreted in the context of expected behavior. For instance, contextual anomalies require considering temporal or spatial attributes.

Table 5.1 summarizes the difference between an anomaly and an outlier:

Aspect	Anomaly	Outlier
Definition	A data point or pattern that does not conform to expected behavior, often with practical significance	A data point that deviates significantly from the rest of the dataset based on statistical or geometric properties
Context	Domain-specific; requires context to determine if the deviation is meaningful (for example, a fraud or error)	Primarily statistical; identified based on data distribution (for example, far from the mean or outside 1.5 * IQR)
Practical Significance	Typically implies a meaningful deviation requiring attention or action (for example, a security breach or equipment failure)	May or may not have practical importance (for example, an unusually high test-score could be an outlier but not problematic)
Usage	Prevalent in applied fields such as fraud detection, cybersecurity, or industrial monitoring where deviations have operational impact	Common in statistical analysis, data cleaning, or exploratory data analysis, to identify data points that skew results
Example	A sudden spike in network traffic at 2 a.m., indicating a potential security breach (context makes it significant)	A student's exam score of 10 in a dataset of scores between 60–90 (could be an error or exceptional performance)

Detection Approach	Employs advanced techniques (for example, Isolation Forest, LOF) and domain-specific rules, often considering contextual attributes	Uses statistical methods (for example, Z-score, IQR) or visualization (for example, boxplots, scatter plots) to find numerically distant points

Table 5.1: *Difference between an Anomaly and an Outlier*

While all anomalies are usually outliers (statistically significant deviations), not all outliers are anomalies unless they are practically or contextually relevant (for example, indicating fraud or errors). This distinction clarifies when to prioritize investigation or action in real-world applications.

Anomalies are often classified as Point Anomalies, Contextual Anomalies, and Collective Anomalies.

Point Anomalies

A point anomaly is a single data point that deviates significantly from the rest of the dataset based on its features or values, without considering any contextual factors. It is the simplest and most common type of anomaly. It is identified by comparing the data point to the overall distribution or pattern of the dataset. Often detected using statistical measures (for example, Z-score, distance from the mean, Grubbs' test or IOR) or machine learning methods (for example, Isolation Forest, One-Class SVM, K-NN). It does not depend on temporal, spatial, or other contextual attributes. Point anomalies are common in applications such as fraud detection (for example, a single suspicious transaction) or quality control (for example, a defective product measurement).

Examples of point anomalies include:

- In a dataset of customer transactions where most purchases are between $10 and $100, a single transaction of $10,000 is a point anomaly as it is statistically distant from the norm.
- In a dataset of body temperatures (mostly 36–38°C), a reading of 42°C is a point anomaly, likely indicating an error or medical issue.

Contextual Anomalies

A contextual anomaly is a data point that is anomalous within a specific context but may appear normal in other contexts. The anomaly depends on contextual attributes, such as time, location, or other situational factors. It requires defining a context (for example, time of day, season, geographic region) to determine whether the data point is abnormal and often involves analyzing the data point relative to a subset of the dataset defined by the context. These types of anomalies are common in time-series or spatially distributed data. Statistical methods like contextual modelling using conditional distributions or time-series analysis, and machine learning methods such as autoencoders, local outlier factor with contextual features or time-series anomaly detection algorithms (ARIMA-based methods) are often used for detecting contextual anomalies. Contextual anomalies are critical in applications such as IoT monitoring (for example, detecting unusual sensor readings based on time of day) or user behavior analysis (for example, detecting fraud based on a user's historical patterns).

Examples of contextual anomalies include:

- A temperature reading of 30°C in a city might be normal in summer but anomalous in winter (context: season).
- A $500 purchase on an e-commerce platform might be normal during the holiday season, but anomalous for a user who typically spends $50 in other months (context: time and user behavior).
- A network login from a foreign country might be normal for a frequent traveler but anomalous for an employee who always logs in locally (context: location).

Collective Anomalies

A collective anomaly occurs when a group of data points, when considered together, exhibits abnormal behavior even though individual points may appear normal. The anomaly lies in the pattern or relationship among the points. Identification of collective anomalies requires analyzing the collective behavior or sequence of data points rather than individual values. It often involves sequential, temporal, or relational data where the anomaly is detected in the group's structure or dynamics. It is more complex to detect as it requires modeling interactions or dependencies among data points. Detection methods include statistical methods like sequence analysis or pattern mining to detect unusual combinations and machine learning methods like recurrent neural networks, graph-based methods from relational data or clustering techniques such as DBSCAN. Collective anomalies are vital in cybersecurity (for example, detecting coordinated attacks), predictive maintenance (for example, identifying subtle trends in sensor data), or social network analysis (for example, detecting coordinated misinformation campaigns).

Examples of collective anomalies include:

- In network security, a series of small, seemingly normal data transfers from a server might be a collective anomaly if their frequency and pattern suggest a distributed denial-of-service (DDoS) attack.
- In a manufacturing process, a sequence of sensor readings that individually fall within normal ranges but together form an unusual trend (for example, a gradual increase in vibration) could indicate an impending equipment failure.
- In financial markets, a group of stock trades that individually seem typical but collectively manipulate market prices could be a collective anomaly.

Three Approaches to Anomaly and Outlier Detection

Anomaly and outlier detection rest on a set of theoretical principles that define how deviations from expected data patterns are identified. These principles will provide the foundation for the algorithms and techniques that are explored later in this chapter and will enable us to model normal behavior and flag anomalies effectively. This section introduces the core perspectives—statistical, distance-based, and density-based—that underpin anomaly detection, and establishes connections to clustering and dimensionality reduction techniques discussed in *Chapter 3, Clustering Techniques* and *Chapter 4, Dimensionality Reduction*. By understanding these theoretical foundations, you will gain insight into why certain methods work and how to choose the right approach for a given problem.

Statistical Approach

The statistical approach assumes that normal data follows a specific probability distribution, often modeled as Gaussian (normal distribution), and anomalies are points that lie in low-probability regions of this distribution. This approach relies on statistical measures to quantify deviations from the expected norm.

- Normal data points are expected to cluster around the mean or median of the distribution, with deviations measured using metrics like the Z-score (standardized distance from the mean) or p-values.
- For multivariate data, assumptions such as multivariate Gaussian distributions are used, where anomalies are points with low probability under the distribution (for example, measured via Mahalanobis distance).

Statistical approaches to anomaly and outlier detection are simple, interpretable, and effective for well-behaved data with clear distributional assumptions. However, they assume that the data follows a known distribution (often unrealistic for complex or high-dimensional data) and struggles with collective anomalies that do not manifest as extreme values.

Distance-Based Approach

The distance-based approach identifies anomalies as data points that are far from their neighbors or the dataset's central tendency via geometric distance metrics such as Euclidean or Mahalanobis distance. This approach is particularly suited for point anomalies and leverages the intuition that normal points are densely packed, while anomalies are isolated.

- Anomalies are points with large distances to their k-nearest neighbors (k-NN) or to the dataset's centroid (mean or median).

- Mahalanobis distance accounts for correlations between features, making it effective for multivariate data.
- Distance-based methods often connect to clustering, as anomalies may be points that do not belong to any cluster.

For instance, in a 2D scatter plot of user login locations, a login from a distant geographic coordinate could be a contextual anomaly if it deviates from the user's typical locations.

Distance-based methods are intuitive, work well for low-dimensional data, and do not require strong distributional assumptions. However, they are computationally expensive for large datasets (due to pairwise distance calculations), sensitive to the curse of dimensionality and are thus less effective for collective anomalies.

Density-Based Approach

The density-based approach identifies anomalies as points in low-density regions of the data, where density is defined by the number of points within a given neighborhood. This approach is effective for detecting both point and contextual anomalies and is closely related to clustering techniques such as DBSCAN.

- Normal points reside in high-density regions (for example, clusters), while anomalies are in sparse regions with fewer neighbors.
- Metrics such as Local Outlier Factor (LOF) compare a point's local density to that of its neighbors, flagging points with significantly lower density as anomalies.
- Density-based methods can capture contextual anomalies by incorporating contextual attributes (for example, time or location) into the density estimation.

For instance, in a dataset of network traffic, a server receiving an unusually low number of requests compared to its neighbors' activity might be flagged by LOF as a contextual anomaly, indicating a potential issue. In a spatial dataset of retail store sales, a store with low sales in a densely populated area (high-density region) could be an anomaly.

Density-based methods are robust to varying data distributions, effective for detecting local anomalies, and adaptable to contextual analysis. However, they are sensitive to parameter choices (for example, neighborhood size), computationally intensive for high-dimensional data, and less suited for collective anomalies unless combined with sequence or graph-based methods.

The statistical, distance-based, and density-based perspectives form the theoretical backbone of anomaly and outlier detection, with each offering unique insights into what constitutes a deviation. By modeling normal behavior through probability distributions, geometric distances, or local densities, these approaches enable the detection of point, contextual, and collective anomalies across diverse applications.

Understanding these foundations will prepare you to select and apply the anomaly detection algorithms, tailoring them to the characteristics of your data and the anomalies you aim to detect.

Overview of Unsupervised Learning in Anomaly Detection Due to Limited Labeled Data

Anomaly detection often operates in environments where labeled data is scarce, thus making unsupervised learning a natural approach for identifying unusual patterns. Unlike supervised learning, which relies on labeled examples of both normal and anomalous instances to train models, unsupervised learning detects anomalies by modeling the inherent structure of the data without requiring prior knowledge of what constitutes an anomaly. This is particularly critical in anomaly detection, as anomalies are rare, diverse, and often unpredictable, resulting in limited or no labeled data for training.

The scarcity of labeled data in anomaly detection stems from the nature of anomalies themselves. Anomalous events, such as fraudulent transactions, network intrusions, or equipment failures, occur infrequently compared to normal behavior, leading to highly imbalanced datasets. Moreover, anomalies can take many forms, ranging from a single outlier (for example, a large transaction) to complex patterns (for example, a coordinated cyberattack), making it impractical to collect comprehensive labeled examples for every possible scenario. In many cases, labeling data is also costly, time-consuming, or infeasible, as it requires expert knowledge or hindsight (for example, confirming fraud after an investigation). Unsupervised learning overcomes these challenges by focusing on the majority behavior of the data, assumed to be normal, and identifying deviations without needing labeled examples.

In unsupervised anomaly detection, algorithms learn the typical patterns, distributions, or clusters within the data and flag instances that deviate significantly from these norms. For example, clustering techniques such as DBSCAN (introduced in *Chapter* 3, *Clustering Techniques*) can identify points that do not belong to any cluster as potential anomalies, while dimensionality reduction methods such as PCA (*Chapter* 4, *Dimensionality Reduction*) can highlight deviations in a reduced feature space. Other methods, such as Isolation Forest or Local Outlier Factor (LOF), model the data's structure to isolate anomalies based on their statistical or density-based properties. By relying solely on the data's intrinsic characteristics, these approaches are versatile and adaptable to diverse domains, from finance to IoT.

While unsupervised learning enables anomaly detection in scenarios where supervised methods are impractical like detecting novel types of fraud or emerging cyber threats; at the same time, the absence of labels complicates model evaluation and increases the risk of false positives, as distinguishing true anomalies from noise or benign outliers requires careful tuning.

Importance of anomaly detection in real-world applications

Anomaly detection is a critical tool in data-driven decision-making, enabling organizations to identify and respond to unusual patterns or events that could signal significant opportunities or risks. By uncovering deviations from expected behavior, anomaly detection empowers industries to enhance security, optimize operations, and prevent costly disruptions. Its versatility and impact are evident across a wide range of real-world applications, including fraud detection, cybersecurity, and industrial monitoring, where timely identification of anomalies can make the difference between success and failure.

In **fraud detection**, anomaly detection is indispensable for safeguarding financial systems. Banks and payment platforms process millions of transactions daily, most of which follow predictable patterns based on customer behavior. Anomalous transactions, such as a sudden large purchase from an unusual location or a series of rapid withdrawals, may indicate credit card fraud, identity theft, or money laundering. By flagging these anomalies in real time, organizations can freeze accounts, notify customers, and prevent financial losses. For example, a point anomaly like a $10,000 transaction on a card typically used for small purchases can trigger immediate investigation, while collective anomalies like a pattern of small, frequent transfers might reveal sophisticated fraud schemes.

In **cybersecurity**, anomaly detection is a frontline defense against threats in complex digital environments. Modern networks generate vast amounts of data, including login attempts, data transfers, and application usage. Anomalies in this data, such as a login from an unrecognized device at an odd hour (a contextual anomaly) or a coordinated spike in traffic suggesting a Distributed Denial-of-Service (DDoS) attack (a collective anomaly), can indicate malware, insider threats, or external intrusions. By detecting these anomalies, security systems can trigger alerts, block suspicious activities, or isolate compromised systems, minimizing damage and ensuring network integrity.

Industrial monitoring leverages anomaly detection to enhance efficiency and reliability in manufacturing, energy, and IoT-driven systems. Sensors in industrial equipment, such as turbines, assembly lines, or smart grids, continuously collect data on metrics like temperature, pressure, or vibration. Anomalous readings, such as a sudden spike in motor temperature (a point anomaly) or a gradual trend of irregular vibrations (a collective anomaly), can signal equipment malfunctions, wear, or impending failures. By identifying these anomalies early on, companies can schedule predictive maintenance, reduce downtime, and avoid costly repairs. For instance, in a smart factory, detecting a contextual anomaly like an abnormal sensor reading during peak production hours can prevent production halts.

Beyond these domains, anomaly detection finds applications in healthcare (for example, detecting abnormal patient vitals), retail (for example, identifying unusual customer behavior), and environmental monitoring (for example, flagging unexpected changes in climate data). The ability to detect anomalies in real time or retrospectively empowers organizations to act swiftly, whether by mitigating risks, optimizing processes, or uncovering novel insights. As datasets grow in size and complexity, the importance of anomaly detection continues to rise, making it a cornerstone of modern data science and a key focus of unsupervised learning, as explored in this chapter.

Algorithms and Techniques for Anomaly and Outlier Detection

Anomaly and outlier detection encompasses a diverse set of algorithms and techniques, each rooted in the theoretical approaches—statistical, distance-based, and density-based. This section explores the key methods used to identify anomalies, organized by their underlying approach: statistical, distance-based, density-based, clustering-based, isolation-based, one-class classification, and neural network-based. These methods address different types of anomalies–point, contextual, and collective–and are suited to various data characteristics and applications. By understanding their strengths and limitations, you can select the right tool for your anomaly detection tasks.

Statistical Methods

In statistical methods, we will cover Z-score, modified Z-score and Grubbs' Test for outlier detection.

Z-Score and Modified Z-Score:

The Z-score measures how many standard deviations a data point is from the mean, assuming a Gaussian distribution. A point with a high Z-score (for example, >3) is flagged as a point anomaly. For example, in a dataset of daily temperatures (mean 20°C, standard deviation 2°C), a reading of 28°C has a Z-score of 4, indicating a potential anomaly. The modified Z-score, which uses the median and median absolute deviation (MAD), is more robust to outliers in non-Gaussian data.

It is suitable for detecting extreme values in univariate data such as unusually high transaction amounts or sensor readings. It is fast, interpretable, and suitable for low-dimensional data. However, it assumes a specific distribution and is less effective for multivariate or complex data.

In *Figure* 5.2, we see the Python implementation of the Z-score for outlier detection and the output plot. In this code, we have used a synthetic dataset of 100 daily temperature readings that was generated, with most values following a normal distribution (mean=20°C, std=2°C) and five manually added outliers (for example, 28°C, 30°C). The data is stored in a pandas DataFrame for easy manipulation. The Z-score is computed as (x - mean) / std for each temperature value. A threshold of **|Z-score|** > 3 is used to identify outliers, which is a common rule for Gaussian data.

```
# Using Z-Score
import numpy as np
import pandas as pd
import matplotlib.pyplot as plt
# Set random seed for reproducibility
np.random.seed(42)
# Step 1: Generate synthetic univariate dataset (e.g., daily temperatures in Celsius)
n_samples = 100
normal_data = np.random.normal(loc=20, scale=2, size=n_samples - 5)  # Mean=20, std=2
outlier_data = np.array([28, 12, 30, 10, 29])  # Manually added outliers
data = np.concatenate([normal_data, outlier_data])
# Convert to pandas DataFrame for easier handling
df = pd.DataFrame(data, columns=['Temperature'])
# Step 2: Calculate Z-scores
# Z-score = (x - mean) / standard deviation
mean = df['Temperature'].mean()
std = df['Temperature'].std()
df['Z_score'] = (df['Temperature'] - mean) / std
# Step 3: Identify outliers (threshold: |Z-score| > 3)
threshold = 3
df['Is_Outlier'] = df['Z_score'].abs() > threshold
# Step 4: Visualize the results
plt.figure(figsize=(10, 5))
plt.scatter(df.index, df['Temperature'], c=df['Is_Outlier'],cmap='coolwarm', label='Data Points')
plt.axhline(y=mean, color='green', linestyle='--', label='Mean')
plt.axhline(y=mean + threshold * std, color='red', linestyle='--',label=f'Threshold (±{threshold} std)')
plt.axhline(y=mean - threshold * std, color='red', linestyle='--')
plt.title('Z-score Outlier Detection for Temperature Data')
plt.xlabel('Index')
plt.ylabel('Temperature (°C)')
plt.legend()
plt.grid(True)
plt.show()
```

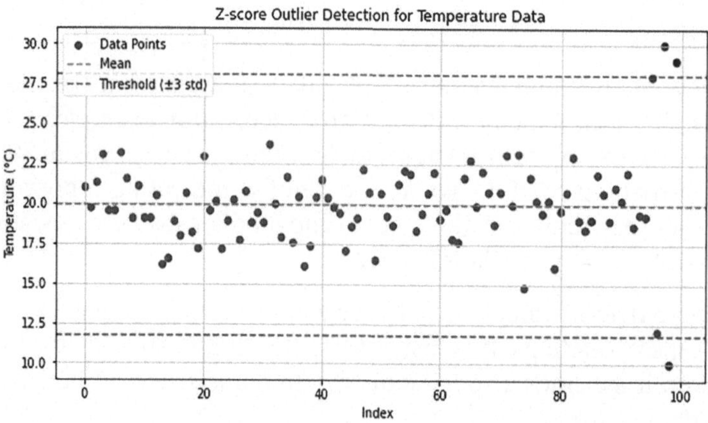

Figure 5.2: *Python Code for Z-score Calculation to Detect Outliers*

Grubbs' Test for Outlier Detection

Grubbs' test is a statistical hypothesis test that identifies a single outlier in a univariate dataset by comparing the maximum deviation from the mean to the expected deviation under a Gaussian distribution. It iteratively removes outliers if multiple are suspected. For instance, in a dataset of machine part measurements, a single unusually large value can be flagged as an outlier if it exceeds the critical value in Grubbs' test.

It is suitable for quality control tasks like identifying defective measurements in a batch of sensor data. It is based on a rigorous statistical foundation and is suitable for small datasets as well. However, it assumes data to be normally distributed and is limited to univariate data. Therefore, it is not suited for contextual or collective anomalies.

Distance-Based Methods

Distance-based methods flag anomalies as points that are far from their neighbors or the dataset's center, using metrics such as Euclidean or Mahalanobis distance. These are effective for point anomalies in low-dimensional data.

k-Nearest Neighbors (k-NN) for Anomaly Detection:

The k-NN algorithm identifies anomalies by calculating the distance from a point to its k-nearest neighbors. Points with large average distances (or distances to the k-th neighbor) are flagged as anomalies, as they are isolated from the majority of the data. It is used often for fraud detection, where a transaction with unusual features (for example, amount, location) is distant from typical transactions. For instance, in a dataset of customer purchases, a transaction with an unusually high amount and a rare product category might have a large k-NN distance, which marks it as a point anomaly.

The k-NN algorithm is intuitive, makes no assumptions about the data distributions, and is adaptable to multivariate data. However, it is computationally expensive for large datasets ($O(n^2)$ for distance calculations), sensitive to the choice of k, and struggles in high-dimensional spaces due to the curse of dimensionality.

Figure 5.3 shows the Python implementation of the K-Nearest Neighbor algorithm for anomaly detection. The code includes data preprocessing, k-NN distance calculation, anomaly detection, and visualization, and is tailored to be accessible for beginners to intermediate learners. It uses a synthetic multivariate dataset (simulating customer transactions) to demonstrate point anomaly detection. The output is visualized in *Figure* 5.4:

```
## K-NN for Anomaly Detection
import numpy as np
import pandas as pd
import matplotlib.pyplot as plt
from sklearn.neighbors import NearestNeighbors
from sklearn.preprocessing import StandardScaler
# Set random seed for reproducibility
np.random.seed(42)
# Step 1: Generate synthetic multivariate dataset (e.g., customer transactions)
# Features: purchase amount, time since last purchase (hours)
n_samples = 100
normal_data = np.random.multivariate_normal(
    mean=[100, 24],  # Mean: $100, 24 hours
    cov=[[1000, 50], [50, 100]],  # Covariance for realistic spread
    size=n_samples - 5)
outlier_data = np.array([[500, 1], [50, 72], [600, 2], [30, 80], [450, 0.5]])  # Outliers
data = np.concatenate([normal_data, outlier_data])

# Convert to pandas DataFrame
df = pd.DataFrame(data, columns=['Amount', 'Time_Since_Last'])

# Step 2: Preprocess data (standardize features)
scaler = StandardScaler()
data_scaled = scaler.fit_transform(df[['Amount', 'Time_Since_Last']])

# Step 3: Apply k-NN to compute distances to k-th nearest neighbor
k = 5  # Number of neighbors
knn = NearestNeighbors(n_neighbors=k)
knn.fit(data_scaled)
distances, _ = knn.kneighbors(data_scaled)
# Use distance to k-th neighbor as anomaly score
anomaly_scores = distances[:, k-1]

# Step 4: Identify outliers (threshold: top 5% of distances)
threshold = np.percentile(anomaly_scores, 95)  # Top 5% as anomalies
df['Anomaly_Score'] = anomaly_scores
df['Is_Anomaly'] = df['Anomaly_Score'] > threshold

# Step 5: Visualize the results
plt.figure(figsize=(10, 6))
plt.scatter(df['Amount'], df['Time_Since_Last'], c=df['Is_Anomaly'],cmap='coolwarm', label='Data Points')
plt.title('k-NN Anomaly Detection for Customer Transactions')
plt.xlabel('Purchase Amount ($)')
plt.ylabel('Time Since Last Purchase (hours)')
plt.colorbar(label='Anomaly (1) / Normal (0)')
plt.grid(True)
# Highlight anomalies with larger markers
anomalies = df[df['Is_Anomaly']]
plt.scatter(anomalies['Amount'], anomalies['Time_Since_Last'], c='red', s=100,label='Anomalies', edgecolors='black')
plt.legend()
```

Figure 5.3: *Python Code to Use K-NN for Anomaly Detection*

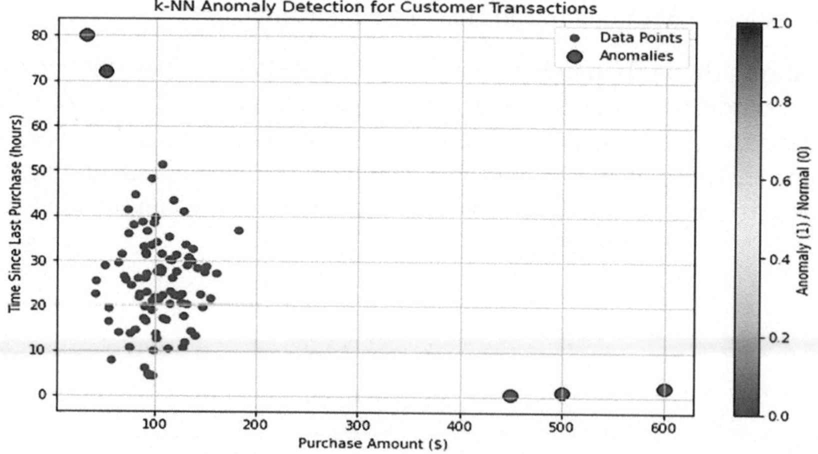

Figure 5.4: *Visualization of Anomalies Detected Using K-NN*

Density-Based Methods

Density-based methods identify anomalies as points in low-density regions, where density is measured by the number of points in a neighborhood. These methods excel at detecting both point and contextual anomalies and re explained as follows:

Local Outlier Factor

Local Outlier Factor (LOF) compares a point's local density (based on the distance to its k-nearest neighbors) to the densities of its neighbors. Points with significantly lower density (high LOF scores) are flagged as anomalies, capturing local deviations in varying-density data. For example, in a dataset of retail sales, a store with low sales in a high-density region (busy area) might have a high LOF score, indicating a contextual anomaly.

LOF is often used for network intrusion detection, where a server with unusually low traffic in a busy network is anomalous. It is robust to varying data densitics, effective for local and contextual anomalies. However, it is sensitive to parameter k and neighborhood size and it is computationally intensive for large datasets.

Connectivity-Based Outlier Factor

Connectivity-Based Outlier Factor (COF) extends LOF by considering the connectivity of points in a neighborhood, using a shortest-path approach to measure density. It is more effective than LOF in datasets with complex structures or non-uniform densities. For example, in a smart grid, a sensor with irregular readings disconnected from the typical pattern of neighboring sensors might be flagged by COF. It is often used in IoT sensor networks, where anomalies arise in spatially or temporally connected data. COF method captures anomalies in structured data and is robust to complex density patterns. However, it has a higher computational complexity than LOF and requires careful parameter tuning.

Figure 5.5 shows the Python implementation of the Connectivity-Based Outlier Factor method for outlier detection. We have generated a synthetic dataset of 100 IoT sensor observations, with two features: temperature (°C) and vibration (mm/s). Most data follow a multivariate normal distribution (mean: 25°C, 5 mm/s), with five manually added outliers (For example, 35°C with 10 mm/s). We will standardize the features using StandardScaler to ensure equal weighting in connectivity calculations, critical for density-based methods. Then, we will use the COF class from the PyOD (https://pyod.readthedocs.io/en/latest/) library to compute anomaly scores with **`n_neighbors=5`** and **`contamination=0.05`** (expecting 5% outliers). Higher scores indicate anomalies. Points labeled as 1 by COF are flagged as anomalies, based on their high anomaly scores. The output is visualized in a scatter plot with normal points in blue and anomalies in red. PyOD is a Python library for detecting anomalies in multivariate data.

```python
#COF using PyOD library
import numpy as np
import pandas as pd
import matplotlib.pyplot as plt
from sklearn.preprocessing import StandardScaler
from pyod.models.cof import COF
# Set random seed for reproducibility
np.random.seed(42)
# Step 1: Generate synthetic multivariate dataset (e.g., IoT sensor data)
# Features: temperature (°C), vibration (mm/s)
n_samples = 100
normal_data = np.random.multivariate_normal(
    mean=[25, 5],  # Mean: 25°C, 5 mm/s
    cov=[[10, 2], [2, 1]],  # Covariance for realistic spread
    size=n_samples - 5)
outlier_data = np.array([[35, 10], [15, 0.5], [40, 12], [10, 0.3], [38, 15]])  # Outliers
data = np.concatenate([normal_data, outlier_data])
# Convert to pandas DataFrame
df = pd.DataFrame(data, columns=['Temperature', 'Vibration'])
# Step 2: Preprocess data (standardize features)
scaler = StandardScaler()
data_scaled = scaler.fit_transform(df[['Temperature', 'Vibration']])
# Step 3: Apply Connectivity-Based Outlier Factor (COF)
k = 5  # Number of neighbors
cof = COF(n_neighbors=k, contamination=0.05)  # Expect 5% outliers
cof.fit(data_scaled)
labels = cof.labels_  # 1 for anomalies, 0 for normal
anomaly_scores = cof.decision_scores_  # Higher scores indicate anomalies
# Step 4: Identify anomalies
df['Anomaly_Score'] = anomaly_scores
df['Is_Anomaly'] = labels == 1  # COF labels anomalies as 1
# Step 6: Visualize the results
plt.figure(figsize=(10, 6))
plt.scatter(df['Temperature'], df['Vibration'], c=df['Is_Anomaly'],
            cmap='coolwarm', label='Data Points')
plt.title('COF Anomaly Detection for IoT Sensor Data')
plt.xlabel('Temperature (°C)')
plt.ylabel('Vibration (mm/s)')
plt.colorbar(label='Anomaly (1) / Normal (0)')
plt.grid(True)
# Highlight anomalies with larger markers
anomalies = df[df['Is_Anomaly']]
plt.scatter(anomalies['Temperature'], anomalies['Vibration'], c='red',
            s=100,label='Anomalies', edgecolors='black')
plt.legend()
```

Figure 5.5: *Python Implementation of COF for Anomaly Detection*

Figure 5.6 shows the visualization of the output of the preceding code.

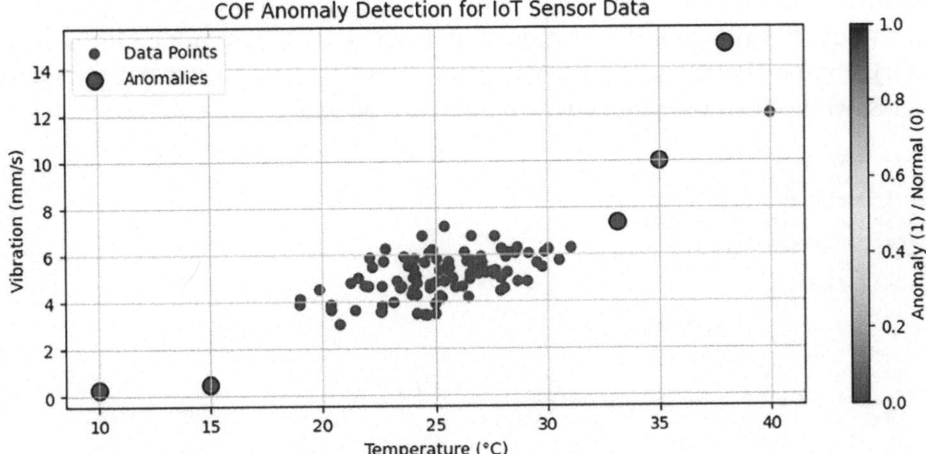

Figure 5.6: *Visualization of Anomalies Using COF Anomaly Detection Method*

Clustering-Based Methods

Clustering-based methods identify anomalies as points that do not belong to any cluster or are far from cluster centroids, leveraging techniques we discussed in *Chapter 3*.

DBSCAN or K-Means to Identify Outliers:

DBSCAN labels points that do not belong to any cluster (noise points) as anomalies. It is ideal for point and contextual anomalies in density-based settings. k-means flags points far from their assigned cluster centroids (For example, high within-cluster distance) as anomalies. For example, in a dataset of user website visits, DBSCAN might label a user with erratic browsing patterns as noise, while k-means might flag a user far from their cluster centroid as an outlier.

DBSCAN or k-means based methods for anomaly detection are suited for tasks such as customer segmentation, where outlier customers with unique purchasing patterns are flagged for further analysis. These methods are intuitive, leverage existing clustering algorithms, and are effective for low-dimensional data. However, DBSCAN is sensitive to density parameters, while k-means assumes spherical clusters and struggles with non-linear patterns or collective anomalies.

Figure 5.7 shows the Python implementation of DBSCAN for anomaly detection. In this code, a synthetic dataset of 100 user website visit observations is generated, with two features: page views per session and average session duration (minutes). Most data follow a multivariate normal distribution (mean: 10 page views, 5 minutes), with five manually added outliers (For example, 20 page views with 0.5 minutes). Features are standardized using StandardScaler to ensure equal weighting in distance calculations, critical for density-based clustering. The DBSCAN class from scikit-learn clusters data with **eps=0.5** (neighborhood radius) and **min_samples=5** (minimum points for a cluster). Points labeled as -1 are noise (anomalies). Noise points (-1) are flagged as anomalies, while clustered points (0 or higher) are normal.

```
import numpy as np
import pandas as pd
import matplotlib.pyplot as plt
from sklearn.cluster import DBSCAN
from sklearn.preprocessing import StandardScaler
# Set random seed for reproducibility
np.random.seed(42)

# Step 1: Generate synthetic multivariate dataset (e.g., user website visits)
# Features: page views per session, average session duration (minutes)
n_samples = 100
normal_data = np.random.multivariate_normal(
    mean=[10, 5],  # Mean: 10 page views, 5 minutes
    cov=[[4, 0.5], [0.5, 1]],  # Covariance for realistic spread
    size=n_samples - 5
)
outlier_data = np.array([[20, 0.5], [2, 15], [25, 0.3], [1, 20], [22, 0.2]])  # Outliers
data = np.concatenate([normal_data, outlier_data])

# Convert to pandas DataFrame
df = pd.DataFrame(data, columns=['Page_Views', 'Session_Duration'])

# Step 2: Preprocess data (standardize features)
scaler = StandardScaler()
data_scaled = scaler.fit_transform(df[['Page_Views', 'Session_Duration']])

# Step 3: Apply DBSCAN for clustering and anomaly detection
eps = 0.5  # Radius of neighborhood
min_samples = 5  # Minimum points to form a cluster
dbscan = DBSCAN(eps=eps, min_samples=min_samples)
labels = dbscan.fit_predict(data_scaled)  # Cluster labels: -1 for noise (anomalies), 0+ for clusters

# Step 4: Identify anomalies (noise points labeled as -1)
df['Cluster_Label'] = labels
df['Is_Anomaly'] = labels == -1  # Anomalies are noise points

# Step 6: Visualize the results
plt.figure(figsize=(10, 4))
# Plot normal points (clustered) with different colors for each cluster
normal_points = df[~df['Is_Anomaly']]
plt.scatter(normal_points['Page_Views'], normal_points['Session_Duration'],
            c=normal_points['Cluster_Label'], cmap='viridis', label='Clustered Points')
# Plot anomalies in red
anomalies = df[df['Is_Anomaly']]
plt.scatter(anomalies['Page_Views'], anomalies['Session_Duration'], c='red', s=100,
            label='Anomalies', edgecolors='black')
plt.title('DBSCAN Anomaly Detection for User Website Visits')
plt.xlabel('Page Views per Session')
plt.ylabel('Average Session Duration (minutes)')
plt.colorbar(label='Cluster Label')
plt.legend()
plt.grid(True)
plt.show()
```

Figure 5.7: *Python Code for DBSCAN for Anomaly Detection*

The output of the preceding code is visualized in *Figure 5.8*:

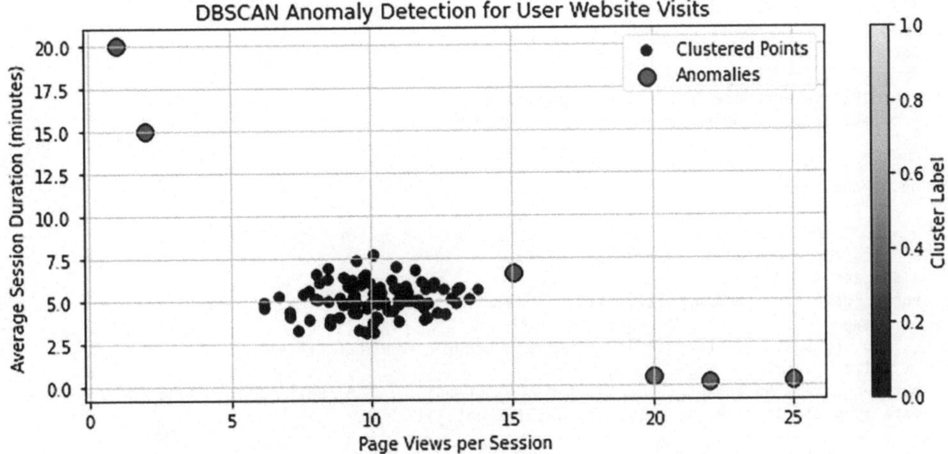

Figure 5.8: *Anomalies Detected by DBSCAN*

Isolation-Based Methods

Isolation-based methods exploit the idea that anomalies are easier to isolate from normal points, using randomized partitioning. Some of these methods are explained as follows:

Isolation Forest and Extended Isolation Forest

Isolation Forest builds random trees to partition the data, isolating points by measuring how few splits are needed to separate them. Anomalies require fewer splits due to their distinctiveness. Extended Isolation Forest improves performance in high-dimensional data by using hyperplanes for partitioning. For example, in a dataset of credit card transactions, a fraudulent transaction might be isolated in a few splits, yielding a low path length in an Isolation Forest.

These methods are useful for large-scale fraud detection, where anomalies are rare and distinct from normal transactions. These methods are scalable to large datasets, are effective for point anomalies, and make minimal assumptions about data distribution. However, they are less effective for contextual or collective anomalies as they are sensitive to tree depth and sample size parameters.

Figure 5.9 shows the Python code for the implementation of the Isolation Forest algorithm for anomaly detection. A synthetic dataset of 100 credit card transactions is generated, with two features: transaction amount ($) and time since last transaction (hours). Most data follow a multivariate normal distribution (mean: $100, 24 hours), with five manually added outliers (for example, $500 in 1 hour).

```
# Isolation Forest
import numpy as np
import pandas as pd
import matplotlib.pyplot as plt
from sklearn.ensemble import IsolationForest
from sklearn.preprocessing import StandardScaler

# Set random seed for reproducibility
np.random.seed(42)

# Step 1: Generate synthetic multivariate dataset (e.g., credit card transactions)
# Features: transaction amount ($), time since last transaction (hours)
n_samples = 100
normal_data = np.random.multivariate_normal(
    mean=[100, 24],  # Mean: $100, 24 hours
    cov=[[1000, 50], [50, 100]],  # Covariance for realistic spread
    size=n_samples - 5)
outlier_data = np.array([[500, 1], [50, 72], [600, 2], [30, 80], [450, 0.5]])  # Outliers
data = np.concatenate([normal_data, outlier_data])

# Convert to pandas DataFrame
df = pd.DataFrame(data, columns=['Amount', 'Time_Since_Last'])

# Step 2: Preprocess data (standardize features)
scaler = StandardScaler()
data_scaled = scaler.fit_transform(df[['Amount', 'Time_Since_Last']])

# Step 3: Apply Isolation Forest for anomaly detection
iso_forest = IsolationForest(n_estimators=100, contamination=0.05, random_state=42)
labels = iso_forest.fit_predict(data_scaled)  # -1 for anomalies, 1 for normal
anomaly_scores = -iso_forest.decision_function(data_scaled)  # Higher scores for anomalies

# Step 4: Identify anomalies
df['Anomaly_Score'] = anomaly_scores
df['Is_Anomaly'] = labels == -1  # Anomalies are labeled as -1

# Step 5: Visualize the results
plt.figure(figsize=(10, 6))
plt.scatter(df['Amount'], df['Time_Since_Last'], c=df['Is_Anomaly'],
            cmap='coolwarm', label='Data Points')
plt.title('Isolation Forest Anomaly Detection for Credit Card Transactions')
plt.xlabel('Transaction Amount ($)')
plt.ylabel('Time Since Last Transaction (hours)')
plt.colorbar(label='Anomaly (1) / Normal (0)')
plt.grid(True)

# Highlight anomalies with larger markers
anomalies = df[df['Is_Anomaly']]
plt.scatter(anomalies['Amount'], anomalies['Time_Since_Last'], c='red', s=100,
            label='Anomalies', edgecolors='black')
plt.legend()
plt.show()
```

Figure 5.9: *Implementation of Isolation Map Algorithm for Anomaly Detection*

Figure 5.10 visualizes the anomalies obtained using the Isolation Forest algorithm implemented in the preceding code:

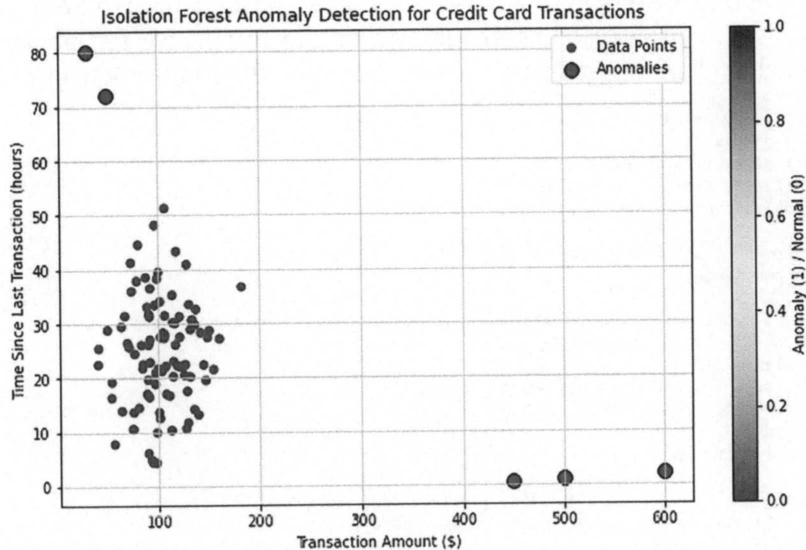

Figure 5.10: *Visualization of Anomalies Detected Using Isolation Forest Algorithm*

One-Class Classification

One-class classification methods learn a boundary around normal data, flagging points outside this boundary as anomalies. Some of these methods are mentioned as follows:

One-Class SVM

One-Class SVM constructs a hyperplane that encloses normal data in a high-dimensional space, using a kernel (for example, RBF) to handle non-linear boundaries. Points far from the hyperplane are flagged as anomalies. For instance, in a dataset of server logs, One-Class SVM might flag an unusual login pattern as an anomaly if it falls outside the learned boundary. It is useful for intrusion detection, where normal network behavior is modeled, and deviations are flagged. The strengths of One-Class SVM are that it is effective for high-dimensional data and is flexible with the use of appropriate kernel functions. However, it is computationally intensive and is sensitive to kernel parameters and scaling.

Figure 5.11 shows the Python code implementing One-Class SVM for anomaly detection. A synthetic dataset of 100 server log observations is generated, with two features: number of logins per hour and average response time (ms). Most data follow a multivariate normal distribution (mean: 20 logins, 100 ms), with five manually added outliers (for example, 50 logins with 500 ms). Features are standardized using StandardScaler to ensure consistent scaling, critical for SVM's distance-based calculations. The OneClassSVM class from scikit-learn is used with an RBF kernel,

nu=0.05 (expecting 5% outliers), and **gamma='scale'** (automatically tuned). Anomalies are labeled as -1, and decision scores are converted to positive for interpretability. Points labeled as -1 are flagged as anomalies, based on their high anomaly scores.

```
import numpy as np
import pandas as pd
import matplotlib.pyplot as plt
from sklearn.svm import OneClassSVM
from sklearn.preprocessing import StandardScaler

# Set random seed for reproducibility
np.random.seed(42)

# Step 1: Generate synthetic multivariate dataset (e.g., server log data)
# Features: number of logins per hour, average response time (ms)
n_samples = 100
normal_data = np.random.multivariate_normal(
    mean=[20, 100],  # Mean: 20 logins, 100 ms
    cov=[[25, 5], [5, 100]],  # Covariance for realistic spread
    size=n_samples - 5
)
outlier_data = np.array([[50, 500], [5, 10], [60, 600], [2, 5], [45, 450]])  # Outliers
data = np.concatenate([normal_data, outlier_data])

# Convert to pandas DataFrame
df = pd.DataFrame(data, columns=['Logins', 'Response_Time'])

# Step 2: Preprocess data (standardize features)
scaler = StandardScaler()
data_scaled = scaler.fit_transform(df[['Logins', 'Response_Time']])

# Step 3: Apply One-Class SVM for anomaly detection
oc_svm = OneClassSVM(kernel='rbf', nu=0.05, gamma='scale')  # nu=0.05 expects 5% outliers
labels = oc_svm.fit_predict(data_scaled)  # -1 for anomalies, 1 for normal
anomaly_scores = -oc_svm.decision_function(data_scaled)  # Higher scores for anomalies

# Step 4: Identify anomalies
df['Anomaly_Score'] = anomaly_scores
df['Is_Anomaly'] = labels == -1  # Anomalies are labeled as -1

# Step 5: Visualize the results
plt.figure(figsize=(10, 6))
plt.scatter(df['Logins'], df['Response_Time'], c=df['Is_Anomaly'],
            cmap='coolwarm', label='Data Points')
plt.title('One-Class SVM Anomaly Detection for Server Log Data')
plt.xlabel('Logins per Hour')
plt.ylabel('Average Response Time (ms)')
plt.colorbar(label='Anomaly (1) / Normal (0)')
plt.grid(True)

# Highlight anomalies with larger markers
anomalies = df[df['Is_Anomaly']]
plt.scatter(anomalies['Logins'], anomalies['Response_Time'], c='red', s=100,
            label='Anomalies', edgecolors='black')
plt.legend()
plt.show()
```

Figure 5.11: *Python Implementation of One-Class SVM for Anomaly Detection*

Figure 5.12 shows the visualization of anomalies detected using the code in *Figure* 5.11. It shows a scatter plot with all data points in the 2D feature space (logins versus response time), with normal points in blue and anomalies in red. Anomalies are highlighted with larger markers for clarity.

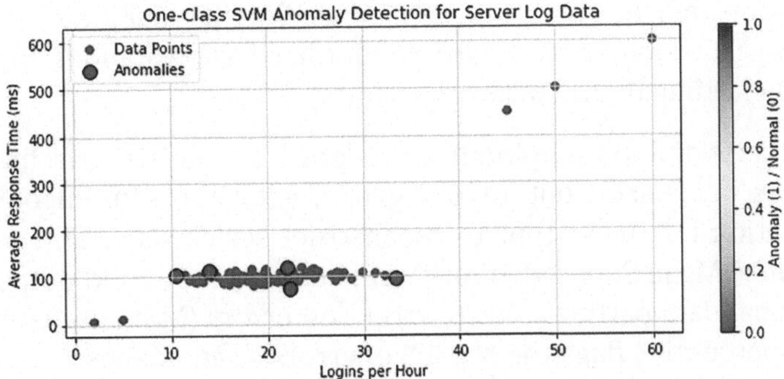

***Figure* 5.12:** *Visualization of Anomalies Detected Using One-Class SVM*

Elliptic Envelope:

Elliptic Envelope fits a multivariate Gaussian distribution to the data and defines an ellipsoid that encloses normal points. Points outside the ellipsoid (based on Mahalanobis distance) are flagged as anomalies. For example, in a dataset of machine measurements, a point with an extreme combination of features might lie outside the ellipsoid, indicating a defect.

It is often used for quality control tasks where sensor data is expected to follow a Gaussian distribution. It is fast, interpretable, and suited for Gaussian-like data. However, it assumes multivariate normality of data and is less effective for non-Gaussian or high-dimensional data.

Neural Network-Based Methods

Neural network-based methods, particularly autoencoders, leverage deep learning to model complex data patterns, detecting anomalies via reconstruction errors. Some of them are mentioned as follows:

Autoencoders for Anomaly Detection:

Autoencoders are neural networks trained to compress and reconstruct data. Normal data is reconstructed with low error, while anomalies (point or contextual) yield high reconstruction errors due to their deviation from learned patterns. Autoencoders are often used for image-based anomaly detection, such as identifying defective products in manufacturing.

Autoencoders are powerful for high-dimensional, complex data (for example, images, time series); they capture non-linear patterns. However, they require significant computational resources as they are sensitive to architecture and training.

Figure 5.13 shows the Python implementation of an autoencoder neural network for anomaly detection. A synthetic dataset of 100 IoT sensor readings is generated, with two features: temperature (°C) and pressure (kPa). Most data follow a multivariate normal distribution (mean: 25°C, 100 kPa), with five manually added outliers (For example, 35°C with 150 kPa). Features are standardized using StandardScaler to ensure consistent scaling, aiding neural network training.

We have used keras to define a simple autoencoder with a 2-8-4-8-2 architecture (input, two hidden layers, bottleneck, output) using ReLU activations for encoding/decoding and linear activation for the output to reconstruct scaled data. The autoencoder is trained to minimize Mean Squared Error (MSE) between input and output, learning to reconstruct normal data patterns. Reconstruction errors (MSE) are computed, and a threshold (95th percentile) flags the top 5% of errors as anomalies.

```
import numpy as np
import pandas as pd
import matplotlib.pyplot as plt
from sklearn.preprocessing import StandardScaler
from tensorflow.keras.models import Model
from tensorflow.keras.layers import Input, Dense
np.random.seed(42)# Set random seed for reproducibility
n_samples = 100# Step 1: Generate synthetic multivariate time-series dataset (e.g., IoT sensor readings)
n_features = 2# Features: temperature (°C), pressure (kPa) over 100 time points
normal_data = np.random.multivariate_normal(
    mean=[25, 100],  # Mean: 25°C, 100 kPa
    cov=[[4, 0.5], [0.5, 10]],  # Covariance for realistic spread
    size=n_samples - 5)
outlier_data = np.array([[35, 150], [15, 50], [40, 200], [10, 30], [38, 180]])  # Outliers
data = np.concatenate([normal_data, outlier_data])
df = pd.DataFrame(data, columns=['Temperature', 'Pressure'])# Convert to pandas DataFrame
# Step 2: Preprocess data (standardize features)
scaler = StandardScaler()
data_scaled = scaler.fit_transform(df[['Temperature', 'Pressure']])
# Step 3: Define and train the autoencoder(Architecture:Input(2)->Hidden(8)->Bottleneck(4)->Hidden(8)->Output(2)
input_layer = Input(shape=(n_features,))
encoded = Dense(8, activation='relu')(input_layer)
encoded = Dense(4, activation='relu')(encoded)
decoded = Dense(8, activation='relu')(encoded)
decoded = Dense(n_features, activation='linear')(decoded)
autoencoder = Model(input_layer, decoded)
autoencoder.compile(optimizer='adam', loss='mse')
# Train the autoencoder
autoencoder.fit(data_scaled, data_scaled, epochs=50, batch_size=16,shuffle=True, verbose=0)
# Step 4: Compute reconstruction errors
reconstructions = autoencoder.predict(data_scaled, verbose=0)
mse = np.mean(np.power(data_scaled - reconstructions, 2), axis=1)  # Mean squared error
# Step 5: Identify anomalies (threshold: top 5% of reconstruction errors)
threshold = np.percentile(mse, 95)  # Top 5% as anomalies
df['Reconstruction_Error'] = mse
df['Is_Anomaly'] = mse > threshold
# Step 6: Visualize the results
plt.figure(figsize=(10, 6))
plt.scatter(df['Temperature'], df['Pressure'], c=df['Is_Anomaly'],cmap='coolwarm', label='Data Points')
plt.title('Autoencoder Anomaly Detection for IoT Sensor Readings')
plt.xlabel('Temperature (°C)')
plt.ylabel('Pressure (kPa)')
plt.colorbar(label='Anomaly (1) / Normal (0)')
plt.grid(True)
# Highlight anomalies with larger markers
anomalies = df[df['Is_Anomaly']]
plt.scatter(anomalies['Temperature'], anomalies['Pressure'], c='red', s=100,label='Anomalies', edgecolors='black')
plt.legend()
plt.show()
# Plot reconstruction errors
plt.figure(figsize=(10, 4))
plt.plot(df['Reconstruction_Error'], label='Reconstruction Error')
plt.axhline(y=threshold, color='red', linestyle='--', label=f'Threshold ({threshold:.4f})')
plt.title('Reconstruction Errors for Anomaly Detection')
plt.xlabel('Sample Index')
plt.ylabel('Mean Squared Error')
plt.legend()
plt.grid(True)
plt.show()
```

Figure 5.13: *Python Code to Implement an Autoencoder Neural Network for Anomaly Detection*

Figure 5.14 shows a scatter plot containing all data points in the 2D feature space (temperature versus pressure), with normal points in blue and anomalies in red, highlighted with larger markers. The second plot shows reconstruction errors versus sample index, displaying the threshold to help you visualize the anomaly detection process.

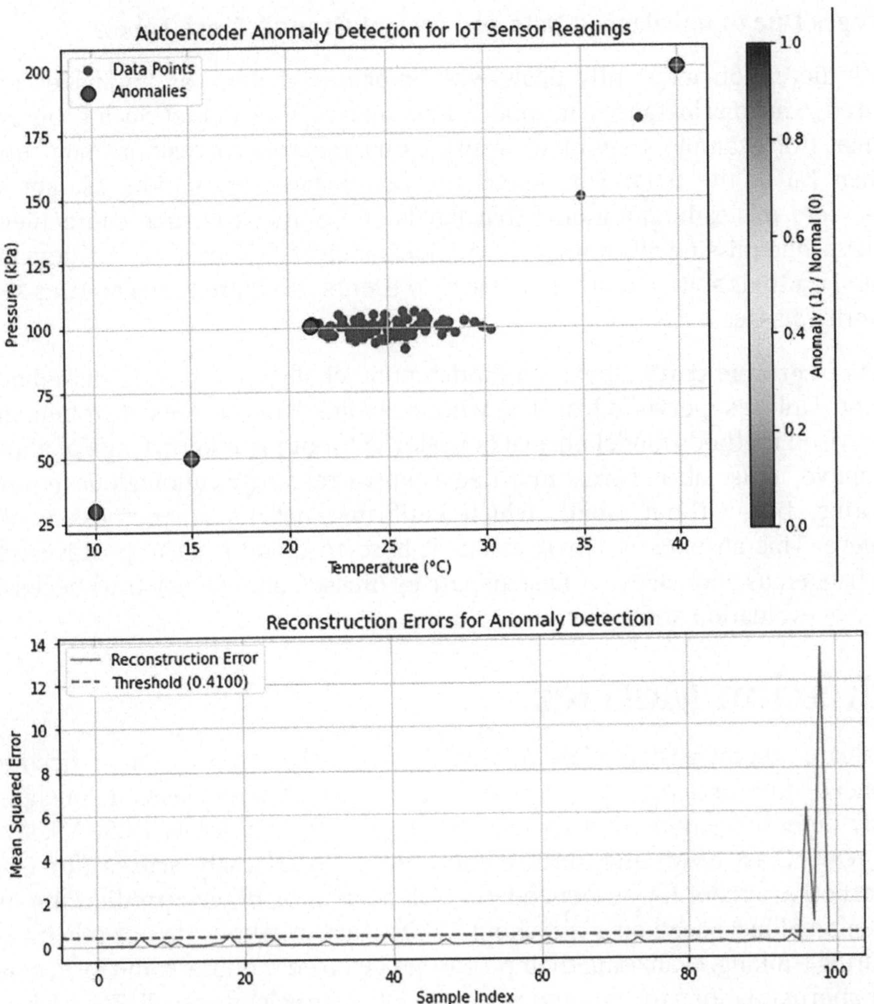

Figure 5.14: *Anomalies Detected Using Autoencoder Neural Network*

Evaluation of Anomaly Detection Methods

Evaluating unsupervised anomaly detection methods is a critical step to ensure their effectiveness in real-world applications, yet it poses unique challenges due to the nature of anomalies and the absence of labeled data. This section explores the difficulties of evaluating methods such as Z-score, k-NN, LOF, COF, DBSCAN, Isolation Forest, One-Class SVM, autoencoders, focusing on imbalanced data and the lack of ground truth labels. It introduces key evaluation metrics—precision, recall, F1-score, ROC-AUC, and precision-recall curves—and discusses validation techniques, including synthetic anomaly generation and cross-validation, to assess performance reliably.

Challenges Due to Imbalanced Data and Lack of Ground Truth Labels

Anomaly detection inherently deals with **imbalanced data**, as anomalies are rare compared to normal instances. In applications such as fraud detection or cybersecurity, anomalies (for example, fraudulent transactions, network intrusions) may constitute less than 1% of the data. This imbalance complicates evaluation, as metrics like accuracy are misleading; a model that labels all points as normal can achieve high accuracy while missing all anomalies. Methods such as LOF or autoencoders must be evaluated on their ability to detect these rare events, which requires metrics sensitive to minority classes.

The **lack of ground truth labels** is a fundamental challenge in unsupervised anomaly detection. Unlike supervised learning, where labeled data provides clear benchmarks, unsupervised methods model normal behavior without prior knowledge of anomalies. For example, an Isolation Forest may flag a sensor reading as anomalous in industrial monitoring, but without labels, which confirms that its correctness is difficult to achieve. This absence of labels makes it hard to quantify false positives (normal points flagged as anomalies) or false negatives (missed anomalies), thus necessitating alternative evaluation strategies.

Evaluation Metrics

To evaluate anomaly detection methods effectively, metrics must account for imbalanced data and prioritize the detection of rare anomalies. In unsupervised anomaly detection, methods such as Z-score, k-NN, LOF, COF, DBSCAN, Isolation Forest, One-Class SVM, and autoencoders produce **anomaly scores** (for example, reconstruction errors for autoencoders, LOF scores) or **binary predictions** (normal versus anomalous) based on a threshold. While these methods do not rely on labeled data during training, evaluating their performance often requires some form of labeled data or approximations to compute metrics such as precision, recall, F1-score, and PR curves.

Availability of Labels for Evaluation:

- **Synthetic Datasets:** In unsupervised settings, synthetic datasets with injected anomalies provide ground truth labels. For example, our autoencoder implementation (*Figure* 5.13) added outliers (for example, 35°C, 150 kPa) to a synthetic IoT dataset, allowing calculation of true positives (correctly flagged outliers), false positives, and so on.

- **Partially Labeled Data:** In real-world scenarios, partial labels may be available (for example, verified fraud cases in a credit card dataset), enabling supervised metrics for evaluation.
- **Post-Hoc Labeling:** After applying an unsupervised method, domain experts may label flagged anomalies (for example, in industrial monitoring), thereby providing ground truth for metrics such as precision and recall.

Anomaly Detection as Binary Classification:

- Unsupervised anomaly detection can be framed as a binary classification problem for evaluation purposes: normal (negative) versus anomalous (positive). Methods produce continuous anomaly scores, and a threshold determines the binary classification (for example, points with high LOF scores are labeled anomalous).
- Metrics such as precision (proportion of flagged anomalies that are true), recall (proportion of true anomalies detected), and F1-score (balancing precision and recall) are computed by comparing these predictions to ground truth labels, when available.

Precision-Recall Curves in Imbalanced Settings:

- Anomaly detection datasets are highly imbalanced (anomalies are rare), making PR curves particularly suitable. Unlike ROC curves, which consider both classes equally, PR curves focus on the minority class (anomalies), aligning with the goal of detecting rare events.
- For example, in Isolation Forest implementation, anomaly scores could be thresholded at various levels to plot precision versus recall, evaluating performance on synthetic outliers.

While training of anomaly detection methods is unsupervised (no labels needed), their evaluation often uses supervised metrics when labels are available or simulated. This is standard in anomaly detection research and practice, as seen in datasets like KDD Cup 1999, where ground truth labels are used to evaluate unsupervised methods such as One-Class SVM.

The following metrics are commonly used, assuming ground truth labels are available (for example, in synthetic datasets or partially labeled real data):

- **Precision:** The proportion of flagged anomalies that are true anomalies (true positives / (true positives + false positives)). High precision indicates few false positives, crucial in applications such as fraud detection, where false alarms are costly.
- **Recall:** The proportion of true anomalies correctly identified (true positives / (true positives + false negatives)). High recall ensures most anomalies are detected, vital in cybersecurity to avoid missing threats.

- **F1-score:** The harmonic mean of precision and recall (2 * (precision * recall) / (precision + recall)). It balances precision and recall, providing a single metric for overall performance, useful when comparing methods such as DBSCAN and autoencoders.
- **Receiver Operating Characteristic - Area Under Curve (ROC-AUC):** Measures the trade-off between true positive rate (recall) and false positive rate across various thresholds. A high ROC-AUC indicates a model's ability to distinguish normal from anomalous points, which is suitable for methods such as Isolation Forest.
- **Precision-Recall Curves:** Plots precision against recall at different thresholds, emphasizing performance on the minority class (anomalies). The area under the precision-recall curve (PR-AUC) is particularly effective for imbalanced data, as it focuses on anomaly detection performance, unlike ROC-AUC, which considers both classes equally.

These metrics require anomaly scores or rankings (For example, reconstruction errors from autoencoders, LOF scores) to set thresholds for classifying points as normal or anomalous. In unsupervised settings where labels are unavailable, these metrics can be applied to synthetic or partially labeled datasets to estimate performance.

Techniques for Validation of Anomaly Detection Methods

Given the lack of ground truth labels, validation techniques are essential to evaluate unsupervised anomaly detection methods. Two common approaches are synthetic anomaly generation and cross-validation, which simulate or approximate labeled scenarios. These approaches are explained as follows:

Synthetic Anomaly Generation

Synthetic anomalies are introduced into a dataset by injecting outliers that deviate from normal patterns. For example, in a dataset of credit card transactions, synthetic fraud cases can be created with unusually high amounts or irregular timing. Methods such as Z-score or One-Class SVM are then evaluated on their ability to detect these injected anomalies.

It provides controlled ground truth labels, allowing the use of precision, recall, and ROC-AUC. It is particularly useful when real labeled data is unavailable. However, synthetic anomalies may not fully represent real-world anomalies, which can be more complex or subtle. Careful design (for example, varying anomaly magnitude) is needed to ensure realism. For example, in our autoencoder implementation (*Figure* 5.13), outliers like a 35°C temperature with 150 kPa pressure were injected to test detection, enabling evaluation with F1-score or PR-AUC.

Cross-Validation

Cross-validation adapts supervised techniques to unsupervised settings by splitting data into training and testing subsets. The model is trained on one subset (assumed mostly normal) and evaluated on another, using anomaly scores to rank points. If partial labels are available, metrics such as recall can be computed; otherwise, proxy metrics (for example, score distribution) are used.

Cross-validation validates model robustness across different data subsets, suitable for methods such as k-NN or Isolation Forest. It helps assess generalization to unseen data, critical for real-world applications. However, it assumes the training set is mostly normal, which may not hold if anomalies are prevalent. Without labels, interpreting results relies on heuristic thresholds or domain knowledge.

Figure 5.15 shows the Python code that implements an Autoencoder for anomaly detection from the Kaggle Credit Card Fraud (https://www.kaggle.com/datasets/mlg-ulb/creditcardfraud) dataset. This dataset contains 284,807 transactions (492 frauds, 0.172% of the data). Features include 28 PCA components and Amount, with Class labels (0: normal, 1: fraud) used only for evaluation. The code includes the computation of evaluation metrics such as ROC-AUC, Precision, Recall and F1-Score. The autoencoder detects fraudulent transactions by learning to reconstruct normal transactions with low error. Fraudulent transactions, being rare and distinct, yield high reconstruction errors and are hence flagged as anomalies. ROC-AUC quantifies the model's ability to distinguish normal from fraudulent transactions across thresholds. We have dropped the Time column from the dataset, standardized features, and split the data into training (normal transactions only) and test sets (mixed normal and fraud) portions. Our autoencoder uses a 29-14-7-14-29 architecture (matching the 29 features) with ReLU activations for encoding/decoding and linear output for reconstruction. It is trained on normal transactions to minimize MSE. To detect anamolies, the autoencoder computes reconstruction errors (MSE) on the test set. A threshold (99.828th percentile, matching the fraud proportion) classifies points as normal or anomalous. For evaluation, we calculate ROC-AUC, precision, recall, and F1-score using true labels.

```
##Autoencoder Anomaly Detection with Evaluation Metrics on Kaggle Credit Card Fraud Dataset
import numpy as np
import pandas as pd
import matplotlib.pyplot as plt
from sklearn.preprocessing import StandardScaler
from sklearn.model_selection import train_test_split
from sklearn.metrics import roc_curve, auc, precision_recall_curve, precision_score, recall_score, f1_score
from tensorflow.keras.models import Model
from tensorflow.keras.layers import Input, Dense
np.random.seed(42)# Set random seed for reproducibility
# Step 1: Load the Kaggle Credit Card Fraud dataset
# Note: Download from https://www.kaggle.com/datasets/mlg-ulb/creditcardfraud  and place in working directory
df = pd.read_csv("creditcard.csv")
# Step 2: Preprocess the data, Drop 'Time' (less relevant for anomaly detection) and separate features and labels
X = df.drop(['Time', 'Class'], axis=1)  # Features: 28 PCA components + Amount
y = df['Class']  # Labels: 0 (normal), 1 (fraud)
scaler = StandardScaler()# Standardize features
X_scaled = scaler.fit_transform(X)
# Split into training (normal only) and test sets
X_train, X_test, y_train, y_test = train_test_split(X_scaled, y, test_size=0.2, random_state=42, stratify=y)
X_train_normal = X_train[y_train == 0]  # Train on normal transactions only
# Step 3: Define and train the autoencoder
n_features = X_train.shape[1]  # 29 features
input_layer = Input(shape=(n_features,))
encoded = Dense(14, activation='relu')(input_layer)
encoded = Dense(7, activation='relu')(encoded)
decoded = Dense(14, activation='relu')(encoded)
decoded = Dense(n_features, activation='linear')(decoded)
autoencoder = Model(input_layer, decoded)
autoencoder.compile(optimizer='adam', loss='mse')
# Train on normal transactions only
autoencoder.fit(X_train_normal, X_train_normal, epochs=50, batch_size=256,shuffle=True, validation_split=0.2, verbose=0)
# Step 4: Compute reconstruction errors
reconstructions = autoencoder.predict(X_test, verbose=0)
mse = np.mean(np.power(X_test - reconstructions, 2), axis=1)  # Mean squared error
# Step 5: Evaluate with ROC-AUC and other metrics, Compute ROC curve and ROC-AUC
fpr, tpr, roc_thresholds = roc_curve(y_test, mse)
roc_auc = auc(fpr, tpr)
# Set threshold (e.g., top 0.172% of errors, matching fraud proportion)
threshold = np.percentile(mse, 99.828)  # 100 - 0.172
predicted_labels = (mse > threshold).astype(int)
# Compute precision, recall, F1-score
precision = precision_score(y_test, predicted_labels)
recall = recall_score(y_test, predicted_labels)
f1 = f1_score(y_test, predicted_labels)
# Compute precision-recall curve
precision_vals, recall_vals, pr_thresholds = precision_recall_curve(y_test, mse)
# Step 6: Print results
print("Evaluation Metrics:")
print(f"ROC-AUC: {roc_auc:.3f}")
print(f"Precision: {precision:.3f}")
print(f"Recall: {recall:.3f}")
print(f"F1-score: {f1:.3f}")
```

Figure 5.15: *Autoencoder for Anomaly Detection along with the Evaluation of its Performance*

Evaluation metrics computed in the preceding code are shown in *Figure* 5.16:

```
Evaluation Metrics:
ROC-AUC: 0.936
Precision: 0.347
Recall: 0.347
F1-score: 0.347
```

Figure 5.16: *Evaluation Metrics for the Code in Figure* 5.17

You can also plot the ROC Curve, Precision-Recall Curve for this Autoencoder anomaly detection code. The plots will look as shown in *Figure* 5.17:

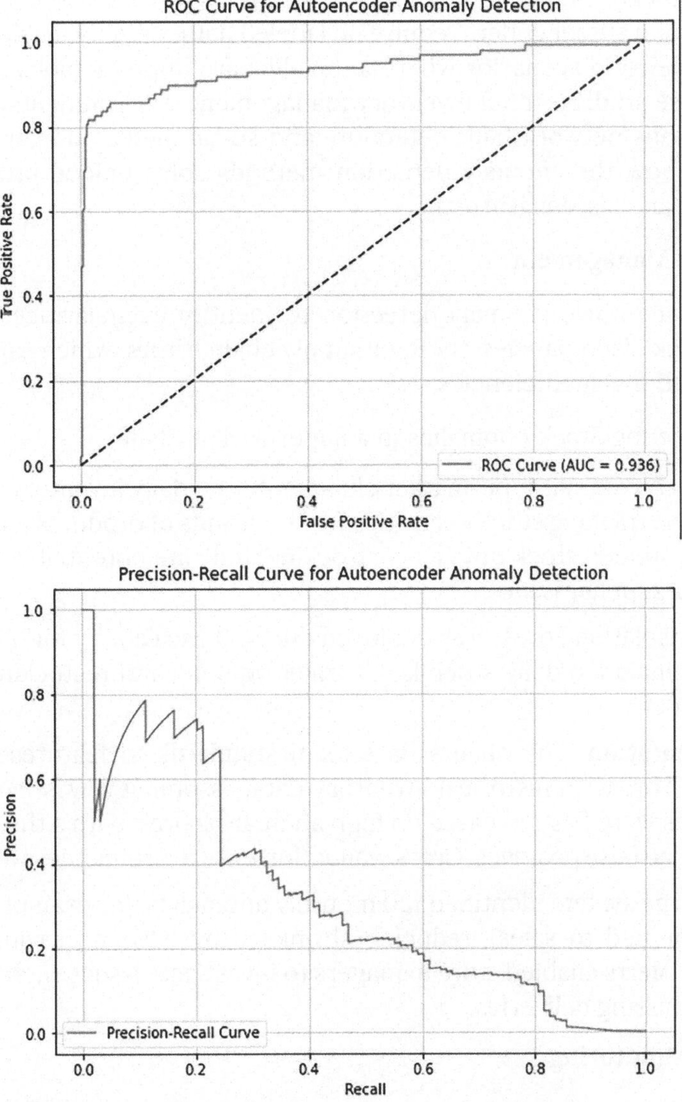

Figure 5.17: *ROC Curve and PR Curve for Autoencoder-based Anomaly Detection*

Each of the methods excels in specific scenarios: statistical methods for simple univariate data, density-based methods for local anomalies, and autoencoders for complex patterns.

Real-World Applications and Case Studies

Unsupervised anomaly detection is a versatile tool for identifying rare events across industries like retail and telecommunications. Unlike supervised methods, the unsupervised approaches such as Z-score, k-NN, LOF, COF, DBSCAN, Isolation Forest, One-Class SVM, and autoencoders require no labeled data, thereby making them ideal for dynamic, real-world scenarios where anomalies are unpredictable. This section presents four case studies–retail inventory management, environmental monitoring, telecommunications network fault detection, and social media anomaly detection–which illustrate how the anomaly detection methods solve unique problems, their business impact, and lessons learned.

Retail Inventory Management

Application: Retailers use anomaly detection to identify irregularities in inventory data, such as stock discrepancies, theft, or supply chain errors, which can lead to lost revenue or operational inefficiencies.

Case Study: Detecting Stock Anomalies in a Supermarket Chain

- **Scenario**: A national supermarket chain monitors daily inventory levels across 500 stores, tracking stock quantities for thousands of products. Anomalies (for example, sudden stock drops, overstocking) indicate potential theft, scanning errors, or supplier issues.
- **Method**: Isolation Forest was deployed due to its scalability for large datasets. Features included daily stock levels, sales volume, and restocking frequency per product.
- **Implementation**: The chain's data team standardized features and trained Isolation Forest on historical inventory data, assuming it was mostly normal. Anomalies were flagged based on high anomaly scores, with a threshold tuned to minimize false positives. Cross-validation ensured robustness across stores.
- **Impact**: The system identified 120 monthly anomalies (for example, 50% stock drops not tied to sales), reducing shrinkage by 15% and saving $2 million annually. Alerts enabled store managers to investigate issues such as employee theft or missing deliveries.

Environmental Monitoring

Application: Environmental agencies use anomaly detection to monitor air or water quality, detecting pollution spikes or sensor malfunctions that threaten ecosystems or public health.

Case Study: Air Quality Anomaly Detection in Urban Areas

- **Scenario**: A city deploys 200 air quality sensors measuring PM2.5, CO, and NO2 levels hourly. Anomalies (for example, sudden PM2.5 spikes, sensor failures) indicate pollution events or equipment issues.
- **Method**: Autoencoders were chosen for their ability to model complex, time-series patterns. Features included sensor readings and meteorological data (for example, wind speed, temperature).

- **Implementation**: An autoencoder was trained on normal sensor data, reconstructing inputs with low error. High reconstruction errors flagged anomalies that were evaluated using synthetic pollution spikes. A PR curve assessed performance on rare events.
- **Impact**: The system detected 10 pollution events monthly (for example, industrial emissions), enabling rapid response from authorities, and identified 5% of sensors as faulty, improving data reliability. Public health alerts reduced hospital admissions by 8% during pollution spikes.

Telecommunications Network Fault Detection

Application: Telecom providers use anomaly detection to identify network faults, such as signal drops or equipment failures, ensuring reliable service in high-traffic networks.

Case Study: Fault Detection in a 5G Network

- **Scenario**: A telecom provider operates a 5G network with 10,000 base stations, collecting metrics such as signal strength, latency, and data throughput. Anomalies indicate hardware failures or interference.
- **Method**: DBSCAN was selected for its ability to cluster normal network behavior and label noise as anomalies. Features included latency, throughput, and error rates.
- **Implementation**: After standardizing metrics, DBSCAN clustered normal base station behavior, flagging noise points as faults. Synthetic anomaly generation simulated failures (for example, 50% throughput drops) to evaluate recall. A threshold on noise points was tuned for high recall.
- **Impact**: The system detected 200 faults monthly, reducing downtime by 20% and improving customer satisfaction. Early alerts saved $500,000 in repair costs annually.

Social Media Anomaly Detection

Application: Social media platforms use anomaly detection to identify unusual user behavior, such as bot activity, spam, or account hijacking, to maintain platform integrity.

Case Study: Bot Detection on a Social Media Platform

- **Scenario**: A social media platform with 50 million users monitors activity metrics such as post frequency, likes, and follower growth. Anomalies (for example, 100 posts/hour) suggest bot accounts or hacking.
- **Method**: One-Class SVM was used to define a boundary around normal user behavior. Features included post frequency, engagement rates, and account age.

- **Implementation**: One-Class SVM (Section 4) was trained on standardized user data, flagging points outside the boundary as anomalies. Synthetic bot activity is injected to compute the F1-score, balancing precision and recall.
- **Impact**: The system flagged 1,000 suspicious accounts daily, reducing spam by 30% and improving user experience. Automated suspensions saved 500 hours of moderation time per month.

These case studies demonstrate the versatility of unsupervised anomaly detection in retail, environmental, telecommunications, and social media applications. By leveraging methods such as Isolation Forest, autoencoders, DBSCAN, and One-Class SVM, organizations can detect rare events, improve operations, and enhance safety without labeled data.

Best Practices and Pitfalls

Unsupervised anomaly detection, as explored through methods such as Z-score, k-NN, LOF, COF, DBSCAN, Isolation Forest, One-Class SVM, and autoencoders, offers powerful solutions for identifying rare events. However, its effectiveness depends on navigating common pitfalls and adopting best practices. This section discusses the pitfalls in anomaly detection methods, such as sensitivity to hyperparameters, false positives, and the curse of dimensionality, and offers the best practices such as ensemble methods, feature engineering, and iterative tuning. It also discusses interpretability, emphasizing how to explain anomalies using feature importance and visualization, ensuring actionable insights for practitioners.

Common Pitfalls

Unsupervised anomaly detection is prone to several pitfalls that can undermine performance if not addressed. Understanding these challenges is crucial for deploying robust models.

- **Sensitivity to Hyperparameters:**
    - Many methods rely on parameters that significantly affect results. For example, DBSCAN's eps and `min_samples` determine cluster formation, while LOF's k (number of neighbors) influences density estimates. Poorly chosen parameters can lead to missed anomalies or excessive noise. Sensitivity complicates automation, especially in dynamic datasets where optimal parameters vary. To mitigate this, use data-driven tuning (for example, cross-validation) and test multiple parameter sets to ensure robustness.

- **False Positives:**
  - False positives–normal points flagged as anomalies–can erode trust in a system. For instance, autoencoders may flag rare but legitimate patterns (for example, high-value transactions in retail) as anomalies due to high reconstruction errors. High false positive rates increase operational costs (for example, manual investigations) and risk overlooking true anomalies. To mitigate this, tune thresholds to balance precision and recall and incorporate domain knowledge to filter false positives.
- **Curse of Dimensionality:**
  - High-dimensional data, which is common in real-world applications, reduces the effectiveness of distance-based methods such as k-NN or LOF. In high dimensions, points appear equidistant, diluting density or distance measures. The curse of dimensionality increases computational cost and degrades anomaly detection accuracy. To mitigate this, apply dimensionality reduction techniques such as Principal Component Analysis before using distance-based methods, or choose methods such as Isolation Forest, which are less sensitive to high dimensions.

Best Practices

To overcome these pitfalls, practitioners can adopt best practices that enhance model performance, scalability, and reliability. Some of these are mentioned as follows:

- **Ensemble Methods:**
  - Combining multiple anomaly detection methods leverages their strengths, thus improving robustness. For example, Isolation Forest's scalability complements LOF's density-based sensitivity, thereby reducing missed anomalies.
  - **Implementation**: Train Isolation Forest and LOF separately, then aggregate their anomaly scores (for example, weighted average) to flag points. Alternatively, use majority voting for binary predictions.
  - **Benefits**: Ensembles mitigate individual method weaknesses, such as LOF's parameter sensitivity or Isolation Forest's focus on point anomalies.
  - **Consideration**: Ensembles increase computational cost, so prioritize methods with complementary strengths.
- **Feature Engineering:**
  - Selecting or creating relevant features enhances model performance. For instance, transforming raw data into domain-specific metrics (for example, transaction frequency instead of raw amounts) improves anomaly detection.

- **Implementation**: Use domain knowledge to engineer features (for example, ratios, time-based aggregates) and apply standardization to ensure equal weighting.
- **Benefit**: Relevant features reduce noise and highlight anomalies, mitigating the curse of dimensionality.
- **Consideration**: Feature engineering requires domain expertise and experimentation, but it significantly boosts accuracy.

- **Iterative Tuning:**
  - Anomaly detection models benefit from iterative refinement of parameters, thresholds, and features based on evaluation feedback. Cross-validation or synthetic anomaly generation can guide tuning.
  - **Implementation**: Test multiple parameter sets (for example, COF's `n_neighbors`, autoencoder's layer sizes) and thresholds, evaluating with metrics such as F1-score or PR-AUC.
  - **Benefits**: Iterative tuning adapts models to specific datasets, thereby improving detection rates and reducing false positives.
  - **Consideration**: Tuning is time-intensive, so automate where possible (for example, grid search) or use domain insights to narrow parameter ranges.

Interpretability

Explaining why a point is flagged as an anomaly is critical for trust and actionability, especially in unsupervised settings where models lack explicit rules. Interpretability techniques such as feature importance and visualization make anomalies understandable to stakeholders.

- **Feature Importance:**
  - Identifying which features contribute most to an anomaly score clarifies the model's reasoning. For example, in Isolation Forest, features with the shortest average path lengths in trees are most influential.
  - **Implementation**: For autoencoders, compute the contribution of each feature to reconstruction error (for example, absolute difference between input and output). For k-NN, analyze distances to neighbors per feature.
  - **Benefits**: Feature importance provides actionable insights (for example, "investigate high latency" in telecom faults) and builds trust in the model.
  - **Consideration**: Importance scores may vary across methods, requiring method-specific techniques.

- **Visualization:**
  - Visualizing anomalies in the feature space or score distribution helps stakeholders understand results. Scatter plots, histograms, and decision boundaries (for example, for One-Class SVM) are effective tools.
  - **Implementation**: Plot anomalies in 2D or show score distributions (for example, reconstruction errors). Highlight anomalies with distinct colors or markers.
  - **Benefits**: Visualizations make complex models accessible, facilitating communication with non-technical stakeholders.
  - **Consideration**: High-dimensional data requires dimensionality reduction for effective visualization, which may oversimplify patterns.

Navigating the pitfalls of unsupervised anomaly detection requires careful planning and robust practices. Ensemble methods, feature engineering, and iterative tuning enhance model performance, while feature importance and visualization ensure interpretable results. By applying these best practices, practitioners can deploy methods such as LOF, Isolation Forest, or autoencoders effectively.

Conclusion

In this chapter, we explored anomaly and outlier detection tasks using unsupervised learning. Anomaly detection is an important task in unsupervised learning, enabling the identification of rare and unusual events in data without the need for labeled examples. This chapter has explored the multifaceted landscape of unsupervised anomaly detection, providing a comprehensive guide to its theory, practice, and real-world impact. We began by laying the theoretical foundations, distinguishing anomalies from outliers and introducing statistical, distance-based, density-based, clustering-based, isolation-based, one-class classification, and neural network-based approaches. Then we discussed and applied methods such as Z-score, k-NN, LOF, COF, DBSCAN, Isolation Forest, One-Class SVM, and autoencoders to synthetic and real datasets, demonstrating their ability to detect anomalies in diverse scenarios. We also discussed the evaluation metrics for anomaly detection methods, along with the best practices and pitfalls.

In the next chapter, we will explore the use of deep neural network architectures for unsupervised learning.

Key Terms

- **Anomaly Detection**: The process of identifying rare and unusual patterns in data that deviate significantly from normal behavior, often using unsupervised methods without labeled data

- **Outlier**: A data point that differs markedly from the majority of the dataset, potentially indicating an anomaly, error, or significant event, as distinguished in theoretical foundations
- **Isolation Forest**: An unsupervised anomaly detection method that isolates points using random splits in a tree-based structure, effective for high-dimensional data due to its scalability
- **Local Outlier Factor (LOF):** A density-based method that identifies anomalies by comparing a point's local density to that of its neighbors, suitable for varying-density datasets
- **One-Class SVM**: A boundary-based method that learns a hyperplane to enclose normal data in a high-dimensional space, flagging points outside as anomalies
- **Autoencoder**: A neural network-based method that compresses and reconstructs data, detecting anomalies by identifying points with high reconstruction errors
- **Precision-Recall Curve (PR-AUC)**: An evaluation metric plotting precision against recall at various thresholds, ideal for assessing anomaly detection in imbalanced datasets
- **Synthetic Anomaly Generation**: A validation technique that injects artificial outliers into a dataset to create ground truth labels for evaluating unsupervised methods
- **Curse of Dimensionality**: A challenge in high-dimensional data where distance and density measures become less meaningful, impacting methods such as k-NN and LOF
- **Feature Importance**: An interpretability technique that identifies the features that contribute the most to an anomaly score; enhances trust and actionability in detection results

Questions

1. Explain the concept of density-based anomaly detection and its significance in identifying anomalies. How does it differ from distance-based methods such as k-NN, and what are its advantages in varying-density datasets?
2. Describe the working of Isolation Forest for anomaly detection. How does it leverage random splits to isolate anomalies, and what makes it particularly suitable for high-dimensional data compared to other methods?
3. What is the key difference between statistical methods such as Z-score and neural network-based methods such as autoencoders for anomaly detection? In which scenarios would each be preferred, and why?

4. Discuss the role of synthetic anomaly generation in evaluating unsupervised anomaly detection methods. How does it address the lack of ground truth labels, and what are its limitations?
5. Explain how DBSCAN can be used for anomaly detection. How does it differ from clustering-based anomaly detection approaches, and what challenges arise when applying it to real-world datasets?
6. Describe the evaluation challenges posed by imbalanced data in anomaly detection. How do metrics such as precision-recall curves help overcome these challenges, and why are they preferred over accuracy?
7. What are the advantages and limitations of using One-Class SVM for anomaly detection? How does its boundary-based approach compare to density-based methods such as LOF, and in which applications is it most effective?
8. Discuss the importance of feature engineering in unsupervised anomaly detection. How can it mitigate the curse of dimensionality, and what role does domain knowledge play in its implementation?
9. Explain how interpretability can be achieved in unsupervised anomaly detection. Why is it critical for real-world applications, and how do techniques such as feature importance and visualization contribute to actionable insights?
10. What are the key lessons from the real-world applications of unsupervised anomaly detection? How do these lessons inform the deployment of methods such as autoencoders or Isolation Forest in new domains?

Multiple Choice Questions

1. Which of the following anomaly detection methods is based on isolating points using random splits in a tree-based structure?
   a. K-NN
   b. LOF
   c. Isolation Forest
   d. One-Class SVM
2. What is a primary challenge in evaluating unsupervised anomaly detection methods?
   a. Overfitting to labeled data
   b. Lack of ground truth labels
   c. High computational cost of supervised metrics
   d. Inability to handle high-dimensional data

3. Which evaluation metric is particularly effective for imbalanced datasets in anomaly detection?

   a. Accuracy

   b. ROC-AUC

   c. PR-AUC

   d. MSE

4. Which validation technique involves injecting outliers into a dataset to create ground truth labels for evaluation?

   a. Cross Validation

   b. Synthetic Anomaly Generation

   c. Grid Search

   d. Feature Selection

5. In which real-world application mentioned in this Chapter is DBSCAN used to cluster normal behavior and label noise points as anomalies?

   a. Retail Inventory Management

   b. Environmental Monitoring

   c. Telecommunications Network Fault Detection

   d. Social Media Anomaly Detection

6. What is a common pitfall in unsupervised anomaly detection that affects methods such as LOF and DBSCAN?

   a. Overreliance on labeled data

   b. Sensitivity to hyperparameters

   c. Inability to scale to large datasets

   d. Lack of interpretability

7. Which best practice involves combining multiple anomaly detection methods to improve robustness?

   a. Feature engineering

   b. Iterative tuning

   c. Ensemble methods

   d. Dimensionality reduction

8. How can interpretability be achieved in anomaly detection to explain why a point is flagged as anomalous?
   a. Increasing model complexity
   b. Using feature importance
   c. Reducing training data
   d. Ignoring false positives
9. Which of these methods is particularly suited for high-dimensional data due to its low sensitivity to the curse of dimensionality?
   a. K-NN
   b. LOF
   c. Isolation Forest
   d. COF
10. What is a key advantage of unsupervised anomaly detection?
    a. Reliance on large, labeled datasets
    b. Ability to detect anomalies without labeled data
    c. Guaranteed high precision in all scenarios
    d. Simplicity in hyperparameter tuning

Answers

1. c
2. b
3. c
4. b
5. c
6. b
7. c
8. b
9. c
10. b

Chapter 6
Deep Unsupervised Learning

Introduction

Unsupervised learning enables the discovery of patterns and structures in unlabeled data, which is an important capability in machine learning methods where labeled data is scarce. In the previous chapters, we explored foundational unsupervised methods, including clustering and dimensionality reduction, which facilitate data grouping and simplification. This chapter introduces deep unsupervised learning, which employs neural networks to model complex data distributions and representations. Techniques such as autoencoders, Variational Autoencoders (VAEs), Generative Adversarial Networks (GANs), autoregressive models, and flow models are examined, which in turn offer advanced capabilities for representation learning and data generation. Through formal explanations and Python-based implementations, this chapter elucidates these methods and their applications such as denoising, synthetic data generation, and probabilistic modeling.

Structure

In this chapter, we will discuss the following topics:

- Introduction to Deep Unsupervised Learning
- Autoencoders
- Latent Variable Models and Variational Autoencoders
- Generative Adversarial Networks
- Autoregressive Models
- Flow Models
- Diffusion Models
- Self-Supervised Learning
- Energy-Based Models

Introduction to Deep Unsupervised Learning

Deep unsupervised learning refers to the use of deep neural networks for discovering patterns from raw data without labels. This means the use of deep neural networks to discover patterns, representations, or data distributions from unlabeled data. Unlike supervised learning, which relies on labeled inputs to predict outputs, deep unsupervised learning operates without explicit guidance and models the underlying structure of the data through methods such as autoencoders, Variational Autoencoders (VAEs), Generative Adversarial Networks (GANs), autoregressive models, and flow models. These techniques enable tasks such as representation learning (for example, extracting meaningful features), data generation (for example, creating synthetic images or text), and density estimation, making them powerful for applications where labeled data is scarce or unavailable like in image denoising, text generation, and anomaly detection. With deep unsupervised learning, we can build generative models that recreate the distributions of training data and with self-supervised learning and large language models that have revolutionized natural language processing.

Important Features of Neural Network Architectures for Unsupervised Learning

Instead of mapping to a given label, neural network architectures for unsupervised learning are designed to reveal structure in the input data itself through self-supervision, latent modeling, reconstruction, or distribution learning.

- **Latent Variable Modeling:** Deep neural network architectures used for unsupervised learning often are designed to discover hidden factors (latent variables) in input data. For example, Variational Autoencoders and GANs. The latent variables explain the input data distribution. These architectures include a latent space (a lower-dimensional or structured representation) that encodes meaningful features of the input data. This is achieved through bottleneck layers (for example, in autoencoders) or probabilistic modeling (for example, in VAEs). The latent space captures essential data characteristics, enabling tasks such as dimensionality reduction, feature extraction, or generative modeling. For instance, VAEs impose a probabilistic structure on the latent space for data generation, that is, VAEs map inputs to a latent distribution (for example, Gaussian), thus allowing sampling for generative tasks.
- **Self-Supervised Signal Generation:** Since the data is unlabeled, the deep neural network creates its own supervisory signal from data (for example, predicting missing parts, transformations, and augmentations), it enables the networks to work without external labels in data.
- **Reconstruction-Based Objectives:** Neural architectures such as autoencoders learn to reconstruct the input, thus forcing it to extract meaningful features from input data.

- **Generative Modeling:** Neural network architectures used for unsupervised learning are built to model the input data distribution itself rather than learning a mapping from data features to target labels. GANs and VAEs are examples of this.
- **Contrastive Learning and Clustering-Friendly Design:** Architectures are modified to bring similar data points close in the latent space and push dissimilar points apart without labels.
- **Encoder-Decoder Structures:** Architectures such as autoencoders and VAEs feature an encoder-decoder framework, where the encoder compresses input data into a latent representation, and the decoder reconstructs or generates data from this representation. This structure supports representation learning (for example, denoising in autoencoders) and generative tasks (for example, image reconstruction in VAEs) without requiring labels. In a denoising autoencoder, the encoder processes noisy inputs, and the decoder reconstructs clean outputs, learning robust features.
- **Adversarial Training Mechanisms:** GANs employ a dual-network architecture with a generator and a discriminator trained using adversarial training. The generator produces synthetic data, while the discriminator evaluates its authenticity, optimizing both via a min-max game. This mechanism enables GANs to learn implicit data distributions without explicit likelihood estimation, generating realistic samples (for example, images, audio, and so on). In a DCGAN, convolutional layers in the generator create images, while the discriminator distinguishes real from fake images.
- **Energy-Based and Score-Based Approaches:** These neural architectures sometimes define an energy landscape over inputs preferring likely patterns and rejecting unlikely ones like in Score-based generative models.
- **Heavy Data Augmentation for Invariance:** These neural networks use heavy data augmentation to help networks learn invariant representations of the data. This is essential because there are no labels to guide invariance otherwise.
- **Specialized Loss Functions:** These neural networks use specialized loss functions like reconstruction error, KL divergence, adversarial loss, contrastive loss, and clustering loss.

Applications of Deep Unsupervised Learning

Deep unsupervised learning finds numerous applications in various domains including:

- Building Generative Models for the creation of new content
- Conditional Synthesis Technology (WaveNet, GAN-pix2pix)
- Compression

- Improve downstream tasks with self-supervised pre-training (For example, production level impact - Google Search powered by BERT)
- Flexible building blocks

In subsequent sections, we will learn about specific neural networks for deep unsupervised learning.

Autoencoders

An autoencoder is a neural network architecture used in unsupervised learning to learn compact representations of unlabeled data. It consists of two neural networks—an encoder network and a decoder network. An encode compresses input data into a lower-dimensional latent space; in other words, it maps the input data to a lower-dimensional latent space representation, compressing the data by learning its essential features. A decoder reconstructs the original data from the latent space representation, while aiming to reproduce the input as accurately as possible.

The training objective of an autoencoder is to minimize the **reconstruction error**, typically measured as the difference between the input data and its reconstructed output (for example, mean squared error or binary cross-entropy). This is achieved by optimizing the neural network to encode the input into a compact latent representation and decode it back to closely match the original data, thereby learning meaningful features without labels. Trained to minimize reconstruction error (for example, mean squared error), autoencoders capture essential data features, enabling tasks such as dimensionality reduction, denoising, and anomaly detection.

Architecture Details

Autoencoders are composed of two neural networks—an encoder and a decoder. Both of these are explained as follows:

Encoder

The encoder neural network in an autoencoder consists of multiple neural network layers, typically fully connected or convolutional, with non-linear activation functions (for example, ReLU, sigmoid). The encoder maps the input data $\mathbf{x} \in \mathbf{R}^n$ to a lower-dimensional latent space representation $\mathbf{z} \in \mathbf{R}^m$, where $m<n$.

The layers progressively reduce dimensionality, culminating in a bottleneck layer that outputs `z`. For example, for a 784-dimensional MNIST image (28x28 pixels), the encoder might consist of dense layers (for example, **784 → 128 → 32**) to produce a 32-dimensional latent vector. Here, the layer that produces the lowest dimensional latent representation of the input data is the bottleneck layer.

The **bottleneck layer** is the neural network layer within the encoder that produces the lowest-dimensional latent representation of the input data, denoted as $\mathbf{z} \in \mathbf{R}^m$, where m is significantly smaller than the input dimension **n**. Positioned between the encoder and decoder, it acts as a compressed intermediary, forcing the autoencoder to capture the most essential features of the data to enable accurate reconstruction. For example, in an autoencoder for MNIST images (784 dimensions), the bottleneck layer might reduce the data to a 32-dimensional vector, thus constraining the information flow, and promoting efficient representation learning for unsupervised tasks such as dimensionality reduction or denoising.

Decoder

The decoder neural network in an autoencoder is architecturally similar to the encoder. It consists of multiple layers (fully connected or convolutional) with non-linear activations to expand the latent vector back to the input dimensionality. The final layer often uses an activation function suitable for the data type. For example, the sigmoid function is used for pixel values in the range [0,1]. For example, for the same MNIST image, the decoder might use dense layers (for example, **32 → 128 → 784**) to reconstruct the 784-dimensional image.

The decoder reconstructs the input data **x`** $\in$ $\mathbf{R}^n$ from the laten representation**z**.

Overall Architecture

The autoencoder forms a sequential pipeline:

```
x -> Encoder(f) -> z -> Decoder(g) -> x`
```

Where **f** and **g** are the encoder and decoder functions, respectively. The latent space acts as a bottleneck, thus forcing the network to learn a compressed yet informative representation of the input.

The training objective is to minimize reconstruction error, which is given by the equation:

Where,

$$\text{Loss} = \frac{1}{N}\sum_{i=1}^{N} \|x_i - x_i'\|^2$$

$\mathbf{x_i}$ is the ith input data sample.

$\mathbf{x_i}$` is the reconstructed output for the ith sample, produced by the decoder from the latent representation.

N is the number of samples in the dataset.

$\|\cdot\|^2$ is the squared Euclidean norm (for example, mean squared error for continuous data).

This loss measures the reconstruction error, optimizing the autoencoder to make *xi'* as close as possible to *xi*.

For example, given an input image $x \in R^n$, the encoder $f: R^n \rightarrow R^m$ (where $m<n$) produces a latent representation $z=f(x)$, and the decoder $g: R^m \rightarrow R^n$ reconstructs the output $x'=g(z)$. The objective is to optimize the parameters of f and g to minimize the reconstruction loss given in the preceding equation.

Variants of Autoencoders

Variants of autoencoders extend the standard architecture to address specific challenges and enhance functionality in unsupervised learning. Denoising autoencoders introduce noise (for example, Gaussian or dropout) to the input data during training, forcing the network to reconstruct clean outputs, thereby improving robustness for tasks such as image denoising. Sparse autoencoders incorporate sparsity constraints, such as L1 regularization on the latent representation, to activate fewer neurons, promoting selective feature learning suitable for high-dimensional data. Contractive autoencoders add a penalty to the loss function to make the learned representations less sensitive to small input perturbations, enhancing generalization. These variants, by modifying the training objective or architecture, broaden the applicability of autoencoders to diverse domains, including anomaly detection and feature extraction, as explored in subsequent sections of this chapter.

Applications of Autoencoders

Autoencoders are useful in numerous domains like:

- In image processing, they compress high-dimensional images or remove noise.
- In anomaly detection, they identify outliers by flagging data with high reconstruction errors.
- In feature learning, they extract representations for downstream tasks, such as classification, when labeled data is limited.

Latent Variable Models and Variational Autoencoders

Latent variable models are a class of probabilistic models that represent observed data through unobserved (latent) variables. Latent variables are a lower dimensional representation of input data. The latent variables capture the hidden structures in unlabeled datasets and the underlying factors generating the data.

Formally, the latent variable models model the joint distribution $p(x,z)=p(x|z)p(z)$, where x is the observed data, z is the latent variable, $p(x|z)$ is the conditional distribution, and $p(z)$ is a prior (for example, Gaussian). These models infer the posterior $p(z|x)$, using techniques such as variational inference or expectation-maximization, to learn representations of data or to generate data. That is, the latent variable models assume that data $x \in R^n$ is generated from latent variables $z \in R^m$, typically with $m<n$, via a conditional distribution $p(x|z)$). The joint distribution is expressed as $p(x,z)=p(x|z)p(z)$, with a prior $p(z)$, often a standard Gaussian $N(0,I)$. Inference requires estimating the posterior $p(z|x)$, which is typically intractable. Variational inference approximates $p(z|x)$ with a parameterized distribution $q(z|x)$, thus optimizing parameters to maximize the likelihood of the observed data.

In unsupervised learning, latent variable models include variational autoencoders, Gaussian mixture models, and hidden Markov models. These can be used for dimensionality reduction, clustering, and generative tasks. Variational Autoencoders (VAEs) represent a key implementation of the latent variable models, extending the autoencoder architecture with probabilistic modeling for generative tasks. *Figure 6.1* shows the general schematic of latent space models in action:

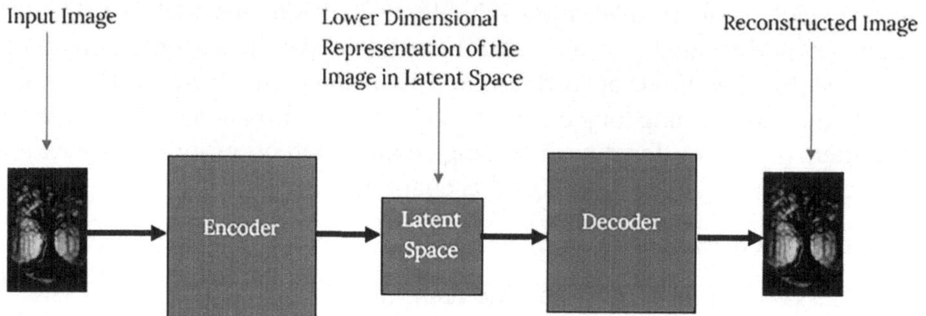

Figure 6.1: *General Schematic of Latent Space Models*

Variational Autoencoders

A **Variational Autoencoder (VAE)** is a deep learning-based latent variable model used in unsupervised learning to learn probabilistic representations of data and perform generative tasks. It extends the autoencoder architecture by imposing a probabilistic structure on the latent space, modeling the joint distribution $p(x,z)=p(x|z)p(z)$, where x is the observed data, z is the latent variable, and $p(z)$ is a prior (typically a standard Gaussian, $N(0,I)$.

VAEs approximate the intractable posterior $p(z|x)$ with a variational distribution $q(z|x)$, optimized to maximize the evidence lower bound (ELBO), which balances data reconstruction and latent space regularization. VAEs are applied in image generation, data imputation, and representation learning.

$$\mathcal{L} = E_{q(z|x)}[\log p(x|z)] - D_{\mathrm{KL}}(q(z|x)\|p(z))$$

The architecture of VAE comprises an encoder, which approximates $q(z|x)$ by outputting parameters (mean and variance) of a Gaussian distribution, and a decoder, which models $p(x|z)$ to reconstruct or generate data. Unlike standard autoencoders, VAEs impose a probabilistic latent space, thereby enabling sampling for generative tasks. The training objective maximizes the Evidence Lower Bound (ELBO):

ELBO objective is used to maximize the log-likelihood of the observed data **log(p(x))** in VAEs, where $x \in R^n$ represents the observed data. Since directly computing **p(x) = ∫p(x|z)p(z)dz** is intractable due to the integration over latent variables $z \in R^m$, VAE uses variational inference to approximate the posterior **p(z|x)** with a tractable distribution **q(z|x)** which is typically a Gaussian distribution. The ELBO provides a lower bound on **log(p(x))**, which the VAE optimizes by maximizing the preceding loss function.

The ELBO consists of two terms: Reconstruction Term and KL-Divergence Term, which are explained as follows:

$$E_{q(z|x)}[\log p(x|z)]$$

- **Reconstruction Term**

  The reconstruction term encourages the VAE to accurately reconstruct the input data by maximizing the expected log-likelihood of x given the latent variable z. The decoder models **p(x|z)**, the probability of generating x from z. The expectation is approximated by sampling **z ~ q(z|x)** using the reparameterization trick **(z =** $\mu + \sigma \odot \epsilon$, where ϵ~**N(0,I))** and computing **log(p(x|z))**.

$$D_{\mathrm{KL}}(q(z|x)\|p(z))$$

- **K-L Divergence Term**

  Kullback-Leibler (KL)-Divergence term regularizes the variational distribution **q(z|x)** to be close to the prior distribution **p(z)** which is typically a Gaussian **N(0,1)**. The Kullback-Leibler (KL) divergence measures the difference between the probability distributions, in this case **q(z}x)** and **p(z)**. **q(z|x)** is the encoder's approximation of the posterior, and **p(z)** is the prior. Minimizing this term ensures that the latent space is structured and enables sampling from **p(z)** for generative tasks. This term enforces a smooth, continuous latent space, preventing overfitting, and allows meaningful interpolation or generation, for example, sampling **z ~ p(z)** to create new images.

The reconstruction term encourages accurate data reconstruction, while the KL-divergence regularizes **q(z|x)** to align with **p(z)**. The reparameterization trick, where $z=\mu+\sigma\odot\epsilon$ with ϵ~**N(0,I)**, ensures differentiable sampling.

Applications of VAEs

VAEs are applied in image generation, data imputation, and representation learning. For example, in image processing, VAEs generate new samples by sampling from the latent space, complementing autoencoders' capabilities. Variants, such as β-VAEs, adjust the KL-divergence weight to enhance generative quality or disentangle latent representations.

Figure 6.2 shows the Python implementation of a variational autoencoder network for the reconstruction of digits from the MNIST dataset. The encoder outputs mean and log-variance for a 32-dimensional latent space, and the decoder reconstructs the image. This code trains a VAE to model MNIST digits, optimizing the ELBO, balancing reconstruction and KL-divergence losses, and visualizes generated samples.

```
import torch
import torch.nn as nn
import torch.optim as optim
from torchvision import datasets, transforms
import matplotlib.pyplot as plt
import numpy as np
# Load and preprocess MNIST dataset
transform = transforms.Compose([transforms.ToTensor()])
train_dataset = datasets.MNIST(root='./data', train=True, download=True, transform=transform)
test_dataset = datasets.MNIST(root='./data', train=False, download=True, transform=transform)
train_loader = torch.utils.data.DataLoader(train_dataset, batch_size=128, shuffle=True)
test_loader = torch.utils.data.DataLoader(test_dataset, batch_size=128, shuffle=False)
# Define VAE model
class VAE(nn.Module):
    def __init__(self):
        super(VAE, self).__init__()
        self.encoder = nn.Sequential(nn.Linear(784, 128),nn.ReLU())
        self.fc_mu = nn.Linear(128, 32)  # Mean of latent space
        self.fc_logvar = nn.Linear(128, 32)  # Log-variance of latent space
        self.decoder = nn.Sequential(nn.Linear(32, 128),nn.ReLU(),nn.Linear(128, 784),nn.Sigmoid())
    def encode(self, x):
        x = x.view(-1, 784)
        h = self.encoder(x)
        return self.fc_mu(h), self.fc_logvar(h)
    def reparameterize(self, mu, logvar):
        std = torch.exp(0.5 * logvar)
        eps = torch.randn_like(std)
        return mu + eps * std
    def decode(self, z):
        return self.decoder(z)
    def forward(self, x):
        mu, logvar = self.encode(x)
        z = self.reparameterize(mu, logvar)
        x_prime = self.decode(z)
        return x_prime, mu, logvar
# Loss function
def vae_loss(reconstructed, x, mu, logvar):
    recon_loss = nn.functional.binary_cross_entropy(reconstructed, x.view(-1, 784), reduction='sum')
    kl_div = -0.5 * torch.sum(1 + logvar - mu.pow(2) - logvar.exp())
    return recon_loss + kl_div
# Initialize model, optimizer
model = VAE()
optimizer = optim.Adam(model.parameters(), lr=0.001)
# Train the VAE
num_epochs = 10
model.train()
for epoch in range(num_epochs):
    total_loss = 0
    for data in train_loader:
        img, _ = data
        optimizer.zero_grad()
        recon, mu, logvar = model(img)
        loss = vae_loss(recon, img, mu, logvar)
        loss.backward()
        optimizer.step()
        total_loss += loss.item()
    avg_loss = total_loss / len(train_loader.dataset)
    print(f'Epoch [{epoch+1}/{num_epochs}], Average Loss: {avg_loss:.6f}')
# Generate and visualize samples
model.eval()
with torch.no_grad():
    z = torch.randn(10, 32)  # Sample from standard normal
    generated = model.decode(z)
# Visualize generated images
plt.figure(figsize=(20, 2))
for i in range(10):
    ax = plt.subplot(1, 10, i + 1)
    plt.imshow(generated[i].reshape(28, 28), cmap='gray')
    plt.title('Generated')
    ax.axis('off')
plt.show()
```

Figure 6.2: *Python Implementation of VAE for Image Reconstruction*

Figure 6.3 shows the output of the preceding code. It shows the images of the reconstructed digits from the representations in the latent space. We can see that the reconstructed images closely resemble the original digit images.

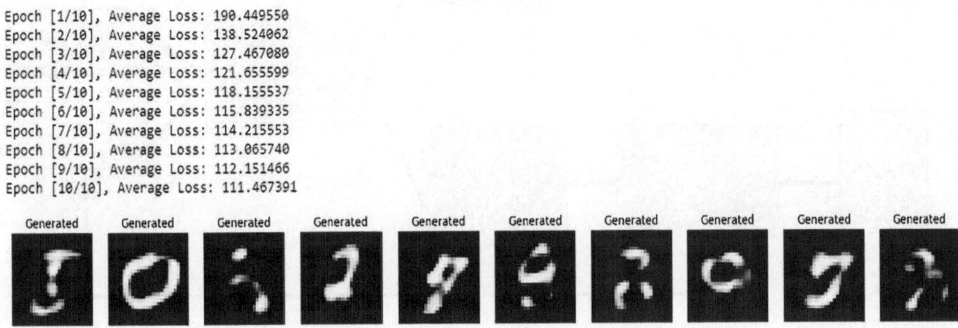

Figure 6.3: *Output of* VAE Code

Next, we will learn about the Generative Adversarial Networks (GANs) model for unsupervised learning.

Generative Adversarial Networks

Generative Adversarial Networks (GANs) are a deep unsupervised learning framework designed to generate realistic data by training two neural networks–a generator and a discriminator–in an adversarial manner. The generator produces synthetic data from random noise, aiming to mimic the true data distribution, while the discriminator evaluates whether inputs are real (from the dataset) or fake (from the generator). Through a min-max optimization process, GANs learn to model the implicit data distribution without explicit likelihood estimation, thus enabling applications such as image generation, data augmentation, and style transfer in an unsupervised manner.

Unsupervised learning aims to extract meaningful patterns and representations from unlabeled data, enabling models to learn underlying structures without explicit supervision. Deep neural networks such as autoencoders, Variational Autoencoders (VAEs), and Generative Adversarial Networks (GANs) leverage unlabeled datasets to model data distributions. An important application of this unsupervised data modeling is Generative tasks. Generative tasks involve creating new data samples that resemble the training distribution (for example, generating realistic images or text).

Architecture of a GAN

The architecture of a GAN consists of two neural networks - a generator and a discriminator trained adversarially to model the data distribution from unlabeled data. *Figure* 6.4 shows this architecture:

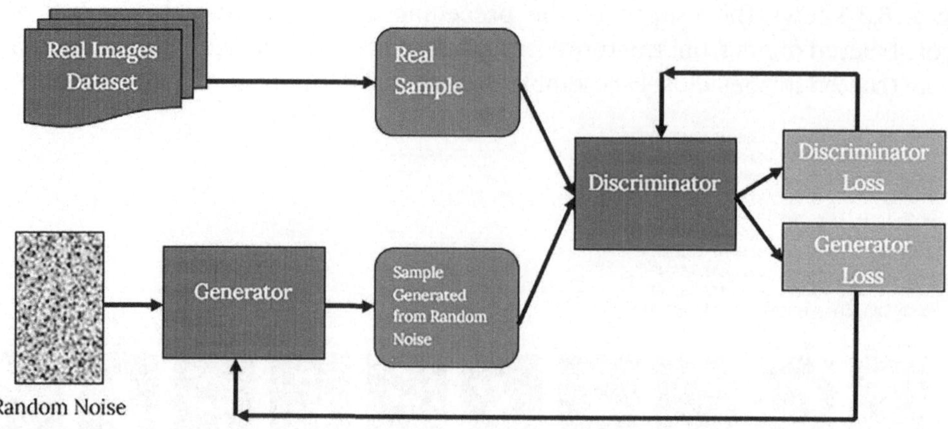

Figure 6.4: *Architecture of a Generative Adversarial Network*

Generator

The generator neural network comprises multiple neural network layers, typically fully connected or convolutional, with non-linear activations (for example, ReLU, LeakyReLU) to model complex transformations. The output layer's activation depends on the data type (for example, **`sigmoid`** for **`[0,1]`** pixel values, **`tanh`** for normalized images). The generator maps a random noise vector $z \in R^m$, sampled from a simple prior distribution **`p(z)`** (for example, standard Gaussian **`N(0,I)`** or uniform distribution) to a synthetic data point $G(z) \in R^n$ that mimics the true data distribution $p_{data}(x)$. The generator learns to produce data that "fools" the discriminator, iteratively improving to approximate $p_{data}(x)$.

For example, for MNIST images (**`n=784`**, **`28x28`** pixels), the generator might use fully connected layers (for example, **`100 → 256 → 512 → 784`**) or convolutional layers (in variants like DCGANs) transforming a 100-dimensional noise vector **`z`** into a 784-dimensional image.

Discriminator

The discriminator also consists of multiple neural network layers, typically fully connected or convolutional, with non-linear activations (for example, LeakyReLU) just like the generator. The final layer uses a sigmoid activation to produce a scalar probability. The discriminator evaluates whether an input $x \in R^n$ is real (from the true dataset, **`x~p data (x)`**) or fake (from the generator, **`x=G(z)`**), outputting a probability **`D(x)∈[0,1]`** where **`D(x)≈1`** for real data and **`D(x)≈0`** for fake data. The discriminator acts as a critic, improving its ability to distinguish real data from synthetic data, and pushing the generator to produce more realistic outputs. For example, for MNIST handwritten digit images, the discriminator might use layers (**`784 → 512 → 256 → 1`**) or convolutional layers, taking a 784-dimensional image and outputting a single probability score.

Adversarial Training

Adversarial training in the context of Generative Adversarial Networks (GANs) is the process of simultaneously training–the generator and the discriminator–in a competitive, zero-sum game manner to model the data distribution. The generator creates synthetic data **G(z)** from random noise **z ~ p(z)**, attempting to "fool" the discriminator. The discriminator then evaluates inputs and distinguishes real data $x \sim p_{data}$**(x)** from fake data **G(z)**, outputting a probability **D(x)**. The training objective optimized the min-max loss function which is formalized as:

$$\min_G \max_D V(D, G) = \mathbb{E}_{x \sim p_{\text{data}}(x)}[\log D(x)] + \mathbb{E}_{z \sim p_z(z)}[\log(1 - D(G(z)))]$$

Where,

G is the Generator.

D is the Discriminator.

$x \sim p_{data}$ is the real data samples.

$z \sim p_z$ is the Latent noise vector.

G(z) is the fake data generated from noise.

D(x) is the probability that x is real.

D(G(z)) is the probability that the generated data is real.

The discriminator (**D**) maximizes the **log(D(x) + log(1-D(G(z)))** to correctly classify real versus fake data. The generator (**G**) minimizes the discriminator's success in identifying fake data, that is **log(1-D(G(z)))**. It tries to trick the discriminator into thinking that **G(z)** is real.

The training process alternates updates. The discriminator is updated using real data x and fake data **G(z)**, and then the generator is updated using the discriminator's feedback on **G(z)**. This alternating update to the discriminator and the generator reaches equilibrium when the generator produces data that is indistinguishable from real data and the discriminator cannot differentiate. That is, **D(G(z)) ≈ 0.5** and **D(x) ≈ D(G(z))**. The discriminator loss is used to update the weights of the discriminator neural network using back propagation and the generator loss is fed back to the generator neural network to update its weights.

The generator and discriminator can use various architectures (for example, convolutional for images, recurrent for sequences), making GANs adaptable to different data types.

Challenges in GAN Training:

- **Mode Collapse**: Mode collapse occurs when the generator produces a limited variety of output and captures only a few modes (subsets) of the true data distribution $p_{data}(x)$. Instead of generating diverse samples, the generator repeatedly outputs similar data points. This reduces the generative quality, as the model fails to represent the full diversity of the dataset. For example, in MNIST, the generator might produce only digits resembling "1" and "7," ignoring other classes. Techniques such as minibatch discrimination feature matching or variants such as Wasserstein GANs (WGANs) to overcome the mode collapse challenge.

- **Training Instability**: Training instability refers to the difficulty in achieving a stable equilibrium between the generator and discriminator. The loss keeps oscillating or diverging instead of reaching a convergence. If the discriminator becomes too strong, it perfectly distinguishes real and fake data, providing no useful gradients for the generator. If a discriminator is too weak, it is easily fooled, halting the improvement of GAN. This can result in poor-quality generated samples or failure to converge. The non-convex nature of the min-max objective, coupled with differing learning rates or capacities of the generator and discriminator, disrupts balanced training. To reduce the training instability, careful tuning of hyperparameters such as learning rates, gradient clipping, label smoothing or alternative loss functions may be used.

GAN Variants

There are three prominent variants of GAN architecture to overcome the training challenges of original GANs. We have explained them as follows:

- **Deep Convolutional GANs (DCGANs):** Deep Convolutional GANs (DCGANs) enhance standard GANs by incorporating Convolutional Neural Network (CNN) layers in both the generator and discriminator, thereby leveraging spatial hierarchies in data to improve image generation quality. The generator transforms a noise vector $z \in R^m$ (for example, 100-dimensional) into an image using transposed convolutional layers (also called deconvolutional layers). These layers upsample low-dimensional features into high-resolution images, while capturing spatial patterns such as edges or textures. The discriminator processes input images (real or fake) using convolutional layers to extract spatial features, followed by pooling or strided convolutions to reduce dimensionality, outputting a probability score. For example, in case of MNIST handwritten digits images (28x28 grayscale images), the generator might use transposed convolutions (for example, **100 → 4x4x64 → 7x7x32 → 28x28x1**) with ReLU activations, while the discriminator uses convolutions (for example, **28x28x1 → 14x14x32 → 7x7x64 → 1**) with LeakyReLU.

  The advantage of using convolutional layers is that they exploit spatial correlations, producing sharper, more realistic images compared to fully connected layers and enabling scalability to higher-resolution images.

- **Wasserstein GANs (WGANs):** Wasserstein GANs (WGANs) introduce a Wasserstein distance-based loss (also called Earth Mover's distance) to stabilize GAN training and mitigate issues such as mode collapse and training instability. The discriminator (called a critic in WGANs) outputs a scalar score rather than a probability, and the loss is the difference in expected scores for real and fake data. A WGAN stabilizes training by providing meaningful gradients even when real and fake data distributions are far apart, reducing the mode collapse challenge. It improves the convergence rate in training and offers a loss metric correlated with sample quality helping with the evaluation of the training. However, WGANs require additional constraints like weight clipping, thereby increasing the computational complexity of the model.
- **Conditional GANs:** Conditional GANs extend GANs by generating data conditioned on labels or attributes, allowing controlled synthesis of specific data types. Both the generator and discriminator receive additional input such as class labels y (for example, digit class in MNIST) or attributes (for example, style, color). The generator produces `G(z, y)`, and the discriminator evaluates `D(x, y)`, ensuring the generated data aligns with the condition. The min-max loss function is modified accordingly. For example, for the MNIST dataset, the generator might take a noise vector **z** and a label **y=5** to generate a "5" digit, while the discriminator checks if the input image matches the label "5", and is real.

Role of GANS in Modelling Implicit Data Distribution

GANs play an important role in modeling implicit data distribution in deep unsupervised learning by learning to generate data that mimics the true distribution, without explicitly defining a likelihood function. The generator produces synthetic data from random noise, and through adversarial training with the discriminator, it implicitly approximates the data distribution $p_{data}(x)$ by optimizing the min-max objective. This approach does not need a predefined probabilistic model, further allowing GANs to capture complex, high-dimensional distributions in data. However, this approach can suffer from training instability.

GANs versus VAEs

In contrast to implicit data modeling in GANs, VAEs use an explicit likelihood approach to model the data distribution through a probabilistic framework. VAEs define a joint distribution $p(x,z) = p(x|z)p(z)$ with a prior $p(z)$ (usually a Gaussian distribution) and a conditional likelihood $p(x|z)$ while maximizing ELBO. This explicit modeling enabled VAEs to capture likelihoods and perform inference (for example, reconstruct data from latent vectors) but limits their ability to generate sharp, high-quality samples compared to GANS. While VAEs provide a structured latent space for tasks like interpolation, GANs can produce realistic outputs by implicitly learning the data distribution through adversarial competition.

Applications of GANs in Unsupervised Learning:

- **Image Generation**: GANs generate realistic images by learning the distribution of an unlabeled image dataset, producing synthetic samples that resemble the training data. This application enables creative tasks (for example, generating artwork) and data synthesis for domains with limited data, leveraging unlabeled images without requiring annotations.
- **Data Augmentation**: GANs augment datasets by generating additional synthetic samples, enhancing the training of downstream machine learning models in unsupervised or semi-supervised settings. Data augmentation mitigates overfitting and addresses data scarcity by exploiting the implicit distribution learned from unlabeled data.
- **Style Transfer and Domain Adaptation**: GANs facilitate style transfer by transforming data from one domain to another (for example, converting photos to paintings) and support domain adaptation by aligning distributions across datasets. These tasks enable unsupervised learning to adapt models to new domains or create visually compelling outputs.
- **Anomaly Detection**: GANs identify anomalies in unlabeled data by modeling the normal data distribution and flagging samples that deviate significantly. This application leverages GANs' ability to capture complex distribution without labels, supporting tasks like quality control or fraud detection.
- **Representation Learning**: GANs learn meaningful latent representations in their generator's latent space, which is useful for downstream tasks like clustering and visualization.

Python Implementation of DCGAN on MNIST Dataset for Image Generation

The Python code shown in *Figures 6.5a, 6.5b, 6.5c, and 6.5d* implements a Deep Convolutional GAN (DCGAN) for generating images resembling the MNIST handwritten digits dataset from PyTorch. The generator uses transposed convolutional layers to map 100-dimensional noise to 64x64 images, and the discriminator employs convolutional layers to classify images as real or fake. The code trains the DCGAN, prints training losses, and visualizes generated digits. We have used the PyTorch library to implement DCGAN. You will need to install the required libraries using pip or conda package managers. If you are using pip, use the following command for installation: `pip install torch torchvision matplotlib`

A portion of the code shown in *Figure 6.5a* imports the required libraries, loads and transforms the MNIST dataset built in PyTorch datasets and defines the Generator component of the DCGAN:

```python
import torch
import torch.nn as nn
import torch.optim as optim
from torchvision import datasets, transforms
import matplotlib.pyplot as plt
import numpy as np

# Set random seed for reproducibility
torch.manual_seed(42)

# Load and preprocess MNIST dataset
transform = transforms.Compose([
    transforms.ToTensor(),
    transforms.Normalize((0.5,), (0.5,))  # Normalize to [-1, 1]
])
train_dataset = datasets.MNIST(root='./data', train=True, download=True,
                               transform=transform)
train_loader = torch.utils.data.DataLoader(train_dataset, batch_size=64,
                                           shuffle=True)

# Define Generator
class Generator(nn.Module):
    def __init__(self):
        super(Generator, self).__init__()
        self.model = nn.Sequential(
            # Input: z [batch, 100, 1, 1]
            nn.ConvTranspose2d(100, 128, 7, 1, 0, bias=False),
            nn.BatchNorm2d(128),
            nn.ReLU(True),
            # State: [batch, 128, 7, 7]
            nn.ConvTranspose2d(128, 64, 4, 2, 1, bias=False),
            nn.BatchNorm2d(64),
            nn.ReLU(True),
            # State: [batch, 64, 14, 14]
            nn.ConvTranspose2d(64, 1, 4, 2, 1, bias=False),
            nn.Tanh()  # Output: [batch, 1, 28, 28] in [-1, 1]
        )

    def forward(self, z):
        z = z.view(-1, 100, 1, 1)  # Reshape noise to [batch, 100, 1, 1]
        return self.model(z)
```

Figure 6.5a: *Python Code for DCGAN Generator*

Figure 6.5b shows the next portion of Python code that implements the Discriminator component of our DCGAN and initializes the generator as well as discriminator classes:

```
# Define Discriminator
class Discriminator(nn.Module):
    def __init__(self):
        super(Discriminator, self).__init__()
        self.model = nn.Sequential(
            # Input: [batch, 1, 28, 28]
            nn.Conv2d(1, 64, 4, 2, 1, bias=False),
            nn.LeakyReLU(0.2, inplace=True),
            # State: [batch, 64, 14, 14]
            nn.Conv2d(64, 128, 4, 2, 1, bias=False),
            nn.BatchNorm2d(128),
            nn.LeakyReLU(0.2, inplace=True),
            # State: [batch, 128, 7, 7]
            nn.Conv2d(128, 1, 7, 1, 0, bias=False),
            nn.Sigmoid()  # Output: [batch, 1, 1, 1]
        )

    def forward(self, x):
        return self.model(x).view(-1, 1)  # Flatten to [batch, 1]

# Initialize models, loss, and optimizers
generator = Generator()
discriminator = Discriminator()
criterion = nn.BCELoss()
g_optimizer = optim.Adam(generator.parameters(), lr=0.0002,
                         betas=(0.5, 0.999))
d_optimizer = optim.Adam(discriminator.parameters(), lr=0.0002,
                         betas=(0.5, 0.999))

# Training parameters
num_epochs = 20
z_dim = 100

```

Figure 6.5b: *Python Code for DCGAN Discriminator*

Figure 6.5c shows the portion of our Python code that runs the training for the discriminator and the generator as well as samples some images from the generator. It prints the training loss for the generator and the discriminator. As shown in *Figure* 6.5*b*, our training will run for 20 epochs, and **`z`** will have **`100`** dimensions.

```
# Train the DCGAN
for epoch in range(num_epochs):
    d_loss_total = 0
    g_loss_total = 0
    for data in train_loader:
        real_imgs, _ = data
        batch_size = real_imgs.size(0)

        # Labels
        real_labels = torch.ones(batch_size, 1)
        fake_labels = torch.zeros(batch_size, 1)

        # Train Discriminator
        d_optimizer.zero_grad()
        real_outputs = discriminator(real_imgs)
        d_real_loss = criterion(real_outputs, real_labels)
        z = torch.randn(batch_size, z_dim)
        fake_imgs = generator(z)
        fake_outputs = discriminator(fake_imgs.detach())
        d_fake_loss = criterion(fake_outputs, fake_labels)
        d_loss = d_real_loss + d_fake_loss
        d_loss.backward()
        d_optimizer.step()
        d_loss_total += d_loss.item()

        # Train Generator
        g_optimizer.zero_grad()
        fake_outputs = discriminator(fake_imgs)
        g_loss = criterion(fake_outputs, real_labels)#Trick discriminator
        g_loss.backward()
        g_optimizer.step()
        g_loss_total += g_loss.item()

    # Print average losses
    avg_d_loss = d_loss_total / len(train_loader)
    avg_g_loss = g_loss_total / len(train_loader)
    print(f'Epoch [{epoch+1}/{num_epochs}], D Loss: {avg_d_loss:.4f},
          G Loss: {avg_g_loss:.4f}')

```

Figure 6.5c: *Python Code for DCGAN Training*

Figure 6.5d shows the portion of DCGAN code that uses a generator to generate images and visualizes the images sampled from the generator:

```python

# Generate and visualize samples
generator.eval()
with torch.no_grad():
    z = torch.randn(10, z_dim)
    generated_imgs = generator(z)

# Visualize generated images
plt.figure(figsize=(20, 2))
for i in range(10):
    ax = plt.subplot(1, 10, i + 1)
    # Denormalize from [-1, 1] to [0, 1] for display
    img = (generated_imgs[i].squeeze() + 1) / 2
    plt.imshow(img, cmap='gray')
    plt.title('Generated')
    ax.axis('off')
plt.show()
```

Figure 6.5d: *Python Code for Visualization of Images Generated by DCGAN*

To run this DCGAN, you need to type the entire code shown in *Figures 6.5a* to *6.5d* in a single Python script. It may take a long time to finish execution depending on your computer's computational resources.

Figure 6.6 shows the output of the preceding code—epoch-wise discriminator and generator loss and the images generated by the DCGAN. To further improve the quality of these images, you can try increasing the number of training epochs and increasing the number of layers in DCGAN components.

```
Epoch [1/20], D Loss: 0.4592, G Loss: 2.7526
Epoch [2/20], D Loss: 0.4741, G Loss: 2.1291
Epoch [3/20], D Loss: 0.5050, G Loss: 2.1544
Epoch [4/20], D Loss: 0.5580, G Loss: 2.0885
Epoch [5/20], D Loss: 0.5726, G Loss: 2.0912
Epoch [6/20], D Loss: 0.5533, G Loss: 2.1689
Epoch [7/20], D Loss: 0.5678, G Loss: 2.2041
Epoch [8/20], D Loss: 0.5491, G Loss: 2.2328
Epoch [9/20], D Loss: 0.5415, G Loss: 2.3058
Epoch [10/20], D Loss: 0.5455, G Loss: 2.3243
Epoch [11/20], D Loss: 0.5212, G Loss: 2.3914
Epoch [12/20], D Loss: 0.5138, G Loss: 2.4360
Epoch [13/20], D Loss: 0.5023, G Loss: 2.4925
Epoch [14/20], D Loss: 0.4898, G Loss: 2.5361
Epoch [15/20], D Loss: 0.4881, G Loss: 2.5597
Epoch [16/20], D Loss: 0.4742, G Loss: 2.6180
Epoch [17/20], D Loss: 0.4741, G Loss: 2.6378
Epoch [18/20], D Loss: 0.4630, G Loss: 2.6709
Epoch [19/20], D Loss: 0.4583, G Loss: 2.7062
Epoch [20/20], D Loss: 0.4426, G Loss: 2.7532
```

Figure 6.6: *Output of DCGAN Implementation*

We will learn about autoregressive models next.

Autoregressive Models

Autoregression is a concept borrowed from time series models where the values of a variable at previous time steps are used to predict its value at the current time step. For example, the temperature of a room at the current time can be predicted by learning a pattern from values of the temperature at previous hours.

Autoregressive models are a class of deep (deep neural networks) unsupervised learning models that implement the autoregressive principle. The autoregressive principle involves modeling the joint probability distribution of data `p(x)`, where `x = [x1, x2, …., xn]` represents a data point (for example, an image's pixels or words in a text sequence), by factorizing it into a product of conditional probabilities as shown in the following equation:

$$p(\mathbf{x}) = \prod_{i=1}^{n} p(x_i | x_1, x_2, \ldots, x_{i-1}) = \prod_{i=1}^{n} p(x_i | \mathbf{x}_{<i})$$

Here with each data dimension xi (each pixel, word or feature) is conditioned on all previous dimensions $x_{1:i-1} = [x_1, x_2, \ldots, x_{i-1}]$, capturing sequential dependencies in the data. The factorization uses the chain rule of probability, assuming an ordering (for example, raster scan for images, left-to-right for text). This formula does not assume conditional independence between the terms x_i and its previous terms.

In an autoregressive generative model using deep neural networks (for example, PixelCNN or RNN, Transformer-based Models), the conditionals are specified as parameterized functions with a fixed number of parameters. We assume the conditional distribution $p_{\theta i}$ `(xi|x<i) = Bern(fi(x1,x2,…,xi-1))` where θ_i denotes the set of parameters used to specify the mean function `fi: {0,1} i-1 -> [0,1]`. The number of parameters of the autoregressive generative model are given by $\Sigma^n_{i=1}|\theta_i$.

General Architectural Principles

Input: A data point $x \in R^n$ (for example, a flattened MNIST image with `n=784` pixels) or structured data (for example, a 28x28x1 image tensor) is the input.

Output: For each dimension `i`, the model outputs parameters of the conditional distribution `p(xi|x1:i-1)`, such as:

- Bernoulli for binary pixels (for example, probability of a pixel being 1)
- Categorical (softmax) for discrete values (for example, 256 grayscale levels)
- Gaussian for continuous values (for example, mean and variance)

Sequential Dependency: The architecture ensures each prediction depends only on prior dimensions, respecting the chosen order (for example, raster scan for images: left-to-right, top-to-bottom).

Neural Network Architectures: Recurrent, convolutional, or transformer-based networks can be used to model complex dependencies, with mechanisms to prevent "future" data leakage.

PixelRNN Architecture

PixelRNN uses recurrent neural networks (RNNs), typically LSTMs, to model long-range sequential dependencies by processing data dimensions one at a time. The input layer accepts the previous dimensions **x1:i-1** or the current pixel's context. For example, for an image from the MNIST dataset, each input is a pixel value (binary or grayscale) at position **i**, with context from prior pixels. Recurrent layers are made up of one or more LSTM layers. These layers process the sequence of pixels in order (for example, row-by-row, column-by-column). Each LSTM cell maintains a hidden state that encodes the context of **x 1:i-1**. For example, for a 28x28 MNIST image, the LSTM processes 784 pixels sequentially, with hidden state size (for example, 256 units) capturing dependencies. The output layer is a fully connected layer that maps the LSTM's hidden state to the parameters of **p(xi|x1:i-1)**. For binary images, the output may be Sigmoid activations as a probability with Bernoulli distribution, for grayscale images, the output may be SoftMax probabilities for 256 classes. In step i, the LSTM takes the previous pixel values (or their embeddings) and updates its hidden state. The output layer predicts **p(xi|x1:i-1)**, therby ensuring no future pixels are used. For example, for the MNIST images, the model predicts each pixel's value given all pixels above and to the left in raster order.

The PixelRNN model captures long-range dependencies across the images and is flexible enough to be applied to any sequential data. However, sequential processing is slow for training and generation and incurs high computational costs.

PixelCNN Architecture

PixelCNN uses convolutional neural networks (CNNs) with masked convolutions to model conditional distributions, enabling parallel processing within each layer for faster training compared to PixelRNN. The input layer is a 2D image tensor (for example it is a 28 * 28 *1 tensor for images in the MNIST dataset), where pixels are processed in raster order. Masked convolutional layers are used to ensure each pixel's prediction depends only on prior pixels (above and to the left of the current pixel). Mask Type A excludes the current pixel from the receptive field used in the first layer to prevent self-dependency. Mask Type B includes the current pixel used in subsequent layers to deeper context. For example, a 3 * 3 convolution with Mask B sets weights to zero for pixels below or to the right of the current pixel while processing an image. Intermediate layers in a PixelCNN are stacked convolutional layers with ReLU activations often with residual connections for deeper models. There are typically 64 to 128 channels per layer to capture complex features. The output layer is a 1 * 1 convolution that maps features to the parameters of **`p(xi|x1:i-1)`**. The output layer may output Sigmoid probabilities for binary images and SoftMax probabilities for grayscale images.

Each layer applies masked convolutions to compute features for all pixels simultaneously, respecting the autoregressive order. The output predicts **`p(xi|x1:i-1)`** for all pixels in parallel during training. For example, for images in the MNIST dataset, PixelCNN predicts the probability of each pixel's value given prior pixels in the raster order, using spatial context from above and left.

PixelCNN uses parallel computation within layers to speed up training compared to PixelRNN and is effective for spatial data like images due to its convolutional structure. However, PixelCNN has a limited receptive field compared to RNN and the generation is sequential as each pixel is sampled one at a time. With deeper layers or dilated convolutions, the receptive field can be improved.

Both PixelRNN and PixelCNN enforce causality (no future data leakage) via RNN sequencing or masked convolutions, ensuring valid autoregressive factorization. The final layer parameterizes flexible distributions (for example, Bernoulli, categorical, or mixtures), tailored to the data type. Architectures can be extended with deeper layers or larger receptive fields for complex data (for example, high-resolution images, and long text sequences). Training of both models can be optimized via Backpropagation to maximize log-likelihood, using teacher forcing (providing true **`x1:i-1`**) during training.

Transformer-Based Architecture

Transformer-based architectures for Autoregressive language modelling often use a decoder-only transformer (for example, GPT) to model sequential dependencies in text or other sequences, leveraging self-attention for long-range context as seen in Large Language Models (LLMs) such as GPT 4o, Gemini, LLaMa, and so on.

Input is a sequence of tokens (for example, words, subwords, or embeddings). For text, tokens are from a vocabulary (for example, 50,000 subwords). For MNIST (less common), pixels could be treated as a sequence of 784 discrete values. An embedding layer maps each token to a dense vector (for example, 512-1024 dimensions), adding positional encodings to encode sequence order. Transformer layers include a causal self-attention layer, feed-forward network and layer normalization. Each token attends to all the prior tokens (not future ones), ensuring autoregressive property. For token i_1, attention weights compute context from **`x1:i-1`**. Feed-forward network is a per-token dense layer with ReLU or GeLU activations. Layer normalization stabilizes training. It is applied before and after attention and feed-forward blocks. The output layer consists of a fully connected layer with SoftMax activation over the vocabulary predicting **`p(xi|x1:i-1)`** as a categorical distribution.

Applications of Autoregressive Models

- **Image Generation**: Autoregressive models such as PixelCNN generate new images by sequentially sampling pixels according to the learned conditional distributions, producing realistic samples from the data distribution. This enables unsupervised creation of synthetic images, useful for data synthesis or creative applications.
- **Text Generation**: Autoregressive models generate coherent text sequences by modeling the probability of each word or character conditioned on previous ones, leveraging the sequential nature of language. Large language models such as GPT, Gemini, and LLaMa are autoregressive models that generate human-quality text. These models often use the Transformer Architecture of neural networks for text modelling and generation.
- **Data Completion**: Autoregressive models complete missing parts of data (for example, occluded image regions, incomplete text) by predicting missing dimensions based on observed ones.
- **Anomaly Detection**: Autoregressive models identify anomalies by assigning low likelihoods to data points that deviate from the learned distribution, leveraging their explicit likelihood formulation.
- **Representation Learning**: Autoregressive models learn meaningful representations in their intermediate layers, capturing sequential dependencies that can be used for downstream tasks like clustering or visualization.

Autoregressive models play a significant role in generative tasks within deep unsupervised learning by modeling data distribution through sequential conditional probabilities to generate new data samples (for example, images, text) from unlabeled data.

Python Implementation of PixelCNN on MNIST Digits Dataset with PyTorch Library

The code in *Figure* 6.7 implements a simple PixelCNN for binarized MNIST digits. The model used masked convolutional layers to predict each pixel's Bernoulli probability given prior pixels in raster order. The training runs for 15 epochs and the output consists of visualization of the synthetic digits. *Figure 6.7a* shows the importing of libraries, loading of the MNIST dataset, and implementation of MaskedConv2d neural network layers:

```python
## Autoregressive Models: PixelCNN
import torch
import torch.nn as nn
import torch.optim as optim
from torchvision import datasets, transforms
import matplotlib.pyplot as plt
import numpy as np

# Set random seed for reproducibility
torch.manual_seed(42)

# Load and preprocess MNIST dataset (binarized)
transform = transforms.Compose([
    transforms.ToTensor(),
    lambda x: (x > 0.5).float()  # Binarize: pixels > 0.5 become 1, else 0
])
train_dataset = datasets.MNIST(root='./data', train=True, download=True, transform=transform)
train_loader = torch.utils.data.DataLoader(train_dataset, batch_size=64, shuffle=True)

# Define Masked Convolutional Layer
class MaskedConv2d(nn.Conv2d):
    def __init__(self, mask_type, *args, **kwargs):
        super(MaskedConv2d, self).__init__(*args, **kwargs)
        self.mask_type = mask_type
        self.register_buffer('mask', self.weight.data.clone())
        self.apply_mask()

    def apply_mask(self):
        _, _, kH, kW = self.weight.size()
        self.mask.fill_(1)
        if self.mask_type == 'A':
            self.mask[:, :, kH//2, kW//2:] = 0  # Exclude current pixel and right
            self.mask[:, :, kH//2+1:] = 0       # Exclude below
        else:  # Mask B
            self.mask[:, :, kH//2, kW//2+1:] = 0  # Exclude right
            self.mask[:, :, kH//2+1:] = 0         # Exclude below

    def forward(self, x):
        self.weight.data *= self.mask
        return super(MaskedConv2d, self).forward(x)

```

Figure 6.7a: *Python Code for Portions of PixelCNN – MaskedConv2d Layer*

Figure 6.7b shows the implementation of the PixelCNN class with multiple **`MaskedConv2d`** layers, **`Conv2d`** layer and **`Sigmoid`** output layer. It initializes the model, loss function and optimizer. Finally, it runs the training for 15 epochs and computes the average loss as well as prints it.

```
# Define PixelCNN Model
class PixelCNN(nn.Module):
    def __init__(self):
        super(PixelCNN, self).__init__()
        self.layers = nn.Sequential(
            # Mask A for first layer (excludes current pixel)
            MaskedConv2d('A', in_channels=1, out_channels=32, kernel_size=3, padding=1),
            nn.ReLU(),
            # Mask B for subsequent layers
            MaskedConv2d('B', 32, 32, kernel_size=3, padding=1),
            nn.ReLU(),
            MaskedConv2d('B', 32, 32, kernel_size=3, padding=1),
            nn.ReLU(),
            # Output layer: predict Bernoulli probability for each pixel
            nn.Conv2d(32, 1, kernel_size=1),
            nn.Sigmoid()  # Probability of pixel being 1
        )

    def forward(self, x):
        return self.layers(x)

# Initialize model, loss, and optimizer
model = PixelCNN()
criterion = nn.BCELoss()
optimizer = optim.Adam(model.parameters(), lr=0.001)

# Training parameters
num_epochs = 15

# Train PixelCNN
for epoch in range(num_epochs):
    model.train()
    total_loss = 0
    for data, _ in train_loader:
        optimizer.zero_grad()
        outputs = model(data)
        loss = criterion(outputs, data)  # BCE loss for log-likelihood
        loss.backward()
        optimizer.step()
        total_loss += loss.item()

    # Print average loss
    avg_loss = total_loss / len(train_loader)
    print(f'Epoch [{epoch+1}/{num_epochs}], Loss: {avg_loss:.4f}')

```

Figure 6.7b: *PixelCNN Class and Training*

Figure 6.7c shows the code for the generation of images sampled using the Autoregressive approach and the Visualization of these images:

```

# Generate samples
model.eval()
num_samples = 10
samples = torch.zeros(num_samples, 1, 28, 28)
with torch.no_grad():
    for i in range(28):
        for j in range(28):
            out = model(samples)
            probs = out[:, :, i, j]
            samples[:, :, i, j] = torch.bernoulli(probs)

# Visualize generated images
plt.figure(figsize=(20, 2))
for i in range(num_samples):
    ax = plt.subplot(1, num_samples, i + 1)
    plt.imshow(samples[i].squeeze(), cmap='gray')
    plt.title('Generated')
    ax.axis('off')
plt.show()
```

Figure 6.7c: *Image Generation and Visualization Using PixelCNN*

```
Epoch [4/15], Loss: 0.1050
Epoch [5/15], Loss: 0.1048
Epoch [6/15], Loss: 0.1046
Epoch [7/15], Loss: 0.1045
Epoch [8/15], Loss: 0.1043
Epoch [9/15], Loss: 0.1042
Epoch [10/15], Loss: 0.1041
Epoch [11/15], Loss: 0.1040
Epoch [12/15], Loss: 0.1040
Epoch [13/15], Loss: 0.1039
Epoch [14/15], Loss: 0.1038
Epoch [15/15], Loss: 0.1038
```

Figure 6.8: *Shows the Loss for Each Training Epoch and a Visualization of Generated Digit Images*

You can see that since the generated digit images are not very good, the quality can be improved with a greater number of training epochs by using a deeper architecture of the neural network layers.

Flow Models

Flow-based models, also known as normalizing flows, are deep unsupervised learning models that use invertible neural networks to transform a complex data distribution (for example, MNIST images) into a simple, tractable distribution (for example, standard normal, `N(0,I)` distribution). By ensuring the transformation is bijective (invertible), these models compute the exact log-likelihood of the data thus enabling both generative tasks (for example, sampling new images) and analytical tasks (for example, density estimation). They are particularly suited for unsupervised learning because they learn from unlabeled data and can model `p(x)` without requiring supervision.

Important Characteristics of Flow-Based Models:

- **Invertible Transformation**: A flow-based model defines a bijective function f:x→z, where `x` is the data (for example, a 28x28 MNIST image) and `z` is a latent variable following a simple distribution (for example, `z~N(0,I)`). The inverse `f`, f^{-1} `:z→x` allows sampling i.e., it allows to generate z from the base distribution and map it to data x. For example, for the MNIST dataset, `f` maps a digit image to a Gaussian latent space and f^{-1} generated a digit from noise.

$$\log p(x) = \log p_z(f(x)) + \log \left| \det \frac{\partial f(x)}{\partial x} \right|$$

- **Exact Likelihood Estimation**: The probability density is computed using the change of variables formula:

  Where `pz` is the base distribution's density (for example a Gaussian distribution) and the determinant term is the Jacobian determinant of the transformation. This explicit likelihood contrasts with the implicit modelling in GANs and approximate likelihood calculation (ELBO) in VAEs.

- **Invertible Neural Networks Architecture**: Flow-based models use invertible neural networks composed of layers designed to be invertible or bijective with tractable Jacobians. Common architectures of these layers include:
  - **Coupling Layers,** which split data into parts, while applying scale and translation to one part of data conditioned on the other part. For example, Real-valued Non-Volume Preserving (RealNVP) architecture.
  - **Autoregressive Flows,** which model dependencies sequentially like autoregressive models except that these are invertible.
  - **Glow Architecture,** which extends Coupling Layers architecture with additional normalization and invertible 1x1 convolutions.

Working of Flow-Based Models

The working of the Flow-based models consists of the following steps:

1. **Forward Pass**: During the forward pass, the data `x` is transformed into a latent space `z` using a transformation `f(x)`. That is `z = f(x)`, computing the log-likelihood using the change of variables formula.

2. **Inverse Pass**: During this pass, the sample `z ~ N(0,1)` is chosen and `x = f⁻¹(z)` is computed to generate new data.

3. **Training**: The objective of training Flow-based models is to maximize the log-likelihood **`log p(x)`**, equivalent to minimizing the negative log-likelihood loss given by the following equation:

$$\mathcal{L} = -E[\log p(x)] = -E\left[\log p_z(f(x)) + \log\left|\det \frac{\partial f(x)}{\partial x}\right|\right]$$

For example, for a binarized MNIST digit image, the RealNVP flow-based model applies a series of coupling layers to map the 28*28-pixel image value to a Gaussian, computing the likelihood for training and sampling new digits via the inverse.

Applications of Flow-Based Models in Unsupervised Learning:

- **Image Generation**: Flow-based models generate new images by sampling from the base distribution and applying the inverse transformation producing realistic images from the learned data distribution.
- **Density Estimation**: Flow-based models compute the exact log-likelihood **`log p(x)`** for any data point, enabling precise density estimation to assess how well data fits the learned distribution.
- **Data Completion**: Flow-based models infer missing parts of data (for example, occluded image regions) by optimizing the likelihood over observed dimensions, leveraging their invertible structure.
- **Representation Learning**: Flow-based models learn meaningful latent representations in their latent space **`z=f(x)`**, which capture the data's inherent structure for downstream tasks like clustering or visualization.
- **Data Augmentation**: Flow-based models generate synthetic data samples to augment training sets, improving the robustness of downstream tasks without requiring additional labeled data.

Diffusion Models

Diffusion models are a powerful class of deep unsupervised learning models that generate data by learning to reverse a process of gradually adding noise to unlabeled data. Unlike Generative Adversarial Networks (GANs), which implicitly model the data distribution, or autoregressive models, which sequentially predict data points, diffusion models use explicit likelihood-based generation just like Variational Autoencoders (VAEs), but diffusion models enable the generation of higher-quality data samples. By modeling the data distribution **p(x)**, diffusion models can be used for generative tasks such as image synthesis, as well as analytical tasks, such as data denoising.

Working of Diffusion Models

Diffusion models operate through two processes: a forward process that adds noise to data and a reverse process that learns to denoise it. In the forward process, a data point x_0 (for example, a 28x28 MNIST image) is incrementally corrupted with Gaussian noise over **T** steps, producing a sequence **x1,x2,…,xT**, where **xT** approximates pure noise **(N(0,I))**. This is defined by a Markov chain with variance schedule βt. The reverse process, which is parameterized by a neural network, learns the conditional distributions p_θ**(xt-1 |xt)**, reconstructing x_0 from noise. The training of a Denoising Diffusion Probabilistic Model (DDPM) minimizes the denoising loss given by the following equation:

$$\mathcal{L}_{\text{simple}} = \mathbb{E}_{\mathbf{x}_0,\epsilon,t}\left[\left\|\epsilon - \epsilon_\theta(\mathbf{x}_t, t)\right\|^2\right]$$

Where,

x_0 is the original clean data sample.

x_t is the noisy data at timestep t, generated by adding noise ϵ.

ϵ is the Gaussian noise sampled from **N(0,I)**.

ϵ_θ is the model's prediction of the noise.

t is the timestep (usually sampled uniformly from **1** to **T**).

This loss function trains the model ϵθ to predict the noise added at each step, which is important for learning the denoising (reverse) process.

Architecture and Training

Diffusion models typically use a **U-Net** architecture, a convolutional network with downsampling, bottleneck, and upsampling layers, augmented with skip connections to preserve spatial details. The U-Net predicts the noise ϵθ(xt,t) conditioned on the time step t, often via simple embeddings (for example, expanding **t** to match the input). Training involves sampling random time steps **t**, adding noise to data **x0** to form x_t, and optimizing the mean squared error between true and predicted noise.

Applications of Diffusion Models

Diffusion models support various unsupervised learning tasks using their generative and denoising capabilities which are explained as follows:

- **Image Generation**: Generating high-quality realistic images
- **Denoising**: Removing noise from corrupted images, enhancing preprocessing
- **Data Augmentation**: Creating synthetic images for downstream tasks, thus improving classifier robustness
- **Anomaly Detection**: Using likelihood-like scores to identify outlier images

Self-Supervised Learning

Self-Supervised Learning (SSL) is a deep unsupervised learning paradigm that leverages the inherent structure of unlabeled data to create supervisory signals, enabling robust representation learning without manual labels. Unlike autoencoders, which focus on reconstruction or Generative Adversarial Networks (GANs), that prioritize sample generation, SSL trains models on pretext tasks–such as predicting image rotations or contrasting augmented views to learn generalizable features. These features support downstream tasks like classification and clustering, thereby bridging unsupervised and supervised learning.

Mechanism of Self-Supervised Learning

Self-supervised learning generates pseudo-labels from the data itself through carefully designed pretext tasks. For example, in the contrastive learning framework (for example, SimCLR), a model learns to maximize the similarity between two augmented views of the same MNIST digit (for example, rotated and cropped versions) while distinguishing them from views of different digits. The objective is often formulated as a contrastive loss, such as the InfoNCE loss:

$$\mathcal{L} = -E\left[\log \frac{\exp(\mathrm{sim}(z_i, z_j)/\tau)}{\sum_{k=1}^{N} \exp(\mathrm{sim}(z_i, z_k)/\tau)}\right]$$

Where

`zi` and `zj` are representations of two views of the same digit

`sim` is a similarity metric (for example, cosine similarity)

τ is a temperature parameter

the sum is over negative samples

Non-contrastive methods, like BYOL, rely on predicting one view's representation from another without negative samples, while masked image modeling (for example,

MAE) reconstructs masked patches of a digit, which is akin to autoencoders but with transformers. These tasks enable the model to learn invariant and discriminative features from unlabeled data.

Architecture and Training

SSL models typically employ deep neural networks, such as convolutional neural networks (CNNs, for example, ResNet) or Vision Transformers (ViTs), to extract representations. For MNIST, a CNN processes 28x28 images, producing feature vectors (for example, 512-dimensional) that capture digit shapes. Transformers used in methods such as MAE treat images as patch sequences, thereby leveraging self-attention to model global context. The architecture includes:

- **Encoder**: Maps input images to representations (for example, a CNN or ViT encoder).
- **Projection Head**: A small network (for example, MLP) maps representations to a space for pretext task optimization, often discarded post-training.

Training involves optimizing the pretext task's loss (for example, InfoNCE for SimCLR) using backpropagation. Data augmentations such as cropping, flipping, or color jittering are important for creating diverse views and ensuring robust features. Compared to VAEs' likelihood optimization or GANs' adversarial training, SSL focuses on feature invariance, requiring large batches or memory banks for contrastive methods.

Applications of Self-Supervised Learning

Self-supervised learning supports the following unsupervised learning tasks and leverages its learned representations:

- **Representation Learning**: Extracts features from input images for clustering or visualization, enhancing unsupervised analysis
- **Pretraining for Downstream Tasks**: Initializes models for classification or detection with limited labeled data, improving performance in semi-supervised settings
- **Anomaly Detection**: Identifies outlier images (for example, malformed shapes) by comparing representation similarities, supporting quality control
- **Data Augmentation**: Generates augmented views of digits to enrich training sets to complement synthetic samples from generative models

These applications highlight SSL's versatility, along with advanced methods such as DINO and MAE enabling state-of-the-art performance.

Energy-Based Models

Energy-Based Models (EBMs) are a class of deep unsupervised learning models that represent the data distribution `p(x)` by assigning an energy score to each data point, with lower energies corresponding to higher probabilities. Unlike Generative Adversarial Networks (GANs), which rely on adversarial training, or self-supervised learning, which uses pretext tasks, EBMs model the unnormalized probability `p(x) ∝ exp(-E(x))`, where `E(x)` is a learned energy function. EBMs are very good in generative tasks, such as synthesizing new data, and analytical tasks such as anomaly detection by leveraging their probabilistic framework.

Mechanism of Energy-Based Models

EBMs define the data distribution through an energy function `E(x; θ)`, parameterized by a neural network with parameters θ. The probability is given by:

$$p(x;\theta) = \frac{\exp(-E(x;\theta))}{Z(\theta)}, \quad Z(\theta) = \int \exp(-E(x;\theta))\,dx$$

Where `Z(θ)` is the normalizing constant (partition function), often intractable to compute directly. For an MNIST digit `x`, a low `E(x)` indicates a high probability configuration (for example, a clear digit 7 from the MNIST dataset), while a high `E(x)` suggests an unlikely one (for example, noise). The log-likelihood is:

$$\log p(x;\theta) = -E(x;\theta) - \log Z(\theta)$$

Training involves maximizing the log-likelihood, which requires approximating the gradient of `log Z(θ)`. Techniques such as Markov Chain Monte Carlo (MCMC) or contrastive divergence sample negative examples (for example, non-digit images) to estimate this gradient, enabling the model to distinguish data from non-data. For our example MNIST digits dataset, EBMs learn to assign low energies to digit-like images, facilitating generation and analysis.

Architecture and Training

EBMs typically use deep neural networks, such as Convolutional Neural Networks (CNNs) or Multilayer Perceptrons (MLPs), to define the energy function `E(x; θ)`. The architecture is flexible, focusing on the following:

- **Energy Network**: Maps input images to a single energy score, capturing data likelihood
- **Sampling Mechanism**: Generates samples via MCMC (for example, Langevin dynamics), adjusting inputs to minimize energy.

$$\mathcal{L} = E_{x\sim p_{\text{data}}}[E(x;\theta)] - E_{x'\sim p_\theta}[E(x';\theta)]$$

Training minimizes the negative log-likelihood which is approximated as:

Where $x \sim p_{data}$ are real images, and $x' \sim p_\theta$ are samples generated by the model.

Applications of Energy-Based Models

Energy-based models support the following unsupervised learning tasks and leverage their energy landscape:

- **Image Generation**: Generate new images y sampling low-energy configurations
- **Anomaly Detection**: Identify high-energy images (for example, malformed shapes) as outliers, enhancing quality control
- **Representation Learning**: Use energy gradients to extract features for clustering or visualization, just like self-supervised learning)
- **Data Denoising**: Minimize energy to reconstruct corrupted images, supporting preprocessing

Conclusion

In this chapter, we explored the deep neural network architectures used in unsupervised learning which are important in the modern machine learning landscape. We learned about autoencoders, generative adversarial networks, variational autoencoders, autoregressive models, flow models, self-supervised learning, and energy-based models. Each approach offers unique strengths: autoencoders and self-supervised learning excel in feature extraction, VAEs and flow-based models provide tractable likelihoods, GANs and diffusion models prioritize sample quality, autoregressive models ensure sequential precision and energy-based models offer flexible probabilistic modeling. However, challenges like the computational intensity of diffusion models, the instability of GAN training, or the sampling complexity of energy-based models still remain. Together, these methods form a comprehensive toolkit for unsupervised learning and are applicable to tasks such as clustering, preprocessing, and generative modeling.

In the next chapter, we will explore the applications of unsupervised learning including advanced applications such as semi-supervised learning and text-to-image generation.

Key Terms

- **Autoencoder**: A neural network that learns to reconstruct input data by encoding it into a compressed latent representation and decoding it back; used for unsupervised feature learning and data denoising.

- **Variational Autoencoder (VAE)**: A generative model that extends autoencoders by modeling a probabilistic latent space, enabling data generation and approximate likelihood estimation through a variational objective
- **Generative Adversarial Network (GAN)**: A framework with a generator and discriminator trained adversarially to produce realistic data samples, modeling the data distribution implicitly without likelihood
- **Autoregressive Model**: A model that generates data by predicting each element conditioned on previous elements, factorizing the joint distribution as a product of conditional probabilities
- **Self-Supervised Learning**: An unsupervised approach that learns robust data representations by solving pretext tasks, such as predicting transformations, without requiring manual labels
- **Energy-Based Model (EBM)**: A model that represents the data distribution using an energy function, where lower energy corresponds to higher probability and is used for generation and analysis
- **Flow-Based Model**: A generative model that uses invertible neural network transformations to map data to a simple base distribution, enabling exact likelihood computation.
- **Diffusion Model**: A generative model that learns to reverse a noise-adding process, denoising data over multiple steps to produce high-quality samples with explicit objectives
- **Contrastive Loss**: A loss function used in self-supervised learning to maximize similarity between representations of different views of the same data while distinguishing them from other data
- **Denoising Loss**: The training objective in diffusion models minimizes the difference between true noise and predicted noise, enabling the model to learn effective data generation

Questions

1. Explain how an autoencoder learns to represent data in an unsupervised manner, along with the roles of its encoder and decoder components.
2. Describe the probabilistic framework of variational autoencoders (VAEs) and how it enables both data generation and likelihood estimation.
3. Discuss the adversarial training process in generative adversarial networks (GANs) and identify at least two challenges that might arise during training.
4. Explain the mechanism by which autoregressive models generate data, highlighting how their sequential approach differs from other unsupervised learning models.

5. Describe the concept of pretext tasks in self-supervised learning and provide two examples of such tasks used to learn robust data representations.
6. Discuss how energy-based models define the probability distribution of data and explain the role of the energy function in their generative process.
7. Explain the principle of invertible transformations in flow-based models and how they allow for exact likelihood computation in unsupervised learning.
8. Describe the forward and reverse processes in diffusion models and explain how they contribute to generating high-quality data samples.
9. Compare the strengths and limitations of flow-based models and diffusion models in the context of unsupervised data generation.
10. Discuss how self-supervised learning can be applied to improve downstream tasks in unsupervised learning, providing at least one specific application example.

Multiple Choice Questions

1. What is the primary objective of an autoencoder in unsupervised learning?
    a. Image Reduction
    b. To reconstruct input data from a compressed representation
    c. Clustering
    d. Data Reduction
2. What distinguishes Variational Autoencoders (VAEs) from standard autoencoders?
    a. Modeling a probabilistic latent space for generation
    b. Adversarial training
    c. Sequential data prediction
    d. Energy-based scoring
3. What is a common challenge in training generative adversarial networks (GANs)?
    a. Exact likelihood computation
    b. Sequential feature extraction
    c. Instability due to adversarial dynamics
    d. Latent space reconstruction

4. How do autoregressive models generate data?
    a. By reconstructing data from latent codes
    b. By predicting each element conditioned on previous elements
    c. By minimizing an energy function
    d. By denoising corrupted data
5. What is the purpose of pretext tasks in self-supervised learning?
    a. To generate new data samples
    b. To learn robust features via tasks like rotation prediction
    c. To compute exact data likelihoods
    d. To assign energy scores to data
6. How do energy-based models define the probability of data?
    a. As a product of conditional probabilities
    b. As a similarity between data views
    c. As a transformation to a base distribution
    d. As an unnormalized exponential of a negative energy function
7. What feature allows flow-based models to compute exact likelihoods?
    a. Invertible transformations with tractable Jacobians
    b. Adversarial generator training
    c. Sequential element prediction
    d. Multi-step denoising
8. What is the main training objective of diffusion models?
    a. Maximizing view similarity
    b. Minimizing the difference between true and predicted noise
    c. Reconstructing compressed data
    d. Assigning low energy to data

9. Which model is most suitable for anomaly detection using likelihoods?
    a. Generative adversarial networks
    b. Flow-based models
    c. Autoencoders
    d. Self-supervised learning
10. Which model typically requires the most computational resources for data sampling?
    a. Variational autoencoders
    b. Flow-based models
    c. Diffusion models
    d. Autoregressive models

Answers

1. b
2. a
3. c
4. b
5. b
6. d
7. a
8. b
9. b
10. c

CHAPTER 7
Applications of Unsupervised Learning

Introduction

This chapter focuses on the real-world applications of unsupervised learning algorithms in various industries. You will learn how unsupervised learning is applied in data-driven decision-making processes in various illustrations such as customer segmentation, market basket analysis, and anomaly detection. The chapter will also provide practical examples of how these techniques can be leveraged in business intelligence, marketing, healthcare, and beyond. In this chapter, we will examine key applications, highlight practical examples, and discuss the challenges and future trends of deploying unsupervised learning in production environments.

Structure

In this chapter, we will discuss the following topics:

- Introduction to Real World Applications of Unsupervised Learning
- Customer Segmentation
- Recommender Systems
- Image and Video Analysis
- Fraud Detection and Cybersecurity
- Market Basket Analysis
- Social Network Analysis
- Genomics and Bioinformatics

- Industrial and IoT Applications
- Challenges and Considerations
- Future Trends in Unsupervised Learning Applications

Introduction to Real World Applications of Unsupervised Learning

Unsupervised learning discovers the structure and patterns in data without the need for labeled examples, which makes it a powerful tool across a wide range of industries. With its ability to extract meaningful patterns from unlabeled data, unsupervised learning drives innovation across a diverse array of industries by addressing challenges where labeled data is scarce or impractical.

In retail and e-commerce industries, clustering techniques such as K-means and deep embedded clustering segment customers based on purchasing behavior, thus supplying key inputs for personalized marketing and optimizing inventory through market basket analysis via association rule mining. Entertainment and media leverage recommender systems powered by matrix factorization and deep models such as variational autoencoders to deliver tailored content on platforms like streaming services. In healthcare, unsupervised learning excels in image analysis, where autoencoders and clustering enhance medical imaging for tasks such as tumor detection, while in genomics, dimensionality reduction and clustering uncover patterns in gene expression data to advance drug discovery. Finance and cybersecurity rely heavily on anomaly detection methods, such as Isolation Forest and deep autoencoders, to identify fraudulent transactions and network intrusions. Social media and marketing benefit from community detection in social network analysis, using graph-based clustering and deep graph models to identify influential groups or track misinformation. In manufacturing and IoT, unsupervised learning supports predictive maintenance by detecting anomalies in sensor data and clustering operational patterns to optimize smart factory processes. Across these sectors, traditional methods like PCA and DBSCAN work alongside deep unsupervised models, such as GANs and self-supervised learning, to tackle scalability and complexity, transforming raw data into actionable insights without the need for extensive labeled datasets.

In the following sections of this chapter, we will discuss the specific use cases, with each demonstrating the impact of unsupervised learning. We begin with customer segmentation, where clustering and deep embedding techniques group consumers for targeted marketing. We explore recommender systems, which use matrix factorization and deep models to power personalized suggestions in e-commerce and streaming platforms. In image and video analysis, unsupervised methods such as autoencoders and clustering enable advancements in medical imaging and object detection. Fraud detection and cybersecurity rely on anomaly detection to identify suspicious activities in finance and network security. Market basket analysis employs association rule mining to uncover product relationships in retail, while social network analysis uses clustering to detect communities and influential nodes. In genomics and bioinformatics, unsupervised learning aids in gene expression analysis and drug discovery. Finally, industrial and IoT applications harness anomaly detection and clustering for predictive maintenance and sensor data analysis. Each application highlights the versatility of unsupervised learning, with practical examples illustrating how traditional and deep learning approaches work together to address industry challenges.

Customer Segmentation

Customer segmentation is an important application of unsupervised learning, as it allows businesses to group customers into meaningful clusters based on shared characteristics, behaviors, and preferences. By using techniques such as clustering and deep unsupervised learning, organizations in retail, e-commerce, marketing, and Customer Relationship Management (CRM) can tailor strategies to specific customer segments, thereby improving engagement and profitability. This section explores how clustering methods such as K-means and DBSCAN, alongside deep learning approaches such as deep embedded clustering, are applied to customer segmentation, with a practical example from the retail industry.

Figure 7.1 shows a sample segmentation of customers of a hypothetical company based on their spending patterns:

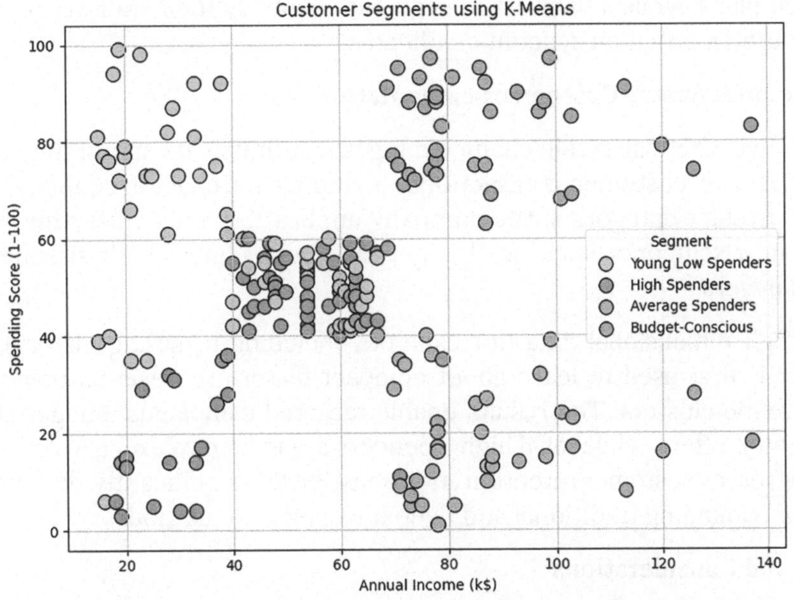

Figure 7.1: *Segmenting Customers as per Their Spending Patterns*

Techniques for Customer Segmentation

Traditional clustering algorithms are widely used for customer segmentation due to their simplicity and effectiveness. K-means clustering groups customers based on features like purchase history, spending patterns, or demographic data, thus minimizing intra-cluster variance. DBSCAN excels at identifying non-spherical clusters and handling outliers, making it suitable for datasets with noisy or irregular customer behavior.

Hierarchical clustering provides a tree-like structure of customer groups that are useful for understanding nested segments. In contrast, deep unsupervised learning approaches like Deep Embedded Clustering (DEC) learn low-dimensional feature representations using autoencoders before applying clustering and end up improving performance on high-dimensional or complex datasets. Dimensionality reduction techniques such as PCA or t-SNE are often used as preprocessing steps to enhance clustering by reducing noise and computational complexity.

Applications in Industry

Customer segmentation has transformative applications across industries. In marketing, segments based on behavior (for example, frequent buyers, seasonal shoppers) allow for targeted campaigns, increasing conversion rates. In e-commerce, clustering customers by browsing patterns or cart abandonment rates inform personalized recommendations and promotions. CRM systems use segmentation to prioritize high-value customers or identify those at risk of churn. For example, a telecommunications company might cluster users by call frequency and data usage to offer tailored plans, while a bank could segment clients by their transaction patterns to detect potential premium account candidates.

Example: Retail Industry Customer Segmentation

Consider a hypothetical retail chain aiming to optimize its marketing strategy. Using a dataset of customer transactions, including purchase frequency, average spend, and product categories, the company applies K-means clustering to group customers into segments such as "budget shoppers," "loyal high-spenders," and "occasional buyers."

To handle high-dimensional data (for example, including browsing history), a deep autoencoder is first used to learn about compact feature representations, followed by DEC to refine clusters. The results enable targeted campaigns: budget shoppers receive discount offers, while loyal high-spenders are invited to exclusive events. This approach increases customer retention and campaign ROI significantly, demonstrating the power of combining traditional and deep unsupervised methods.

Challenges and Considerations

Customer segmentation faces challenges like selecting the optimal number of clusters (for example, using the elbow method for K-means) and ensuring the interpretability of results for business stakeholders. Deep learning approaches require significant computational resources and might produce less interpretable clusters compared to traditional methods. Additionally, ethical concerns arise when segmentation involves sensitive demographic data, necessitating careful handling to avoid bias or privacy violations.

Future Directions in Customer Segmentation

Future advances in customer segmentation are aimed at enhancing precision, scalability and adaptability in understanding consumer behavior. Some of these advances are:

- **Integration of Multimodal Data for Holistic Segmentation**: Future customer segmentation will leverage unsupervised learning to integrate diverse data types, such as text (reviews, social media posts), images (product photos, user-generated content), audio (call center recordings), and behavioral data (clickstreams, purchase history). Advanced clustering techniques like multimodal deep clustering will learn joint representations across these modalities, enabling richer customer profiles. For example, combining visual preferences from Instagram posts with textual sentiment from reviews could reveal nuanced segments, such as "eco-conscious fashion enthusiasts." This approach enhances personalization in marketing by capturing complex customer identities.
- **Self-Supervised Learning for Enhanced Feature Discovery**: Self-supervised learning, a subset of unsupervised learning, will drive advances by automatically generating pseudo-labels from unlabeled customer data. Techniques such as contrastive learning (for example, SimCLR) will extract robust features from unstructured data, such as customer interactions or social media activity, without requiring manual labels. This will improve segmentation by identifying subtle patterns, such as micro-segments of customers with unique lifestyle preferences, thereby enabling businesses to target niche markets with tailored campaigns.
- **Real-time and Dynamic Segmentation Advances** in scalable unsupervised learning algorithms, such as online deep clustering, will enable real-time customer segmentation. These methods process streaming data (for example, live website interactions or app usage) to update clusters dynamically as customer behaviors evolve. For instance, a retail platform could instantly re-segment users during a flash sale based on their browsing patterns, thus optimizing personalized offers. This shift from static to dynamic segmentation enhances responsiveness in fast-paced markets.
- **Graph-Based Segmentation for Network Insights**: Graph-based unsupervised learning, using techniques such as Graph Neural Networks (GNNs), will advance

customer segmentation by modeling relationships within customer networks. For example, analyzing social connections or co-purchasing patterns can identify influential customers or communities with shared preferences. This is particularly valuable for viral marketing, where targeting "trendsetter" segments can amplify campaign impact. GNNs will uncover hidden relational structures, thereby improving segment accuracy.

- **Explainable and Interpretable Segmentation Future:** Unsupervised learning models will prioritize interpretability to make customer segmentation actionable for businesses. Techniques such as attention-based clustering or post-hoc explanation methods will highlight key features driving each segment, such as specific purchase triggers or demographic traits. For example, a model might explain that a segment of "budget-conscious tech buyers" is defined by frequent price comparisons and discount searches. This transparency will bridge the gap between technical models and business decision-making.
- **Personalized Micro-Segmentation with Generative Models**: Generative models, such as variational autoencoders and diffusion models, enable hyper-personalized micro-segmentation by learning fine-grained customer representations. These models can generate synthetic customer profiles to augment sparse data, allowing businesses to identify ultra-specific segments, like "urban cyclists seeking sustainable gear." This enhances precision in targeting, particularly for niche products or services.
- **Federated Unsupervised Learning for Privacy-Preserving Segmentation**: With growing privacy concerns, federated learning will adapt unsupervised methods to perform customer segmentation across decentralized datasets without sharing raw data. For instance, retailers could collaborate to segment customers based on shared patterns (for example, shopping trends) while keeping individual data on local servers. This approach ensures compliance with regulations like GDPR while enabling robust segmentation.
- **Temporal and Contextual Segmentation**: Advances in temporal clusterings, such as recurrent neural network-based unsupervised models, will capture time-dependent customer behaviors. For example, segmenting customers based on seasonal purchasing patterns or life-stage changes (for example, new parents) will become more precise. Contextual clustering will also account for external factors, like economic trends or cultural events, to create adaptive segments that reflect current market dynamics.
- **Scalable Segmentation for Massive Datasets**: As customer data grows, scalable unsupervised learning frameworks like sparse neural networks, will handle massive datasets efficiently. These advancements allow businesses to segment millions of customers in near real-time, while supporting applications in global e-commerce or social media platforms where scale is critical.

- **Hybrid Human-AI Segmentation Systems**: Future systems will combine unsupervised learning with human-in-the-loop approaches, where domain experts refine segments iteratively. For example, marketers could adjust cluster boundaries based on business goals, while unsupervised models suggest new segments based on emerging patterns. This hybrid approach balances automation with strategic insight, improving segmentation relevance.

Customer segmentation highlights the versatility of unsupervised learning in transforming raw customer data into actionable business strategies. Through clustering, businesses can uncover nuanced customer groups, driving personalization and efficiency.

Recommender Systems

Recommender systems are another important application of unsupervised learning, that power personalized experiences in e-commerce, streaming platforms, and social media by predicting user preferences without explicit labels. These systems leverage techniques like matrix factorization and deep unsupervised learning models like variational autoencoders and autoencoders to analyze user-item interactions and uncover latent patterns. This section will explore how unsupervised learning drives collaborative filtering and content-based recommendation, their applications across industries, and a practical example from a streaming service.

Techniques for Recommender Systems

Recommender systems primarily rely on two approaches: collaborative filtering and content-based filtering, both of which benefit from unsupervised learning. Collaborative filtering uses user-item interaction data (for example, ratings, clicks) to identify patterns. A key technique is matrix factorization, such as Singular Value Decomposition (SVD), which decomposes a user-item rating matrix into latent factor matrices representing user preferences and item characteristics. This reduces dimensionality and captures underlying relationships, enabling predictions for unrated items. Non-negative Matrix Factorization (NMF) is another variant, which ensures interpretable, positive latent factors. In contrast, content-based filtering clusters items based on features (for example, movie genres, product descriptions) using algorithms such as K-means or DBSCAN.

Deep unsupervised learning enhances these approaches. Autoencoders learn compact representations of user or item data, improving scalability for large datasets. Variational Autoencoders (VAEs) model probabilistic latent spaces, capturing uncertainty in user preferences. Deep Collaborative Filtering integrates neural networks with matrix factorization, such as in Neural Collaborative Filtering (NCF), which combines user and item embeddings for more accurate predictions. Self-supervised learning can pre-train models on auxiliary tasks, such as predicting masked ratings, to improve performance with sparse data.

Applications in Industry

Recommender systems are ubiquitous across industries. In e-commerce, platforms such as Amazon use collaborative filtering to suggest products based on purchase history, increasing sales through cross-selling. Streaming services such as Netflix and Spotify rely on hybrid systems combining collaborative and content-based filtering to recommend movies or songs, enhancing user retention. Social media platforms, such as YouTube, cluster users by viewing habits to suggest videos, driving engagement. In news aggregation, recommender systems personalize article feeds based on reading patterns. These applications demonstrate how unsupervised learning transforms sparse, high-dimensional data into tailored user experiences.

Figure 7.2 shows recommendations for Amazon.com's e-commerce platform based on a customer's interests:

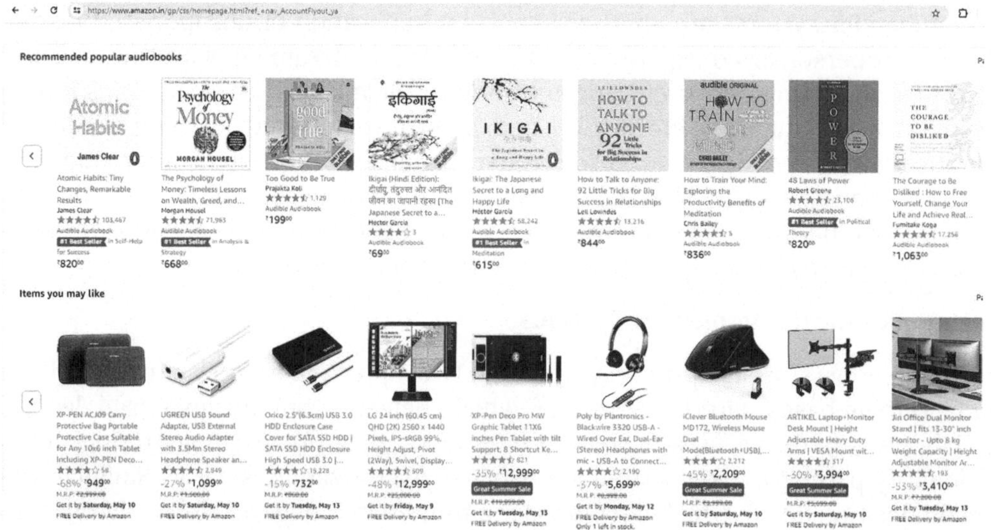

Figure 7.2: *Amazon.com Recommendations*

Example: Streaming Service Recommendations

Consider a hypothetical streaming platform aiming to recommend movies to its users. The platform has a user-item interaction matrix with ratings for watched movies, but most entries are missing due to sparse user activity. Using SVD, the system decomposes the matrix into latent factors, capturing user preferences (for example, affinity for action films) and movie attributes (for example, genre).

To handle millions of users, a deep autoencoder compresses user profiles into low-dimensional embeddings, which are then clustered using K-means to group similar users. For new users with limited data, a VAE-based model generates probabilistic recommendations by modeling uncertainty in preferences. This hybrid approach—combining SVD for collaborative filtering and deep models for scalability—results in a significant increase in user engagement, as users discover relevant content faster. The system also incorporates content-based filtering by clustering movies based on metadata (for example, director, genre), ensuring robust recommendations for niche films.

Challenges and Considerations

Recommender systems face several challenges. Sparsity in user-item matrices can limit prediction accuracy, though deep models such as VAEs mitigate this by learning robust latent representations. Cold-start problems, such as recommendations for new users or items with no interaction history, require content-based or hybrid approaches. Scalability is a concern for platforms with millions of users, necessitating efficient algorithms and distributed computing. Interpretability of recommendations is critical for user trust, but deep models often produce opaque results. Ethical issues, such as reinforcing filter bubbles or biases in recommendations, require careful design to ensure fairness and diversity. For example, over-relying on collaborative filtering might repeatedly suggest popular items and marginalize niche content.

Future Directions in Recommender Systems

These advances in unsupervised learning are shaping the future of recommender systems:

- **Graph-based Learning**: Unsupervised learning by leveraging Graph Neural Networks (GNNs) will model complex relationships between users, items, and their interactions as graphs. By clustering nodes based on connectivity patterns, these systems will uncover latent communities or influence networks, such as groups of users who co-purchase similar products. This can enhance recommendations in social commerce, where targeting "trend-following" user clusters can boost campaign effectiveness.
- **Self-supervised Learning**: It will enhance recommender systems by generating pseudo-labels from unlabeled user interaction data, such as browsing histories or implicit feedback. Techniques such as contrastive learning (for example, inspired by SimCLR) will extract fine-grained user and item embeddings, improving recommendation quality in sparse data scenarios. This will allow systems to identify niche user segments, such as "indie game enthusiasts," even with limited explicit feedback, enhancing personalization for long-tail content.
- **Multimodal Recommender Systems**: Unsupervised learning will increasingly integrate multimodal data, such as text (user reviews, product descriptions), images (product visuals, user-generated content), audio (podcasts, music preferences), and behavioral data (clicks, dwell time), to create richer user and item representations. Advanced clustering and embedding techniques, like multimodal autoencoders, will learn unified representations across these data types, enabling more accurate recommendations. For example, a streaming

platform could recommend movies by combining visual trailer analysis with user comments, thus capturing nuanced preferences like "visually stunning sci-fi epics."

- **Dynamic and Contextual Recommendations**: Future recommender systems will use online unsupervised learning to adapt recommendations in real-time based on evolving user behavior and contextual factors, such as time, location, or device. Temporal clustering models will capture shifting preferences, enabling platforms such as e-commerce sites to recommend seasonal products (for example, winter gear) or context-specific items (for example, workout gear during fitness app usage). This dynamic approach will improve relevance and user engagement in fast-changing environments.
- **Explainable Recommendations**: Unsupervised learning will prioritize interpretability to make recommendations transparent and trustworthy. Techniques like attention-based clustering will highlight key factors driving recommendations such as specific user behaviors or item attributes (for example, "recommended because you frequently browse eco-friendly products"). Explainable models will improve user trust and allow businesses to align recommendations with strategic goals, such as promoting sustainable products.
- **Privacy-Preserving Recommendations with Federated Learning**: With increasing privacy regulations, federated unsupervised learning will enable recommender systems to learn user embeddings across decentralized datasets without sharing raw data. For instance, mobile apps can collaboratively build recommendation models while keeping user data on-device. Clustering techniques adapted for federated settings will help generate personalized recommendations while complying with laws like GDPR, making it critical for global platforms.
- **Micro-Segmentation with Generative Models**: Generative models, such as variational autoencoders or diffusion models, will enable micro-segmentation by learning detailed user and item representations. These models can generate synthetic user profiles to augment sparse data, allowing recommender systems to target highly specific segments, like "vintage vinyl collectors." This will improve recommendation precision for niche markets and enhance diversity in content discovery.
- **Cross-Domain and Transferable Recommendations**: Unsupervised learning can facilitate cross-domain recommender systems by transferring learned representations across different platforms or industries. For example, clustering user preferences from a music streaming service could inform book recommendations on an e-reader platform by identifying shared taste patterns. Techniques like domain-adaptive clustering will enable seamless knowledge transfer and expand recommendation use cases.

- **Scalable Recommendations for Massive Datasets**: As user and item catalogs grow, scalable unsupervised learning frameworks such as distributed clustering or sparse neural networks will handle massive datasets efficiently. These advancements will support real-time recommendations for platforms with billions of users, like social media or global e-commerce, ensuring low latency and high accuracy even at scale.
- **Human-in-the-Loop Recommendation Refinement**: Future recommender systems will integrate unsupervised learning with human-in-the-loop approaches, allowing domain experts or users to refine recommendation clusters interactively. For instance, a retailer can adjust segment boundaries to prioritize high-margin products, while unsupervised models suggest emerging user trends. This hybrid approach will balance automation with human insight, thus improving recommendation relevance and business outcomes.

Recommender systems highlight the power of unsupervised learning in delivering personalized experiences. By combining matrix factorization with deep models, these systems address sparsity and scalability while driving impact in e-commerce, streaming, and social media.

Image and Video Analysis

Unsupervised learning plays a prominent role in computer vision when the labeled data is scarce. Some of its important applications include image clustering, feature learning, image segmentation, anomaly detection, dimensionality reduction and visualization, generative modeling, self-supervised learning, unsupervised object detection, style transfer, image translation and so on.

Image clustering involves grouping similar images (for example, unsupervised image organization, face grouping in Google Photos). It is used in medical imaging to categorize similar tissue patterns. Feature learning involves learning useful image representations without labels (for example, SimCLR, MoCo, DINO). It helps in transfer learning and reduces the need for labeled data. Image Segmentation involves the use of unsupervised techniques (like clustering pixels based on color/texture) to segment objects without labels.

Anomaly detection refers to identifying unusual or rare visual patterns and detects manufacturing defects, medical anomalies, and so on. Unsupervised object detection involves discovering and localizing objects without bounding box labels. Style transfer and image translation involve learning mappings between different visual domains like day to night and sketch-to-photo via models such as CycleGAN.

Image and video analysis is an interesting application of unsupervised learning in computer vision, enabling the extraction of meaningful patterns from visual data without requiring extensive labeled datasets. By leveraging techniques like clustering, dimensionality reduction, and deep unsupervised learning models, such as autoencoders, variational autoencoders, and Generative Adversarial Networks (GANs), these methods power advancements in fields like medical imaging, autonomous driving, and content creation. This section will explore how unsupervised learning facilitates image segmentation, object detection, and feature extraction in computer vision, with a detailed example from medical imaging.

Techniques for Image and Video Analysis

Unsupervised learning techniques are critical for processing high-dimensional image and video data. Clustering groups similar images or video frames based on pixel intensities or extracted features. For instance, K-means clustering segments images into regions with similar colors or textures, while DBSCAN identifies irregularly shaped regions, useful for isolating objects in cluttered scenes.

Dimensionality reduction simplifies complex visual data for analysis. Principal Component Analysis (PCA) reduces image dimensions while preserving variance, while aiding visualization or clustering. t-SNE and UMAP create low-dimensional embeddings for exploratory analysis, such as visualizing image datasets.

Deep unsupervised learning has revolutionized image and video analysis. Autoencoders learn compact representations of images by reconstructing input data, enabling denoising or feature extraction. Variational Autoencoders (VAEs) model probabilistic latent spaces, which are useful for generating synthetic images or interpolating between visual styles. Generative Adversarial Networks (GANs) create realistic images or enhance low-resolution videos by pitting a generator against a discriminator.

Self-supervised learning pretrains models on tasks such as predicting image rotations or frame sequences, improving downstream tasks with limited labeled data. For video, temporal clustering groups frames based on motion patterns, while convolutional autoencoders capture spatiotemporal features, therefore enabling action recognition or anomaly detection.

Applications in Industry

Unsupervised learning drives innovation across diverse domains. In medical imaging, clustering and autoencoders segment MRI or CT scans to identify abnormalities like tumors, which reduces the need for manual annotations. In autonomous driving, unsupervised methods cluster sensor data or segment road scenes, aiding object detection in real-time.

Surveillance systems use anomaly detection to flag unusual activities in video feeds, leveraging deep models like VAEs. In entertainment, GANs generate realistic visual effects or upscale video quality, while clustering organizes media libraries by content similarity. Retail employs image analysis to categorize products based on visual features, enhancing search and recommendation systems. These applications highlight the versatility of unsupervised learning in handling unstructured visual data.

Figure 7.3 shows an encoder-decoder setup for medical image segmentation. This image is from the Nature article titled *Segment Anything in Medical Images*.

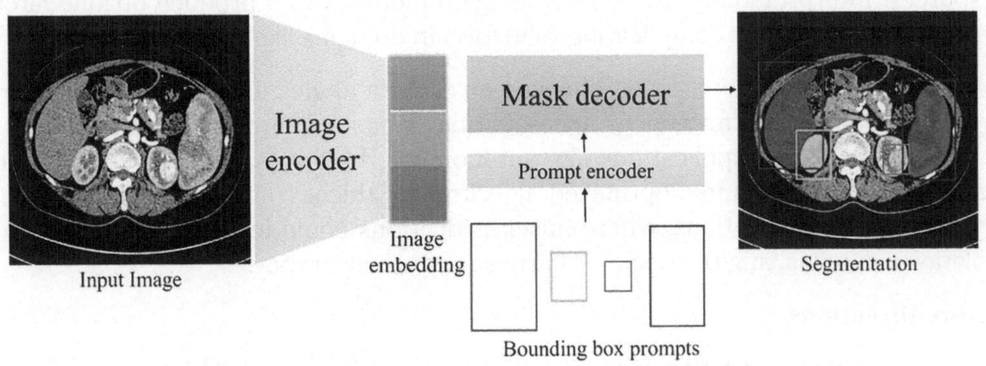

Figure 7.3: *Medical Image Segmentation Using Segment Anything Model (Source: Segment anything in medical images, Nature Communications, Jan 2024, https://www.nature.com/articles/s41467-024-44824-z)*

Example: Medical Imaging for Tumor Detection

Consider a hypothetical hospital aiming to detect brain tumors in MRI scans. The dataset consists of thousands of unlabeled scans, which makes supervised learning impractical due to the high cost of expert annotations.

The hospital employs a pipeline combining traditional and deep unsupervised methods. First, PCA reduces the dimensionality of MRI pixel data, while retaining 95% of variance to simplify subsequent analysis. Meanwhile, K-means clustering segments each scan into regions based on pixel intensity, identifying potential tumor areas as distinct clusters. To improve accuracy, a convolutional autoencoder is trained to reconstruct MRI scans, learning robust feature representations to capture subtle anomalies. The latent embeddings from the autoencoder are clustered using DBSCAN, which isolates irregularly-shaped tumor regions as outliers.

For enhanced precision, a VAE models the distribution of normal brain tissue, allowing anomaly detection to flag scans with significant deviations as potential tumors. Finally, self-supervised learning pretrains the model on a proxy task (for example, predicting scan orientations), improving feature extraction for rare tumor cases. This pipeline achieves a higher detection sensitivity reducing false negatives and enabling radiologists to prioritize high-risk cases. The system also visualizes tumor regions using UMAP embeddings, aiding interpretability for medical staff. By integrating clustering, dimensionality reduction, and deep models, this approach demonstrates the power of unsupervised learning in critical healthcare applications.

Challenges and Considerations

Image and video analysis with unsupervised learning faces significant challenges. The high dimensionality of visual data demands computationally intensive models, particularly for deep learning approaches like GANs, which require substantial GPU resources. Interpretability is a hurdle, as deep models often produce opaque latent representations, hence complicating validation in domains like healthcare.

Data variability, such as lighting changes or camera angles, can degrade clustering or reconstruction performance, necessitating robust preprocessing. Scalability is critical for real-time applications like autonomous driving, where processing high-frame-rate videos requires optimized algorithms. Ethical concerns arise in medical or surveillance applications, where misclassifications could lead to harm or privacy violations, emphasizing the need for fairness and transparency.

Future Directions

Several emerging trends are expanding the scope of unsupervised learning in image and video analysis in the following ways:

- **Multimodal Visual Analytics with Integrated Data**: Unsupervised learning can combine image and video data with other modalities, such as text (captions, metadata), audio (soundtracks, narration), and sensor data (motion, depth), to create holistic representations. Techniques like multimodal clustering or cross-modal autoencoders enable richer analytics, such as automatically grouping video clips by thematic content (for example, "outdoor adventure vlogs") based on visuals, audio, and descriptions. This enhances applications in content recommendation, video summarization, and social media analytics.
- **Self-Supervised Learning for Robust Feature Extraction**: Self-supervised learning will drive advancements in image and video analytics by learning robust visual representations from unlabeled datasets. Techniques such as contrastive learning (for example, MoCo, SimCLR) or masked image modeling (for example, inspired by MAE) can extract features from raw visual data, while allowing the user to detect objects or understand scenes without manual annotations. For instance, self-supervised models can identify recurring objects in surveillance footage, improving anomaly detection in smart cities.
- **Real-Time Video Analytics with Dynamic Clustering**: Online unsupervised learning algorithms, such as streaming clustering or incremental deep clustering, enable real-time analysis of video streams. These methods dynamically group video frames or segments based on content, such as identifying crowd patterns in live event footage. This supports applications like real-time traffic monitoring, where systems instantly detect congestion or accidents, thereby enhancing responsiveness in dynamic environments.

- **Graph-Based Visual Analytics for Relational Insights:** Graph-based unsupervised learning, using Graph Neural Networks (GNNs), will model relationships within visual data, such as object interactions in images or temporal connections in videos. For instance, clustering nodes in a graph of video frames could reveal narrative structures or recurring scenes, which is helpful during video summarization or event detection. This approach is valuable in applications like sports analytics, where understanding player interactions across frames can improve strategic insights.
- **Explainable Visual Analytics for Trustworthy Insights:** Future unsupervised learning models will prioritize interpretability to make image and video analytics actionable. Techniques like attention-based clustering or saliency maps can highlight regions of images or video frames driving analytical outcomes, such as identifying key objects in a scene. For example, in medical imaging, an explainable model can pinpoint areas of a scan indicating anomalies, thereby increasing trust among clinicians and supporting diagnostic workflows.
- **Privacy-Preserving Analytics with Federated Learning:** Federated unsupervised learning can enable image and video analytics across decentralized datasets, while preserving privacy. For instance, hospitals can collaboratively train models to cluster medical images for disease patterns without sharing patient data. Unsupervised techniques like federated clustering can ensure compliance with regulations, such as HIPAA or GDPR, making it critical for healthcare and security applications.
- **Generative Models for Synthetic Visual Analytics:** Generative models, such as diffusion models or Generative Adversarial Networks (GANs), can advance image and video analytics by creating synthetic visual data to augment sparse datasets. These models can generate realistic scenarios (for example, simulated traffic accidents) for training analytics systems and improve robustness in rare-event detection. Applications include autonomous driving, where synthetic videos enhance scene understanding under diverse conditions.
- **Temporal and Contextual Video Understanding Advances:** In temporal unsupervised learning, such as recurrent neural network-based clustering or transformer-based sequence modeling, will capture time-dependent patterns in videos. For example, clustering video segments based on activity progression could identify phases of a surgical procedure in medical videos, aiding in automated monitoring or training. Contextual analytics will also incorporate external factors, like environmental conditions, to refine insights.
- **Scalable Analytics for Massive Visual Datasets:** As image and video datasets grow, scalable unsupervised learning frameworks, leveraging distributed computing or sparse neural networks, will process massive visual corpora efficiently. These advancements will support large-scale applications, such as analyzing petabytes of satellite imagery for environmental monitoring or

clustering user-generated videos on social platforms, while ensuring low latency and high accuracy.

These advancements promise to enhance the accuracy and applicability of unsupervised learning in computer vision.

Image and video analysis highlight the transformative potential of unsupervised learning in processing complex visual data. Thus, by combining clustering and dimensionality reduction with deep models such as autoencoders and VAEs, these methods enable breakthroughs in medical imaging, autonomous systems, and entertainment.

Fraud Detection and Cybersecurity

Fraud detection and cybersecurity are critical domains where unsupervised learning excels at identifying unusual patterns in data, such as fraudulent transactions or network intrusions, without relying on labeled examples. By leveraging anomaly detection techniques and deep unsupervised learning models such as autoencoders and variational autoencoders, can effectively detect of rare and evolving threats. This section explores how unsupervised learning powers fraud detection in finance and cybersecurity in network monitoring, with a practical example from credit card fraud detection.

Techniques for Fraud Detection and Cybersecurity

Unsupervised learning is well-suited for anomaly detection, a core component of fraud and cybersecurity applications. Isolation Forest isolates anomalies by constructing random decision trees, efficiently detecting outliers in high-dimensional datasets like transaction logs. One-Class SVM models the distribution of normal data, flagging deviations as potential fraud or intrusions. Clustering-based anomaly detection, using algorithms like DBSCAN, identifies outliers as data points that do not belong to any cluster, useful for detecting unusual network traffic patterns.

Deep unsupervised learning enhances these approaches. Autoencoders learn to reconstruct normal data, with high reconstruction errors indicating anomalies. For example, an autoencoder trained on legitimate transactions will struggle to reconstruct fraudulent ones. Variational Autoencoders (VAEs) model probabilistic latent spaces, thereby enabling anomaly scoring based on likelihoods.

Self-supervised learning pre-trains models on tasks like predicting transaction sequences, and improving anomaly detection in sparse or dynamic datasets. Dimensionality reduction techniques like PCA preprocess data to reduce noise and computational complexity, thus enhancing the performance of both traditional and deep methods.

Applications in Industry

Unsupervised learning drives critical applications in multiple sectors. In banking and finance, anomaly detection identifies fraudulent credit card transactions, insurance claims, or money laundering by analyzing spending patterns or account activities. In e-commerce, it detects account takeovers or fake reviews by flagging irregular user behaviors. In cybersecurity, unsupervised methods monitor network traffic to detect intrusions, malware, or denial-of-service attacks. For instance, telecom companies use anomaly detection to identify unauthorized access to infrastructure, while cloud service providers leverage it to secure user data. These applications demonstrate how unsupervised learning can adapt to tackle evolving threats in real-time.

Example: Credit Card Fraud Detection

Consider a financial institution aiming to detect fraudulent credit card transactions in a dataset of millions of transactions, where only a tiny fraction is fraudulent. Using Isolation Forest, the system isolates transactions with unusual features such as high amounts or atypical merchant categories, achieving fast detection with minimal computational overhead. To handle complex patterns, a convolutional autoencoder is trained on normal transaction sequences, learning to reconstruct features such as transaction time, location, and amount. Fraudulent transactions yield high reconstruction errors, flagging them for review.

For improved sensitivity, a VAE models the distribution of legitimate transactions, assigning low probability scores to anomalies. PCA preprocesses the data, reducing dimensionality while preserving 90% of variance, making clustering feasible. DBSCAN then groups transactions, identifying outliers as potential fraud. This hybrid performs much better, enabling the institution to freeze suspicious accounts quickly and reduce losses. The system also provides interpretable anomaly scores, thus aiding manual review by fraud analysts.

Challenges and Considerations

Fraud detection and cybersecurity face several challenges. Imbalanced data, where anomalies are rare, can lead to high false positives and thus requires careful threshold tuning. Evolving threats demand adaptive models that generalize well. Scalability is critical for processing high-velocity transactions or network data in real-time and often necessitating distributed systems. Interpretability is essential as stakeholders need to understand why a transaction or event was flagged, particularly in regulated industries like finance. Ethical concerns arise when profiling user behavior, thereby risking privacy violations or biased detections, all of which calls for transparent and fair algorithms.

Future Directions

Prominent trends in the domain of fraud detection and cybersecurity using unsupervised learning methods include:

- **Graph-Based Anomaly Detection for Networked Threats**: Graph-based anomaly detection using graph autoencoders, models relationships between users, or devices improves the detection of coordinated attacks. When Graph-based unsupervised learning use Graph Neural Networks (GNNs), they model relationships in cybersecurity data such as user-device interactions or transaction networks to uncover complex fraud patterns. Clustering nodes in a graph may reveal coordinated attacks like botnets or money laundering rings by identifying anomalous connectivity patterns. This approach enhances detection in applications like cryptocurrency fraud, where relational insights are important.

- **Privacy-Preserving Detection with Federated Learning**: Federated learning enables collaborative training across institutions while preserving data privacy, which is critical for financial and cybersecurity applications. For example, banks could jointly train anomaly detection models on transaction data while keeping customer information local, complying with regulations like GDPR. Unsupervised techniques like federated clustering can identify shared fraud patterns such as cross-bank scams, thereby enhancing collective security.
- **Generative Models for Synthetic Attack Simulation**: Adversarial robustness, inspired by GANs, strengthens models against attacks designed to evade detection. Generative models, such as generative adversarial networks or diffusion models, create synthetic attack scenarios to improve anomaly detection systems. By generating realistic fraud patterns or malware behaviors, these models augment training data, enabling unsupervised systems to better recognize rare or novel threats. This is valuable in applications such as penetration testing or training fraud detection systems for emerging financial scams.
- **Real-Time Anomaly Detection with Streaming Algorithms**: Real-time streaming analytics integrates unsupervised learning with edge computing, enabling instant threat detection in IoT or 5G networks. Online unsupervised learning such as streaming clustering or incremental anomaly detection models can enable real-time threat identification in high-velocity data streams, such as payment transactions or network traffic. These methods will dynamically update anomaly thresholds as new data arrives, hence allowing systems to detect fraud during a transaction or identify a Distributed Denial-of-Service (DDoS) attack as it unfolds. This is critical for applications in e-commerce and critical infrastructure protection.
- **Temporal and Contextual Anomaly Detection**: Advances in temporal unsupervised learning, such as recurrent neural network-based clustering or transformer-based sequence modeling, can capture time-dependent patterns in cybersecurity data. For example, clustering user activities over time could detect account takeovers by identifying deviations from normal behavior like sudden high-value transactions. Contextual models also incorporate external factors such as threat intelligence feeds to refine anomaly detection in dynamic threat landscapes.

- **Scalable Detection for Large-Scale Systems**: As cyber threats grow in volume and complexity, scalable unsupervised learning frameworks by leveraging distributed computing or sparse neural networks, can process massive datasets efficiently. These advancements support real-time anomaly detection in large-scale systems such as cloud infrastructures or global payment networks, ensuring low latency and high accuracy even under heavy data loads.
- **Human-in-the-Loop Threat Validation**: Future systems can combine unsupervised learning with human-in-the-loop approaches, allowing security analysts to refine anomaly detection outputs interactively. For instance, unsupervised models can cluster suspicious network activities, while analysts validate or adjust clusters based on domain expertise. This hybrid approach improves detection accuracy in high-stakes applications, such as protecting critical infrastructure or combating Advanced Persistent Threats (APTs).
- **Explainable Anomaly Detection for Actionable Insights**: Future unsupervised learning models will prioritize interpretability to make fraud and cybersecurity alerts actionable. Techniques such as attention-based anomaly detection or feature importance analysis can highlight specific data points driving alerts whenever unusual activity is detected. For instance, an explainable model could clarify why a login attempt was flagged, which enables security teams to respond effectively and builds trust in automated systems.
- **Self-Supervised Learning for Adaptive Threat Detection**: Self-supervised learning can enhance fraud detection by learning robust representations from unlabeled cybersecurity data, such as network packets or transaction histories. Techniques like contrastive learning (for example, inspired by SimCLR) can identify subtle anomalies in sparse or noisy datasets and detect novel threats like zero-day exploits pretty early on. For example, self-supervised models can flag unusual API calls in cloud environments, thus improving resilience against emerging attack vectors.
- **Multimodal Anomaly Detection for Comprehensive Threat Identification**: Unsupervised learning can integrate multimodal data, such as network traffic logs, user behavior (keystrokes, mouse movements), text (emails, chat logs), and system metadata, to detect fraud and cyber threats holistically. Advanced clustering techniques like multimodal autoencoders or cross-modal embeddings, can identify anomalies across these data types, such as detecting phishing attempts by combining suspicious email content with unusual login patterns. This improves detection accuracy in applications such as financial fraud prevention and enterprise security.

Fraud detection and cybersecurity highlight the power of unsupervised learning in identifying rare and dynamic threats. By combining anomaly detection techniques with deep models, these methods can safeguard financial systems and networks.

Market Basket Analysis

Market Basket Analysis (MBA) is a powerful application of unsupervised learning that uncovers relationships between items purchased together, enabling retailers to optimize product placement, promotions, and inventory. By using association rule mining techniques and integrating clustering and deep unsupervised learning, MBA provides actionable insights into consumer behavior. In this section, we will explore how algorithms such as Apriori and FP-growth, enhanced by deep embeddings, drive MBA in retail, with a practical example from a supermarket.

Techniques for Market Basket Analysis

The core of MBA lies in association rule mining, which identifies frequent itemsets and generates rules of the form "`if {item A}, then {item B}`." The Apriori algorithm identifies frequent itemsets by iteratively scanning transaction data, using metrics such as support (frequency of itemsets), confidence (likelihood of rule accuracy), and lift (strength of association). FP-growth (Frequent Pattern growth) improves efficiency by constructing a compact FP-tree, reducing computational overhead for large datasets. These methods excel at discovering patterns like "customers buying bread often buy butter."

Clustering complements MBA by grouping similar transactions or customers. For instance, K-means clusters transactions based on purchased item categories, revealing distinct shopping patterns. Deep unsupervised learning enhances MBA for complex datasets. Autoencoders learn low-dimensional embeddings of transaction data, capturing latent relationships between items. Deep-embedded clustering groups transactions in this latent space, improving pattern discovery in high-dimensional or sparse data. Dimensionality reduction, such as PCA, preprocesses item features to streamline analysis.

Applications in Industry

MBA has wide-ranging applications in retail and beyond. In supermarkets, it informs product placement (for example, placing complementary items such as chips and salsa together) and cross-selling strategies. E-commerce platforms use MBA to suggest related products, such as recommending phone cases with smartphones. Subscription services analyze usage patterns to bundle offerings, like pairing streaming content with merchandise. In healthcare, MBA identifies co-occurring medical procedures in patient records, aiding resource planning. These applications demonstrate how MBA translates transactional data into strategic decisions that boost sales and customer satisfaction.

Example: Supermarket Product Bundling

Consider a supermarket chain analyzing transaction data to optimize product bundling. The dataset includes thousands of daily transactions, each listing purchased items.

Using the Apriori algorithm, the supermarket identifies frequent itemsets, discovering rules like "`{diapers, baby wipes} → {baby-formula}`" with high confidence, indicating a strong association. To handle the large dataset, FP-growth constructs an FP-tree to reduce processing time significantly compared to Apriori.

To uncover nuanced patterns, a convolutional autoencoder encodes transaction data into a low-dimensional latent space, capturing relationships between item categories (for example, snacks and beverages). K-means clustering groups transactions in this space, revealing segments such as "health-conscious shoppers" or "party planners." These clusters inform targeted promotions like bundling organic produce for health-conscious customers. PCA preprocesses item features, ensuring efficient clustering. The analysis leads to a store layout where complementary items are colocated, thereby increasing basket size and sales revenue. The supermarket also launches bundled promotions, like snack combos for party planners, which further drives customer engagement.

Challenges and Considerations

MBA faces several challenges. Scalability is a concern, as large transaction datasets require efficient algorithms like FP-growth or distributed computing. Sparsity in data, where many item combinations are rare, can lead to weak rules, necessitating robust preprocessing. Interpretability of rules is important for actionable insights, but complex datasets may produce numerous trivial rules (for example, "`milk → bread`"). Deep learning models, while powerful, increase computational costs and may reduce interpretability compared to traditional methods. Ethical concerns arise when MBA informs dynamic pricing or profiling, risking customer trust if perceived as manipulative.

Future Directions

Advances in unsupervised learning are enhancing MBA. A few prominent illustrations include the following:

- **Multimodal Basket Analysis with Integrated Data**: Unsupervised learning can combine transaction data with multimodal sources such as customer reviews, browsing histories, and social media interactions to uncover richer purchasing patterns. Advanced clustering techniques, like multimodal embeddings, can reveal nuanced associations such as linking eco-friendly product purchases with sustainability-focused online behavior. This enhances cross-selling strategies in retail and e-commerce by identifying holistic customer preferences.
- **Real-Time and Dynamic Basket Analysis**: Online unsupervised learning such as streaming clustering enables real-time market basket analysis on live transaction streams. These methods dynamically update item associations as purchasing behaviors shift, allowing retailers to offer instant personalized promotions (for example, suggesting complementary products during

checkout). This is critical for fast-paced environments like online marketplaces, improving responsiveness and sales.

- **Graph-Based Analysis for Relational Insights**: Graph-based unsupervised learning, using Graph Neural Networks (GNNs), can model complex relationships between products, customers, and transactions as graphs. Clustering nodes can uncover hidden patterns, such as product bundles purchased by specific customer segments or seasonal trends. This can optimize inventory management and marketing campaigns, particularly for large retailers with diverse product catalogs.
- **Privacy-Preserving Analysis with Federated Learning**: Federated unsupervised learning can enable market basket analysis across decentralized datasets, such as transactions from multiple retailers or regions, without sharing sensitive customer data. Clustering techniques adapted for federated settings can identify shared purchasing patterns while complying with privacy regulations like GDPR. This is vital for collaborative retail networks or global e-commerce platforms.
- **Scalable Analysis for Massive Transaction Datasets**: Scalable unsupervised learning frameworks, leveraging distributed computing or sparse neural networks, can process massive transaction datasets efficiently. These advancements can support market basket analysis for global retailers or platforms with billions of transactions, enabling rapid identification of purchasing patterns at scale such as trending product combinations during holiday seasons.

Market basket analysis highlights unsupervised learning's ability to uncover item relationships and driving strategic decisions in retail. By combining association rule mining with clustering and deep embeddings, MBA delivers measurable business value as shown in the supermarket example. Challenges such as scalability and ethical concerns highlight areas for innovation.

Social Network Analysis

Social Network Analysis (SNA) employs unsupervised learning to uncover structures and relationships within networks, such as online platforms or organizational graphs, by identifying communities and influential nodes. Using clustering techniques, graph-based algorithms, and deep unsupervised learning models like graph autoencoders, SNA powers applications in marketing, misinformation detection, and organizational studies. This section will explore how unsupervised learning drives community detection and influence analysis, with a practical example from X/Twitter community analysis.

Techniques for Social Network Analysis

SNA relies heavily on clustering to group nodes (for example, users) with similar connections. Louvain method, a graph-based clustering algorithm, maximizes modularity to detect communities by optimizing the density of intra-community edges. Spectral clustering uses graph Laplacian eigenvalues to partition networks, effective for sparse graphs. DBSCAN can identify communities of varying densities, handling noise in loosely connected networks. Dimensionality reduction, such as t-SNE or UMAP, embeds high-dimensional graph data into lower dimensions for visualization or clustering.

Deep unsupervised learning enhances SNA for large-scale networks. Graph Autoencoders (GAEs) learn node embeddings by reconstructing graph adjacency matrices and capturing structural patterns. When Graph Convolutional Networks (GCNs) are trained via self-supervised tasks like link prediction in an unsupervised setting, they can generate robust embeddings for clustering. Variational Graph Autoencoders (VGAEs) model probabilistic node representations to improve community detection in noisy networks. Self-supervised learning pre-trains models on tasks like predicting missing edges and enhancing performance with limited data.

Figure 7.4 shows a social network diagram showing friendship ties between a set of users of Facebook.

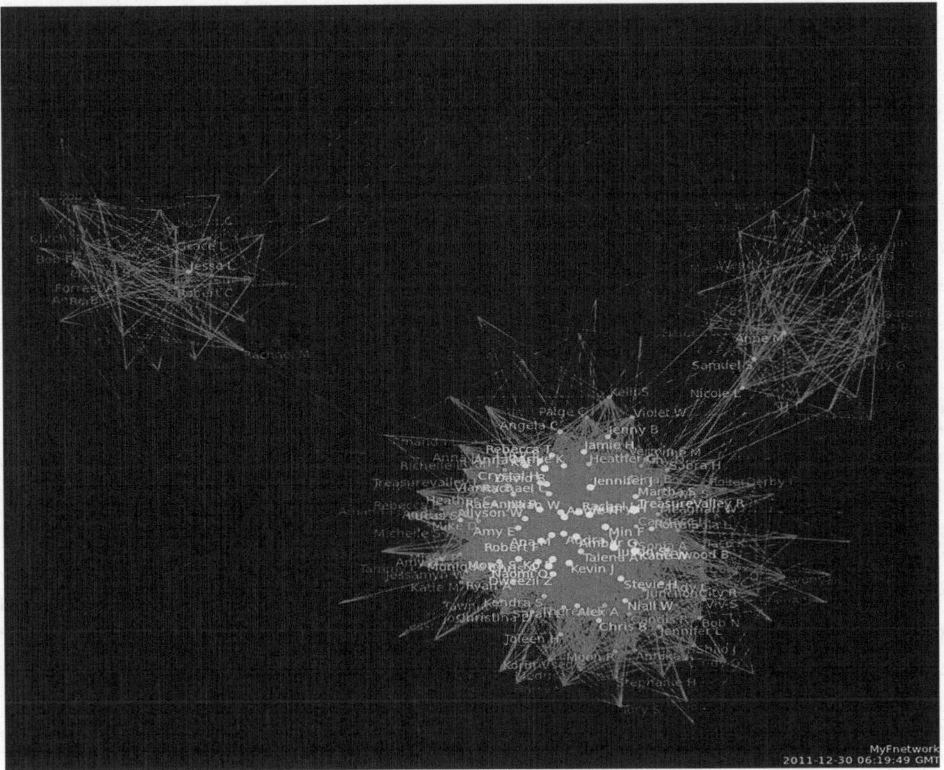

Figure 7.4: *A Network of Facebook Friends (Source: https://en.wikipedia.org/wiki/Social_network_analysis#/media/File:Kencf0618FacebookNetwork.jpg (CC BY-SA 3.0 License))*

Applications in Industry

SNA has diverse applications. In marketing, identifying communities on social media platforms like Twitter helps target campaigns to influential groups. Misinformation detection uses community detection to trace the spread of false narratives, enabling platforms to intervene. Organizational analysis maps employee networks to optimize collaboration or identify key decision-makers. In public health, SNA tracks disease spread by analyzing contact networks. Recommendation systems leverage SNA to suggest connections or content based on community affiliations, enhancing user engagement.

Example: X (Formerly Twitter) Community Analysis

Consider a hypothetical social media analytics firm analyzing X (previously Twitter) data to identify communities for a marketing campaign. The dataset is a graph of 100,000 users, with edges representing follows or retweets. The Louvain method detects communities by maximizing modularity, grouping users into clusters such as "tech enthusiasts" or "sports fans." To handle the graph's complexity, a Graph Autoencoder learns low-dimensional node embeddings, preserving structural properties like node degree. Spectral clustering then groups these embeddings to reveal finer-grained communities.

For visualization, UMAP projects embeddings into 2D, allowing marketers to inspect community structures. To identify influential users, the firm applies PageRank, a graph-based ranking algorithm within each community, pinpointing key opinion leaders. Self-supervised learning pre-trains the GAE on a link prediction task, improving embedding quality for sparse regions of the graph. This pipeline identifies 15 distinct communities, with the top influencers driving 30% of engagement. The firm targets ads towards these communities to increase campaign click-through rates. The approach thus demonstrates how traditional and deep unsupervised methods uncover actionable network insights.

Challenges and Considerations

SNA faces several challenges today. Scalability is critical for large networks with millions of nodes, requiring efficient algorithms or distributed computing. Dynamic networks, where connections evolve (for example, X follows), demand adaptive models to capture temporal changes. Interpretability of communities is essential for actionable insights, but deep models like GAEs may produce opaque embeddings. Noise in social data, such as fake accounts, can distort clustering, necessitating robust preprocessing. Ethical concerns arise in applications such as targeted marketing or misinformation tracking, where profiling of the communities raises the risks of privacy violations or bias amplification.

Future Directions

Advances in unsupervised learning are shaping SNA. Here are some of these future directions:

- **Graph-Based Community Detection with Enhanced Scalability**: Graph-based unsupervised learning, by leveraging advanced graph neural networks, can improve community detection in massive social networks by clustering nodes based on structural and attribute similarities. These methods can scale to billions of nodes (for example, users on X or Facebook), uncovering hidden groups such as coordinated misinformation networks or niche hobbyist communities. This can support applications in cybersecurity and market segmentation.
- **Privacy-Preserving Analysis with Federated Learning**: Federated unsupervised learning enables social network analysis across decentralized datasets, such as user interactions on multiple platforms, without sharing sensitive data. Federated graph clustering can identify shared network patterns, like cross-platform influencer networks while complying with privacy regulations like GDPR. This is vital for collaborative analysis in advertising or countering online threats.
- **Explainable Network Insights for Actionable Outcomes**: Unsupervised learning models will prioritize interpretability, using techniques like attention-based graph clustering to highlight key factors driving community formation, such as influential users or trending topics. For example, an explainable model could clarify why a group forms around a specific hashtag, while aiding marketers in crafting targeted campaigns. This transparency enhances trust and usability in applications like policy analysis and brand management.
- **Multimodal Social Network Analysis**: Unsupervised learning will integrate diverse data types, such as user interactions (likes, shares), text (posts, comments), images (profile pictures, shared media), and metadata (timestamps, locations), to model social networks comprehensively. Advanced clustering techniques, like multimodal graph embeddings, will uncover nuanced communities, such as groups united by shared interests and visual aesthetics on platforms like Instagram. This enhances applications in targeted advertising and trend forecasting.
- **Dynamic and Real-Time Network Analysis**: Online unsupervised learning, such as streaming graph clustering, enables real-time analysis of evolving social networks, capturing shifting relationships and influence patterns. For instance, platforms can instantly detect emerging influencer communities during viral events, enabling timely marketing campaigns. This dynamic approach is critical for social media platforms and crisis monitoring, where rapid insights are necessary.

Social network analysis illustrates unsupervised learning's ability to reveal community structures and influence in complex graphs. By combining clustering with deep graph models, SNA drives impact in marketing and misinformation detection, as shown in the X/Twitter example.

Genomics and Bioinformatics

Genomics and bioinformatics use unsupervised learning to uncover patterns in complex biological data, such as gene expression profiles and protein sequences, driving advancements in personalized medicine and drug discovery. By applying clustering, dimensionality reduction, and deep unsupervised learning models such as autoencoders and self-supervised learning, these fields extract meaningful insights from high-dimensional, unlabeled datasets. This section explores how unsupervised learning facilitates gene expression analysis, biological sequence clustering, and drug discovery, with a practical example of drug discovery.

Techniques for Genomics and Bioinformatics

Unsupervised learning is ideal for analyzing high-dimensional biological data. Clustering groups similar genes or samples based on expression levels. K-means clustering partitions gene expression data into functional groups, while hierarchical clustering reveals nested relationships, useful for phylogenetic analysis. DBSCAN identifies clusters of varying densities, handling noisy genomic datasets. Dimensionality reduction simplifies complex data for visualization and analysis. Principal Component Analysis (PCA) reduces gene expression dimensions, capturing major sources of variance. t-SNE and UMAP create low-dimensional embeddings for visualizing sample relationships, such as tumor subtypes. Deep unsupervised learning enhances the analysis of large-scale genomic data. Autoencoders learn compact representations of gene expression or sequence data, enabling denoising or feature extraction. Variational Autoencoders (VAEs) model probabilistic latent spaces, useful for generating synthetic biological data or identifying rare variants. Self-supervised learning pretrains models on tasks like predicting masked DNA sequences and improving performance on downstream tasks with limited labeled data. Graph-based methods, such as graph autoencoders, model protein interaction networks, and clustering proteins by functional similarity. *Figure* 7.5 shows protein structure analysis using clustering. (Source: https://iiif.elifesciences.org/lax/39397/elife-39397-fig4-v2.tif/full/617,/0/default.jpg, Creative Commons License).

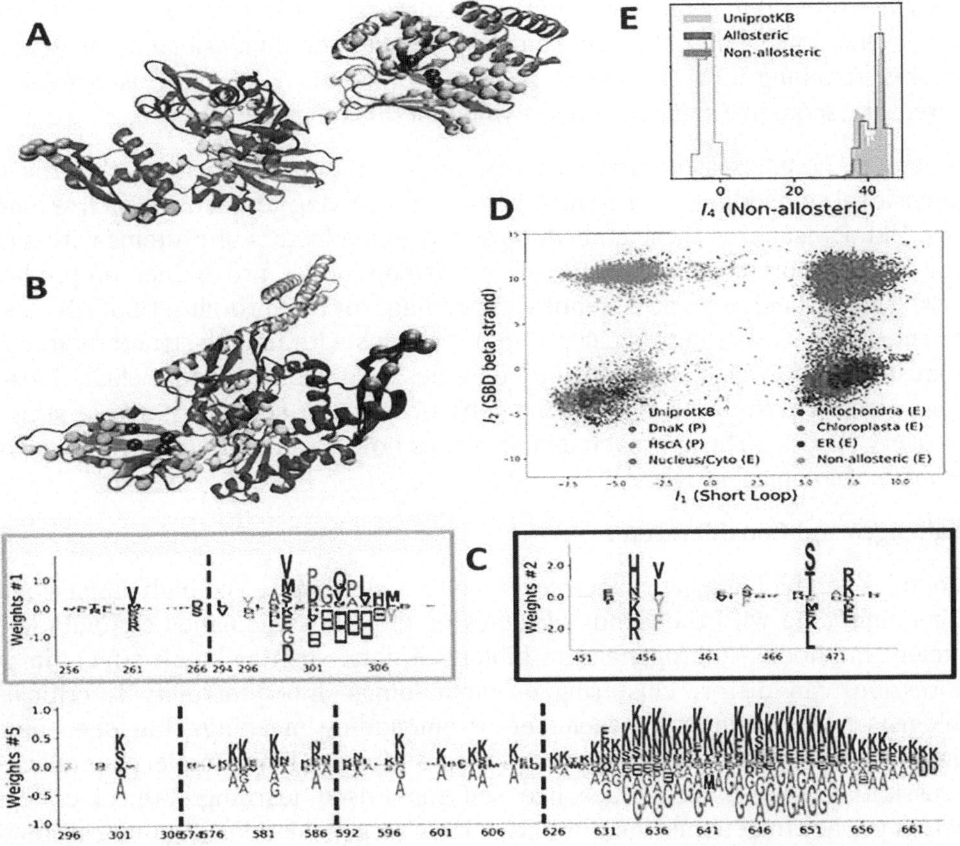

Figure 7.5: *Protein Structure Analysis Using Clustering (Source: https://iiif.elifesciences.org/lax/39397/elife-39397-fig4-v2.tif/full/617,/0/default.jpg)*

Applications in Industry

Unsupervised learning powers critical applications in genomics and bioinformatics. In personalized medicine, clustering gene expression data identifies patient subtypes, guiding tailored treatments. Drug discovery uses unsupervised methods to cluster compounds by molecular properties or predict protein interactions. Functional genomics applies clustering to annotate gene functions based on co-expression patterns. In metagenomics, unsupervised learning groups microbial sequences from environmental samples, aiding biodiversity studies. Cancer research uses dimensionality reduction and clustering to classify tumors, informing prognosis and therapy. These applications highlight unsupervised learning's ability to handle complex, unlabeled biological data.

Example: Drug Discovery with Protein Structure Analysis

Consider a hypothetical pharmaceutical company aiming to identify drug candidates targeting a protein associated with Alzheimer's disease. The dataset includes thousands of protein sequences and their structural features, but no labeled data on drug interactions. Using PCA, the company reduces the dimensionality of structural features, retaining 90% of variance to simplify analysis. K-means clustering groups proteins by sequence similarity, identifying functional families.

To capture complex structural patterns, a convolutional autoencoder learns low-dimensional embeddings of protein structures, preserving key features such as binding sites. UMAP visualizes these embeddings, revealing clusters of proteins with similar drug-binding potential. A self-supervised learning model, pre-trained on predicting masked amino acid sequences, refines embeddings for rare proteins. DBSCAN clusters the embeddings, isolating a small group of proteins with unique structural motifs as promising drug targets. This pipeline identifies a candidate protein cluster, leading to a major increase in hit rate during subsequent drug screening, accelerating the discovery process. The approach demonstrates how unsupervised learning uncovers actionable biological insights.

Challenges and Considerations

Genomics and bioinformatics face several challenges today. The high dimensionality of genomic data with thousands of genes or sequences demands computationally efficient methods. Heterogeneity in biological data, such as batch effects in gene expression, can distort clustering or embeddings. Interpretability is critical, as biologists need to understand cluster or embedding meanings, but deep models might lack transparency. Data scarcity for rare diseases limits model generalization, necessitating robust techniques like self-supervised learning. Ethical concerns, such as privacy in genomic data or bias in drug target selection, require careful data handling and fair algorithms.

Future Directions

We have listed future advances in the field of genomics and bioinformatics as follows:

- **Multimodal Genomic Analysis**: Unsupervised learning can integrate diverse biological data types, such as DNA sequences, RNA expression profiles, epigenomic markers, and proteomic data, to uncover comprehensive patterns. Advanced clustering techniques, such as multimodal autoencoders or joint embeddings, can identify hidden biological subtypes, such as distinct cancer patient groups based on combined genomic and proteomic profiles. This enhances applications in precision medicine and drug discovery by enabling tailored treatments.
- **Self-Supervised Learning for Robust Feature Discovery**: Self-supervised learning can extract meaningful features from vast, unlabeled genomic datasets such as raw sequencing reads or single-cell RNA data. Techniques like contrastive learning or masked sequence modeling can identify biologically relevant patterns such as gene regulatory networks, without any manual

annotations. This improves tasks such as cell type identification or variant effect prediction, which will further accelerate research in rare diseases and developmental biology.

- **Dynamic and Temporal Genomic Analysis:** Unsupervised learning models, such as temporal clustering or transformer-based sequence analysis, can capture time-dependent patterns in genomic data such as gene expression changes during disease progression or development.
- **Graph-Based Analysis for Biological Networks**: When Graph-based unsupervised learning leverages graph neural networks, it can model complex biological relationships, such as protein-protein interactions or gene regulatory networks. Clustering nodes in these graphs will uncover functional modules or disease-related pathways, enhancing applications in systems biology. For instance, identifying tightly connected gene clusters could reveal novel targets for cancer therapies.

Genomics and bioinformatics highlight unsupervised learning's ability to extract patterns from complex biological data. By combining clustering and dimensionality reduction with deep models, these methods drive drug discovery and personalized medicine, as shown in the protein analysis example.

Industrial and IoT Applications

Industrial and Internet of Things (IoT) applications harness unsupervised learning to analyze vast streams of sensor data, enabling predictive maintenance, fault detection, and operational optimization in manufacturing, energy, and smart infrastructure. By leveraging anomaly detection, clustering, and deep unsupervised learning models like autoencoders, these methods identify equipment failures and uncover patterns in complex IoT systems. This section explores how unsupervised learning drives predictive maintenance and sensor data analysis, with a practical example from a smart factory.

Techniques for Industrial and IoT Applications

Unsupervised learning is critical for processing high-frequency, unlabeled sensor data. Anomaly detection identifies deviations from normal equipment behavior. Isolation Forest detects outliers in sensor readings, such as abnormal vibrations, while One-Class SVM models normal operating conditions, flagging anomalies like temperature spikes. Clustering groups similar operational states. K-means clusters sensor data to identify distinct machine modes (for example, idle, high-load), and DBSCAN isolates irregular patterns in noisy IoT streams.

Deep unsupervised learning enhances the analysis of complex, high-dimensional data. Autoencoders learn to reconstruct normal sensor readings, with high reconstruction errors indicating faults. Variational Autoencoders (VAEs) model probabilistic distribution of sensor data, enabling robust anomaly scoring. Self-supervised learning pre-trains models on tasks like predicting future sensor values, and improving performance in dynamic environments. Dimensionality reduction, such as PCA, preprocesses multivariate sensor data to reduce noise and computational load, aiding clustering and visualization.

Applications in Industry

Unsupervised learning powers critical industrial and IoT applications. In manufacturing, predictive maintenance uses anomaly detection to schedule repairs before equipment failures, reducing downtime. Energy systems monitor wind turbines or power grids, detecting faults in real-time. Smart cities analyze IoT data from traffic sensors or water systems to optimize resource use. Logistics leverages clustering to optimize fleet operations by grouping similar vehicle performance patterns. Agriculture uses IoT sensors to detect anomalies in soil or crop conditions, enhancing yield. These applications demonstrate unsupervised learning's ability to transform raw sensor data into actionable insights.

Example: Smart Factory Fault Detection

Consider a hypothetical smart factory with IoT sensors monitoring machinery, generating data on vibration, temperature, and pressure. The goal is to detect faults to prevent costly shutdowns. Using Isolation Forest, the system identifies anomalous vibration patterns, flagging potential bearing failures. To handle multivariate data, PCA reduces sensor dimensions, retaining 95% of the variance for efficient processing. K-means clustering groups machine states (for example, normal, overheating), enabling operators to monitor operational modes.

For complex patterns, a convolutional autoencoder learns to reconstruct normal sensor sequences, with high reconstruction errors indicating faults like motor misalignment. A VAE models the distribution of healthy machine states, assigning low probability scores to anomalies. Self-supervised learning pre-trains the model from predicting next-minute sensor values, improving the detection of rare faults. This pipeline detects the majority of critical faults many hours in advance, thereby reducing unplanned downtime and maintenance costs. UMAP visualizes sensor clusters, aiding engineers in diagnosing issues.

Challenges and Considerations

Industrial and IoT applications face challenges. Data volume and velocity from IoT devices demand scalable, real-time processing, often requiring edge computing. Heterogeneity in sensor types and formats complicates analysis, necessitating robust preprocessing. Interpretability is critical, as engineers need clear explanations for flagged anomalies, but deep models can be opaque. False positives in anomaly detection risk unnecessary maintenance, requiring careful threshold tuning. Ethical concerns arise in workforce monitoring (for example, wearable IoT devices), where data misuse could infringe on privacy, emphasizing the need for transparent policies.

Future Directions

Important advances in industrial and IoT applications are:

- **Multimodal IoT Data Analysis**: Unsupervised learning will integrate diverse IoT data streams, such as sensor readings (temperature, vibration), video feeds, audio signals (machine sounds), and operational logs, to uncover comprehensive system insights. Advanced clustering techniques, such as multimodal embeddings or autoencoders, will detect patterns across these data types such as identifying equipment failure precursors in manufacturing plants. This enhances predictive maintenance and process optimization.
- **Real-Time Anomaly Detection in IoT Networks**: Online unsupervised learning, such as streaming clustering or incremental anomaly detection, will enable real-time monitoring of IoT devices and industrial systems. These methods dynamically identify anomalies in sensor data like unusual power consumption in smart grids or equipment malfunctions in factories, and allow immediate interventions. This is critical for minimizing downtime and ensuring operational continuity in Industry 4.0 settings.
- **Privacy-Preserving IoT Analytics with Federated Learning**: Federated unsupervised learning will enable collaborative analysis across distributed IoT devices or industrial sites without sharing sensitive data. Federated clustering will identify shared patterns, such as equipment wear trends across multiple factories while complying with data privacy regulations. This will be vital for cross-organizational initiatives, such as optimizing supply chains or energy networks.

Industrial and IoT applications demonstrate unsupervised learning's power in transforming sensor data into predictive insights. These methods optimize manufacturing and smart systems, as shown in the smart factory example.

Challenges and Considerations

The diverse applications of unsupervised learning like spanning customer segmentation, recommender systems, image and video analysis, fraud detection, market basket analysis, social network analysis, genomics, and industrial/IoT systems, demonstrate its transformative potential. However, deploying these techniques involves significant challenges. This section explores prominent hurdles in scalability, interpretability, data quality, and ethical considerations, to guide effective implementation of unsupervised learning applications in real-world settings.

Scalability and Computational Complexity

Unsupervised learning often processes large, high-dimensional datasets, posing scalability challenges. In recommender systems, matrix factorization or deep models like variational autoencoders handle millions of user-item interactions, requiring distributed computing or GPU acceleration. Image and video analysis demands intensive computation for convolutional autoencoders or GANs, especially for real-time applications like autonomous driving. Social network analysis struggles with massive graphs, where algorithms like Louvain or graph autoencoders scale poorly without optimized frameworks. Industrial/IoT applications process high-velocity sensor streams, necessitating edge computing for real-time anomaly detection. Solutions such as dimensionality reduction (for example, PCA) or efficient algorithms (for example, FP-growth in market basket analysis) mitigate these issues, but computational bottlenecks remain a hurdle for large-scale deployment.

Interpretability and Explainability

Interpretability is critical for stakeholder trust, particularly in sensitive domains. During fraud detection, explaining why a transaction was flagged as anomalous using deep autoencoders is challenging due to their opaque latent representations. Genomics requires biologists to understand gene clusters, but deep models like VAEs may obscure biological meaning. Customer segmentation needs clear cluster descriptions for marketing teams, yet deep-embedded clustering can produce abstract results. Traditional methods, such as K-means or Isolation Forest, offer better interpretability, but lack the accuracy of deep models. Techniques like visualizing embeddings with UMAP or rule-based explanations in market basket analysis improve transparency, but balancing accuracy and interpretability remains an important challenge.

Data Quality and Preprocessing

Unsupervised learning is sensitive to data quality issues. Sparsity affects recommender systems and market basket analysis, where missing interactions or rare item combinations weaken patterns. Noise in image and video data, such as varying lighting, degrades clustering or reconstruction. Heterogeneity in genomics, like batch effects in gene expression, distorts clusters. Dynamic data in social networks or IoT systems requires models to adapt to evolving patterns. Robust preprocessing, such as normalization, outlier removal, or self-supervised learning for feature enhancement, is essential. However, over-preprocessing risks losing critical information and hence requires careful data engineering.

Ethical and Privacy Concerns

Ethical challenges arise when unsupervised learning informs decision-making. Customer segmentation and social network analysis risk profiling users based on sensitive attributes, potentially leading to discrimination or privacy violations. Fraud detection might falsely flag legitimate users, causing inconvenience or bias against certain demographics. Genomics handles sensitive patient data, where breaches or misuse could harm individuals. Industrial/IoT applications monitoring worker performance via sensors raise surveillance concerns. Fairness, transparency, and compliance with regulations like GDPR are critical. Techniques such as federated learning or differential privacy, applicable in genomics or IoT, help mitigate risks, but ethical deployment remains a complex challenge.

Generalization and Robustness

Ensuring generalization across diverse or evolving datasets is difficult. In fraud detection, new fraud schemes require adaptive anomaly detection. Social network analysis must handle shifting user behaviors. Genomics faces challenges with rare disease data, thus limiting model robustness. Self-supervised learning and generative models like VAEs improve generalization, but overfitting to specific datasets or failure to capture rare events remains a concern. Robust validation, such as cross-dataset testing, is essential but often limited by data availability.

The challenges of scalability, interpretability, data quality, ethics, and generalization underscore the complexities of applying unsupervised learning in real-world contexts. From recommender systems to IoT, these hurdles require careful algorithm selection, robust preprocessing, and ethical considerations. Hence, it is important to address them and ensure that you fully realize the potential of unsupervised learning

Future Trends in Unsupervised Learning Applications

Unsupervised learning has transformed fields such as customer segmentation, recommender systems, image analysis, fraud detection, market basket analysis, social networks, genomics, and industrial/IoT applications. As challenges like scalability, interpretability, and ethics persist, emerging trends are poised to expand its capabilities. The recent trends in unsupervised learning include hybrid models, multimodal learning, federated learning and generative AI. These trends leverage the advances in unsupervised learning techniques including clustering, dimensionality reduction, anomaly detection, and deep unsupervised learning. This section will explore these innovations, their potential to address current limitations, and their impact on future applications.

Hybrid Models Combining Supervised and Unsupervised Learning

Hybrid models integrating unsupervised and supervised learning are gaining traction to address data scarcity and improve performance. In recommender systems, unsupervised matrix factorization pre-trains embeddings, which supervised models fine-tune with sparse ratings, enhancing personalization. In fraud detection, unsupervised anomaly detection identifies outliers, which supervised classifiers refine with limited labeled fraud cases, improving accuracy. Genomics uses unsupervised clustering to group patient subtypes, guiding supervised drug response predictions. These hybrids mitigate the cold-start problem in recommender systems and improve robustness in dynamic domains like fraud, promising more accurate and adaptable solutions.

Multimodal Learning for Integrated Data Analysis

Multimodal learning, which processes diverse data types (for example, text, images, audio), is revolutionizing unsupervised applications. In image and video analysis, models like vision transformers with self-supervised learning integrate video frames and audio for tasks like video summarization. Social network analysis combines graph structures with user posts or images, using multimodal graph autoencoders to detect communities with richer contexts. Market basket analysis incorporates product images or descriptions alongside transaction data, enhancing association rules. Genomics integrates gene expression with clinical or imaging data for holistic disease profiling. By leveraging cross-modal patterns, multimodal learning addresses data heterogeneity and enables comprehensive insights.

Federated Learning for Privacy-Preserving Analysis

Federated learning enables collaborative model training across decentralized datasets, addressing privacy concerns. In genomics, hospitals share unsupervised model updates without exchanging sensitive patient data, improving gene clustering for rare diseases. Fraud detection benefits as banks train anomaly detection models on local transaction data, aggregating insights to detect global fraud patterns. Industrial/IoT applications use federated learning to train autoencoders across factories, preserving proprietary sensor data. Social network analysis applies it to analyze user interactions across platforms without centralizing private data. Federated learning ensures ethical deployment, thereby making it critical for sensitive domains.

Generative AI and Synthetic Data Generation

Generative models like GANs and diffusion models are expanding unsupervised learning by creating synthetic data. In image and video analysis, diffusion models generate high-quality medical images, augmenting datasets for rare conditions. Genomics uses VAEs to simulate gene expression profiles, addressing data scarcity. Fraud detection employs GANs to generate synthetic fraud scenarios, improving model robustness. Customer segmentation leverages synthetic customer profiles to test marketing strategies. These models mitigate data limitations and enable stress-testing but require careful validation to ensure synthetic data reflects real-world distribution.

Real-Time and Edge-Based Unsupervised Learning

Real-time processing and edge computing are critical for dynamic applications. Industrial/IoT applications deploy lightweight autoencoders on edge devices for instant anomaly detection in sensors, reducing latency. Fraud detection uses streaming clustering to monitor transactions in real-time. Image analysis applies edge-based clustering for autonomous vehicles, enabling rapid obstacle detection. Optimized algorithms and hardware acceleration address scalability challenges, thus making unsupervised learning viable for time-sensitive use cases.

Explainable and Robust Models

Advances in explainable AI are improving interpretability. In social network analysis, attention-based graph models highlight influential nodes in communities. Genomics uses interpretable embeddings to explain gene clusters. Fraud detection adopts rule-based anomaly explanations alongside deep models. Robustness is enhanced through adversarial training, ensuring models such as GANs or VAEs generalize to new data in dynamic fields such as fraud or IoT. These trends enhance trust and reliability in unsupervised applications.

Future trends in unsupervised learning, such as hybrid models, multimodal learning, federated learning, generative AI, real-time processing, and explainable models, promise to overcome current challenges and expand applications.

Conclusion

In this chapter, we explored the applications of unsupervised learning across diverse real-world domains. Unsupervised learning drives business value in applications such as customer segmentation, where K-means and deep embedded clustering are used to personalize marketing; and recommender systems, where we leveraged matrix factorization and VAEs for tailored suggestions. Image and video analysis uses autoencoders for medical imaging, while fraud detection employs anomaly detection to secure finance and cybersecurity. As for market basket analysis, it can uncover product relationships with association rules, while social network analysis identifies communities via graph-based clustering. Genomics advances drug discovery through gene clustering, and industrial/IoT applications optimize operations with predictive maintenance. We also covered challenges like scalability, interpretability, data quality, and ethics that highlight the need for careful implementation of unsupervised learning methods. We discussed the future trends in unsupervised learning including hybrid models, multimodal learning, and federated learning.

In the next chapter, we will delve into its specialized applications in natural language processing, where similar techniques unlock patterns in textual data.

Key Terms

- **Customer Segmentation**: The process of grouping customers into clusters based on shared traits, such as purchasing habits, using unsupervised learning techniques like clustering; can be used in targeted marketing and customer relationship management.
- **Topic Modeling**: The identification of underlying themes or topics in large text datasets using unsupervised learning methods like Latent Dirichlet Allocation; can be used in applications such as in document analysis and information retrieval.
- **Anomaly Detection**: The process of identifying rare or unusual data points in unsupervised learning by often using techniques like Isolation Forest; can be used in cybersecurity and fraud detection.
- **Image Denoising**: The removal of noise or artifacts from images using unsupervised learning models like autoencoders; can be used in applications such as in enhancing medical imaging and improving photograph quality.
- **Data Visualization**: The projection of high-dimensional data into lower-dimensional spaces for visual interpretation using unsupervised learning techniques like t-SNE; can be used in bioinformatics and financial analysis.
- **Synthetic Data Generation**: The creation of artificial data that resembles real-world distributions using unsupervised learning models like Generative Adversarial Networks; can be used in applications such as data augmentation and simulation.
- **Recommendation Systems**: The grouping of similar users or items to provide personalized suggestions using unsupervised learning techniques like matrix factorization; can be used in e-commerce and streaming services.
- **Feature Learning**: The automatic extraction of meaningful data representations from raw inputs using unsupervised learning models like autoencoders; can be used in applications such as improving predictive modeling and computer vision.
- **Geographic Clustering**: The grouping of spatial data points into clusters based on proximity or similarity using unsupervised learning techniques like DBSCAN; is used for urban planning and disaster response
- **Text Summarization**: The extraction of key ideas or themes from large text corpora using unsupervised learning methods like topic modeling; can be used for news aggregation and automated report generation

Questions

1. Explain how autoencoders are applied in unsupervised learning for image denoising. Describe the process and discuss why this application is valuable in real-world scenarios such as medical imaging.

2. Discuss the role of K-Means clustering in customer segmentation for marketing. How does this unsupervised learning technique help businesses tailor their strategies, and what challenges might arise during its implementation?

3. Describe how Principal Component Analysis (PCA) is used to reduce dimensionality in high-dimensional datasets. Provide an example of a specific application such as facial recognition, and explain the benefits of this approach.

4. Explore the application of Generative Adversarial Networks (GANs) in generating realistic synthetic images. How do GANs achieve this, and what are some ethical considerations when using GAN-generated content in industries like entertainment or advertising?

5. Elaborate on how topic modeling, such as Latent Dirichlet Allocation (LDA), is applied in unsupervised learning to analyze large collections of text documents. Provide a real-world example, such as a news article analysis, and discuss its impact on information retrieval.

6. Describe the use of unsupervised learning for anomaly detection in cybersecurity, particularly in identifying unusual network traffic patterns. How do techniques like Isolation Forest contribute to this application, and what are the potential limitations?

7. Explain how t-SNE is applied in unsupervised learning to visualize high-dimensional data, such as gene expression datasets. Discuss the steps involved, and why this visualization is critical for researchers in fields like bioinformatics.

8. Discuss the application of variational autoencoders in generating new creative content, such as music or artwork. How do VAEs differ from traditional autoencoders in this context, and what makes them suitable for creative industries?

9. Describe how DBSCAN is used in unsupervised learning for clustering spatial data, such as identifying geographic hotspots in urban planning. Explain the advantages of DBSCAN over other clustering methods in this application.

10. Explain how unsupervised learning techniques, such as clustering or matrix factorization, are applied in recommender systems to group similar items or users. Provide an example from an e-commerce platform, and discuss how this enhances user experience and business outcomes.

Multiple Choice Questions

1. What is a common application of autoencoders in unsupervised learning for image processing?
   a. Image Classification
   b. Image Denoising
   c. Object Detection
   d. Image Segmentation
2. How is K-Means clustering typically applied in marketing?
   a. Predicting Customer Purchases
   b. Customer Segmentation
   c. Price Optimization
   d. Inventory Management
3. What is a key application of clustering algorithms like K-Means in unsupervised learning?
   a. Dimensionality Reduction
   b. Image Denoising
   c. Customer Segmentation
   d. Feature Extraction
4. Which application of Principal Component Analysis (PCA) is most relevant in unsupervised learning?
   a. Reducing Data Dimensionality for Visualization
   b. Data Classification
   c. Generating Synthetic Data
   d. Clustering Similar Items

5. What is a key application of Generative Adversarial Networks (GANs) in unsupervised learning?
    a. Outlier Detection
    b. Generating Realistic Images
    c. Data Compression
    d. Feature Selection
6. How is topic modeling, such as Latent Dirichlet Allocation (LDA), commonly applied in unsupervised learning?
    a. Image Enhancement
    b. Anomaly Detection
    c. Visualizing High-Dimensional Data
    d. Extracting Themes from Text Documents
7. Which unsupervised learning application is most associated with anomaly detection in cybersecurity?
    a. Clustering User Behavior
    b. Identifying Unusual Network Traffic Patterns
    c. Generating Synthetic Data
    d. Reducing Feature Dimensions
8. How are Variational Autoencoders (VAEs) applied in unsupervised learning for creative industries?
    a. Classifying Art Styles
    b. Reducing Image Resolution
    c. Generating New Designs or Artworks
    d. Clustering Similar Images
9. What is the primary application of DBSCAN in unsupervised learning for spatial data analysis?
    a. Generating Synthetic Locations
    b. Identifying Clusters of Geographic Points
    c. Compressing Location Data
    d. Predicting Movement Patterns

10. How is unsupervised learning applied in recommender systems?
    a. Predicting User Ratings
    b. Classifying User Preferences
    c. Grouping Similar Items or Users for Recommendations
    d. Optimizing Pricing Models

Answers

1. b
2. b
3. c
4. a
5. b
6. d
7. b
8. c
9. b
10. c

CHAPTER 8
Unsupervised Learning for Natural Language Processing

Introduction

In this chapter, we will dive into the intersection of unsupervised learning and Natural Language Processing (NLP). We will explore how unsupervised learning techniques help unlock hidden patterns in text. From traditional methods like Latent Semantic Analysis and topic modelling to cutting-edge transformer-based models like BERT, this chapter will cover the tools and knowledge to enable you to tackle real-world NLP problems using Python. We will also delve into some foundational approaches, modern advancements and practical applications such as document clustering, semantic search and topic discovery, zero-shot learning and cross-lingual NLP. The hands-on examples using Python libraries like scikit-learn, transformers will guide you through building robust unsupervised NLP pipelines.

Structure

In this chapter, we will discuss the following topics:

- Introduction to Unsupervised Learning in NLP
  - Text-Preprocessing and Text Representation
  - Document Clustering
  - Topic Modelling using LSA and DDA
- Word Embeddings: Word2Vec, GloVe, FastText
- Unsupervised NLP with Neural Models – BERT
  - Unsupervised Finetuning and Adaptation

- Practical Considerations and Challenges of Unsupervised Learning in NLP
- Recent Trends in Unsupervised NLP

Introduction to Unsupervised Learning in NLP

Unsupervised learning deals with techniques for discovering the patterns from unlabelled data. In the field of Natural Language Processing (NLP), this capability is valuable, given the vast and unstructured nature of text data present on the internet in the form of social media posts, customer reviews, news articles, scientific papers and so on. This text often is unlabelled. Unsupervised learning techniques can be used to discover patterns in them, such as the topics the text is about, semantically-related text, the sentiment carried by the text and so on.

Unsupervised learning techniques in NLP can scale well and adapt to diverse text datasets. Unlike supervised learning methods, which need costly and labor-intensive manual labelling of data, unsupervised learning methods can process raw text to extract meaningful insights. These methods are especially important when labelled data is scare, such as in tasks involving the analysis of low-resource languages text and discovering new and emerging trends in real-time data streams. Unsupervised learning techniques like clustering algorithms are used to group similar text documents, while dimensionality reduction techniques like t-SNE and UMAP are used to visualize high dimensional text representations.

Historically, NLP was carried out using statistical methods like Latent Semantic Analysis (LSA) and Latent Dirichlet Allocation (LDA), which model word co-occurrences or probabilistic topic distributions. These approaches while effective for tasks like document similarity and topic discovery, often struggle with capturing deep semantic relationships. Text embedding techniques like Word2Vec (https://code.google.com/archive/p/word2vec/) and GloVe (https://nlp.stanford.edu/projects/glove/) represent words of text as dense vectors that encode semantic meaning.

Recent, transformer-based models like BERT and GPT have revolutionized unsupervised NLP through self-supervised pre-training, where models learn from vast corpora of text by predicting masked word or sentence relationships. As of the year 2025, these models power state-of-the-art applications, from zero-shot classification to cross-lingual tasks and continue to evolve with innovations in efficiency and multimodal learning.

Unsupervised methods like topic modeling and word embeddings have significantly transformed tasks such as text classification, sentiment analysis, and information retrieval by enabling the extraction of meaningful patterns and representations from unlabeled text data.

Important Unsupervised Learning Methods in NLP

- **Topic Modeling:** Topic modeling identifies latent themes or topics in a collection of documents by analyzing word co-occurrence patterns. Each topic is a distribution over words and each document is a mixture of topics. Important methods for topic modelling include Latent Dirichlet Allocation (LDA), Non-negative Matrix Factorization (NMF), Latent Semantic Analysis (LSA).
- **Word Embeddings**: Word embeddings map words to dense, low-dimensional vectors capturing semantic relationships (for example, "king" is close to "queen"). These are learned in an unsupervised manner from large text corpora. Important methods for learning word embeddings include Word2Vec, GloVe, FastText.
- **Document Clustering**: Document clustering groups similar documents, sentences, or words based on their features, which are often derived from word embeddings or document-term matrices. Important algorithms for document clustering are K-means, hierarchical clustering, DBSCAN.
- **Dimensionality Reduction**: Reduces high-dimensional text-representation (for example, document-term matrices or embeddings) to lower dimensions for visualization or downstream tasks. Important methods for dimensionality reduction include principal component analysis, t-SNE, UMAP.
- **Language Model Pre-training** (Unsupervised or Self-Supervised): Modern NLP relies on large-scale language models pre-trained on massive text corpora in an unsupervised or self-supervised manner, while learning contextual representations of words or sentences. Important models trained using self-supervised learning are BERT (Bidirectional Encoder Representation from Transformers), GPT (Generative Pre-Trained Transformer), Sentence-BERT, and so on.
- **Text Denoising/Anomaly Detection/Text Generation**: Autoencoders are neural networks that learn compressed representations of text by reconstructing input data (for example, document embeddings or bag-of-words vectors). Variational autoencoders can be used to generate text, denoising autoencoders can reconstruct clean text from noisy inputs learning robust text features.

Most of the above methods require careful text preprocessing (for example, tokenization, stop word removal, lemmatization) to ensure quality results. Methods like LDA and K-means scale well for large datasets, while t-SNE and hierarchical clustering may be computationally intensive. Since unsupervised methods lack ground truth, evaluation relies on metrics like coherence (for topics), silhouette scores (for clustering), or qualitative analysis. Topic modeling and clustering produce interpretable results, while embeddings and autoencoders require additional steps to derive human-readable insights.

These methods form the backbone of unsupervised NLP, enabling tasks like text exploration, summarization, and semantic analysis. By combining them (for example, clustering document embeddings from BERT), you can discover deeper insights from unstructured text data.

We have already learned about Clustering methods in *Chapter* 3, Dimensionality Reduction techniques in *Chapter* 4, and anomaly detection methods in *Chapter* 5. In this chapter, we will focus on the methods for Topic Modeling, while learning about Word Embeddings and Self-supervised pre-training of large language models.

Early unsupervised learning techniques in NLP focused on text preprocessing (for example, tokenization, stemming) and simple representations like bag-of-words or TF-IDF. Clustering methods such as K-means and hierarchical clustering, enable document grouping, while Latent Semantic Analysis (LSA) uses singular value decomposition to uncover latent topics. Probabilistic models like Latent Dirichlet Allocation (LDA) have further advanced topic modeling by capturing document-topic distributions. These traditional approaches laid the groundwork for understanding text structure and semantics, paving the way for modern embeddings and self-supervised methods used in large language models.

Text Pre-Processing

Text Preprocessing is the initial step of cleaning and standardizing raw text to make it suitable for representation and analysis. It includes tasks like tokenization (splitting text into words or sub-words), stemming (reducing words to their root form, for example, "running" to "run"), and lemmatization (mapping words to their dictionary form, for example, "better" to "good"). Other steps may involve removing punctuation, stop words, or special characters and normalizing case to ensure consistency. Preprocessing reduces noise and vocabulary size, thereby making unsupervised learning more effective.

Tokenization, Stemming, Lemmatization

Tokenization is the process of breaking down raw text into smaller units, called tokens, typically words, subwords, or punctuation marks. For example, the sentence "The cats are running!" might be tokenized into `["The", "cats", "are", "running", "!"]`. Tokenization handles challenges such as punctuation, contractions, and language-specific rules, and often serves as the first step in preparing text for NLP tasks. Tools like NLTK or spaCy provide robust tokenizers for various languages.

Stemming is a heuristic process that reduces words to their root or base form by removing suffixes, often producing non-words. For instance, "running" and "runner" might both stem to "run," while "better" might become "bett." Algorithms like the

Porter or Snowball stemmer are commonly used. Stemming simplifies text by reducing vocabulary size but can be imprecise due to its rule-based nature.

Lemmatization reduces words to their dictionary form, or lemma, using linguistic knowledge such as part-of-speech and context. For example, "running" becomes "run," and "better" becomes "good." Unlike stemming, lemmatization ensures valid words but is more computationally intensive and requires language-specific resources. It is more accurate for capturing semantic meaning in NLP tasks.

While lemmatization is more accurate, it is computationally intensive and requires language-specific resources. Both stemming and lemmatization reduce vocabulary size and improve the consistency of text representations for unsupervised tasks.

Text Representation

Text Representation in NLP refers to the process of converting unstructured text into a structured, numerical format that machine learning algorithms can process. It involves transforming words, sentences, or documents into mathematical representations, such as vectors, which capture linguistic properties like frequency, semantics, or context. Common methods include Bag-of-Words (BoW), TF-IDF, and word embeddings, where each varies in complexity and the ability to preserve meaning.

Bag-of-Words (BoW) and Term Frequency-Inverse Document Frequency (TF-IDF)

The Bag-of-Words (BoW) model represents text as a collection of words, ignoring grammar and word order. Each document is encoded as a vector, where each dimension corresponds to a word in the vocabulary, and the value represents its frequency (or presence). For example, given a vocabulary {"cat", "dog", "run"}, the sentence "Cat run" might be represented as `[1, 0, 1]`. BoW is simple and effective for tasks like document clustering but discards contextual information, thus treating "dog chases cat" and "cat chases dog" as identical.

Term frequency-inverse document frequency (TF-IDF) builds on BoW by weighing words based on their importance. Term frequency (TF) measures how often a word appears in a document, while inverse document frequency (IDF) reduces the weight of common words (for example, "the") that appear across many documents. The TF-IDF score for a word is calculated as:

$$[\ \text{TF-IDF(t, d)} = \text{TF(t, d)} \times \log\left(\frac{N}{\text{DF}(t)}\right)]$$

Where

`t` is the term, d is the document

`N` is the total number of documents

`DF(t)` is the number of documents containing term t.

TF-IDF highlights discriminative words, thereby making it useful for tasks like information retrieval and topic modeling. Libraries like scikit-learn provide efficient implementations for constructing BoW and TF-IDF representations.

Limitations of Early Text Representations

Despite their utility, early text representation methods have significant drawbacks. BoW and TF-IDF treat words as independent units and ignore word order and context, which results in the loss of semantic meaning. For example, they cannot distinguish between "*I love coding*" and "*I hate coding*" beyond the presence of "love" or "hate." These methods also suffer from high dimensionality as the vocabulary size grows with the corpus, resulting in sparse vectors that increase computational complexity. Additionally, they struggle with polysemy (words with multiple meanings) and synonymy as they assign distinct representations to synonyms and the same representation to a word regardless of its context. These limitations motivated the development of dense, context-aware representations like word embeddings.

Document Clustering

Document clustering enables the grouping of similar documents or text snippets without predefined labels. Using text representations like Bag-of-Words (BoW) or TF-IDF, clustering techniques such as K-means and hierarchical clustering organize text data into meaningful clusters, facilitating tasks like document organization.

K-Means Algorithm for Document Clustering

K-means clustering is a popular, efficient algorithm that partitions documents into a predefined number of clusters, (K), by minimizing the variance within each cluster. The algorithm starts by randomly initializing (K) centroids, assigns each document to the nearest centroid based on a distance metric (for example, Euclidean or cosine distance) and iteratively updates centroids until convergence. In NLP, documents are typically represented as TF-IDF vectors, where each dimension corresponds to a term in the vocabulary. For example, a collection of news articles might be clustered into (K = 5) groups, revealing topics like politics, sports, or technology.

K-means is computationally efficient and scales well to large datasets, which makes it suitable for document clustering tasks. Applications include organizing large corpora such as grouping Wikipedia articles by topic or clustering customer reviews by themes. However, K-means requires specifying (K) in advance, which can be challenging without prior knowledge. It also assumes spherical clusters and struggles with high-dimensional, sparse text data and often requiring dimensionality reduction techniques such as PCA to improve performance.

Python Code for Applying K-Means for Document Clustering

Figure 8.1 shows the Python code for implementing the K-Means algorithm to cluster text documents from the 20 newsgroups text datasets. This dataset contains around 18000 newsgroups posts on 20 topics split into two subsets—training and testing. (**`http://qwone.com/~jason/20Newsgroups/`**). We use the **`sklearn.datasets.fetch_20newsgroups`** function to download the data archive from the original website, extract the archive contents and call the **`sklearn.datasets.load_files`** on both training and testing subsets of data. We are extracting documents belonging to only three categories—science-electronics, science-medicine and science-space—from the 20 topics present in the dataset. TF-IDF is used to vectorize text before fitting K-Means to the text vectors. Comments in the code explain each important step.

```
import numpy as np
from sklearn.datasets import fetch_20newsgroups
from sklearn.feature_extraction.text import TfidfVectorizer
from sklearn.cluster import KMeans
from wordcloud import WordCloud
import matplotlib.pyplot as plt
from time import time
# Load the 20newsgroups dataset with selected categories -electronics, medicine, and space
categories = ["sci.electronics", "sci.med", "sci.space"]
dataset = fetch_20newsgroups(
    remove=("headers", "footers", "quotes"),  # Remove metadata to focus on content
    subset="all",  # Use all data (train + test) for clustering
    categories=categories,shuffle=True,random_state=42,)
# Extract true labels and compute category sizes
labels = dataset.target  # Ground truth labels (0: electronics, 1: med, 2: space)
unique_labels, category_sizes = np.unique(labels, return_counts=True)  # Count documents per category
true_k = unique_labels.shape[0]  # Number of unique categories (3)
print(f"{len(dataset.data)} documents - {true_k} categories")  # Print dataset summary
# Vectorize text data using TF-IDF
vectorizer = TfidfVectorizer(max_df=0.5,min_df=5,stop_words="english")
t0 = time()  # Start timing vectorization
X_tfidf = vectorizer.fit_transform(dataset.data)  # Transform text to TF-IDF matrix
print(f"vectorization done in {time() - t0:.3f} s")  # Print time taken
print(f"n_samples: {X_tfidf.shape[0]}, n_features: {X_tfidf.shape[1]}")  # Print matrix dimensions
print(f"Matrix Sparsity is: {X_tfidf.nnz / np.prod(X_tfidf.shape):.3f}")  # Print matrix sparsity
# Perform K-means clustering with multiple random seeds
for seed in range(4):
    kmeans = KMeans(n_clusters=true_k,max_iter=100,n_init=10,random_state=seed).fit(X_tfidf)
    cluster_ids, cluster_sizes = np.unique(kmeans.labels_, return_counts=True)  # Count documents per cluster
    print(f"Number of elements assigned to each cluster: {cluster_sizes}")  # Print cluster sizes
print("True number of documents in each category according to the class labels:"f"{category_sizes}")
#top terms per cluster (Use centroid values (TF-IDF weights) to identify important terms)
centroids = kmeans.cluster_centers_.argsort()[:, ::-1]  # Sort indices by centroid values (descending)
terms = vectorizer.get_feature_names_out()  # Get vocabulary terms
for i in range(true_k):
    print("Cluster %d:" % i, end='')  # Print cluster number
    for ind in centroids[i, :10]:  # Print top 10 terms
        print(' %s' % terms[ind], end='')
# Generate word clouds for each cluster, use centroid weights to determine word sizes in the clouds
plt.figure(figsize=(15, 5))
for i in range(true_k):
    # Create a dictionary of terms and their centroid weights for the word cloud
    term_weights = {terms[ind]: kmeans.cluster_centers_[i, ind] for ind in centroids[i, :50]}  # Top 50 terms
    # Generate word cloud with specified parameters
    wordcloud = WordCloud(width=400, height=300,background_color='white',max_words=50,
                          random_state=42).generate_from_frequencies(term_weights)
    # Plot word cloud in a subplot (1 row, 3 columns)
    plt.subplot(1, true_k, i + 1)  # Select subplot for cluster i
    plt.imshow(wordcloud, interpolation='bilinear')  # Display word cloud
    plt.title(f'Cluster {i}')  # Set title as Cluster 0, 1, or 2
    plt.axis('off')
plt.tight_layout() |
plt.savefig('kmeans_wordclouds.png')
```

Figure 8.1: *Python Code for K-Means Algorithm for Document Clustering*

Figure 8.2 shows the output of above code including the word clouds for each of the three document clusters. According to this output, the three categories of our data contain a total of 2,961 documents with 6,751 features. It also shows number of elements assigned to each cluster. The number of clusters is equal to the number of categories in the data, that is 3. The following Word cloud representation shows the top 50 words in each of the three document clusters:

```
2961 documents - 3 categories
vectorization done in 0.250 s
n_samples: 2961, n_features: 6751
Matrix Sparsity is: 0.007
Number of elements assigned to each cluster: [2418   71  472]
Number of elements assigned to each cluster: [2465   71  425]
Number of elements assigned to each cluster: [2424  466   71]
Number of elements assigned to each cluster: [2140  750   71]
True number of documents in each category according to the class labels:[984 990 987]
Cluster 0: space like know just use thanks does don edu usedCluster 1: people don know like msg just doctor good think diseaseC
luster 2: shameful surrender cadre dsl n3jxp chastity skepticism geb intellect pitt
```

Figure 8.2: *Word Clouds Showing Top 50 Words in Each Document Cluster*

Topic Modelling Using Latent Semantic Analysis (LSA)

Latent Semantic Analysis (LSA), also known as Latent Semantic Indexing (LSI), is an unsupervised learning technique used in Natural Language Processing (NLP) to uncover latent (hidden) relationships between words, documents, and concepts in a text corpus. LSA leverages linear algebra, specifically Singular Value Decomposition (SVD), to reduce the dimensionality of high-dimensional text representations such as term-document matrices created from Bag-of-Words (BoW) or Term Frequency-Inverse Document Frequency (TF-IDF). By projecting these matrices into a lower-dimensional "semantic space," LSA captures underlying patterns and relationships like synonyms or topical similarities, which are not explicit in the original data. For example, LSA might reveal that "car" and "automobile" are related by placing them close together in the semantic space, even if they don't co-occur frequently in documents.

The process works as follows:

1. **Construct a Term-Document Matrix**: Represent the corpus as a matrix where rows are terms (words) and columns are documents, with entries indicating term frequencies or TF-IDF weights.

2. **Apply SVD**: Decompose the matrix into three components: `A = UΣVT`, where `U` represents term-to-concept relationships, `Σ` contains singular values indicating concept importance, and `VT` represents document to concept relationships.

3. **Reduce Dimensionality**: Keep only the top k singular values and corresponding vectors to create a lower-dimensional approximation of the original matrix and capture the most significant latent concepts.

4. **Interpret the Semantic Space**: The reduced matrix represents documents and terms in a k-dimensional space where similarity (for example, cosine similarity) reflects semantic relationships.

LSA assumes that words with similar meanings appear in similar contexts (the distributional hypothesis), allowing it to model semantic structure without labeled data. However, LSA assumes linear relationships in the data, which may not capture complex semantic patterns. It doesn't model word order or local context, unlike modern embeddings. The latent dimensions (concepts) are not always easily interpretable as distinct topics. These limitations led to the rise of probabilistic models (for example, LDA) and word embeddings which capture richer context in text.

Python Implementation of LSA on 20 News Groups Text Dataset

In *Figure* 8.3, we see the Python implementation of LSA on 20 news groups' text dataset with three categories—**`sci.electronics`**, **`sci.med`**, **`sci.space`**. The text is vectorized using TF-IDF. We have applied LSA with TruncatedSVD to reduce the TF-IDF matrix to 3 components that is, 3 latent topics capturing the most significant semantic patterns in text. Here, TruncatedSVD is used because it is efficient for sparse matrices like TF-IDF. Our code prints the top 10 terms per topic based on the **`lsa.components_`** matrix, which maps terms to topics. Higher weights indicate stronger associations with a topic (for example, "space, nasa" for a space-related topic). We generate a word cloud for each topic using the top 50 terms' weight from **`lsa.components_`**. Larger words indicate higher weights or topic importance. The output also prints dataset statistics, vectorization time, LSA time, matrix shapes, explained variance ration and top terms in text.

```
import numpy as np # For numerical operations and array handling
from sklearn.datasets import fetch_20newsgroups # To load the 20newsgroups dataset
from sklearn.feature_extraction.text import TfidfVectorizer # For TF-IDF vectorization
from sklearn.decomposition import TruncatedSVD # For LSA via Singular Value Decomposition
from wordcloud import WordCloud # For generating word cloud visualizations
import matplotlib.pyplot as plt # For plotting word clouds
from time import time # To measure processing time
# Load the 20newsgroups dataset with selected categories
categories = ["sci.electronics", "sci.med", "sci.space"]
dataset = fetch_20newsgroups(remove=("headers", "footers", "quotes"), # Remove metadata to focus on content
    subset="all", categories=categories, shuffle=True, random_state=42,)
# Print dataset summary
print(f"{len(dataset.data)} documents - {len(categories)} categories")
# Vectorize text data using TF-IDF
# TF-IDF converts text to numerical vectors, emphasizing important words
vectorizer = TfidfVectorizer(max_df=0.5,min_df=5,stop_words="english")
t0 = time() # Start timing vectorization
X_tfidf = vectorizer.fit_transform(dataset.data) # Transform text to TF-IDF matrix
print(f"Vectorization done in {time() - t0:.3f} s")
print(f"n_samples: {X_tfidf.shape[0]}, n_features: {X_tfidf.shape[1]}")
print(f"Sparsity: {X_tfidf.nnz / np.prod(X_tfidf.shape):.3f}")
# Apply Latent Semantic Analysis (LSA) using Truncated SVD
# Reduce the TF-IDF matrix to a lower-dimensional semantic space
n_components = 3 # Number of latent topics (set to number of categories for simplicity)
lsa = TruncatedSVD(n_components=n_components, random_state=42) # Initialize LSA model
t0 = time() # Start timing LSA
X_lsa = lsa.fit_transform(X_tfidf) # Transform TF-IDF matrix to latent space
print(f"LSA done in {time() - t0:.3f} s")
print(f"Reduced matrix shape: {X_lsa.shape}")
# Print explained variance ratio to show how much information is retained
explained_variance = lsa.explained_variance_ratio_.sum()
print(f"Explained variance ratio of {n_components} components: {explained_variance:.3f}")
# Extract and print top terms for each latent topic
# Use LSA components to identify terms with highest weights per topic
terms = vectorizer.get_feature_names_out() # Get vocabulary terms
components = lsa.components_ # Term-to-topic matrix
for i in range(n_components):
    print(f"Topic {i}:", end='')
    top_term_indices = components[i].argsort()[::-1][:10]#Sort terms by their weights -| Top 10 terms
    for idx in top_term_indices:
        print(f" {terms[idx]}", end='')
# Generate word clouds for each latent topic - Use component weights to determine word sizes in the clouds
plt.figure(figsize=(15, 5)) # Create a figure with width 15, height 5
for i in range(n_components):
    # Create a dictionary of terms and their weights for the word cloud
    term_weights = {terms[idx]: components[i, idx] for idx in components[i].argsort()[::-1][:50]} # Top 50 terms
    wordcloud = WordCloud(width=400,height=300,background_color='white',max_words=50,
                          random_state=42).generate_from_frequencies(term_weights)
    plt.subplot(1, n_components, i + 1) # Select subplot for topic i
    plt.imshow(wordcloud, interpolation='bilinear') # Display word cloud
    plt.title(f'Topic {i}') # Set title as Topic 0, 1, or 2
    plt.axis('off') # Hide axes for clean visualization
plt.tight_layout() # Adjust spacing between subplots
```

Figure 8.3: Python Code for LSA on 20 News Groups Dataset

Figure 8.4 shows the output of the preceding code and the word clouds corresponding to the three prominent latent semantic topics:

```
2961 documents - 3 categories
Vectorization done in 0.270 s
n_samples: 2961, n_features: 6751
Sparsity: 0.007
LSA done in 0.022 s
Reduced matrix shape: (2961, 3)
Explained variance ratio of 3 components: 0.018
Topic 0: space like don know just think does people use eduTopic 1: geb shameful surrender cadre dsl pitt n3jxp chastity skepti
cism intellectTopic 2: space nasa shuttle launch orbit moon mission earth satellite program
```

***Figure 8.4:** Word Clouds Corresponding to Latent Semantic Analysis of 20 News Groups Dataset*

Probabilistic Models in NLP

Probabilistic models in NLP are unsupervised learning techniques that model text data as probabilistic distributions over latent structures, such as topics or concepts, to uncover hidden patterns without requiring labeled data. Unlike deterministic methods like LSA, which rely on linear algebra, probabilistic models such as LDA and Probabilistic Latent Semantic Analysis (PLSA) treat documents as mixtures of topics, where each topic is a distribution over words. These models use statistical inference to estimate these distributions, making them particularly effective for tasks like topic modeling, document clustering, and text summarization. By capturing the uncertainty and variability in text, probabilistic models provide interpretable results such as topics represented by dominant words, and are well-suited for handling the complexity and ambiguity of natural language. They have a significant influence on modern NLP approaches like embeddings and transformer-based models.

LDA for Topic Modeling

Topic modeling is an unsupervised learning technique in NLP that aims to discover latent themes or topics within a collection of documents, thereby enabling the organization and interpretation of large, unlabeled text corpora. By assuming that documents are mixtures of topics and that topics are distributions over words, topic modeling identifies patterns of word co-occurrence to reveal underlying semantic structures. For example, in a news corpus, topic modeling might uncover topics like "politics" or "sports," represented by words such as "election, government" or "game, team." This approach is useful for tasks like document clustering, information retrieval, and text summarization, as it provides interpretable insights without requiring manual annotations. Probabilistic models like LDA and PLSA are prominent techniques used for topic modeling, offering a robust framework for capturing the probabilistic relationships between documents, topics, and words.

Latent Dirichlet Allocation (LDA) is a generative probabilistic model. Unlike Latent Semantic Analysis (LSA), which uses linear algebra to learn semantic structures in text, LDA models documents as mixtures of topics, where each topic is a probability distribution over words, and each document is a distribution over topics. This approach assumes that words in a document are generated by first selecting a topic (for example, "space exploration") and then choosing words associated with that topic (for example, "nasa," "orbit"). LDA employs Bayesian inference typically via variational methods or Gibbs sampling, to estimate these distributions, which makes it highly interpretable and effective for unsupervised tasks. For example, in a given corpus of news articles, LDA might identify topics like "medicine," "electronics," or "space," where each topic is represented by words like "disease, doctor," "circuit, chip," or "nasa, shuttle," respectively.

Mechanics of LDA: Generative Process in LDA

The mechanics of LDA involve constructing a generative process: for each document, a distribution over topics is drawn from a Dirichlet distribution, and for each word, a topic is sampled followed by a word from that topic's distribution. The model optimizes parameters to maximize the likelihood of observing the corpus, resulting in a topic-document matrix (which topics are prominent in each document) and a topic-word matrix (which words define each topic). In practice, LDA is implemented using libraries like scikit-learn or Gensim, requiring a pre-processed text corpus, typically represented as a Bag-of-Words (BoW) matrix. Key hyperparameters include the number of topics ((k)), which must be specified, and Dirichlet priors ((alpha) for document-topic and (beta) for topic-word distributions), which control the sparsity of the mixtures.

Given K number of topics, D number of documents and V number of unique words in those documents (Vocabulary size):

For each document d in the corpus, LDA:

1. Learns a distribution over K topics for document d: $\theta_d \sim \text{Dirichlet}(\alpha)$.
2. For each word w_{di} in document d:
    a. It draws a topic $z_{di} \sim \text{Categorical}(\theta_d)$.
    b. It draws a word $w_{di} \sim \text{Categorical}(\beta_{zdi})$.
    Where $\beta_k \sim \text{Dirichlet}(\eta)$ gives the word distribution for topic k.

From the observed data (words in documents) it infers:

- Topic-Word distributions β_k

- Document-topic distributions $\boldsymbol{\theta}_d$
- Topic assignments for each word $\mathbf{z}_{di}$

The inference is made using approximate methods like Gibbs Sampling, or variational Bayes. The output of LDA is topics, document-topic matrix, and topic-word matrix. Each topic is a probability distribution over words, each document is a mixture of topics, every topic assigns probabilities to words.

LDA is commonly used for **topic discovery**, such as identifying themes in news articles or social media posts (for example, analyzing discussions on social media platforms). It supports **document clustering** by grouping documents with similar topic distributions, thus aiding in information organization. LDA can also be used for **text summarization**, where key topics guide the selection of representative sentences, and **recommendation systems**, where topic similarity informs content suggestions. For instance, applying LDA to the 20newsgroups dataset might reveal distinct topics corresponding to categories such as **`sci.med`** or **`sci.space`**. Compared to LSA, LDA offers better interpretability due to its probabilistic framework but is computationally more intensive and sensitive to hyperparameter choices, such as the number of topics or preprocessing quality (for example, stop word removal).

Python Implementation of LDA for Topic Distribution from Documents

Popular Python libraries for topic modeling include:

- **Gensim**: A robust library for LDA and other topic modeling algorithms, known for scalability
- **scikit-learn**: Offers NMF and LSA implementations when integrated with other machine learning tools
- **BERTopic**: A modern approach leveraging transformer-based embeddings for improved topic coherence

Figure 8.5 shows the Python code for Latent Dirichlet Allocation (LDA) algorithm for topic modeling on 20 News Groups Text dataset. We are using LDS from gensim Python. spaCy Python library is used for text preprocessing including tokenization, lemmatization and stopword removal. LDA processes texts as lists of tokens. In this code, we have used gensim library to create a dictionary and Bag-of-Words corpus, then we will train an LDA model with 5 topics. The code prints the topics with their top words and the library pyLDAvis generates an interactive HTML visualization showing topic distributions and term relevance in the input text.

The dataset used is the 20 Newsgroups Dataset from scikit-learn. It is a benchmark dataset for tasks like topic modeling, text classification and clustering. Each document in the dataset is a single newsgroup post containing free-form text.

You will need to install the following Python libraries on your computer to run this code: spacy, gensim, scikit-learn, pyLDAvis, umap-learn, matplotlib. Use the following pip command to install:

```
pip install spacy gensim scikit-learn pyLDAvis umap-learn matplotlib
```

You will also need to download spacy's core NLP pipeline for English. Use this command to download this pipeline once you have installed spacy:

```
python -m spacy download en_core_web_sm
```

```
import spacy  # Import spaCy for text preprocessing
import gensim  # Import gensim for LDA topic modeling
import gensim.corpora as corpora  # Import corpora for dictionary and corpus creation
from gensim.models import LdaModel  # Import LdaModel for training LDA
from sklearn.datasets import fetch_20newsgroups  # Import 20 Newsgroups dataset
import pyLDAvis  # Import pyLDAvis for interactive topic visualization
import pyLDAvis.gensim_models as gensimvis  # Import gensim integration for pyLDAvis
# Load spaCy model for preprocessing, disabling parser and NER for efficiency
nlp = spacy.load("en_core_web_sm", disable=["parser", "ner"])
# Load a subset of 20 Newsgroups dataset (train split, specific categories)
# Categories chosen to demonstrate diverse topics; headers/footers/quotes removed for cleaner text
newsgroups = fetch_20newsgroups(subset="train", categories=["sci.space", "comp.graphics",
                                                            "talk.politics.misc"],
                                remove=("headers", "footers", "quotes"))
texts = newsgroups.data  # Extract text data from dataset
# Define function to preprocess texts: tokenize, remove stopwords, lemmatize
def preprocess_texts(texts):
    processed_texts = []  # Initialize list to store processed texts
    for doc in texts:  # Iterate through each document
        doc_nlp = nlp(doc.lower())  # Convert to lowercase and process with spaCy
        # Keep only alphabetic tokens, exclude stopwords and short tokens
        tokens = [token.lemma_ for token in doc_nlp if token.is_alpha and not token.is_stop and len(token) > 2]
        processed_texts.append(tokens)  # Append tokenized document to list
    return processed_texts  # Return list of processed texts

# Preprocess the text corpus
processed_texts = preprocess_texts(texts)
# Create a dictionary mapping words to unique IDs
dictionary = corpora.Dictionary(processed_texts)
# Convert each document to a Bag-of-Words representation (word ID, frequency pairs)
corpus = [dictionary.doc2bow(text) for text in processed_texts]
# Train LDA model with 5 topics, 10 passes for convergence, and auto-tuned alpha
lda_model = LdaModel(corpus=corpus, id2word=dictionary, num_topics=5, random_state=42, passes=10, alpha="auto")
# Print top topics with their word distributions
print("LDA Topics:")
for idx, topic in lda_model.print_topics(-1):  # Iterate through all topics
    print(f"Topic {idx}: {topic}")  # Print topic index and top words with weights
# Prepare interactive visualization for LDA topics
vis_data = gensimvis.prepare(lda_model, corpus, dictionary)  # Generate visualization data
pyLDAvis.save_html(vis_data, "lda_visualization2.html")  # Save visualization as HTML file
```

Figure 8.5: *Python Implementation of LDA Algorithm for Topic Modeling*

The output of the LDA code is shown in *Figure* 8.6. The figure shows the top five topics in the dataset along with the prominent words for each topic:

```
LDA Topics:
Topic 0: 0.009*"image" + 0.005*"graphic" + 0.005*"system" + 0.005*"datum" + 0.005*"launch" + 0.004*"include" + 0.003*"software" + 0.003*"new" + 0.003*"package" + 0.003*"available"
Topic 1: 0.010*"people" + 0.009*"think" + 0.009*"president" + 0.008*"go" + 0.007*"stephanopoulos" + 0.007*"know" + 0.007*"say" + 0.006*"work" + 0.006*"government" + 0.005*"job"
Topic 2: 0.018*"space" + 0.006*"nasa" + 0.005*"orbit" + 0.005*"year" + 0.005*"mission" + 0.005*"system" + 0.004*"earth" + 0.004*"lunar" + 0.004*"launch" + 0.004*"time"
Topic 3: 0.005*"jpeg" + 0.004*"like" + 0.003*"man" + 0.003*"homosexual" + 0.003*"think" + 0.003*"people" + 0.003*"satellite" + 0.003*"system" + 0.003*"high" + 0.003*"time"
Topic 4: 0.013*"file" + 0.012*"image" + 0.008*"program" + 0.007*"know" + 0.007*"use" + 0.006*"jpeg" + 0.006*"color" + 0.006*"format" + 0.006*"thank" + 0.005*"bit"
```

Figure 8.6: *Top 5 Topics Identified and Prominent Words for Each Topic*

This code also creates an interactive visualization to demonstrate the topics and most relevant terms in each topic and their distribution. *Figure* 8.7 shows the snapshot of this interactive visualization:

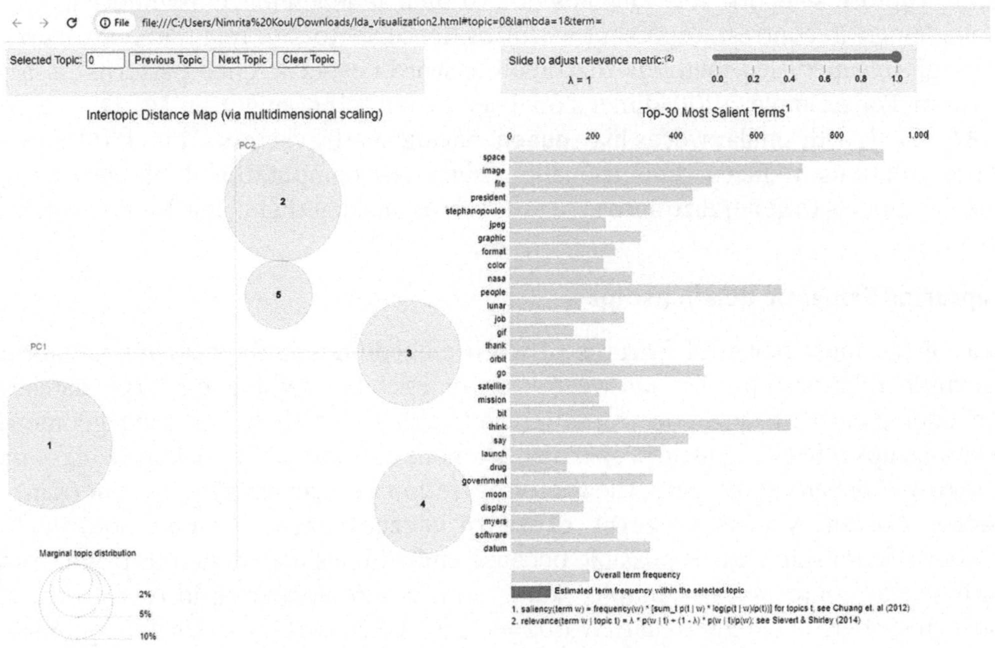

***Figure* 8.7:** *LDA Visualization of Topics in Dataset*

Word Embeddings

Word embeddings represent a transformative advancement in Natural Language Processing (NLP), moving beyond the limitations of traditional text representations like Bag-of-Words (BoW) or TF-IDF to capture the semantic meaning of words in a dense, continuous vector space. Unlike earlier discrete representations which treat words as isolated units with no inherent relationships, word embeddings encode words as low-dimensional vectors (for example, 100–300 dimensions) where proximity in the vector space reflects semantic similarity. This enables embeddings to capture relationships like synonyms, analogies, and contextual nuances, revolutionizing tasks such as text classification, sentiment analysis, and machine translation. By leveraging unsupervised learning on large text corpora, word embeddings learn these representations without labeled data, making them a cornerstone of modern NLP.

From Discrete to Dense Vector Representations

Traditional text representations such as BoW and TF-IDF, rely on discrete, high-dimensional vectors where each dimension corresponds to a specific word in the vocabulary. For instance, in a BoW model, the word "`king`" might be represented as a one-hot vector with a single non-zero entry, ignoring its relationship to words such as "`queen`" or "`prince`." These representations are sparse, computationally expensive, and fail to capture semantic relationships due to their independence assumption. Word embeddings, in contrast, represent words as dense vectors of real numbers, learned through unsupervised methods that analyze word co-occurrence patterns in large corpora. For example, a 100-dimensional vector for "`king`" might be `[0.23, -0.15, 0.87, ...]`, with similar words like "`queen`" having nearby vectors. This shift to dense representations reduces dimensionality, improves computational efficiency, and enables models to generalize across related words, making them ideal for downstream NLP tasks.

Capturing Semantic Relationships

One of the most powerful features of word embeddings is their ability to capture semantic relationships through vector arithmetic. By training on large datasets, embeddings learn to position words in the vector space such that their geometric relationships reflect linguistic properties. A famous example is the analogy "`king - man + woman ≈ queen`." In this case, the vector operation `vector(king) - vector(man) + vector (woman) yields a vector close to vector(queen)`, thereby capturing the gender relationship. This is possible because embeddings are trained to place words with similar contexts (for example, "`king`" and "`queen`" appearing in royal contexts) close together. Techniques like Word2Vec and GloVe achieve this by optimizing objectives based on word co-occurrence, such as predicting a word given its context or modeling global word co-occurrence statistics. It is because of these semantic relationships that applications such as word similarity detection (for example, "car" is close to "automobile"), analogy solving, and even cross-lingual mappings, which have significantly advanced NLP's ability to understand and process language.

Word Embeddings Using Word2Vec

Word2Vec is an unsupervised learning algorithm that generates dense, low-dimensional word embeddings–vector representations of words that capture their semantic and syntactic properties based on their context in a text corpus. Developed by Tomas Mikolov and colleagues at Google in 2013, Word2Vec uses neural networks to learn these embeddings by predicting word relationships, offering two model architectures: Continuous Bag-of-Words (CBOW), which predicts a target word from its context words, and Skip-gram, which predicts context words given a target word. By training on large, unlabeled text datasets, Word2Vec positions words in a vector space (typically 50–300 dimensions), where semantically similar words (for example, "`king`" and "`queen`") are closer together, thus enabling operations like analogies (for example, "`king - man + woman ≈ queen`")

Python Code to Learn Word Embeddings using Word2Vec

Figure 8.8 shows the code for computing word embeddings on the 20newsgroups dataset. We have used the documents from three categories only **sci-electronics**, **sci-med**, **sci-space**. This code requires that you should have installed the following Python libraries—**gensim**, **nltk**, **wordcloud**—and downloaded **punkt** tokenizer via NLTK. The code first tokenizes documents into lists of words using NLTK's **word_tokenize**, converting to lowercase for consistency. This prepares the data for Word2Vec, which requires tokenized text. The code then trains a skip-gram Word2Vec model via gensim to learn word vectors (each vector has 100 dimensions), then we compute the top 5 similar words for selected terms ("**nasa**," "**doctor**," "**circuit**"), demonstrating semantic relationships (for example, "**nasa**" might be similar to "**shuttle**," "**orbit**" with high cosine similarity scores). We visualize the word embeddings using t-SNE to project a subset of word vectors (selected terms and their similar words) into 2D space. Code also prints dataset statistics, vocabulary size, word similarities.

```
import numpy as np  # For numerical operations and array handling
from sklearn.datasets import fetch_20newsgroups  # To load the 20newsgroups dataset
from gensim.models import Word2Vec  # For training Word2Vec embeddings
from sklearn.manifold import TSNE  # For 2D visualization of word vectors
import matplotlib.pyplot as plt  # For plotting
from nltk.tokenize import word_tokenize  # For tokenizing text
import nltk  # For NLP utilities
nltk.download('punkt')  # Download tokenizer data
categories = ["sci.electronics", "sci.med", "sci.space"]
dataset = fetch_20newsgroups(remove=("headers", "footers", "quotes"),
print(f"{len(dataset.data)} documents - {len(categories)} categories")
# Preprocess text: tokenize documents into lists of words:Word2Vec requires tokenized text (lists of words) as input
tokenized_docs = [word_tokenize(doc.lower()) for doc in dataset.data]  # Convert to lowercase and tokenize
# Train Word2Vec model to learn word embeddings, use skip-gram model
model = Word2Vec(sentences=tokenized_docs, vector_size=100, window=5,sg=1,min_count=5,workers=4,seed=42)
print(f"Word2Vec training complete. Vocabulary size: {len(model.wv)}")
#Demonstrate semantic relationships:compute similarities for selected terms relevant to dataset categories
example_words = ["nasa", "doctor", "circuit"]
for word in example_words:
    if word in model.wv:
        print(f"Words similar to '{word}':")
        similar_words = model.wv.most_similar(word, topn=5)  # Get top 5 similar words
        for similar_word, similarity in similar_words:
            print(f"  {similar_word}: {similarity:.3f}")
    else:
        print(f"'{word}' not in vocabulary")
# Demonstrate analogy: king - man + woman ≈ queen, Test an analogy relevant to the dataset (e.g., space-related)
try:
    analogy_result = model.wv.most_similar(positive=["nasa", "doctor"], negative=["space"], topn=1)
    print(f"Analogy 'nasa' - 'space' + 'doctor' ≈ {analogy_result[0][0]} (similarity: {analogy_result[0][1]:.3f})")
except KeyError as e:
    print(f"Analogy not computed: {e} not in vocabulary")
# Visualize word embeddings using t-SNE- Select a subset of words to avoid overcrowding
selected_words = []
for word in example_words:
    if word in model.wv:
        selected_words.append(word)
        # Add top 5 similar words for each example word
        selected_words.extend([w for w, _ in model.wv.most_similar(word, topn=5)])
selected_words = list(set(selected_words))  # Remove duplicates
word_vectors = np.array([model.wv[word] for word in selected_words])  # Get word vectors
# Reduce dimensionality to 2D using t-SNE
tsne = TSNE(n_components=2, random_state=42, perplexity=5, n_iter=1000)
word_vectors_2d = tsne.fit_transform(word_vectors)
# Plot word embeddings in 2D
plt.figure(figsize=(10, 8))
plt.scatter(word_vectors_2d[:, 0], word_vectors_2d[:, 1], c='blue', s=50)
for i, word in enumerate(selected_words):
    plt.annotate(word, (word_vectors_2d[i, 0], word_vectors_2d[i, 1]), fontsize=10)
plt.title("Word2Vec Embeddings Visualized with t-SNE")
plt.xlabel("t-SNE Component 1")
plt.ylabel("t-SNE Component 2")
plt.grid(True)
```

Figure 8.8: *Python Code to Learn Word Embeddings from 20newsgroups Text Dataset Using Word2Vec*

Figure 8.9 shows the output of preceding code along with the t-SNE plots of the word embeddings:

```
2961 documents - 3 categories
Word2Vec training complete. Vocabulary size: 8402
Words similar to 'nasa':
  ames: 0.813
  exploration: 0.778
  hubble: 0.760
  agency: 0.757
  flight: 0.755
Words similar to 'doctor':
  wife: 0.824
  she: 0.824
  ent: 0.820
  friend: 0.818
  woman: 0.812
Words similar to 'circuit':
  impedance: 0.883
  signal: 0.867
  output: 0.862
  voltage: 0.858
  device: 0.851
Analogy 'nasa' - 'space' + 'doctor' ≈ asked (similarity: 0.716)
```

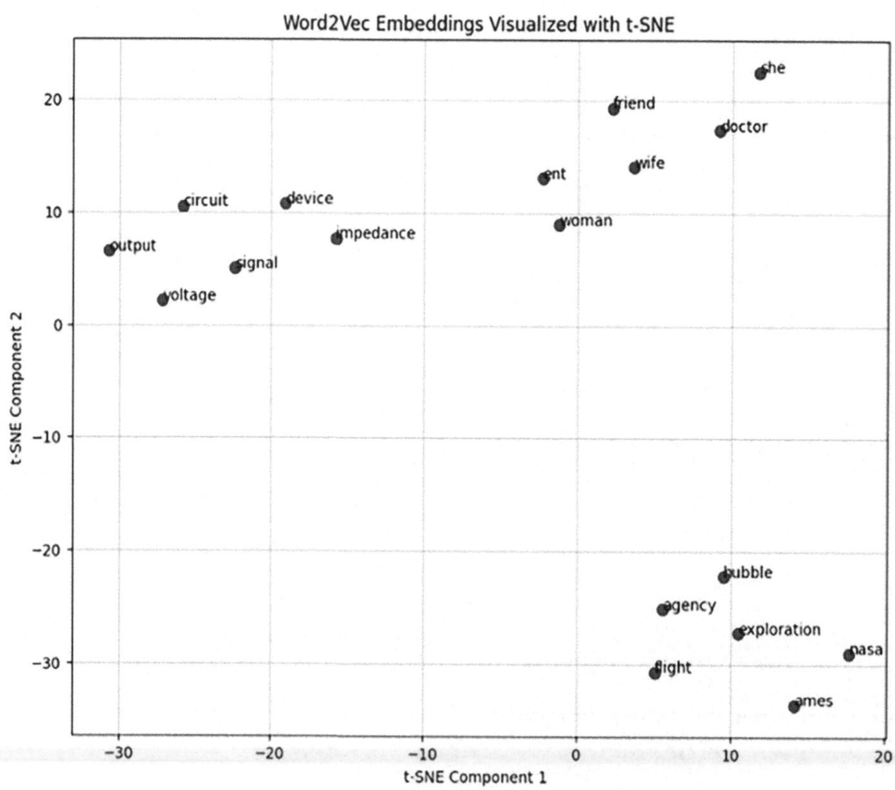

Figure 8.9: *Output of Word2Vec for Learning Word Embeddings from 20newsgroups Text Dataset*

Word Embeddings using GloVe (Global Vectors for Word Representations)

GloVe (Global Vectors for Word Representation) is an unsupervised learning algorithm for generating word embeddings. Developed by researchers at Stanford (https://nlp.stanford.edu/projects/glove/) in 2014, GloVe combines the strengths of local context-based methods (like Word2Vec) and global statistical methods by using word co-occurrence statistics across an entire text corpus. It constructs a co-occurrence matrix that counts how often words appear together within a specified context window, and then factorizes this matrix using a weighted least-squares objective to produce word vectors. The resulting embeddings place semantically similar words (for example, "`king`" and "`queen`") close together in the vector space, thereby enabling tasks like word similarity, analogies (for example, "`king - man + woman ≈ queen`"), and downstream NLP applications such as text classification and sentiment analysis. Unlike Word2Vec, which relies on predictive neural networks, GloVe uses a count-based approach which makes it particularly effective for capturing global corpus-wide patterns.

Word Embeddings using FastText

FastText is an advanced unsupervised learning algorithm for generating word embeddings and extends the capabilities of Word2Vec by incorporating subword information to create robust vector representations. Developed by Facebook AI Research in 2016 (https://github.com/facebookresearch/fastText), FastText represents words as bags of character n-grams (substrings of 3–6 characters), which allows it to capture morphological structure and handle rare or Out-of-Vocabulary (OOV) words more effectively than Word2Vec or GloVe. Like Word2Vec, FastText uses a predictive model (either Continuous Bag-of-Words or Skip-gram) to learn low-dimensional dense vectors (typically 100–300 dimensions) from unlabeled text corpora, positioning semantically similar words (for example, "`doctor`" and "`physician`") close together in the vector space. Its subword approach enables FastText to generate embeddings for unseen words by combining n-gram vectors, making it particularly valuable for morphologically rich languages and noisy datasets like social media posts. FastText's ability to capture both semantic relationships and word structure has made it a powerful tool for NLP tasks such as text classification, sentiment analysis, and word similarity detection.

Unlike Word2Vec, which treats each word as an atomic unit, FastText breaks words into character n-grams. For example, the word "`running`" might be represented by n-grams like "`run`," "`unn`," "`nni`," "`nin`," "`ing`." The word's embedding is the sum of its n-gram vectors, enabling FastText to generalize to words with shared morphemes (for example, "`runner`" and "`running`" have similar vectors). Compared to GloVe's count-based approach, FastText's predictive model and subword focus handle rare words and typos efficiently as it can infer embeddings for words not seen during training. This makes FastText particularly suited for domains with diverse vocabularies. FastText also supports analogy tasks (for example, "`king - man + woman ≈ queen`.)

FastText is computationally more intensive than Word2Vec due to the n-gram processing and its embeddings may be less effective for capturing long-range semantic relationships compared to GloVe. Despite these trade-offs, FastText's versatility and robustness make it a significant advancement in unsupervised NLP.

Python Code for using FastText to compute embeddings of the 20 News Groups Dataset

Figure 8.10 shows the Python code that uses FastText algorithm from gensim library to compute the word embeddings for text from 20 New Groups Dataset. As before, we have used the text documents from the categories – **`sci.electronics`**, **`sci.med`**, **`sci.space`** only. The text is tokenized before passing it to the FastText. We have visualized the t-SNE-transformed vector embeddings of text for readability.

```
import numpy as np
from sklearn.datasets import fetch_20newsgroups
from gensim.models import FastText  # For training FastText embeddings
from sklearn.manifold import TSNE  # For 2D visualization of word vectors
from nltk.tokenize import word_tokenize
import matplotlib.pyplot as plt
import nltk
nltk.download('punkt')
categories = ["sci.electronics", "sci.med", "sci.space"]
dataset = fetch_20newsgroups(remove=("headers", "footers", "quotes"),  # Remove metadata to focus on content
    subset="all", categories=categories,shuffle=True, random_state=42,)
print(f"{len(dataset.data)} documents - {len(categories)} categories")
tokenized_docs = [word_tokenize(doc.lower()) for doc in dataset.data]  # Convert to lowercase and tokenize
# Train FastText model to learn word embeddings- Use skip-gram model with subword n-grams
model = FastText(sentences=tokenized_docs, vector_size=100,window=5,sg=1,min_count=5,min_n=3,max_n=6,workers=4,seed=42)
print(f"FastText training complete. Vocabulary size: {len(model.wv)}")
# Demonstrate semantic relationships: compute similarities for selected terms
example_words = ["nasa", "doctor", "circuit"]
for word in example_words:
    if word in model.wv:
        print(f"Words similar to '{word}':")
        similar_words = model.wv.most_similar(word, topn=5)  # Get top 5 similar words
        for similar_word, similarity in similar_words:
            print(f"  {similar_word}: {similarity:.3f}")
    else:
        print(f"'{word}' not in vocabulary")
# Demonstrate handling of out-of-vocabulary (OOV) words
oov_word = "microchips"  # Example word not necessarily in training data
if oov_word in model.wv:
    print(f"'{oov_word}' is in vocabulary")
else:
    print(f"'{oov_word}' not in vocabulary, but embedding generated:")
    similar_words = model.wv.most_similar(oov_word, topn=5)  # Get similar words for OOV
    for similar_word, similarity in similar_words:
        print(f"  {similar_word}: {similarity:.3f}")
# Visualize word embeddings using t-SNE
selected_words = []
for word in example_words + [oov_word]:
    selected_words.append(word)
    if word in model.wv or word == oov_word:
        selected_words.extend([w for w, _ in model.wv.most_similar(word, topn=5)])
selected_words = list(set(selected_words))  # Remove duplicates
word_vectors = np.array([model.wv[word] for word in selected_words])  # Get word vectors
tsne = TSNE(n_components=2, random_state=42, perplexity=5, n_iter=1000)
word_vectors_2d = tsne.fit_transform(word_vectors)
plt.figure(figsize=(10, 8))
plt.scatter(word_vectors_2d[:, 0], word_vectors_2d[:, 1], c='blue', s=50)
for i, word in enumerate(selected_words):
    plt.annotate(word, (word_vectors_2d[i, 0], word_vectors_2d[i, 1]), fontsize=10)
plt.title("FastText Embeddings Visualized with t-SNE")
plt.xlabel("t-SNE Component 1")
plt.ylabel("t-SNE Component 2")
plt.grid(True)
```

Figure 8.10: *Computing Word Embeddings Using FastText*

The output of the preceding code and the plot of embeddings is shown in *Figure* 8.11:

```
2961 documents - 3 categories
FastText training complete. Vocabulary size: 8402
Words similar to 'nasa':
  nasp: 0.912
  nasal: 0.875
  asa: 0.869
  nasa/jsc/gm2: 0.843
  spacelab: 0.827
Words similar to 'doctor':
  friend: 0.873
  girlfriend: 0.869
  friendly: 0.861
  doc: 0.858
  doctors: 0.844
Words similar to 'circuit':
  circuitry: 0.963
  circuits: 0.951
  switch: 0.858
  amplify: 0.855
  filter: 0.853
 'microchips' is in vocabulary
```

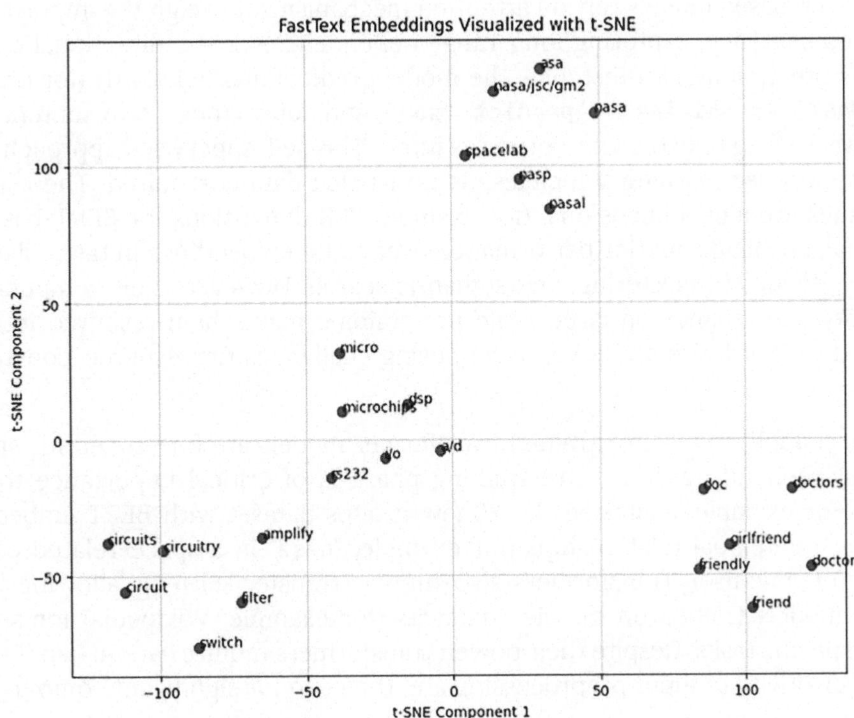

Figure 8.11: *t-SNE Visualization of FastText Embeddings for Selected Words from the 20 News Groups' Dataset*

Unsupervised NLP with Neural Models

The advent of transformer-based deep neural network architectures has revolutionized unsupervised natural language processing, enabling the creation of contextual embeddings that capture nuanced semantic and syntactic relationships in text. Unlike traditional methods like Latent Semantic Analysis (LSA) or static word embeddings (Word2Vec, GloVe, FastText), which produce fixed vectors for words regardless of context, modern neural network-based approaches generate representations that are context-sensitive and dynamic.

Models like BERT (Bidirectional Encoder Representations from Transformers), which was introduced in 2018, leverage self-supervised learning objectives such as masked language modeling to pre-train on vast unlabeled corpora, learning rich representations without human annotations. These embeddings excel in tasks like text classification, question answering, and sentiment analysis by adapting word meanings based on surrounding text (for example, "bank" differs in "river bank" vs. "bank account").

Transformer-based models rely on attention mechanisms to weigh the importance of words in a sentence, capturing long-range dependencies and bidirectional context. In BERT's pre-training, for instance, the model predicts masked words (for example, **`"The [MASK] is shining" → predict "sun"`**) and determines if two sentences are consecutive, using only the text corpus as input. This self-supervised approach aligns with unsupervised learning principles, as no labeled data is required. The resulting embeddings are high-dimensional (for example, 768 dimensions for BERT-base) and contextual, enabling superior performance over static embeddings in tasks like word similarity, document clustering, and semantic search. However, their computational complexity and reliance on large-scale pre-training make them resource-intensive compared to Word2Vec or GloVe, while posing challenges for resource-constrained settings.

In practical applications, pre-trained transformer models are fine-tuned for specific tasks, but their unsupervised pre-training phase is of critical importance to their success. For example, analyzing the 20newsgroups dataset with BERT embeddings can reveal contextual relationships (for example, "**`nasa`**" in a space-related context vs. an acronymic use). Transformers also support transfer learning, allowing you to leverage models trained on massive datasets (for example, Wikipedia) for smaller, domain-specific tasks. Despite their power, transformers require careful handling due to their sensitivity to input preprocessing and the need for significant computational resources.

BERT

BERT (Bidirectional Encoder Representations from Transformers) is a language representation models that is pre-trained to learn deep bidirectional representations from unlabeled text (unsupervised learning). BERT is bidirectional which means, it is conditioned on the input text from left to right and right to left jointly in all layers. Thus, you can fine-tune a pre-trained BERT model with only one additional output layer to create accurate models for downstream tasks like question-answering, language inference, and so on, because only a few parameters need to be learned from scratch for the downstream task. Fine-tuning can be done using unsupervised learning. Additionally, pre-trained model can benefit from transfer learning based on supervised datasets for tasks like machine translation or natural language inference.

BERT Input Representation

BERT represents input text tokens in such a manner that it can jointly understand the tokens as well as their context. The input to BERT consists of a combination of embeddings that represent tokens, their position, and the sentence they belong to.

BERT takes a single sentence or a pair of sentences as input:

- For a **single sentence**:
  `[CLS] Sentence A [SEP]`
- For **sentence pair tasks** (for example, question answering and entailment):

  `[CLS] Sentence A [SEP] Sentence B [SEP]`

`[CLS]` is a special token that indicates the start of input.

`[SEP]` is a special token that means "sentence separator". It is used between sentences at the end of previous sentence.

Embeddings Used:

Each input token is represented by the sum of the following three embeddings:

a. **Token Embeddings**

   These are WordPiece embeddings (subword units). Each token (for example, **`"running" → "run", "##ning"`**) is mapped to a vector from a fixed vocabulary.

b. **Segment Embeddings**

   These indicate which sentence a token belongs to:

   - **`Sentence A → segment ID 0`**
   - **`Sentence B → segment ID 1`**

   This helps BERT distinguish between pairs of sentences.

c. **Position Embeddings**

These indicate the position of each token in the input sequence (position 0, 1, 2...).

BERT does **not** use recurrence or convolution, so the position embeddings provide the order of tokens.

Each token's final input representation is:

Final Embedding = Token Embedding + Segment Embedding + Position Embedding

This representation is passed onto the transformer layers.

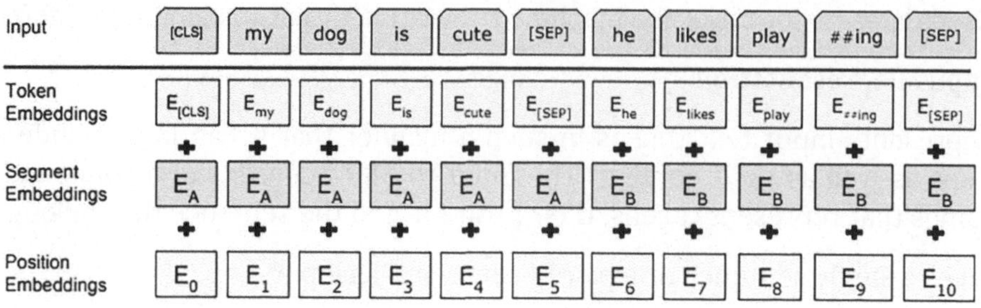

Figure 8.12: *Input Representation in BERT (Source Credits: BERT: Pre-training of Deep Bidirectional Transformers for Language Understanding, https://arxiv.org/pdf/1810.04805)*

BERT Pre-training

BERT's architecture is a multilayer bidirectional Transformer encoder. BERT is trained in two steps—pre-training and fine-tuning. During pre-training, the BERT model is trained on unlabeled data for different pre-training tasks. For fine-tuning, BERT model is first initialized with the pre-trained parameters and all of the parameters are fine-tuned using labeled data from downstream tasks. Therefore, every downstream task has separate fine-tuned models, though they are initialized with the same pre-trained parameters.

During pre-training BERT is trained using two unsupervised tasks—Masked Language Modeling and Next Sentence Prediction (NSP).

Task 1: Masked Language Modeling

To train the deep bidirectional representations of text, some percentage (15% of all WordPiece tokens in each sequence in case of BERT) of input tokens (a token is the smallest processable unit of text data) is masked. The tokens to be masked are chosen randomly. Masking some input tokens means they are not visible to the neural network; the task of the neural network is then to predict those masked tokens. This task is self-supervised learning. Accuracy of this prediction is computed based on the original input text.

Task 2: Next Sentence Prediction (NSP)

For tasks like question-answering, and natural language inference, the model needs to understand the relationship between two sentences. This relationship is not learned during masked language modeling. To enable the model to understand the relationships between two sentences the model is pre-trained with the task of predicting the binarized next sentence. The training data for this task is generated from any monolingual corpus. Pairs of sentences (A, B) are chosen for each pre-training example, such that 50% of the time B is the actual next sentence that follows A (labeled as IsNext), and 50% of the time it is a random sentence from the corpus (labeled as NotNext).

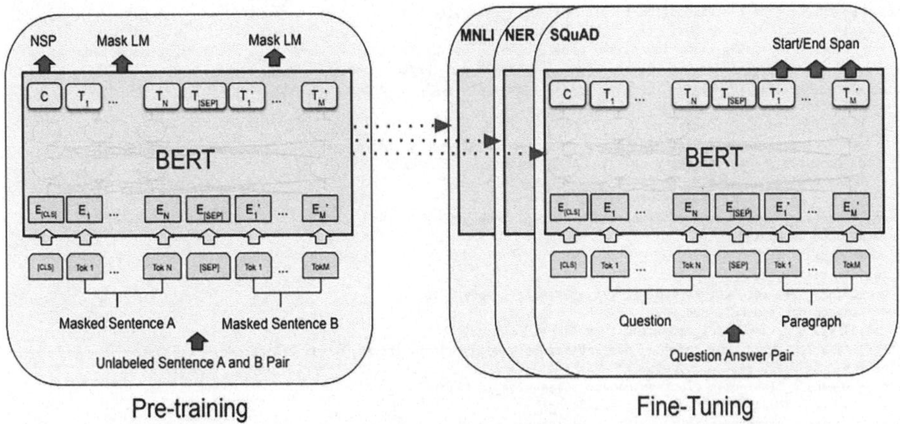

***Figure* 8.13:** *BERT Pre-training and Fine-tuning (Source Credits: BERT: Pre-training of Deep Bidirectional Transformers for Language Understanding, https://arxiv.org/pdf/1810.04805)*

BERT Fine-tuning

A pre-trained BERT model can be fine-tuned using single text as well as text pairs by swapping out the appropriate inputs or input-output pairs. BERT uses self-attention mechanism to compute bidirectional cross-attention between two sentences of text. For each downstream task, task specific inputs and outputs are input into BERT and all the parameters are updated end-to-end.

Recently, more efficient transformers (for example, DistilBERT, ALBERT) and models optimized for specific domains (for example, BioBERT for medical texts) have been developed for learning representations of text and other NLP tasks.

The Python Code to learn word embeddings

This code shown in *Figure* 8.14 uses `transformers` library from Hugging Face to extract contextual embeddings (768-dimensional embeddings) from a pre-trained BERT model (bert-base-uncased), where BertTokenizer is used to tokenize the text. Then the code uses those embeddings for clustering similar documents from 2newsgroups dataset. It also visualizes the clusters in 2D t-SNE projection.

```
import numpy as np
from sklearn.datasets import fetch_20newsgroups  # To load the 20newsgroups dataset
from transformers import BertTokenizer, BertModel  # For BERT model and tokenizer (PyTorch backend)
import torch  # PyTorch for tensor operations
from sklearn.cluster import KMeans  # For K-means clustering
from sklearn.manifold import TSNE  # For 2D visualization
from sklearn.metrics import silhouette_score  # For clustering evaluation
import matplotlib.pyplot as plt
categories = ["sci.electronics", "sci.med", "sci.space"]# Load the 20newsgroups dataset with selected categories(e.g., electr
dataset = fetch_20newsgroups(remove=("headers", "footers", "quotes"),subset="all",
    categories=categories, shuffle=True,random_state=42)
n_docs = 100 # Limit to 100 documents for computational efficiency(BERT processing is resource-intensive)
texts = dataset.data[:n_docs]
print(f"Processing {len(texts)} documents - {len(categories)} categories")
device = torch.device("cuda")
tokenizer = BertTokenizer.from_pretrained('bert-base-uncased') #Intitialize BERT tokenizer and model
model = BertModel.from_pretrained('bert-base-uncased').to(device)  # Move model to GPU/CPU
model.eval()  # Set model to evaluation mode (no training)
def get_document_embedding(text, tokenizer, model, device, max_length=128):# Function to get BERT document embeddings
    inputs = tokenizer(text,return_tensors='pt',max_length=max_length,truncation=True,padding=True)  # Tokenize input text
    inputs = {key: val.to(device) for key, val in inputs.items()}# Move inputs to the same device as the model
    with torch.no_grad(): # Get BERT embeddings
        outputs = model(**inputs)
        embeddings = outputs.last_hidden_state  # Shape: (1, seq_len, hidden_size=768)
    token_embeddings = embeddings[0, 1:-1, :]  # Remove special tokens
    if token_embeddings.size(0) == 0:  # Handle empty sequences
        return np.zeros(model.config.hidden_size)
    doc_embedding = token_embeddings.mean(dim=0).cpu().numpy()  # Shape: (768,)
    return doc_embedding
doc_embeddings = []
for text in texts:
    embedding = get_document_embedding(text, tokenizer, model, device)
    doc_embeddings.append(embedding)
doc_embeddings = np.array(doc_embeddings)  # Shape: (n_docs, 768)
print(f"Extracted embeddings for {len(doc_embeddings)} documents in {time() - t0:.2f} seconds")
n_clusters = 3# Apply K-means clustering- Use 3 clusters to match the number of categories
kmeans = KMeans(n_clusters=n_clusters,random_state=42,n_init=10)
cluster_labels = kmeans.fit_predict(doc_embeddings)
print(f"K-means clustering complete with {n_clusters} clusters")
tsne = TSNE(n_components=2,random_state=42,perplexity=min(30, len(doc_embeddings)-1),n_iter=1000)
embeddings_2d = tsne.fit_transform(doc_embeddings)
colors = ['blue', 'red', 'green']
for cluster in range(n_clusters):
    mask = cluster_labels == cluster
    plt.scatter(embeddings_2d[mask, 0],embeddings_2d[mask, 1],c=colors[cluster],label=f'Cluster {cluster}',s=30)
plt.title("K-means Clusters of BERT Document Embeddings (t-SNE)")
```

Figure 8.14: *Word Embeddings Using BERT Model and Document Clustering Using Those Embeddings*

Figure 8.15 shows the clustering plot obtained by clustering the documents based on their BERT embeddings:

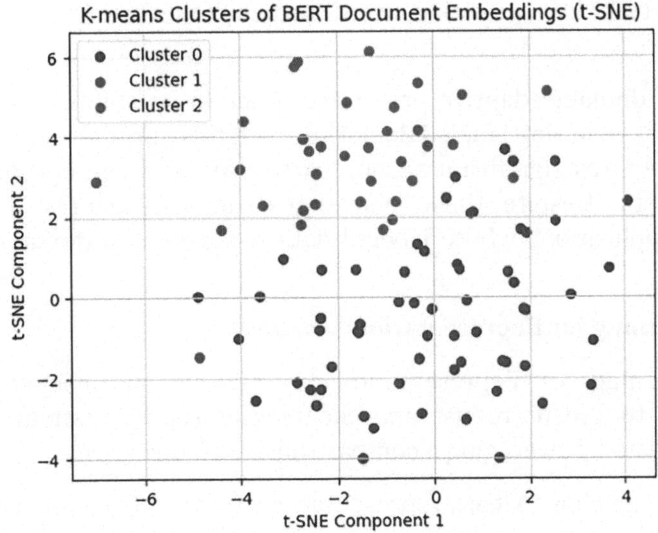

***Figure 8.15:** Clustering Plot Obtained by Clustering Documents Based on Their BERT Embeddings*

Unsupervised Fine-tuning and Adaptation

As natural language processing evolves, the ability to adapt powerful pre-trained models to specialized domains or tasks without relying on labeled data has become a very important application of unsupervised learning. Unsupervised fine-tuning and adaptation refine Large Language Models (LLMs), such as BERT, to better handle niche applications such as scientific literature analysis, legal document processing, or sentiment clustering of social media posts, while preserving the unsupervised paradigm. These techniques leverage self-supervised learning objectives to tailor model representations using unlabeled domain-specific corpora, enhancing performance on downstream tasks like clustering, similarity detection, or topic modeling. We will talk about two key approaches: domain-adaptive pre-training and contrastive learning, which extend the transformer-based methods for natural language processing tasks.

Domain-Adaptive Pre-training

Domain-adaptive pre-training refines a general-purpose pre-trained model like BERT by continuing its self-supervised training on a specialized, unlabeled corpus. For instance, a model pre-trained on a broad dataset like Wikipedia can be further trained on a collection of scientific articles to create a domain-specific variant, such as BioBERT for biomedical texts or SciBERT for scientific literature. This process typically involves the same self-supervised objectives used in initial pre-training, such as masked language modeling, and next sentence prediction. By exposing the model to domain-specific vocabulary, syntactic patterns, and contextual nuances, domain-adaptive pre-training aligns its embeddings to the target domain, improving performance on tasks like clustering scientific documents or extracting entities from legal texts.

The strength of domain-adaptive pre-training lies in its ability to enhance model relevance without requiring labeled data. However, this approach is computationally intensive and requires significant resources to process large corpora and update model parameters. Despite these challenges, domain-adaptive pre-training is invaluable for applications where labeled data is scarce and domain knowledge is critical.

Contrastive Learning for Representation Learning

Contrastive Learning for Representation Learning is an unsupervised learning technique used to create robust and meaningful representations (for example, embeddings) of data by leveraging a comparison-based objective.

Contrastive learning aims to learn representations by teaching a model to distinguish between similar (positive) and dissimilar (negative) pairs of data points. The core idea is to position similar items closer together in the embedding space and push dissimilar items farther apart, without needing explicit labels. In NLP, this often involves sentences, documents, or text snippets, where the goal is to create embeddings that reflect semantic similarity (for example, two sentences about "**nasa**" in the 20newsgroups dataset should have similar embeddings if they discuss space exploration).

The process relies on a **self-supervised** objective, meaning the training signal is derived from the data itself. For example, positive pairs might be two augmented versions of the same sentence, while negative pairs are different sentences from the dataset.

Positive Pairs are two representations of the same data point that are created through augmentation. In NLP, augmentations include applying dropout masks, synonym replacement, or back-translation. For instance, SimCSE (Simple Contrastive Sentence Embedding) generates positive pairs by passing the same sentence through a transformer (for example, BERT) with different dropout masks, producing slightly varied embeddings. Negative Pairs are representations of different data points, often other sentences or documents in the same batch. A similarity function, typically cosine similarity, measures the closeness of embeddings in the vector space.

By optimizing a loss function, such as the **InfoNCE** (Noise-Contrastive Estimation) loss, the model learns to maximize the similarity of positive pairs while minimizing the similarity of negative pairs, resulting in embeddings that capture meaningful patterns.

Contrastive learning often uses transformer-based models. It encodes input text into embeddings (for example, using the [CLS] token or averaged token embeddings), which are then optimized via the contrastive objective. For example, SimCSE fine-tunes BERT to produce sentence embeddings that are directly usable for downstream tasks.

Practical Considerations and Challenges of Unsupervised Learning in NLP

Implementing unsupervised natural language processing techniques involves navigating a range of practical challenges that can significantly impact model performance and applicability. From preparing raw text data to scaling algorithms for large corpora, evaluating results without labeled data, and addressing ethical concerns, practitioners must make informed decisions to ensure robust and responsible outcomes. We will explore four critical areas–data preprocessing, scalability, evaluation, and ethical considerations—for applying unsupervised NLP methods effectively in real-world scenarios.

Data Preprocessing

Effective data preprocessing is the foundation of successful unsupervised NLP as it transforms raw text into a format suitable for modeling. Important steps like text cleaning, tokenization, normalization should be carried out properly. Preprocessing decisions depend on the task and dataset. For example, clustering 20newsgroups documents benefits from aggressive cleaning to remove metadata, but preserving technical terms like "circuit" is crucial for topic coherence. Practitioners must balance thorough cleaning with retaining relevant information and experiment with multiple preprocessing pipelines to optimize model performance.

Scalability

Scaling unsupervised NLP methods to large datasets, such as millions of social media posts or extensive document corpora, poses significant computational challenges. Techniques like K-means, LDA, and Word2Vec are manageable on a single machine, but they become resource-intensive with larger datasets. Transformer-based models like BERT exacerbate this issue due to their high memory and processing demands, and thus require substantial hardware for even moderate-sized corpora.

Distributed computing frameworks, such as Dask and Apache Spark, offer solutions for scalability. Dask enables parallel processing of large datasets on a single machine or cluster by breaking tasks into smaller chunks, thereby making it suitable for preprocessing or training models like Word2Vec on large text corpora. Spark, designed for big data, supports distributed implementations of algorithms like LDA or K-means, allowing practitioners to process datasets across multiple nodes. For transformer-based models, distributed training with frameworks like Horovod or PyTorch's `DistributedDataParallel` can leverage multiple GPUs to handle large-scale fine-tuning or embedding extraction. However, scaling introduces trade-offs. Distributed systems require careful data partitioning to avoid communication overhead, and some algorithms (for example, LDA) may lose coherence when parallelized excessively. Additionally, managing infrastructure costs and ensuring fault tolerance are critical in production environments. You can mitigate these challenges by sampling representative subsets of data for initial experimentation or using lightweight models (for example, DistilBERT instead of BERT) for faster processing.

Evaluation

Evaluating unsupervised NLP models is challenging due to the absence of ground-truth labels, unlike supervised tasks with clear metrics like accuracy. Methods like topic modeling (LDA, PLSA) and clustering (K-means, BERT-based clustering) require alternative metrics to assess quality. **Coherence scores**, such as the `C_v` or `UMass` metrics, evaluate topic models by measuring the semantic coherence of top words in each topic. For example, an LDA model on the 20newsgroups dataset should produce topics where words like "`nasa`," "`satellite`," and "`orbit`" co-occur, indicating a coherent space-related theme. Higher coherence scores suggest more interpretable topics, guiding model tuning (for example, adjusting the number of topics).

Intrinsic evaluation methods, like perplexity for topic models, assess how well a model fits the data, but they may not correlate with human interpretability. **Extrinsic evaluation**, where unsupervised outputs feed into downstream tasks (for example, using clustered documents for search), provides practical insights but also requires additional setup.

Evaluation challenges include metric subjectivity and task dependency. For instance, a high coherence score for LDA may not guarantee useful topics for a specific application, and silhouette scores may mislead the user if the clusters are non-spherical. You should combine multiple metrics, validate results with domain experts, and iteratively refine models based on qualitative feedback.

Ethical Considerations

Unsupervised NLP models, while powerful, can perpetuate biases present in their training data, leading to ethical concerns. Word embeddings (for example, Word2Vec, GloVe, FastText) and transformer-based models (for example, BERT) often learn biases from corpora, such as gender or racial stereotypes embedded in word associations. For example, a Word2Vec model trained on a biased corpus might associate "`engineer`" more closely with "`male`" than "`female`," influencing downstream tasks like resume screening. Similarly, BERT embeddings trained on social media data like X posts may reflect societal biases, thus affecting clustering or sentiment analysis outcomes.

Bias mitigation strategies are essential to address these issues. **Data auditing** involves examining training corpora for biased content, such as stereotypical language in the 20newsgroups dataset, and curating more balanced datasets. **Debiasing techniques**, like projecting embeddings to remove gender-related dimensions (for example, Hard Debiasing for Word2Vec), can reduce bias in static embeddings. For transformers, fine-tuning on diverse, representative corpora or using contrastive learning with fairness-aware objectives can mitigate bias. **Regular evaluation** with fairness metrics such as measuring embedding distances for sensitive attributes (for example, gender, ethnicity), ensures that models do not amplify harmful associations.

Beyond bias, ethical considerations include **privacy**, as unsupervised models trained on user-generated content may inadvertently memorize sensitive information, and **transparency**, as complex models like BERT are often opaque, complicating accountability. Practitioners must prioritize ethical guidelines, such as anonymizing data, documenting model limitations, and engaging with stakeholders to ensure responsible deployment.

Recent Trends in Unsupervised NLP

Unsupervised natural language processing continues to evolve rapidly, driven by innovations in self-supervised learning, multimodal integration, and scalable architectures. As of 2025, these trends build on the techniques such as probabilistic models, word embeddings, and transformer-based approaches like BERT, while addressing practical challenges like scalability and ethics. Let us look at some of these recent trends:

- **Enhanced self-supervised learning** has advanced with models like successors to T5 and RoBERTa, which use refined objectives such as span-based masking or contrastive pretraining to learn richer representations from unlabeled text. These models improve tasks like clustering documents by capturing nuanced semantic relationships, thus requiring less domain-specific fine-tuning than earlier methods.
- **Multimodal unsupervised learning** integrates text with other data such as images or audio using frameworks like CLIP or DALL-E variants. For example, aligning text from social media posts with accompanying images enables unsupervised semantic analysis across modalities, thereby enhancing applications like content categorization.
- **Efficient scaling of large language models** leverages techniques like sparse attention and model distillation to deploy massive models (for example, open-source successors to LLaMA) on resource-constrained environments, making unsupervised NLP accessible for tasks like topic modeling on large social media datasets.

These trends reduce reliance on labeled data, improve generalization, and address ethical concerns by incorporating fairness-aware pre-training, though challenges like computational costs and bias mitigation remain. As these methods mature, they expand the potential of unsupervised NLP and enable practitioners to tackle diverse, real-world text analysis tasks with greater accuracy and efficiency.

Conclusion

In this chapter, we covered unsupervised NLP techniques, starting with techniques for text representation. Then we discussed techniques such as Linear Discriminant Analysis, Linear Semantic Analysis for discovering hidden themes or topics from unlabeled text data. We learned techniques for learning word embeddings such as Word2Vec, GloVe, and FastText, transformer-based methods like BERT and advanced approaches like contrastive learning and domain adaptation. We also saw some practical challenges such as preprocessing, scalability, evaluation, and ethics. Finally, we learned about the recent trends in unsupervised natural language processing.

In the next chapter, we will delve into evaluation of unsupervised learning models in depth.

Key Terms

- **Latent Dirichlet Allocation (LDA):** A probabilistic model that discovers latent topics in a text corpus by assigning words to topics and documents to topic mixtures, used for topic modeling in datasets
- **Word Embeddings:** Dense vector representations of words capturing semantic relationships, generated by methods like Word2Vec, GloVe, or FastText for tasks such as similarity detection
- **FastText:** A word embedding method that extends Word2Vec by incorporating subword information, thereby improving handling of out-of-vocabulary words in texts like 20newsgroups
- **BERT:** A transformer-based model using self-supervised pre-training to generate contextual embeddings, while adapting word representations based on surrounding text for tasks like clustering
- **Contrastive Learning:** An unsupervised technique that learns representations by maximizing similarity between positive pairs (for example, augmented sentences) and minimizing it for negative pairs, as in SimCSE
- **Domain-Adaptive Pretraining:** Fine-tuning a pre-trained model like BERT on a domain-specific unlabeled corpus such as scientific texts to enhance performance on specialized tasks without labeled data
- **Text Preprocessing:** Preparing raw text for NLP by cleaning (for example, removing metadata), tokenizing (splitting into words), and normalizing (for example, lemmatizing) using tools like spaCy or NLTK
- **Silhouette Score:** A metric for evaluating clustering quality, which measures how well-separated clusters are, with higher values indicating better-defined clusters in tasks like K-means on 20newsgroups

- **Multimodal Unsupervised Learning:** An approach integrating text with other modalities (for example, images) using models like CLIP, enabling unsupervised analysis of combined data from social media platforms
- **Bias Mitigation:** Strategies to reduce biases in unsupervised NLP models, such as debiasing word embeddings or curating balanced corpora, to ensure fair outcomes in applications

Questions

1. Explain how Latent Dirichlet Allocation (LDA) discovers topics in a text corpus like the 20newsgroups dataset. Describe the role of its probabilistic assumptions and how it differs from Latent Semantic Analysis (LSA) in terms of methodology and output.
2. Describe the process of generating word embeddings using Word2Vec, including the skip-gram and Continuous Bag-of-Words (CBOW) models. How does FastText improve upon Word2Vec, particularly for handling out-of-vocabulary words in the dataset?
3. Discuss how BERT's contextual embeddings differ from static embeddings like GloVe. Provide an example of how BERT's embeddings could enhance a task like clustering documents in a dataset compared to GloVe.
4. Explain the concept of contrastive learning as used in SimCSE for unsupervised sentence embeddings. How does it optimize embeddings for semantic similarity, and why might it outperform standard BERT embeddings?
5. Describe the key steps in preprocessing text data for unsupervised NLP tasks such as clustering or topic modeling, using a sample dataset. Discuss the roles of text cleaning, tokenization, and normalization, and how tools like spaCy or NLTK support these steps
6. Discuss the scalability challenges of applying unsupervised NLP methods, like LDA or BERT, to large datasets. How can distributed computing frameworks like Apache Spark or Dask address these challenges and what trade-offs might arise?
7. Explain the difficulties in evaluating unsupervised NLP models, such as topic models or clustering, due to the lack of ground-truth labels. Describe how coherence scores for LDA and silhouette scores for clustering can be used to assess model quality, using the 20newsgroups dataset as an example.
8. Address the ethical concerns associated with biases in unsupervised NLP models, such as Word2Vec or BERT. Provide examples of how biases might manifest in embeddings and suggest mitigation strategies.

9. Describe the role of domain-adaptive pretraining in unsupervised fine-tuning, as discussed in Section 5.1. How can it improve the performance of a model like BERT on a specialized corpus, such as scientific texts from the 20newsgroups dataset?

10. Discuss one recent trend in unsupervised NLP, such as multimodal unsupervised learning. Explain how it extends the capabilities of traditional text-only methods and provide a potential application using text and image data from social media platforms.

Multiple Choice Questions

1. What is the primary goal of Latent Dirichlet Allocation (LDA) in unsupervised NLP?
   a. To cluster documents based on their semantic similarity
   b. To generate dense word embeddings for semantic tasks
   c. To discover latent topics in a collection of documents
   d. To normalize text data for preprocessing

2. Which word embedding method captures subword information to handle out-of-vocabulary words?
   a. Word2Vec
   b. GloVe
   c. FastText
   d. LSA

3. How does BERT differ from static embeddings like Word2Vec in representing words?
   a. BERT uses fixed vectors for each word regardless of context.
   b. BERT generates contextual embeddings based on surrounding text.
   c. BERT relies on probabilistic topic assignments.
   d. BERT requires labeled data for training.

4. What is a key advantage of contrastive learning, as used in SimCSE, for unsupervised NLP?
   a. It requires extensive labeled datasets for training.
   b. It produces embeddings optimized for semantic similarity.

   c. It simplifies text preprocessing by removing tokenization.
   d. It reduces the dimensionality of input text.
5. Which preprocessing step is critical for preparing the 20newsgroups dataset for unsupervised NLP?
   a. Adding metadata to enhance document context
   b. Removing headers, footers, and quotes to reduce noise
   c. Converting all text to uppercase for consistency
   d. Including stop-words to preserve semantic meaning
6. What metric is commonly used to evaluate the quality of clusters in unsupervised NLP tasks?
   a. Accuracy
   b. Perplexity
   c. Silhouette score
   d. F1-score
7. Which distributed computing framework can scale unsupervised NLP methods like LDA to large datasets?
   a. spaCy
   b. NLTK
   c. Apache Spark
   d. t-SNE
8. What is a major ethical concern in unsupervised NLP models like Word2Vec or BERT?
   a. High computational cost of training
   b. Biases in embeddings learned from training data
   c. Lack of interpretability in probabilistic models
   d. Inability to handle large datasets
9. Which recent trend in unsupervised NLP integrates text with other data modalities, such as images?
   a. Enhanced self-supervised learning
   b. Multimodal unsupervised learning

   c. Efficient scaling of large models
   d. Domain-adaptive pretraining
10. What is a key challenge in evaluating unsupervised NLP models like LDA?
   a. Reliance on labeled ground-truth data
   b. Lack of metrics for assessing model quality
   c. Absence of ground-truth labels for comparison
   d. Overfitting to training data

Answers

1. c
2. c
3. b
4. b
5. b
6. c
7. c
8. b
9. b
10. c

Chapter 9
Evaluating Unsupervised Learning Models

Introduction

In this chapter, we will focus on the unique challenges of evaluating unsupervised learning models, where ground truth labels are often absent, we will also provide practical guidance for assessing model performance in various contexts including clustering, dimensionality reduction and NLP tasks. Unlike supervised learning, where metrics such as accuracy or F1-score provide clear benchmarks, unsupervised methods like clustering, dimensionality reduction and topic modelling require a blend of intrinsic, extrinsic and qualitative techniques to gauge their effectiveness. We will also explore practical tools and strategies for measuring the success of unsupervised learning solutions.

Structure

This chapter will cover the following topics:

- Evaluation Challenges in Unsupervised Learning
- Intrinsic Evaluation Metrics
- Extrinsic Evaluation Metrics
- Case Study: Evaluating Word Embeddings in a Text Classification Task
- Qualitative Evaluation Techniques
- Practical Considerations
- Advanced Evaluation Techniques

- Best Practices and Common Pitfalls in Evaluation of Unsupervised Learning Methods
- Recent Trends in Unsupervised Model Evaluation

Evaluation Challenges in Unsupervised Learning

Evaluating unsupervised learning models is a challenging task. Unlike supervised learning, where labeled data provides clear benchmarks like accuracy, precision, or recall, unsupervised learning operates without ground truth labels. So, answering the question: "*How do we know if our model is accurate?*" is more difficult in case of unsupervised learning models. For example, in clustering tasks, there is no definitive answer to whether a group of data points forms a "correct" cluster, as the definition of a good cluster often depends on subjective goals or domain-specific needs. Similarly, in dimensionality reduction or topic modeling, the quality of the output–whether it is a low-dimensional representation or a set of topics–relies on how well it serves the intended application, which can vary widely.

In supervised learning, evaluation is relatively intuitive: you compare model predictions to known labels and compute metrics like accuracy (for example, 95% of predictions match the labels) or F1-score for imbalanced datasets. These metrics are a concrete measure of success because the ground truth is explicitly defined. In contrast, unsupervised learning tasks like K-means clustering, Principal Component Analysis (PCA), or Latent Dirichlet Allocation (LDA) produce outputs without predefined correct answers. For instance, a clustering model might group customers into segments, but without labeled data, how can one determine if those segments are meaningful? Metrics like silhouette score or coherence attempt to quantify quality, but they often require careful interpretation and may not fully capture the model's utility in a specific context.

This lack of a universal standard makes evaluation in unsupervised learning tricky, requiring creative performance metrics and careful interpretation of results. The choice of evaluation metric must align closely with the task at hand, whether it is clustering, dimensionality reduction, generative modeling, or Natural Language Processing (NLP).

For clustering, we use metrics that measure how tight and well-separated clusters are, such as the Davies-Bouldin index. For dimensionality reduction, we use metrics that tell us how much variance is preserved, as with the PCA's explained variance ratio. In NLP tasks like topic modeling, coherence scores assess the interpretability of topics. Misaligning metrics with tasks can lead to misleading conclusions, for instance, using a clustering metric to evaluate a generative model's output would be inappropriate. This task-specific alignment ensures that evaluation reflects the model's practical utility, whether it is grouping customers for marketing, reducing data dimensions for visualization, or generating coherent topics for text analysis.

Importance of Evaluating Unsupervised Models Properly

Proper evaluation is critical for deploying unsupervised learning models effectively. Consider the example of a company using clustering to segment customers for targeted advertising: poor evaluation might result in meaningless segments, wasting resources on ineffective campaigns. In NLP, a topic model with low coherence can produce uninterpretable topics and undermine insights from a news corpus. In healthcare, dimensionality reduction on patient data must preserve critical information for accurate diagnostics. Robust evaluation ensures models deliver actionable results. Next, we will learn about a range of evaluation techniques–intrinsic, extrinsic, and qualitative–to help you assess unsupervised models effectively and deploy them successfully in real-world scenarios.

Intrinsic Evaluation Metrics

Intrinsic evaluation metrics assess the quality of unsupervised learning models based solely on their output and the input data, without relying on external tasks or labels. These metrics are essential for tasks like clustering, dimensionality reduction, generative models, and NLP applications as they provide a way to quantify model performance when ground truth is unavailable.

Clustering Metrics

Clustering aims to group similar data points, and intrinsic metrics evaluate how well these groups are formed based on cohesion (how tight clusters are) and separation (how distinct clusters are from one another). The three widely used metrics to evaluate the effectiveness of clusters learned by clustering techniques are:

- **Silhouette Score**: Measures how similar a data point is to its own cluster compared to other clusters. That is, it measures how well each data point fits within its assigned cluster compared to other clusters. The value of Silhouette score ranges from -1 to +1. A high average silhouette score indicates compact and distinct clusters. +1 means a well clustered data point, which refers to the point that is close to its own cluster centre and far away from the others. 0 means that the point is on or very close to the decision boundary between clusters, while -1 means that the point is misclassified into the wrong cluster. The overall score of the dataset is the mean of all individual `s(i)` scores in the dataset.

For a data point i:

- **a(i)** is the average distance between the point "**i**" and all other points in the same cluster (intracluster distance).
- **b(i)** is the smallest average distance between "**i**" and all points in any other cluster (nearest-cluster distance).

Then, the Silhouette Score for point "**i**" is:

$$s(i) = \frac{b(i) - a(i)}{\max(a(i), b(i))}$$

The overall score is the mean of all individual **s(i)** scores in the dataset. Silhouette score can be used to choose optimal number of clusters as well. Try different values of K and pick the one with highest average Silhouette score.

- **Davies-Bouldin Index**: It measures how well-separated and compact the clusters are. Lower values indicate better clustering, with compact clusters far apart. This metric quantifies cluster quality by comparing the average distance within clusters to the distance between cluster centroids.

Steps to Calculate the Davies-Bouldin Index

For a clustering result with k clusters:

1. For each cluster "**i**", compute Si the average distance of all points in cluster "**i**" to its centroid. This is the intra-cluster scatter.
2. For every pair of clusters "**i**" and "**j**", compute Mij the distance between the centroids (that is, the inter-cluster distance).
3. Compute the similarity measure **Rij** between clusters "**i**" and "**j**" as:

$$R_{ij} = \frac{S_i + S_j}{M_{ij}}$$

4. For each cluster "**i**", define:

$$R_i = \max_{j \neq i} R_{ij}$$

5. The Davies-Bouldin Index is the average of all **Ri**:

$$DBI = \frac{1}{k} \sum_{i=1}^{k} R_i$$

Here, **`Si`** measures the compactness of a cluster, **`Mij`** measures the separation between clusters. A lower DBI means that the clusters are compact and well separated, a higher DBI means overlapping or poorly formed clusters.

The Davies-Bouldin index can be used to compare different clustering algorithms or number of clusters (for example in K-means clustering algorithm).

- **Calinski-Harabasz Index**: The Calinski-Harabasz Index (CHI), which is also called the Variance Ratio Criterion, is an internal clustering evaluation metric. It measures how well the data points are clustered based on the ratio of between-cluster dispersion to within-cluster dispersion. Higher values indicate better-defined clusters. Between cluster dispersion, $B_{k,}$ measures how far apart cluster centroids are from the overall data centroid, it should be high. Within-cluster dispersion, W_k, measures how close data points are to their own cluster centroid (it should be small).

  For a dataset of **n** points partitioned into **k** clusters:

$$\text{CHI} = \frac{\text{Tr}(B_k)}{\text{Tr}(W_k)} \cdot \frac{n-k}{k-1}$$

  Where,

  $\text{Tr}(B_k)$ is the trace of the between-cluster dispersion matrix

  $\text{Tr}(W_k)$ is the trace of the within-cluster dispersion matrix

  n is the total number of data points

  k is the number of clusters

  The Calinski-Harabasz Index is especially useful for choosing the optimal number of clusters k in a clustering technique.

Figure 9.1 shows the Python code for computing the Silhouette score, the Davies Bouldin score, and the Calinski-Harabasz index for the clusters obtained using K-means clustering algorithm on a synthetic dataset using **`make_blobs`** module in sklearn library. We can see the values of the scores obtained in the same figure. We see a high value of Silhouette score (0.792), Davies-Bouldin Index of 0.291, and Calinsk-Harabasz Index of 3386.415 indicating good clustering performance on the dataset.

```
import os
os.environ["OMP_NUM_THREADS"] = "2"
from sklearn.cluster import KMeans
from sklearn.datasets import make_blobs
from sklearn.metrics import silhouette_score, davies_bouldin_score, calinski_harabasz_score
import numpy as np
```

```
#Generate synthetic data
X, _ = make_blobs(n_samples=300, centers=4, cluster_std=1, random_state=42)
```

```
#Apply K-means clustering
kmeans = KMeans(n_clusters=4, random_state=42)
labels = kmeans.fit_predict(X)
```

```
#Compute intrinsic metrics
sil_score = silhouette_score(X, labels)
db_score = davies_bouldin_score(X, labels)
ch_score = calinski_harabasz_score(X, labels)

print(f"Silhouette Score: {sil_score:.3f}")
print(f"Davies-Bouldin Index: {db_score:.3f}")
print(f"Calinski-Harabasz Index: {ch_score:.3f}")
```

```
Silhouette Score: 0.792
Davies-Bouldin Index: 0.291
Calinski-Harabasz Index: 3386.415
```

Figure 9.1: *Python Code for Computing the Silhouette Score, Davies Bouldin Score, and the Calinski-Harabasz Index*

Dimensionality Reduction Metrics

Dimensionality reduction techniques, like Principal Component Analysis (PCA) or autoencoders aim to compress data while preserving its structure. Intrinsic metrics evaluate how much information is retained in the dataset after dimensionality reduction or how well the data is reconstructed from the reduced dimensionality dataset. Let us look at some important metrics for dimensionality reduction:

- **Explained Variance Ratio (PCA)**: It measures the proportion of the dataset's variance captured by each principal component. For PCA, the sum of explained variance ratios across components indicates how much information is preserved after dimensionality reduction. A value close to 1 suggests minimal information loss.

If λ_i is the eigenvalue corresponding to the ith principal component, the explained variance ratio for component '`i`' is given by:

$$= \frac{\lambda_i}{\sum_{j=1}^{d} \lambda_j}$$

The sum of explained variance ratios across all components equals 1. It decides how many components are enough to retain most of the data's information. Explained variance ration directly measures how well the data's variability is preserved, without relying on any external tasks or labels.

Figure 9.2 shows the computation of explained variance ratio for PCA:

```
## Explained Variance Ratio
from sklearn.decomposition import PCA
from sklearn.datasets import make_classification
import numpy as np

# Generate synthetic data
X, _ = make_classification(n_samples=200, n_features=10, n_informative=5, random_state=42)

# Apply PCA
pca = PCA(n_components=2)
X_transformed = pca.fit_transform(X)

# Compute explained variance ratio
explained_variance = pca.explained_variance_ratio_
print(f"Explained Variance Ratio: {explained_variance}")
print(f"Total Variance Explained: {np.sum(explained_variance):.3f}")
```

```
Explained Variance Ratio: [0.31659442 0.22280016]
Total Variance Explained: 0.539
```

Figure 9.2: *Computation of Explained Variance Ratio for PCA*

- **Reconstruction Error (Autoencoders)**: It quantifies the difference between the original data and its reconstructed version after encoding and decoding and is represented by:

$$\textbf{Reconstruction Error} = \| X - X` \|^2$$

Where **X** is the original data and **X`** is the reconstructed data after dimensionality reduction and inverse transformation. Reconstruction error is often measures as Mean Square Error or Cross Entropy Loss.

- **Preservation of Pairwise Distances:** It measures how well distances between data points are preserved after projection. Trustworthiness and Continuity are a measure of preservation of pairwise distances.
- **Trustworthiness**: It measures how well the local neighborhood relationships in the low-dimensional space reflect those in the original high-dimensional space.

High trustworthiness means that points close in the low-dimensional space were also close in the original space. Low trustworthiness means the dimensionality reduction has introduced many false neighbors (that is, new neighbors that were not originally nearby).

- **Continuity:** It measures how many neighbors in the original space are not preserved in the low dimensional space. Continuity is complementary to trustworthiness. Continuity measures how well the original neighbors of each data point are preserved in the low-dimensional space.

- o It checks whether the true nearest neighbors (in high-dimensional space) are still close in the low-dimensional representation.
- o If many original neighbors are missing in the low-dimensional neighborhood, continuity is low.

- **Mean Relative Rank Errors (MRRE):** It computes the relative error in the rank of neighbors before and after reduction and is useful for checking how well neighborhood structures are retained.
- **Local Continuity Meta-Criterion (LCMC):** It measures how well local neighborhoods are preserved globally. It is often used to choose the best number of dimensions '**d**' for a dimensionality reduction technique.
- **Shepard Diagram Correlation:** This metric correlates pairwise distances before and after dimensionality reduction. A high correlation value implies that the structure of the data is preserved well.

Generative Model Metrics

Intrinsic evaluation metrics for unsupervised generative models (like VAEs, GANs, diffusion models, and so on) assess the quality and diversity of generated samples without relying on external tasks or labels. These metrics focus on the internal characteristics of the generated data distribution compared to the original data.

- **Log-Likelihood Loss:** Log-likelihood measures how likely it is for a given data point to come from the distribution learned by a generative model. It tells you how well a probabilistic generative model explains your data. Higher values mean the model's learned distribution matches the reality well. In generative modelling, your model learns a probability distribution **pθ(x)** over data **x**. Once the model is trained, we might wish to know the efficacy of this model at explaining the observed data.

  The likelihood of a dataset is the product of probabilities:

$$L(\theta) = \prod_{i=1}^{n} p_\theta(x_i)$$

  Since multiplication of small numbers that represent probabilities is numerically unstable and hard to interpret, so we will take the logarithm of probabilities and sum them up instead of multiplying. The resultant equation we get is the log likelihood which is demonstrated as follows:

$$\log L(\theta) = \sum_{i=1}^{n} \log p_\theta(x_i)$$

A higher value of log-likelihood means that the model assigns higher probability to the observed data. Log-likelihood often is used to evaluate models like VAEs, autoregressive models and normalizing flows (models that allow direct computation of **p(x)**). In VAEs, we approximate the log-likelihood using Evidence Lower Bound (ELBO) as computing exact **log p(x)** is intractable.

- **Reconstruction Error**: Reconstruction Error measures the difference between the original input data and the output produced by a model that tries to reconstruct it, typically an autoencoder. If your model truly understands the data structure, it should be able to compress and then reconstruct the input with minimal loss.
- For models like autoencoders and variational autoencoders, the reconstruction error is given by:

Reconstruction Error = difference (x, x`)

Where **x** is the input to the encoder. Encoder maps **x** to latent space **z**. **x`** is the output of the decoder produced by reconstructing from **z**. The reconstruction error can be measured as mean squared error for continuous data types (images, real valued vectors).

- **Mean Squared Error:**

$$\text{MSE} = \frac{1}{n}\sum_{i=1}^{n}(x_i - \hat{x}_i)^2$$

Reconstruction Error can be measured as binary cross entropy loss for binary data or probabilities which is shown in the following formula:

$$\text{BCE} = -\sum_{i=1}^{n}\left[x_i \log(\hat{x}_i) + (1 - x_i)\log(1 - \hat{x}_i)\right]$$

A low value of reconstruction error means that the model has learned to represent the data well. A high value means that the model failed to capture key features of data or compressed the data too much.

- **Fréchet Inception Distance (FID)**: Measures how similar the distribution of generated images is to the distribution of real images–not pixel-by-pixel, but in terms of semantic features extracted by a deep neural network. It compares the statistics like mean and covariance of real and generated image features in a deep feature space.

  The real and generated images are passed through a pre-trained network such as Inception v3 (for image classification task), the feature vectors are extracted from the middle layer (pooling layer). Then the means and covariance are computed from these feature vectors of real as well as generated images. The Frechet Distance, also called the Wasserstein-2 Distance, between these two multivariate Gaussian is then calculated as follows:

Where, **μr ,Σr** are the mean and covariance of the feature vectors of real images, **μg,Σg** are the mean and covariance of the feature vectors of generated images.

$$\text{FID} = ||\mu_r - \mu_g||^2 + \text{Tr}\left(\Sigma_r + \Sigma_g - 2(\Sigma_r\Sigma_g)^{1/2}\right)$$

Frechet distance measures whether the generated images are realistic in quality and are they diverse enough to represent the real data. A low value of FID means that the generated images are visually similar to real images, and the distribution of features is well matched. FID operates in a deep feature space, which aligns better with human perception of image similarity. FID assumes that the feature distributions are Gaussian, which is not always the case. It requires a large sample size (such as 10,000 images) for stability.

- **Model Score:** It evaluates the mode collapse in GANs and compares how many distinct models (clusters/categories) the generator captures compared to the true data.

NLP-Specific Metrics

For NLP tasks such as topic modeling, intrinsic metrics assess the quality of learned representations, like topics or embeddings.

- **Coherence Score:** They evaluate the interpretability of topics in such models. The coherence score measures the co-occurrence of top words in topics using Normalized Point-wise Mutual Information (NPMI), with higher scores (for example, 0 to 1) indicating more coherent topics. UMass coherence, an alternative to coherence score, uses log-based co-occurrence measures and typically ranges from negative values to 0, with higher (less negative) scores being better. A high coherence score means these words are related and interpretable. A low coherence score means the words are random or incoherent.

Various methods are used to compute coherence score including – cosine similarity, Point-wise Mutual Information (PMI), Normalized Point-wise Mutual Information (NPMI), Boolean sliding window counts.

A few popular coherence metrics are:

C_V: Uses NPMI and cosine similarity based on a sliding window over the corpus

C_UCI: Is based on PMI

C_NPMI: Is normalized PMI, the scores range between -1 and 1

C_UMass: Is based on document co-occurrence, uses a reference corpus

Figure 9.3 shows the Python code to compute coherence scores between given text data:

```
## Coherence Scores
from gensim.models import LdaModel
from gensim.corpora import Dictionary
from gensim.models.coherencemodel import CoherenceModel
import numpy as np

# Sample tokenized documents
documents = [["cat", "dog", "pet"], ["cat", "kitten", "cow"], ["cat", "kitten", "pet"]]
dictionary = Dictionary(documents)
corpus = [dictionary.doc2bow(doc) for doc in documents]

# Train LDA model
lda = LdaModel(corpus, num_topics=2, id2word=dictionary, random_state=42)

# Compute C_v coherence
coherence_model = CoherenceModel(model=lda, texts=documents,
                                 dictionary=dictionary, coherence='c_v')
coherence_score = coherence_model.get_coherence()
print(f"C_v Coherence Score: {coherence_score:.3f}")
```

```
C_v Coherence Score: 0.226
```

Figure 9.3: *Python Code to Compute Coherence Scores*

- **Perplexity:** Perplexity is a measure of how well a probabilistic model predicts a sample.

  In language modeling, it quantifies how well the model predicts the next word in a sequence.

  Given a sequence of words **x1,x2,…,xN**, and a model assigning probability **p(xi|x1,…,xi-1)** to each word, **perplexity** is defined as:

$$\text{Perplexity} = \exp\left(-\frac{1}{N}\sum_{i=1}^{N}\log p(x_i|x_1,\ldots,x_{i-1})\right)$$

Perplexity is the exponential of the average negative log-likelihood per word. Minimizing perplexity is equivalent to maximizing the average log-likelihood. It is like the average number of choices the model considers at each step. Lower perplexity means better predictive performance of the model. For example, a perplexity = 10 means that the model is uncertain about choosing uniformly among 10 options at each step. A perplexity = 1, means that the model predicts without any ambiguity. Perplexity is used to evaluate language models during training and testing.

Figure 9.4 shows the Python code to compute perplexity for LDA model using the Gensim library:

```
# Perplexity
from gensim.models import LdaModel
from gensim.corpora import Dictionary
import numpy as np

# Sample tokenized documents (split into training and test sets)
train_documents = [
    ["cat", "dog", "pet", "animal"],
    ["car", "truck", "vehicle", "road"],
    ["cat", "kitten", "pet", "furry"],
    ["car", "bike", "vehicle", "transport"]
]
test_documents = [
    ["dog", "pet", "animal"],
    ["car", "vehicle", "road"]
]

# Create dictionary and corpus for training
dictionary = Dictionary(train_documents)
train_corpus = [dictionary.doc2bow(doc) for doc in train_documents]
test_corpus = [dictionary.doc2bow(doc) for doc in test_documents]

# Train LDA model
lda = LdaModel(corpus=train_corpus, num_topics=2, id2word=dictionary, random_state=42, passes=10)

# Compute perplexity on test corpus
log_perplexity = lda.log_perplexity(test_corpus)
perplexity = np.exp(-log_perplexity)  # Convert log perplexity to perplexity
print(f"Perplexity: {perplexity:.3f}")
```

```
Perplexity: 40.039
```

Figure 9.4: *Computing Perplexity of LDA Model*

Choosing the Right Intrinsic Metric

Each metric serves a specific purpose: silhouette score and Davies-Bouldin index are ideal for clustering, explained variance ratio suits PCA, FID is tailored for generative models, and coherence scores are critical for NLP tasks. However, no single metric is universally perfect—silhouette score may mislead with non-convex clusters, and perplexity does not always correlate with human interpretability. Combining multiple metrics and understanding their limitations is the key to robust evaluation.

Extrinsic Evaluation Metrics

While intrinsic metrics assess unsupervised learning models based on their internal structure, extrinsic evaluation metrics measure how well the model's outputs perform in downstream tasks. This approach is very valuable in unsupervised learning, where the lack of ground truth labels makes direct assessment challenging. By using the outputs of unsupervised models such as clusters, reduced dimensions, or embeddings as features in supervised tasks, we can quantify their utility with familiar metrics like accuracy or F1-score.

Using Downstream Tasks for Evaluation

Extrinsic evaluation involves applying the results of an unsupervised model to a practical, often supervised, task to assess their effectiveness. For example, clusters from a K-means model might be used as features for customer churn prediction, or embeddings from a dimensionality reduction technique like PCA could be used to enhance a classification model. In NLP, word or document embeddings (for example, from Word2Vec or BERT) can be fed into classifiers for tasks like sentiment analysis or topic classification. The performance of the downstream task–measured with standard supervised metrics–serves as a proxy for the quality of the unsupervised model's output. This approach is powerful because it ties evaluation directly to real-world applications, therefore ensuring the model's outputs are meaningful and actionable.

Task-Specific Metrics

The choice of metric depends on the downstream task. Common supervised metrics include:

- **Accuracy**: Accuracy of a model is the proportion of correct predictions. Accuracy is a suitable metric for balanced datasets. It is calculated as:

  Accuracy = Number of Correct Predictions/Total Number of Predictions

- **F1-Score**: It is the harmonic mean of precision and recall and works well for imbalanced datasets. F1-Score is given by:

  F1-Score = 2*[(Precision * Recall) / (Precision + Recall)]

  Where precision is the ratio of true positives to predicted positives, and recall is the ratio of true positives to actual positives.

- **Area under the ROC Curve (AUC-ROC)**: It measures the trade-off between true positive rate and false positive rate, useful for binary classification tasks.

These metrics evaluate how well the unsupervised model's outputs contribute to solving the downstream task. For instance, high accuracy in a classification task using cluster labels as features suggests that the clustering captured meaningful patterns.

Selecting Appropriate Downstream Tasks

Choosing the right downstream task is very important for successful extrinsic evaluation. The task should align with the intended application of the unsupervised model. For example, if an unsupervised model generates document embeddings for a news recommendation system, a relevant downstream task might involve classifying articles by topic or predicting user engagement. Similarly, for a clustering model applied to customer segmentation, a downstream task could be predicting customer lifetime value using cluster labels as features.

The key is to select tasks that reflect real-world use cases, as this ensures the evaluation is both practical and meaningful. However, care must be taken to avoid tasks that are too simplistic or overly complex, as they may misrepresent the model's utility.

Practical Considerations

When implementing extrinsic evaluation, several factors must be considered to ensure reliable results:

- **Feature Integration**: The outputs of the unsupervised model (for example, clusters, embeddings) must be appropriately integrated into the downstream task. For instance, cluster labels can be used as categorical features, while embeddings may require normalization or transformation to suit the supervised model's input requirements.
- **Model Selection for Downstream Task**: The choice of supervised model for the downstream task can impact evaluation. Simple models like logistic regression or decision trees are often preferred to isolate the contribution of the unsupervised model's outputs, avoiding the influence of overly complex supervised models.
- **Dataset Quality**: The quality and size of the labeled dataset used for the downstream task are crucial. A small or noisy dataset may lead to unreliable metrics, obscuring the unsupervised model's performance.
- **Reproducibility**: Ensure that the evaluation pipeline is reproducible by fixing random seeds and documenting preprocessing steps. This is especially important when comparing multiple unsupervised models.

Example: Evaluating Word Embeddings

To illustrate extrinsic evaluation, consider a Word2Vec model trained on a corpus of product reviews. To evaluate the quality of its word embeddings, the embeddings can be used as features in a sentiment analysis task. A logistic regression classifier is trained on a labeled dataset of reviews (positive or negative), using the embeddings as input features. The classifier's performance, measured by metrics like F1-score or AUC-ROC, reflects the quality of the embeddings. For instance, an F1-score of 0.85 suggests that the embeddings capture semantic relationships relevant to sentiment, while a lower score might indicate poor embedding quality.

Challenges in Extrinsic Evaluation

Extrinsic evaluation is faced with many challenges. First, it requires access to labeled data for the downstream task, which may not always be available, especially in domains where unsupervised learning is used precisely because labeled data is scarce. Second, the performance of the downstream task depends not only on the unsupervised model's outputs but also on the supervised model and task design. Poor performance might reflect issues with the downstream model rather than the unsupervised model. Finally, extrinsic evaluation can be computationally expensive, as it involves training and testing supervised models for each downstream task.

Best Practices

To maximize the effectiveness of extrinsic evaluation, we should follow these best practices:

- **Use Multiple Tasks**: Evaluate the unsupervised model across multiple downstream tasks to gain a comprehensive understanding of its utility. For example, test embeddings on both classification and regression tasks to assess their versatility.
- **Benchmark against Baselines**: Compare the unsupervised model's performance to baseline features, such as random embeddings or simple clustering methods, to quantify its added value.
- **Iterate and Refine**: Use insights from extrinsic evaluation to refine the unsupervised model. For instance, if clusters perform poorly in a downstream task, revisit the clustering algorithm or hyperparameters.
- **Document Task Design**: Clearly document the downstream task setup, including dataset details, supervised model choice, and preprocessing steps, to ensure transparency and reproducibility.

Python Implementation of Extrinsic Evaluation with Clustering

The code in *Figure* 9.5 uses Telco Customer Churn dataset from Kaggle (https://www.kaggle.com/datasets/blastchar/telco-customer-churn?resource=download) to demonstrate extrinsic evaluation of a K-means clustering model by using cluster labels as features in a downstream churn prediction task. You should first download the dataset csv file (**`WA_Fn-UseC_-Telco-Customer-Churn.csv`**) and place it in your working directory. The dataset contains features like customer demographics, services and a Churn column (Yes/No) which we have mapped to column **`churn_label`** (1/0).

This code handles both numerical and categorical features, preprocesses them and evaluates the model using accuracy and F-score. Data pre-processing that we have applied includes dropping missing values, mapping categorical Churn variable to numerical **`churn_label`** column, exclusion of **`customerID`** column as it is non-informative, removing **`Churn`** and **`churn_label`** columns from features list, using **`ColumnTransformer`** to scale numerical features (**`tenure`**, **`MonthlyCharges`**), using one-hot encoding to encode categorical features (**`Contract`** and **`InternetService`**). Then, we will apply K-means clustering with 5 clusters. The downstream task uses cluster labels as an additional feature alongside pre-processed features to train a logistic regression model for churn prediction. The evaluation of the logistic regression model involves computing accuracy and F1-score. We see that the accuracy and F1-score are 0.807 and 0.604, respectively.

```
import pandas as pd
import numpy as np
from sklearn.cluster import KMeans
from sklearn.linear_model import LogisticRegression
from sklearn.metrics import accuracy_score, f1_score
from sklearn.preprocessing import StandardScaler, OneHotEncoder
from sklearn.compose import ColumnTransformer

# Load the Telco Customer Churn dataset
data = pd.read_csv("WA_Fn-UseC_-Telco-Customer-Churn.csv")
# Preprocess: Handle missing values and convert 'TotalCharges' to numeric
data["TotalCharges"] = pd.to_numeric(data["TotalCharges"], errors="coerce")
data["TotalCharges"] = data["TotalCharges"].fillna(data["TotalCharges"].median())

# Map 'Churn' to 'churn_label' (Yes=1, No=0)
data["churn_label"] = data["Churn"].map({"Yes": 1, "No": 0})

# Define features (X) and target (y)
X = data.drop(columns=["Churn", "churn_label", "customerID"])
y = data["churn_label"]

# Identify categorical and numerical columns
categorical_cols = X.select_dtypes(include=["object"]).columns
numerical_cols = X.select_dtypes(exclude=["object"]).columns

# Preprocessing pipeline: Scale numerical, encode categorical
preprocessor = ColumnTransformer(
    transformers=[
        ("num", StandardScaler(), numerical_cols),
        ("cat", OneHotEncoder(drop="first", sparse_output=False), categorical_cols)])
X_preprocessed4864 = preprocessor.fit_transform(X)

# Apply K-means clustering
kmeans = KMeans(n_clusters=5, random_state=42)
clusters = kmeans.fit_predict(X_preprocessed4864)

# Add cluster labels as a feature
X_with_clusters = np.hstack([X_preprocessed4864, clusters.reshape(-1, 1)])

# Train logistic regression on cluster-enhanced features
clf = LogisticRegression(random_state=42, max_iter=1000)
clf.fit(X_with_clusters, y)

# Evaluate performance
y_pred = clf.predict(X_with_clusters)
accuracy = accuracy_score(y, y_pred)
f1 = f1_score(y, y_pred)

print(f"Accuracy: {accuracy:.3f}")
print(f"F1-Score: {f1:.3f}")
```

```
Accuracy: 0.807
F1-Score: 0.604
```

Figure 9.5: *Extrinsic Evaluation of K-Means Clustering Results Using a Classifier*

Let us next look at extrinsic evaluation of word embeddings in a text classification task.

Case Study: Evaluating Word Embeddings in a Text Classification Task

This case study demonstrates how to evaluate the quality of pre-trained word embeddings, such as those generated by Word2Vec and BERT, via extrinsic evaluation in a downstream text classification task. By applying these embeddings as features in a sentiment analysis task, we will assess their ability to capture semantic patterns relevant to the task, using standard supervised metrics like accuracy and F1-score.

Dataset

We will use the IMDb movie reviews dataset, a popular benchmark for sentiment analysis, containing 50,000 labeled reviews (positive or negative). The dataset is accessible via Hugging Face's datasets library or public repositories like Kaggle. Each review is a text string and the task is to predict the binary sentiment label (0 for negative, 1 for positive).

Methodology

We will compare two unsupervised embedding models:

- **Word2Vec**: A shallow embedding model trained on a large corpus (for example, Google News) to produce static word-level embeddings. We average word embeddings to represent each review.
- **BERT**: A transformer-based model that generates contextualized embeddings. We extract sentence-level embeddings from BERT's [CLS] token or by pooling hidden states.

The embeddings are used as features in a logistic regression classifier to predict sentiment. The classifier's performance (accuracy and F1-score) serves as a proxy for the embeddings' quality. This approach mirrors real-world applications where embeddings enhance downstream tasks like sentiment analysis or topic classification.

Python Implementation

The Python code shown in *Figure* 9.6 and *Figure* 9.7 demonstrates the process using the IMDb dataset. You can download the IMDB dataset from Kaggle (https://www.kaggle.com/datasets/lakshmi25npathi/imdb-dataset-of-50k-movie-reviews). The IMDb dataset contains 50,000 movie reviews labeled as positive or negative. We will use a subset (1,000 reviews) for efficiency in our code implementation.

Our code loads pre-trained Word2Vec embeddings via Gensim and BERT embeddings via Hugging Face Transformers library. You should have a HuggingFace (https://huggingface.co/) account and have to provide your HuggingFace access token (https://huggingface.co/settings/tokens) to access models from HuggingFace. Our code also preprocesses the data, trains a logistic regression model, and evaluates performance.

The GoogleNews-vectors-negative300.bin (https://www.kaggle.com/datasets/leadbest/googlenewsvectorsnegative300) file is a pre-trained Word2Vec model released by Google, containing word embeddings trained on a large corpus of Google News articles (approximately 100 billion words). The file contains 300-dimensional word vectors for approximately 3 million words and phrases, generated using the Word2Vec algorithm (skip-gram with negative sampling). These embeddings capture semantic relationships between words, where similar words (for example, "king" and "queen") have vectors that are close in the vector space. It is a binary file (**`.bin`**) optimized for use with the Gensim library in Python. You should install the gensim library using the commnd **`pip install gensim`**.

The uncompressed **`.bin`** file is approximately 3.4 GB, while the compressed **`.bin.gz`** version is about 1.5 GB. In this case study, we are evaluating word embeddings (like Word2Vec) in a downstream text classification task using the IMDb dataset. The GoogleNews-vectors-negative300.bin file provides pre-trained embeddings that can be used directly to represent words in movie reviews, hence allowing us to assess their quality via metrics like accuracy and F1-score in sentiment analysis. This case study shows how extrinsic evaluation measures embedding utility, thereby aiding model selection in unsupervised learning.

```
import pandas as pd
import numpy as np
from sklearn.linear_model import LogisticRegression
from sklearn.metrics import accuracy_score, f1_score
from sklearn.preprocessing import StandardScaler
import gensim.downloader as api
from transformers import BertTokenizer, BertModel
import torch
from datasets import load_dataset

# Load IMDb dataset
df = pd.read_csv("IMDB Dataset.csv")
df = df.sample(n=1000, random_state=42).reset_index(drop=True)  # Subset
texts = df["review"].tolist()
labels = df["sentiment"].map({"positive": 1, "negative": 0}).tolist()

# --- Word2Vec Embeddings ---
word2vec = api.load("word2vec-google-news-300")  # Downloads ~1.5 GB model

def get_word2vec_embedding(text):
    words = text.lower().split()
    embeddings = [word2vec[word] for word in words if word in word2vec]
    return np.mean(embeddings, axis=0) if embeddings else np.zeros(300)

word2vec_embeddings = np.array([get_word2vec_embedding(text) for text in texts])

# --- BERT Embeddings ---
tokenizer = BertTokenizer.from_pretrained("bert-base-uncased")
model = BertModel.from_pretrained("bert-base-uncased")

def get_bert_embedding(text):
    inputs = tokenizer(text, return_tensors="pt", max_length=512, truncation=True, padding=True)
    with torch.no_grad():
        outputs = model(**inputs)
    return outputs.last_hidden_state[:, 0, :].numpy().flatten()  # Use [CLS] token

bert_embeddings = np.array([get_bert_embedding(text) for text in texts])
```

Figure 9.6: *Partial Python Code for Extrinsic Evaluation of Word Embeddings. Shows reading of IMDb dataset, download of Google's pretrained word2vec model and getting word embeddings from BERT Base Uncased embedding model from HuggingFace Transformers library.*

Figure 9.7 shows the remaining code:

```
bert_embeddings = np.array([get_bert_embedding(text) for text in texts])

# --- Downstream Classification ---
scaler = StandardScaler()
word2vec_embeddings_scaled = scaler.fit_transform(word2vec_embeddings)
bert_embeddings_scaled = scaler.fit_transform(bert_embeddings)

# Train and evaluate logistic regression with Word2Vec
clf_word2vec = LogisticRegression(random_state=42, max_iter=1000)
clf_word2vec.fit(word2vec_embeddings_scaled, labels)
y_pred_word2vec = clf_word2vec.predict(word2vec_embeddings_scaled)
word2vec_accuracy = accuracy_score(labels, y_pred_word2vec)
word2vec_f1 = f1_score(labels, y_pred_word2vec)

# Train and evaluate logistic regression with BERT
clf_bert = LogisticRegression(random_state=42, max_iter=1000)
clf_bert.fit(bert_embeddings_scaled, labels)
y_pred_bert = clf_bert.predict(bert_embeddings_scaled)
bert_accuracy = accuracy_score(labels, y_pred_bert)
bert_f1 = f1_score(labels, y_pred_bert)

# Print results
print("Word2Vec Performance:")
print(f"Accuracy: {word2vec_accuracy:.3f}")
print(f"F1-Score: {word2vec_f1:.3f}")
print("\nBERT Performance:")
print(f"Accuracy: {bert_accuracy:.3f}")
print(f"F1-Score: {bert_f1:.3f}")
```

Figure 9.7: *Remaining Python Code for Extrinsic Evaluation of Word Embeddings. This portion of the code shows evaluation of embeddings using logistic regression with word2vec.*

Figure 9.8 shows the results of the Python code. We can see that word2vec embeddings have an accuracy of 0.969 and F1-score of 0.968 while BERT embeddings have an accuracy of 1.0 and F1-score of 1.0. Thus, BERT embeddings are more accurate than word2vec embeddings.

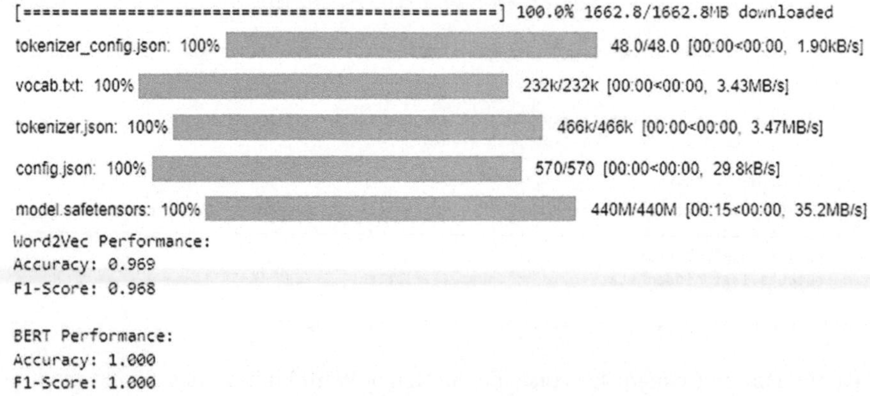

Figure 9.8: *Performance of Word2Vec and BERT Embeddings with Logistic Regression Classifier*

Next, we will discuss the qualitative evaluation techniques.

Qualitative Evaluation Techniques

While intrinsic and extrinsic metrics provide quantitative insights into unsupervised learning model performance, qualitative evaluation techniques offer a complementary perspective by leveraging human interpretation and visualization. These methods are particularly valuable in unsupervised learning, where the absence of ground truth labels makes it challenging to assess whether a model's outputs (for example, clusters and embeddings) are meaningful. Qualitative evaluation involves inspecting model outputs through visualizations, case studies, or expert reviews to assess their interpretability, coherence, and alignment with domain knowledge.

Common Qualitative Techniques

Qualitative evaluation involves several approaches, each suited to different unsupervised tasks:

- **Visualization**: Visualizing high-dimensional outputs in 2D or 3D space assesses whether clusters or embeddings form distinct, meaningful groups. Techniques like t-SNE or PCA are commonly used to project data for inspection. For example, in clustering, well-separated clusters in a scatter plot suggest good model performance.
- **Case Studies and Manual Inspection**: Examining individual outputs (for example, cluster members and generated text) allows domain experts to judge their relevance. For instance, in topic modeling, reviewing top words per topic can reveal whether topics are coherent and interpretable.
- **User Studies**: Involving end-users or domain experts to evaluate outputs ensures alignment with practical needs. For example, in a recommendation system, users might assess whether suggested items are relevant.
- **Comparative Analysis**: Comparing outputs from multiple models (for example, different clustering algorithms) side-by-side can highlight qualitative differences, such as cluster granularity or embedding quality.

These techniques are subjective but provide insights that metrics alone might miss, such as whether clusters capture intuitive patterns or embeddings reflect semantic relationships.

Applications in Unsupervised Learning

Qualitative evaluation is widely used across the following unsupervised tasks:

- **Clustering**: Visualizing clusters helps assess separation and cohesion. Manual inspection of cluster members can reveal whether they share meaningful characteristics (for example, customer segments in the Telco dataset).

- **Dimensionality Reduction**: Visualizing reduced dimensions (for example, PCA on embeddings) checks if similar items are grouped together.
- **Topic Modeling**: Reviewing top words or documents per topic ensures that topics are interpretable and distinct.
- **Word Embeddings**: Visualizing embeddings in 2D space can show whether semantically related words are proximate, as explored in the IMDb case study.

Challenges of Qualitative Evaluation

Qualitative evaluation has the following limitations:

- **Subjectivity**: Interpretations vary across evaluators, and thus require clear criteria or multiple reviewers to reduce bias.
- **Scalability**: Manual inspection is time-consuming for large datasets, limiting its feasibility.
- **Domain Expertise**: Effective evaluation often requires domain knowledge to judge output relevance.
- **Visualization Limitations**: High-dimensional data may lose important details when projected to 2D or 3D, potentially misleading interpretations.

Despite these challenges, qualitative methods are essential for validating unsupervised models in real-world contexts.

Practical Considerations for Effective Qualitative Evaluation

To conduct effective qualitative evaluation, you should:

- **Select Appropriate Tools**: Use robust visualization libraries (for example, Matplotlib, Seaborn) or interactive tools (for example, Plotly) for clarity.
- **Involve Stakeholders**: Engage domain experts or end-users early to define evaluation criteria.
- **Combine with Quantitative Metrics**: Use qualitative insights alongside intrinsic and extrinsic metrics for a holistic assessment.
- **Document Findings**: Record observations systematically to support model improvements or comparisons.

Python Implementation of Visualization of Clusters

Figure 9.9 shows the Python code for visualization of clusters obtained using K-means algorithm from the Telco Customer Churn dataset using t-SNE to assess cluster quality qualitatively. The visualization determines if clusters form distinct groups, indicating meaningful customer segments.

```python
#Qualitative Visualization Techniques
import pandas as pd
import numpy as np
from sklearn.cluster import KMeans
from sklearn.preprocessing import StandardScaler, OneHotEncoder
from sklearn.compose import ColumnTransformer
from sklearn.manifold import TSNE
import matplotlib.pyplot as plt
import seaborn as sns

# Load Telco Customer Churn dataset
data = pd.read_csv("WA_Fn-UseC_-Telco-Customer-Churn.csv")
data = data.dropna()
X = data.drop(columns=["Churn", "customerID"])  # Features for clustering

# Identify categorical and numerical columns
categorical_cols = X.select_dtypes(include=["object"]).columns
numerical_cols = X.select_dtypes(exclude=["object"]).columns

# Preprocessing pipeline
preprocessor = ColumnTransformer(
    transformers=[
        ("num", StandardScaler(), numerical_cols),
        ("cat", OneHotEncoder(drop="first", sparse_output=False), categorical_cols)
    ]
)
X_preprocessed = preprocessor.fit_transform(X)

# Apply K-means clustering
kmeans = KMeans(n_clusters=5, random_state=42)
clusters = kmeans.fit_predict(X_preprocessed)

# Visualize clusters using t-SNE
tsne = TSNE(n_components=2, random_state=42)
X_tsne = tsne.fit_transform(X_preprocessed)

# Plot
plt.figure(figsize=(8, 6))
sns.scatterplot(x=X_tsne[:, 0], y=X_tsne[:, 1], hue=clusters, palette="deep", s=50)
plt.title("t-SNE Visualization of K-means Clusters (Telco Dataset)")
plt.xlabel("t-SNE Component 1")
plt.ylabel("t-SNE Component 2")
plt.legend(title="Cluster")
plt.show()
```

Figure 9.9: *Visualization of Clusters for Telco Customer Churn Dataset for Qualitative Evaluation*

In *Figure* 9.10, we can see the corresponding clusters visualized. They look neatly separated with very little overlap.

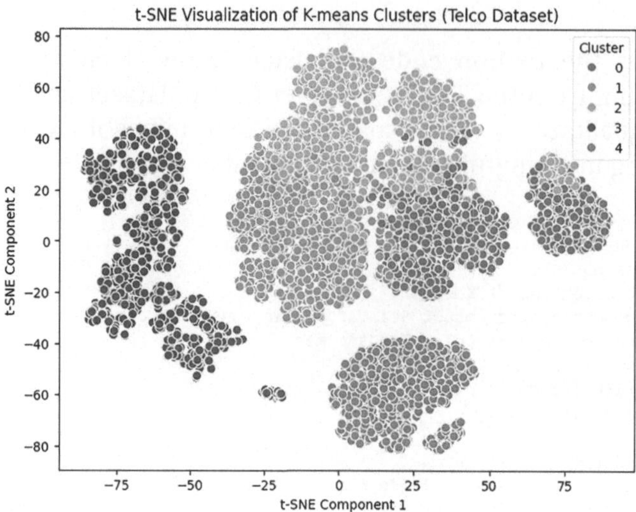

Figure 9.10: *Clusters from Telco Customer Churn Dataset Shows Well Separated Clusters*

Practical Considerations

Evaluating unsupervised learning models is a complex task that requires careful consideration of metrics, data characteristics, computational constraints, and domain context.

Choosing the Right Metric for the Task

Selecting appropriate evaluation metrics depends on the unsupervised learning task and its intended application:

- **Intrinsic Metrics**: Use intrinsic metrics (for example, silhouette score, Davies-Bouldin index) when assessing the internal structure of model outputs, such as cluster cohesion or embedding quality. These are ideal for early model development or when ground truth labels are unavailable. For example, in the Telco dataset clustering, a high silhouette score indicates well-separated customer segments.
- **Extrinsic Metrics**: Opt for extrinsic metrics (for example, accuracy, F1-score in downstream tasks) when evaluating how model outputs perform in real-world applications. These are critical for validating utility, as seen in the IMDb sentiment analysis case study, where BERT embeddings yielded higher F1-scores than Word2Vec. Extrinsic evaluation is preferred when labeled data for a downstream task is accessible.

- **When to Choose**: Use intrinsic metrics for quick, label-free assessments or when exploring multiple models. Reserve extrinsic metrics for final validation or when stakeholders prioritize task-specific performance. Combine both with qualitative techniques (for example, t-SNE visualization) for a comprehensive evaluation.

Handling Noise and Outliers

Noise and outliers can significantly distort unsupervised model evaluation. Outliers may skew cluster centroids in K-means or inflate variance in embeddings, leading to misleading intrinsic metrics. For instance, in the Telco dataset, extreme customer spending values could disrupt clustering.

Strategies to mitigate the impact of noise and outliers:

- **Preprocessing**: Apply robust scaling (for example, RobustScaler) or remove outliers using statistical methods (for example, IQR-based filtering) before evaluation.
- **Robust Metrics**: Use metrics less sensitive to outliers, such as median-based distances instead of mean-based ones.
- **Model Adjustments**: Employ algorithms that handle noise, like DBSCAN for clustering, which treats outliers as noise points.
- **Qualitative Checks**: Visualize outputs (for example, t-SNE plots) to identify outliers and assess their impact on model performance.

Scalability Issues with Large Datasets

Evaluating unsupervised models on large datasets poses scalability challenges. For example, Computing the silhouette score, which requires pairwise distance calculations, is computationally expensive ($O(n^2)$ complexity) for datasets with millions of samples, unlike the modest-sized Telco dataset. The solutions to scalability issues can be through sampling, approximation of metrics and distributed computing.

- **Sampling**: Evaluate on a representative subset of the data. For instance, randomly sample 10,000 points from a large dataset for silhouette score computation.
- **Approximate Metrics**: Use approximate methods such as mini-batch K-means for clustering or approximate nearest neighbors for embedding evaluation.
- **Distributed Computing**: Leverage frameworks like Spark or Dask to parallelize metric calculations on large datasets.

There is a trade-off when using sampling and approximation. Sampling or approximation may reduce evaluation accuracy, so we should validate results on smaller, controlled subsets when possible.

Trade-Offs between Computational Cost and Evaluation Quality

Evaluation quality often conflicts with computational cost:

- **High-Quality Evaluation**: Comprehensive evaluation (for example, full silhouette score, multiple downstream tasks) provides robust insights but is resource intensive. For example, BERT embeddings in the IMDb case study required significant GPU resources.
- **Low-Cost Alternatives**: Simpler metrics (for example, inertia for K-means) or qualitative visualizations (for example, t-SNE on a sample) are faster but less thorough.
- **Balancing Act**: Prioritize high-quality evaluation for critical models or final validation. Use low-cost methods during development or hyperparameter tuning. For large datasets, combine sampling with approximate metrics to manage costs.
- **Hardware Considerations**: Access to GPUs or cloud resources can mitigate costs, but ensure that evaluation pipelines are optimized for efficiency (for example, batch processing for BERT).

Addressing Subjectivity

Subjectivity is a challenge, especially in qualitative evaluation. Interpretations of visualizations or manual inspections vary across evaluators. For instance, one expert might find Telco clusters meaningful, while another sees overlap as problematic. This subjectivity can be addressed using following measures:

- **Incorporating Domain Expertise:**
  - **Engage Experts Early**: Involve domain specialists (for example, marketing teams for Telco customer segments) to define evaluation criteria, ensuring that outputs align with business goals.
  - **Structured Reviews**: Use standardized rubrics for manual inspections, such as scoring cluster coherence on a 1-5 scale.
  - **Multiple Evaluators**: Collect feedback from multiple experts to reduce bias and average subjective scores.

- **Combining with Metrics**: Ground subjective insights with quantitative metrics (for example, silhouette score alongside t-SNE plots) to balance objectivity and interpretability.

In the next section, we will talk about advanced evaluation techniques.

Advanced Evaluation Techniques

As unsupervised learning models are increasingly deployed in complex applications, advanced evaluation techniques become essential to ensure reliability, robustness, and generalizability. Sophisticated approaches like stability-based evaluation, robustness to hyperparameters, and cross-validation analogs for unsupervised learning, address challenges like model consistency and sensitivity, thereby providing deeper insights into model performance beyond standard metrics.

Stability-Based Evaluation

Stability-based evaluation assesses how consistent a model's outputs are across multiple runs with different random initializations or data subsets. Unsupervised models, such as K-means or topic models, often depend on random seeds, leading to variability in results. A stable model produces similar outputs (for example, clusters, topics) despite such variations, indicating reliability.

- **Approach**: Run the model multiple times with different random seeds, then compare outputs using metrics like Adjusted Rand Index (ARI) for clustering or topic coherence for topic modeling. High ARI scores suggest consistent cluster assignments.
- **Application**: Stability analysis can verify if K-means customer segments remain consistent across runs, ensuring dependable business insights.
- **Challenges**: Stability evaluation is computationally intensive, requiring multiple model fits. It also assumes that consistent outputs are desirable, which may not hold for inherently ambiguous tasks.

Robustness to Hyperparameters

Hyperparameter choices, such as the number of clusters in K-means or topics in LDA, significantly impact unsupervised model performance. Robustness analysis evaluates how sensitive a model is to these choices, identifying configurations that yield stable, high-quality outputs.

- **Approach:** Perform sensitivity analysis by varying hyperparameters (for example, `n_clusters` in K-means) and measuring performance with intrinsic metrics (for example, silhouette score) or extrinsic metrics (for example, downstream task accuracy). Robust models maintain performance across a range of values.

- **Application:** Testing K-means with different values of `n_clusters` can reveal if clustering quality is sensitive to the number of segments.
- **Challenges:** Sensitivity analysis requires extensive experimentation, increasing computational cost. It also demands careful selection of evaluation metrics to avoid misleading conclusions.

Cross-Validation Analogs for Unsupervised Learning

Unlike supervised learning, unsupervised learning lacks ground truth labels, making traditional cross-validation challenging. However, analogs like split-based evaluation can approximate this process by assessing model generalizability across data subsets.

- **Approach:** Split the dataset into training and holdout sets. Train the model on the training set and then evaluate its outputs on the holdout set using intrinsic metrics (for example, silhouette score on holdout clusters) or extrinsic metrics (for example, downstream task performance). Alternatively, use multiple random splits to simulate k-fold cross-validation.
- **Application:** For example, in the IMDb case study we covered in this chapter, embeddings could be trained on a subset of reviews and evaluated on a holdout set for sentiment classification, ensuring generalizability.
- **Challenges:** Splits may not capture data heterogeneity, and intrinsic metrics on holdout sets may not fully reflect model quality. Extrinsic evaluation requires labeled holdout data, which may be scarce.

Practical Considerations When Using Advanced Techniques

- **Computational Cost:** Advanced techniques are resource-intensive. Use sampling or parallel processing to manage large datasets like the Telco dataset.
- **Metric Selection:** Combine stability, robustness, and split-based metrics with qualitative insights (for example, t-SNE visualizations) for a holistic view.
- **Interpretation:** Stability and robustness do not guarantee correctness; cross-reference with domain knowledge or extrinsic tasks.
- **Tooling:** Leverage libraries like scikit-learn for clustering metrics or Gensim for topic modeling stability.

Figure 9.11 shows the stability analysis on K-means algorithm applied to Telco customer Churn dataset:

```
# Stability Analysis
import pandas as pd
import numpy as np
from sklearn.cluster import KMeans
from sklearn.preprocessing import StandardScaler, OneHotEncoder
from sklearn.compose import ColumnTransformer
from sklearn.metrics import adjusted_rand_score
import matplotlib.pyplot as plt
# Load Telco Customer Churn dataset
data = pd.read_csv("WA_Fn-UseC_-Telco-Customer-Churn.csv")
data = data.dropna()
X = data.drop(columns=["Churn", "customerID"])  # Features
# Identify categorical and numerical columns
categorical_cols = X.select_dtypes(include=["object"]).columns
numerical_cols = X.select_dtypes(exclude=["object"]).columns
# Preprocessing pipeline
preprocessor = ColumnTransformer(
    transformers=[
        ("num", StandardScaler(), numerical_cols),
        ("cat", OneHotEncoder(drop="first", sparse_output=False), categorical_cols)])
X_preprocessed = preprocessor.fit_transform(X)
# Stability analysis: Run K-means multiple times
n_runs = 10
n_clusters = 5
cluster_labels = []
for i in range(n_runs):
    kmeans = KMeans(n_clusters=n_clusters, random_state=i)
    labels = kmeans.fit_predict(X_preprocessed)
    cluster_labels.append(labels)
# Compute pairwise Adjusted Rand Index (ARI)
ari_scores = []
for i in range(n_runs):
    for j in range(i + 1, n_runs):
        ari = adjusted_rand_score(cluster_labels[i], cluster_labels[j])
        ari_scores.append(ari)
# Summarize stability
mean_ari = np.mean(ari_scores)
std_ari = np.std(ari_scores)
print(f"Mean ARI: {mean_ari:.3f}")
print(f"Standard Deviation of ARI: {std_ari:.3f}")

# Visualize ARI scores
plt.figure(figsize=(8, 6))
plt.hist(ari_scores, bins=10, edgecolor="black")
plt.title("Distribution of Adjusted Rand Index Scores (K-means Stability)")
plt.xlabel("ARI Score")
plt.ylabel("Frequency")
plt.show()
```

Figure 9.11: *Stability Analysis of K-Means Algorithm on Telco Customer Churn Dataset*

Figure 9.12 shows the ARI score obtained by running the code shown in *Figure* 9.11:

```
Mean ARI: 0.840
Standard Deviation of ARI: 0.169
```

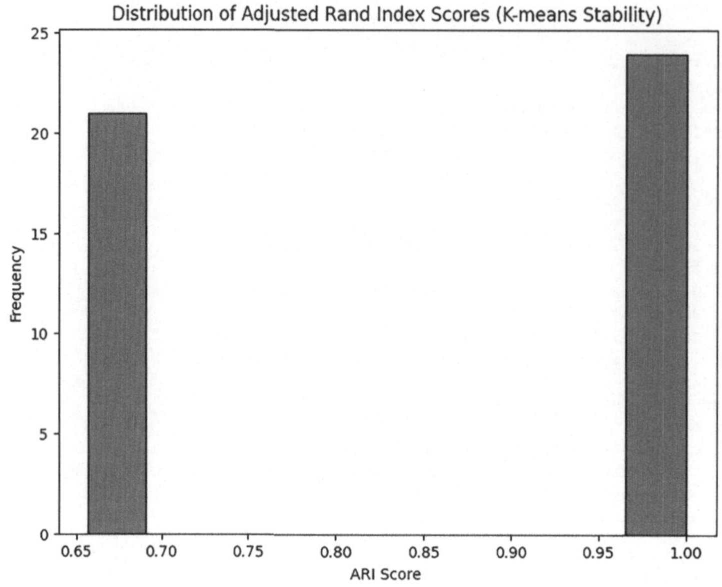

Figure 9.12: *The ARI Score to Measure K-Means Stability*

Best Practices and Common Pitfalls in Evaluation of Unsupervised Learning Methods

Evaluating unsupervised learning models requires careful consideration to ensure reliable, meaningful, and reproducible results. Building on the evaluation techniques discussed in this chapter–intrinsic, extrinsic, qualitative, and advanced methods. In this section, we will talk about the best practices for robust evaluation and common pitfalls to avoid. By adhering to these guidelines, practitioners can achieve a balanced and comprehensive assessment of their models.

Avoiding Misleading Metrics

Relying on a single metric can lead to misleading conclusions, especially when the metric's assumptions do not align with the data or task. Some of these misleading metrics are mentioned as follows along with the corresponding best practice to tackle them:

- **Pitfall**: Over-reliance on the silhouette score for clustering evaluation is a common error. The silhouette score assumes convex, well-separated clusters, which might not hold for non-convex or overlapping clusters (for example, customer segments in the Telco dataset with complex patterns). A high silhouette score might falsely suggest good clustering, while a low score might penalize valid but non-convex structures.

- **Best Practice**: Use metrics that match the task's characteristics. For non-convex clusters, consider the Davies-Bouldin index or qualitative visualizations like t-SNE. For embeddings, as in the IMDb case study, avoid relying solely on intrinsic metrics (for example, cosine similarity) and validate with extrinsic tasks like sentiment classification.
- **Strategy**: Always cross-check metrics with domain knowledge or qualitative insights to ensure that they reflect meaningful patterns.

Combining Multiple Metrics for a Holistic Evaluation

No single metric can capture all aspects of an unsupervised model's performance. Combining multiple metrics provides a more comprehensive assessment.

- **Best Practice**: Integrate intrinsic, extrinsic, and qualitative metrics tailored to the task. For example, in the Telco dataset, evaluate K-means clustering with the silhouette score (intrinsic), downstream churn prediction accuracy (extrinsic), and t-SNE visualization (qualitative). Similarly, in the IMDb case study, BERT embeddings were assessed with F1-score (extrinsic) and visualized for semantic relationships (qualitative).
- **Benefits**: Multiple metrics reveal trade-offs, such as high intrinsic quality but poor downstream performance, and guide model refinement.
- **Pitfall**: Ignoring complementary metrics can skew evaluation. For instance, focusing only on intrinsic metrics for clustering may miss whether clusters are actionable in business contexts.
- **Strategy**: Define a metric suite early, including at least one metric from each evaluation type, and compare results to identify strengths and weaknesses.

Documenting Evaluation Choices for Reproducibility

Clear documentation of evaluation choices ensures reproducibility and transparency, critical for collaboration and validation.

- **Best Practice**: Record all evaluation details, including:
  - Metrics used (for example, silhouette score, F1-score)

    - Data preprocessing steps (for example, outlier removal, scaling in the Telco example)
    - Model parameters (for example, `n_clusters=5` for K-means, random seeds)
    - Dataset splits or sampling methods (for example, 1,000 IMDb reviews)
    - Software versions (for example, scikit-learn, transformers)
- **Pitfall**: Failing to document choices can lead to irreproducible results or misinterpretation. For example, omitting the random seed in K-means stability analysis might cause inconsistent cluster assignments.
- **Strategy**: Use tools like Jupyter notebooks or version control (for example, Git) to log code, parameters, and results. Include comments in code and a dedicated evaluation log in project reports.

Balancing Quantitative Metrics with Qualitative Insights

Quantitative metrics provide objectivity, but qualitative insights ensure interpretability and relevance especially in unsupervised learning where ground truth is absent.

- **Best Practice**: Combine quantitative metrics with qualitative techniques to validate model outputs. For instance, in the Telco dataset, a high silhouette score for K-means should be confirmed with t-SNE visualizations and manual inspection of cluster members (for example, tenure, contract type). In the IMDb case study, BERT's high F1-score was supported by visualizing embedding distributions.
- **Pitfall**: Overemphasizing quantitative metrics can overlook practical utility. A clustering model with excellent intrinsic scores may produce uninterpretable segments, while qualitative-only evaluation risks subjectivity.
- **Strategy**: Use quantitative metrics for initial screening and optimization, then apply qualitative methods (for example, visualizations, expert reviews) to confirm alignment with domain goals. Involve stakeholders to bridge the gap between metrics and real-world needs.

In summary, the best practices to adopt are to use a suite of intrinsic, extrinsic, and qualitative metrics to capture different aspects of model performance, validate your assumptions, document thoroughly all evaluation choices including preprocessing, parameters and software versions for reproducibility, leverage quantitative metrics for objectivity and qualitative methods for interpretability, involve domain experts as needed, and use evaluation results to refine models, adjusting hyperparameters or preprocessing based on combined insights. The common pitfalls to avoid include metrics like silhouette score without qualitative validation, as they may mislead for complex data and the failure to document random seeds or preprocessing steps will hinder result replication; quantitative metrics alone may miss practical relevance, especially without domain expertise, high intrinsic scores do not guarantee downstream utility; always cross-check with extrinsic tasks or visualizations.

Effective evaluation of unsupervised learning models requires a balanced approach, combining diverse metrics, thorough documentation, and qualitative validation. By avoiding common pitfalls like misleading metrics and ensuring reproducibility, practitioners can build reliable models that deliver actionable insights.

Recent Trends in Unsupervised Model Evaluation

As unsupervised learning advances, particularly in deep learning and self-supervised paradigms, new evaluation techniques are emerging to address the growing complexity and diversity of models. In this section, we discuss the emerging trends in evaluation of unsupervised learning models.

Emerging Metrics for Deep Unsupervised Learning

Deep unsupervised models, such as Generative Adversarial Networks (GANs) and Variational Autoencoders (VAEs), require specialized metrics to evaluate their output quality, as traditional metrics like silhouette score or F1-score are often inapplicable.

- **Fréchet Inception Distance (FID)**: Widely used for generative models, FID measures the similarity between feature distributions of generated and real images, extracted using a pre-trained Inception V3 model. Lower FID scores indicate higher-quality generated images, capturing both diversity and realism.
- **Other Metrics**: For text generation, metrics like BLEU or ROUGE are adapted, while for embeddings, coherence scores (for example, topic coherence in LDA) are evolving to assess deep self-supervised representations.
- **Application**: FID is critical for evaluating GANs in computer vision, ensuring that generated images align with real-world distributions, unlike the clustering or embedding tasks in the Telco or IMDb examples.
- **Challenges**: These metrics can be computationally expensive and sensitive to feature extractors, and thus require careful implementation.

Evaluation in Self-Supervised Learning

Self-Supervised Learning (SSL), prevalent in NLP and computer vision, leverages pretext tasks to learn representations without labels, necessitating novel evaluation strategies.

- **Lessons from NLP**: In NLP, SSL models like BERT are evaluated via fine-tuning on downstream tasks (for example, sentiment classification) or probing tasks that assess learned features (for example, part-of-speech tagging). Linear probing, where a simple classifier is trained on frozen embeddings, quantifies representation quality.
- **Lessons from Computer Vision**: In vision, SSL models like SimCLR or MoCo are evaluated by fine-tuning or k-nearest neighbors (k-NN) classification on datasets like ImageNet. Transferability to diverse tasks (for example, object detection) is a key metric.
- **Relevance**: SSL evaluation bridges unsupervised and supervised paradigms, emphasizing extrinsic metrics (for example, F1-score) and robustness across tasks, as seen in the IMDb case study's BERT performance.
- **Challenges**: SSL evaluation requires access to labeled downstream datasets, which may not always be available and fine-tuning can obscure the quality of learned representations.

Trends in Automated Evaluation Frameworks

Automated evaluation frameworks streamline the assessment of unsupervised models, improving reproducibility and scalability. Let us look at some features of automated evaluation frameworks:

- **EvalAI**: A platform for hosting machine learning challenges, EvalAI supports custom metrics for unsupervised tasks, enabling standardized comparisons across models. It is particularly useful for generative models or SSL benchmarks.
- **Custom Toolkits**: Libraries such as PyTorch Metric Learning or Hugging Face's evaluate module offer pre-built metrics for embeddings, clustering, and generative models. These toolkits automate metric computation, reducing implementation errors.
- **Application**: Automated frameworks could standardize Telco clustering evaluations or IMDb embedding assessments, ensuring consistent metrics across experiments.
- **Challenges**: These frameworks may lack flexibility for niche tasks, and users must understand underlying metrics to avoid misinterpretation.

Future Directions

The field is moving toward standardized evaluation protocols to address the lack of consensus in unsupervised learning evaluation.

- **Standardized Benchmarks**: Initiatives like the Unsupervised Learning Benchmark (ULB) propose datasets and metrics for consistent evaluation, similar to ImageNet for supervised learning.
- **Unified Metrics**: Efforts to develop unified metrics that combine intrinsic, extrinsic, and qualitative aspects are gaining traction, aiming to reduce reliance on task-specific measures.
- **Open Challenges**: Standardizing evaluation for diverse tasks (for example, clustering, generative modeling, SSL) remains complex, requiring community agreement on metrics and datasets.
- **Vision**: Standardized protocols would enable fair comparisons, as seen in supervised learning, and accelerate progress in unsupervised applications like customer segmentation or text generation.

Recent trends in unsupervised model evaluation, from FID for generative models to automated frameworks like EvalAI, reflect the field's rapid evolution. Self-supervised learning and standardized protocols are shaping robust evaluation practices. By embracing these trends, practitioners can ensure their models are reliable, scalable, and ready for real-world challenges.

Conclusion

In this chapter, we covered the diverse landscape of evaluation techniques, providing a comprehensive toolkit for assessing unsupervised learning models in the absence of ground truth labels. From intrinsic metrics like silhouette score, to extrinsic metrics, we have seen how quantitative measures quantify model structure and utility. Qualitative techniques such as t-SNE visualizations offer interpretability, while advanced methods like stability analysis and emerging metrics like Fréchet Inception Distance address reliability and modern deep learning paradigms.

In the next chapter, we will learn about deployment of unsupervised learning models into production environments.

Key Terms

- **Intrinsic Evaluation**: Assessing the internal quality of unsupervised model outputs (for example, clusters, embeddings) using metrics like silhouette score, without labeled data. For example, evaluating Telco dataset clusters for cohesion and separation.

- **Extrinsic Evaluation**: Measuring the performance of unsupervised model outputs in a downstream supervised task, such as accuracy or F1-score. For example, Using Telco cluster labels for churn prediction or IMDb embeddings for sentiment classification.
- **Qualitative Evaluation:** Human-driven assessment of model outputs through visualization or manual inspection to ensure interpretability. For example, t-SNE visualization of Telco clusters to check for distinct customer segments.
- **Silhouette Score:** An intrinsic metric measuring cluster quality by comparing intra-cluster cohesion to inter-cluster separation. For example, commonly used in Telco clustering, although it is limited for non-convex clusters.
- **Adjusted Rand Index (ARI):** A metric for stability analysis that quantifies similarity between cluster assignments across multiple model runs. For example, Assessing K-means stability in the Telco dataset.
- **Fréchet Inception Distance (FID)**: A metric for generative models that measures similarity between feature distributions of real and generated images. For example, used in the synthetic image example to evaluate GAN output quality.
- **Self-Supervised Learning (SSL):** A learning paradigm using pretext tasks to generate representations, evaluated via fine-tuning or probing. For example, BERT embeddings in the IMDb case study, assessed through sentiment classification.
- **Stability Analysis**: Evaluating model consistency across multiple runs with different random seeds, often using ARI. For example, checking if Telco K-means clusters remain consistent across runs.
- **Robustness to Hyperparameters**: Assessing how sensitive a model's performance is to changes in hyperparameters, like the number of clusters. For example, Testing K-means with varying `n_clusters` in the Telco dataset.
- **Automated Evaluation Frameworks:** Tools like EvalAI or Hugging Face's evaluate module that streamline metric computation for unsupervised tasks. For example, potentially standardizing Telco clustering or IMDb embedding evaluations.

Questions

1. Explain the difference between intrinsic and extrinsic evaluation metrics for unsupervised learning models, using the Telco Customer Churn dataset as an example. How would you decide which type of metric to prioritize for evaluating K-means clustering in this context?

2. Describe how the IMDb sentiment analysis case study used extrinsic evaluation to compare Word2Vec and BERT embeddings. Why did BERT outperform Word2Vec, and how does this reflect the strengths of contextual embeddings?
3. Discuss the role of qualitative evaluation techniques, such as t-SNE visualization, in assessing unsupervised learning models. How did the t-SNE example in the Telco dataset help interpret K-means clustering results, and what are the limitations of this approach?
4. In the context of handling noise and outliers, as discussed in the practical considerations section, explain how outliers can affect clustering evaluation in the Telco dataset. Describe one preprocessing strategy to mitigate this issue and its impact on evaluation metrics.
5. Elaborate on the concept of stability-based evaluation for unsupervised models, as introduced in the advanced techniques section. How was the Adjusted Rand Index (ARI) used to assess K-means stability in the Telco dataset, and why is stability important for practical applications?
6. Describe the challenge of scalability in evaluating unsupervised models on large datasets. Using the Telco dataset example, suggest two strategies to address computational issues when computing the silhouette score for a large customer dataset.
7. Explain why over-reliance on the silhouette score can be misleading, as highlighted in the best practices section. Provide an example scenario using the Telco dataset where the silhouette score might fail, and suggest an alternative evaluation approach.
8. Discuss the importance of combining multiple metrics for a holistic evaluation of unsupervised models. How did the Telco clustering example integrate intrinsic, extrinsic, and qualitative metrics, and what benefits does this approach provide?
9. Describe the Fréchet Inception Distance (FID) metric introduced in the recent trends section. How does it differ from traditional metrics like silhouette score, and why is it suitable for evaluating generative models in computer vision?
10. Explain the significance of standardized evaluation protocols as a future direction for unsupervised learning, as discussed in the recent trends section. How could such protocols improve the evaluation of models like those used in the Telco and IMDb examples, and what challenges might arise in their development?

Multiple Choice Questions

1. What is the primary purpose of intrinsic evaluation metrics in unsupervised learning?
   a. To assess model performance in a downstream supervised task
   b. To measure the internal structure and quality of model outputs without labels
   c. To visualize model outputs for qualitative interpretation
   d. To evaluate model stability across multiple runs
2. In the Telco Customer Churn example, how were clusters evaluated extrinsically?
   a. By using cluster labels as features in a logistic regression model for churn prediction
   b. By computing the silhouette score
   c. By visualizing clusters with t-SNE
   d. By comparing cluster stability across multiple runs
3. What is a key advantage of qualitative evaluation techniques such as t-SNE visualization?
   a. They provide objective, numerical scores for model performance.
   b. They allow human interpretation of model outputs for interpretability.
   c. They are computationally inexpensive for large datasets.
   d. They guarantee reproducibility across runs.
4. Why is over-reliance on the silhouette score problematic, as noted in the best practices section?
   a. It is too computationally expensive for small datasets.
   b. It cannot be combined with qualitative methods.
   c. It requires labeled data for computation.
   d. It assumes convex clusters, which may not suit all data distributions.

5. In the IMDb sentiment analysis case study, why did BERT embeddings outperform Word2Vec?
   a. BERT uses static embeddings, while Word2Vec uses contextual embeddings.
   b. BERT captures contextual relationships, while Word2Vec uses static embeddings.
   c. Word2Vec requires more computational resources.
   d. BERT was evaluated with intrinsic metrics only.
6. What is a key challenge in handling noise and outliers during unsupervised evaluation?
   a. Noise improves intrinsic metric scores.
   b. Outliers can skew cluster centroids or embedding variance.
   c. Outliers are automatically handled by all unsupervised algorithms.
   d. Noise has no impact on qualitative visualizations.
7. How does stability-based evaluation assess unsupervised models?
   a. By measuring consistency of outputs across multiple runs with different random seeds
   b. By visualizing outputs in 2D space
   c. By fine-tuning models on downstream tasks
   d. By computing pairwise distances for all data points
8. What is the Fréchet Inception Distance (FID) used for?
   a. Evaluating clustering quality in datasets like Telco
   b. Computing coherence scores for NLP embeddings
   c. Assessing the stability of K-means clustering
   d. Measuring similarity between real and generated image distributions

9. What is a recommended best practice for ensuring reproducibility in unsupervised model evaluation?
   a. Rely solely on qualitative visualizations.
   b. Use only one metric to simplify analysis.
   c. Document all evaluation choices, including metrics and preprocessing steps.
   d. Avoid combining quantitative and qualitative methods.
10. What future direction in unsupervised evaluation was highlighted in the recent trends section?
   a. Developing standardized evaluation protocols for unsupervised tasks
   b. Eliminating qualitative evaluation techniques
   c. Focusing exclusively on intrinsic metrics
   d. Reducing the use of automated evaluation frameworks

Answers

1. b
2. a
3. b
4. d
5. b
6. b
7. a
8. d
9. c
10. a

CHAPTER 10
Deploying Unsupervised Learning Models into Production

Introduction

Deploying unsupervised learning models into production is a critical step in transforming data-driven insights into real-world impact. In this chapter, we will explore the end-to-end process of deploying unsupervised learning models, from preparation and infrastructure setup to integration, monitoring, and maintenance. By addressing practical considerations, and providing actionable best practices, we aim to equip readers with the tools and knowledge to successfully bring clustering, anomaly detection, and other unsupervised techniques into production environments, and ensure robust and reliable performance in dynamic, real-world applications.

Structure

In this chapter, we will cover the following topics:

- Introduction to Model Deployment
- Preparing Unsupervised Models for Deployment
- Infrastructure for Deployment
- API Development and Integration
- Integrating Models into Production Systems
- Monitoring and Maintenance of Deployed Models

- Tools and Frameworks for Deployment
- Ethical and Practical Considerations in Model Deployment

Introduction to Model Deployment

Deploying unsupervised learning models into production marks the transition from experimental analysis to actionable, real-world solutions. Unlike traditional data analysis, where insights are derived and interpreted in controlled environments, integrates models into live systems to process dynamic data and deliver continuous value.

Unsupervised learning models, such as those used for clustering, anomaly detection or dimensionality reduction, uncover hidden patterns in data without relying on labeled outputs. This makes them powerful tools for applications like customer segmentation, fraud detection, and exploratory data analysis, but also introduces unique challenges in ensuring reliability, scalability, and interpretability in production settings.

The importance of production-ready unsupervised models cannot be underestimated. In business contexts, these models drive decisions that impact revenue, efficiency, and customer satisfaction. For example, a clustering model might group customers for targeted marketing campaigns, while an anomaly detection model can identify unusual transactions to prevent fraud. Deploying such models effectively ensures that organizations can act on these insights in real time or at scale, transforming raw data into strategic advantages. However, without proper deployment strategies, even the most sophisticated models risk becoming impractical and fail to deliver consistent and trustworthy results.

Deploying unsupervised learning models differs significantly from supervised learning due to the absence of ground truth labels. In supervised learning, clear performance metrics like accuracy or F1-score guide model validation and monitoring. In contrast, unsupervised models require alternative evaluation methods, such as silhouette scores for clustering or pseudo-labels for anomaly detection, which can complicate deployment. Additionally, unsupervised models often deal with evolving data patterns, necessitating the presence of robust mechanisms to handle data drift and maintain performance over time. These differences demand specialized approaches for preparation, infrastructure, and maintenance, which we will explore in this chapter.

Common use cases for unsupervised learning in production include:

- **Customer Segmentation**: Clustering customers based on purchasing behavior to tailor marketing strategies
- **Anomaly Detection**: Identifying outliers in financial transactions, network traffic, or manufacturing processes to flag potential issues

- **Recommendation Systems**: Grouping similar items or users to suggest relevant products or content
- **Data Exploration**: Reducing dimensionality for visualization or preprocessing in large-scale data pipelines

This chapter will guide you through the end-to-end process of deploying unsupervised learning models, covering preparation, infrastructure, integration, monitoring, and ethical considerations. After understanding these steps, you will be equipped to bridge the gap between model development and real-world impact.

Preparing Unsupervised Models for Deployment

Before an unsupervised learning model can be deployed into production, it must be carefully prepared to ensure reliability, efficiency, and compatibility with target systems. This preparation involves evaluating and validating the model's performance, optimizing it for scalability and robustness, and ensuring that it can be seamlessly integrated into production environments. Unlike supervised models, unsupervised models lack labeled data, which introduces unique challenges that require specialized techniques. In this section, we will explore the steps followed during model evaluation and validation, model optimization, and serialization and portability.

Model Evaluation and Validation

Evaluating unsupervised learning models is inherently challenging due to the absence of ground truth labels, which makes traditional metrics like accuracy or mean squared error inapplicable. Instead, evaluation relies on indirect measures of model quality, tailored to the specific task, such as clustering or anomaly detection. The goal is to assess whether the model uncovers meaningful patterns and performs reliably on unseen data.

Challenges in Evaluating Unsupervised Models

The lack of ground truth labels complicates the assessment of unsupervised models. For clustering, there is no definitive way to determine if the discovered clusters align with meaningful real-world categories. For anomaly detection, distinguishing true anomalies from normal variations without labeled examples is difficult. These challenges require a combination of quantitative metrics, qualitative analysis, and domain expertise to validate model performance before deployment.

Metrics for Clustering

Clustering models, such as k-means or DBSCAN, are evaluated using metrics that measure the quality of cluster assignments:

- **Silhouette Score**: Measures how similar an object is to its own cluster compared to other clusters, ranging from -1 to 1. A higher score indicates well-separated and cohesive clusters
- **Davies-Bouldin Index**: Evaluates the average similarity between clusters, where lower values indicate better-defined clusters with minimal overlap
- **Inertia**: Used in k-means, this measures the sum of squared distances of samples to their nearest cluster center, with lower values indicating tighter clusters (though it is sensitive to the number of clusters)

These metrics assess clustering quality but should be complemented with domain-specific validation, such as checking if customer segments align with business goals.

Metrics for Anomaly Detection

Anomaly detection models, such as isolation forests or autoencoders, often rely on pseudo-labels or partial labels for evaluation:

- **Precision, Recall, and F1-Score**: If a small subset of labeled anomalies is available, these metrics can evaluate the model's ability to identify true anomalies while minimizing false positives.
- **Area under the Receiver Operating Characteristic Curve (AUC-ROC)**: Measures the trade-off between true positive and false positive rates; is useful when anomalies are rare.
- **Reconstruction Error**: For models like autoencoders, high reconstruction errors on test data can indicate anomalies, with thresholds set based on validation data.

These metrics require careful interpretation, as they depend on the quality of pseudo-labels or assumptions about anomaly distributions.

Visualizing Model Outputs for Validation

Visualization is a powerful tool for validating unsupervised models, especially when quantitative metrics are ambiguous. For clustering, techniques such as t-SNE or PCA can project high-dimensional data into 2D or 3D spaces to visually inspect cluster separation and cohesion. For anomaly detection, scatter plots or time-series visualizations can highlight outliers against normal data points. These visualizations, combined with domain knowledge, confirm that the model's outputs are meaningful and actionable.

Model Optimization

To ensure unsupervised models perform efficiently in production, they must be optimized for computational complexity, scalability, and robustness. Production environments often involve large-scale data, real-time processing, or resource-constrained settings; therefore, optimization is very important.

Reducing Computational Complexity for Scalability

Unsupervised models, such as those based on distance calculations (for example, k-means) or density estimation (for example, DBSCAN), can be computationally expensive. To improve scalability, you can use the following measures:

- Use approximate algorithms, like mini-batch k-means, to process large datasets in smaller chunks.
- Leverage parallel processing or distributed computing frameworks (for example, Apache Spark) for models like hierarchical clustering.
- Optimize hyperparameters, such as the number of clusters or tree depth in isolation forests, to balance performance and speed.

Handling High-Dimensional Data

High-dimensional data can slow down models and increase memory usage. Dimensionality reduction techniques mitigate these issues. The methods for dimensionality reduction improve efficiency and reduce noise, thus enhancing model performance in production.

Ensuring Robustness to Noise and Missing Data

Production data is often noisy or incomplete, which can degrade model performance. To ensure robustness:

- Preprocess data with techniques like imputation (for example, mean or median imputation for missing values) or robust scaling to handle outliers.
- Use models inherently robust to noise, such as DBSCAN for clustering or robust PCA for dimensionality reduction.
- Test models on synthetic noisy datasets during development to simulate real-world conditions.

Serialization and Portability

To deploy unsupervised models, they must be serialized into a format that can be easily loaded and executed in production environments. Serialization ensures models are portable and compatible with diverse systems.

Saving Models Using Formats Like Pickle, ONNX, or PMML

- **Pickle**: A Python-specific serialization format, widely used for scikit-learn models like k-means or isolation forests. It is simple but less secure and not cross-platform.
- **ONNX (Open Neural Network Exchange)**: A platform-agnostic format suitable for deep learning-based unsupervised models (for example, autoencoders). It supports interoperability across frameworks such as TensorFlow and PyTorch. If deploying across different environments (for example, from a local Python environment to a cloud-based system), use portable formats like ONNX to avoid dependency mismatches.
- **PMML (Predictive Model Markup Language)**: A standard for sharing models across platforms; useful for traditional machine learning models but less common for unsupervised tasks

Choosing the right format depends on the deployment environment and compatibility requirements. Unlike supervised models, unsupervised models like clustering or autoencoders may require additional metadata, such as cluster centroids or encoder weights, to be saved alongside the model. Ensure that any preprocessing steps (for example, scaling or normalization) are also serialized to maintain consistency between training and inference.

Figure 10.1 shows the Python code for serialization of a K-means clustering model trained with scikit-learn using joblib library. The model is saved in a pickle file named "**`kmeans_model.pkl`**":

```
from sklearn.cluster import KMeans
from sklearn.datasets import load_iris
import joblib

# Load sample dataset
iris = load_iris()
data = iris.data  # Only features, no labels

# Train the model
model = KMeans(n_clusters=3, random_state=42)  # Iris has 3 classes
model.fit(data)

# Save the model
joblib.dump(model, 'kmeans_model.pkl')
```

Figure 10.1: *Serialization of a K-means Model Using Pickle Format Using Joblib Library*

Testing the Serialized Model and Ensuring Compatibility with Deployment Environments

Production systems may use different programming languages, hardware, or cloud platforms. To ensure compatibility in heterogeneous environments, you should:

- Test serialized models in the target environment to verify functionality.
- Use standardized formats like ONNX for cross-platform deployment.
- Package dependencies (for example, Python libraries) using tools like Docker to create consistent runtime environments.

Before deployment, rigorously test the serialized model to ensure it performs as expected. Load the model in a staging environment and validate its outputs using a representative dataset. These tests often consist of:

- **Input Validation**: Verify that the model handles production-like input data correctly, including edge cases and missing values.
- **Output Consistency**: For clustering models, check that cluster assignments remain stable for similar inputs. For dimensionality reduction models, ensure that transformed outputs align with expectations.
- **Performance Testing**: Measure inference time and resource usage to ensure the model meets production requirements.

By addressing these preparation steps–evaluation, optimization, and serialization, you lay a strong foundation for deploying unsupervised learning models that are robust, efficient, and ready for real-world challenges.

Infrastructure for Deployment

Deploying unsupervised learning models into production requires a robust infrastructure to ensure scalability, reliability, and accessibility. The infrastructure encompasses the platform where the model runs, the tools used to package and manage it, and the interfaces that connect it to other systems. In this section, we will discuss three key elements of infrastructure for model deployment: choosing a deployment platform, containerization for consistent environments, and API development for seamless integration. These elements collectively ensure that unsupervised models perform effectively in real-world applications.

Choosing a Deployment Platform

The choice of deployment platform significantly impacts a model's performance, cost, and ease of maintenance. The choice depends on factors like the model's computational requirements, the organization's infrastructure, data privacy needs, scalability demands, and budget constraints. The platform must align with the application's requirements, such as latency, scalability, and data security.

Commonly used deployment platform options include cloud-based solutions, containerization, on-premises deployments, serverless architectures, and edge based deployments for real-time use cases.

Cloud-Based Solutions

Cloud platforms like Amazon Web Services (AWS), Google Cloud Platform (GCP), and Microsoft Azure Machine Learning offer scalable, managed environments for deploying unsupervised models and offer scalability for large datasets. These platforms simplify the deployment process by offering preconfigured infrastructure, scalability, and integration with other cloud services.

Some prominent cloud platforms include:

- **AWS**: Services like SageMaker for model hosting, Lambda for serverless inference, and Elastic Kubernetes Service (EKS) for containerized deployments provide flexibility for clustering or anomaly detection models.
- **Google Cloud**: Vertex AI simplifies model deployment and monitoring, while BigQuery integrates with data pipelines for batch processing of unsupervised tasks.
- **Azure**: Azure Machine Learning supports end-to-end workflows, with Azure Kubernetes Service (AKS) for scaling and Blob Storage for handling large datasets.

Benefits of Cloud-Based Deployment

- **Ease of Use**: Cloud platforms provide tools for model hosting, monitoring, and scaling with minimal setup. For example, AWS SageMaker allows you to deploy a scikit-learn K-means model with a few API calls, handling endpoint creation and auto-scaling automatically.
- **Scalability**: Cloud platforms can dynamically scale resources to handle varying inference loads, which is useful for applications like real-time customer segmentation where request volumes may fluctuate.
- **Integration**: These platforms integrate with data storage (for example, AWS S3, Google Cloud Storage) and monitoring tools, simplifying data pipelines and performance tracking for unsupervised models.
- **Managed Services**: Features like automated model retraining and drift detection are particularly valuable for unsupervised models, which may require periodic updates to adapt to changing data distributions.

Challenges of Cloud-Based Deployment

- **Cost**: Cloud platforms can be expensive, especially for high-throughput applications or models requiring GPU resources. Careful cost monitoring is essential.

- **Vendor Lock-In**: Reliance on proprietary tools may limit portability across platforms.
- **Data Privacy**: For sensitive data, ensure compliance with regulations like GDPR or HIPAA, which may require additional configurations (for example, private VPCs).

Cloud platforms are ideal for organizations with existing cloud infrastructure, those needing rapid deployment, or applications requiring high scalability, such as deploying a clustering model for e-commerce customer segmentation across millions of users but they incur ongoing costs and require careful management of data privacy.

On-Premises Deployment Considerations

For organizations with strict data privacy or regulatory requirements, deploying models on local servers (on-premises) may be necessary. On-premises deployment involves hosting models on dedicated hardware within the organization's data center. However, it is important to ensure that the hardware capabilities (for example, CPU/GPU) match the model's computational needs. Therefore, one would need to factor in the following considerations during on-premises deployment:

- **Infrastructure Setup**: Requires dedicated hardware, such as GPU servers for deep learning-based models (for example, autoencoders) or high-memory systems for large-scale clustering.
- **Maintenance**: In-house teams must manage software updates, security patches, and hardware scalability, increasing operational overhead.

Benefits of On-Premises Deployment

- **Data Control**: On-premises deployment ensures that sensitive data like customer profiles for clustering never leaves the organization's infrastructure, thereby addressing privacy concerns.
- **Customization**: Organizations can tailor hardware (for example, GPUs for deep learning-based autoencoders) and software configurations to the model's needs.
- **Cost Predictability**: Unlike cloud platforms, on-premises deployment avoids variable usage-based costs, which can be advantageous for stable workloads.

Challenges of On-Premises Deployment

- **High Upfront Costs**: Purchasing and maintaining hardware, such as servers with sufficient CPU/GPU capacity, requires significant investment.
- **Scalability Limitations**: Scaling on-premises infrastructure is slower and more expensive than cloud-based solutions, which potentially limits responsiveness to demand spikes.

- **Maintenance Burden**: IT teams must manage hardware, software updates, and network configurations, which diverts resources from model development.

On-premises deployments offer control but demand significant resources and expertise compared to cloud solutions. It is often preferred in industries like finance or healthcare where data cannot leave local servers due to compliance (for example, GDPR, HIPAA), or for applications with predictable workloads, such as internal fraud detection using anomaly detection models.

Serverless Architectures

Serverless platforms such as AWS Lambda, Google Cloud Functions, or Azure Functions, allow deployment without managing servers, and automatically handle scaling and resource allocation for your models.

Benefits of Serverless Architectures

- **Zero Server Management**: Serverless platforms abstract infrastructure management, allowing developers to focus on model logic.
- **Cost Efficiency**: Pay only for actual inference requests, which is ideal for sporadic workloads, such as occasional anomaly detection in log data.
- **Auto-Scaling**: Serverless platforms scale seamlessly with request volume, ensuring performance for unpredictable traffic patterns.

Challenges of Serverless Architectures

- **Cold Start Latency**: Serverless functions may experience delays during initialization, which can impact latency-sensitive applications.
- **Resource Constraints**: Limited memory and execution time (for example, AWS Lambda's 15-minute timeout) may restrict complex unsupervised models like deep autoencoders.
- **Dependency Management**: Large models or dependencies (for example, scikit-learn, PyTorch) may exceed serverless platform size limits, requiring optimization or external storage.

Serverless deployment is suitable for lightweight unsupervised models with intermittent usage, such as a clustering model for periodic customer analytics in a small-scale application.

Edge Deployment for Real-Time Applications

Edge deployment involves running models on edge devices, such as IoT devices, mobile phones, or embedded systems, to enable real-time inference close to the data source. This approach is particularly relevant for unsupervised learning models in latency-sensitive or bandwidth-constrained applications. Edge deployment enables low-latency inference for real-time applications like IoT anomaly detection or mobile app recommendations. For example, deploying an anomaly detection model on a factory sensor to flag equipment failures or a clustering model on a mobile app for personalized content.

The hardware required to run lightweight models include edge devices like Raspberry Pi, NVIDIA Jetson, or mobile devices, requiring optimization for limited compute resources. Edge deployment needs that the models must be compact (for example, using quantization or pruning) to fit memory constraints and updates must be managed remotely.

Benefits of Edge Deployment

- **Ultra-Low Latency**: Processes data locally and minimizes latency, which makes it ideal for real-time applications like anomaly detection in industrial sensors or clustering in autonomous vehicles
- **Bandwidth Efficiency**: Reduces the need to transmit large datasets to centralized servers, critical for IoT or mobile applications with limited connectivity
- **Offline Capability**: Enables inference in disconnected environments, such as remote monitoring systems using isolation forests
- **Data Privacy**: Keeps sensitive data on the device, enhancing privacy for applications like personalized customer profiling on mobile apps

Challenges of Edge Deployment

- **Resource Constraints**: Edge devices have limited computational power, memory, and storage, requiring model optimization (for example, quantization, pruning) for lightweight unsupervised models like K-means or simplified autoencoders.
- **Model Updates**: Updating models on distributed edge devices is complex, often requiring Over-the-Air (OTA) update mechanisms.
- **Heterogeneity**: Edge devices vary in hardware and operating systems, thus necessitating cross-platform compatibility.
- **Monitoring**: Monitoring model performance across distributed devices is challenging, requiring lightweight telemetry solutions.

Edge deployment is ideal for real-time applications with strict latency or connectivity constraints, such as anomaly detection in IoT sensors, clustering in smart cameras, or dimensionality reduction in wearable devices. It is best suited for lightweight models or scenarios where data privacy is paramount.

Containerization

By using tools like Docker and Kubernetes, containerization packages the model, its dependencies, and preprocessing steps into portable, isolated containers. This approach ensures that the models run consistently across development, testing, and production environments.

Benefits of Containerization

- **Portability**: Containers run consistently across different environments, from local servers to cloud clusters, reducing issues like dependency mismatches.
- **Isolation**: Each model runs in its own container, which prevents conflicts between different models or applications.
- **Scalability**: Kubernetes can orchestrate containers to handle load balancing, auto-scaling, and fault tolerance, which makes it suitable for high-traffic applications like anomaly detection in IoT systems.
- **Flexibility**: Containers can be deployed on-premises, in the cloud, or in hybrid environments, thereby offering versatility for organizations with diverse infrastructure.

Challenges of Containerization

- **Complexity**: Setting up and managing containers, especially with Kubernetes, requires expertise in DevOps practices.
- **Resource Overhead**: Containers consume more resources than serverless deployments, which may be a concern for lightweight models.
- **Maintenance**: Regular updates to container images and orchestration configurations are needed to address security vulnerabilities and performance issues.

Using Docker for Consistent Environments

Docker creates lightweight, isolated containers that encapsulate the model and its dependencies. Use Docker to package the model, its dependencies, and preprocessing steps into a container. Kubernetes can then be used for orchestration and scaling.

Using Docker ensures consistency between development and production environments, avoiding issues like version mismatches (for example, Python or library versions). A Docker image might include a Python environment with scikit-learn for k-means clustering or PyTorch for autoencoders, along with necessary preprocessing scripts. Example Workflow includes building a Docker image with the serialized model (for example, in pickle or ONNX format), install dependencies via a `requirements.txt` file, and define an entry point to serve predictions.

Docker simplifies deployment by providing a reproducible environment, especially for cloud or on-premises setups.

Kubernetes for Orchestration and Scaling

Kubernetes orchestrates multiple Docker containers to manage scalability, fault tolerance, and load balancing:

- **Scaling**: Automatically scales containers based on demand, such as handling increased traffic for a recommendation system.
- **Orchestration**: Manages container deployment across clusters, ensuring high availability and efficient resource use.
- **Use Case**: Deploying a clustering model for real-time customer segmentation across multiple regions, with Kubernetes balancing requests across containers.

Kubernetes is particularly valuable for large-scale deployments, complementing Docker by automating complex management tasks.

Containerization is ideal for organizations with complex deployment needs, those requiring consistent environments across multiple platforms, or those deploying multiple unsupervised models.

Considerations for Choosing a Deployment Platform for Unsupervised Learning Models

Unsupervised learning models introduce the following considerations when choosing a deployment platform:

- **Computational Requirements**: Models like deep autoencoders or large-scale clustering may require GPU support, which is readily available in cloud platforms like AWS SageMaker, but may necessitate specialized hardware for on-premises deployment.
- **Data Volume and Velocity**: High-throughput applications like real-time anomaly detection in streaming data, benefit from the scalability of cloud or containerized solutions, while serverless may suffice for low-frequency tasks.
- **Monitoring Needs**: Unsupervised models require monitoring for drift in data distributions (for example, changes in cluster structures). Cloud platforms often provide built-in monitoring tools, while on-premises and containerized deployments may require custom solutions.
- **Retraining Pipelines**: Ensure the platform supports automated retraining pipelines, as unsupervised models might need periodic updates to adapt to

evolving patterns. Cloud platforms and Kubernetes excel in integrating with orchestration tools like Airflow.

- **Latency Requirements**: Edge deployment excels for ultra-low latency real-time applications, while cloud and containerized solutions are better for near-real-time or scalable workloads.

A Decision Framework to Choose the Right Platform

To choose the right platform, consider the following questions:

- **What are the performance requirements?** For low-latency, high-throughput applications, cloud or containerized solutions are preferable.
- **What are the data privacy needs?** On-premises deployment is best for sensitive data, while cloud platforms require compliance measures.
- **What is the expected workload?** Serverless is cost-effective for sporadic usage, while cloud or containerized solutions suit continuous workloads.
- **What is the team's expertise?** Cloud platforms and serverless require less DevOps knowledge than containerized or on-premises deployments.
- **What is the budget?** Balance upfront costs (on-premises) against usage-based costs (cloud, serverless).
- **What are the latency requirements**? Edge deployment is best for ultra-low latency real-time applications; cloud and containerized solutions suit near-real-time needs.

Thus, by carefully evaluating these factors, you can select a deployment platform that aligns with the technical and business requirements of your unsupervised learning model.

API Development and Integration

To make unsupervised models accessible to applications, they are typically exposed through APIs using frameworks such as Flask, FastAPI, Django, Streamlit and so on, which allow systems to send input data and receive predictions. APIs must handle input preprocessing, model inference, and output formatting efficiently.

Exposing Models via REST APIs

To make unsupervised learning models accessible to applications, exposing them through REST APIs is a common and effective approach. A REST API allows client applications, such as web or mobile apps, to send input data to the model and receive predictions or transformations in a standardized format, typically JSON.

Designing the API

A well-designed REST API for an unsupervised learning model should be intuitive, secure, and efficient. Important design considerations include:

- **Endpoint Structure**: Define clear endpoints, such as /predict for clustering or anomaly detection models, or /transform for dimensionality reduction models like PCA or autoencoders.
- **Input Format**: Accept input data in a structured format, such as a JSON array or object, which matches the model's expected input shape. For example, a clustering model might expect a list of numerical features.
- **Output Format**: Return meaningful outputs, such as cluster labels, anomaly scores, or reduced-dimensional representations, in a consistent JSON structure.
- **Error Handling**: Implement validation to handle invalid inputs, such as missing features or incorrect data types, and return appropriate error messages.

Proper API design ensures seamless integration with applications, making model outputs actionable for end users.

Tools Like Flask, FastAPI, or TensorFlow Serving

Several tools simplify API development for unsupervised models:

- **Flask**: A lightweight Python framework for building REST APIs. Suitable for simple deployments, such as serving a k-means model for customer segmentation.
- **FastAPI**: A modern, high-performance framework with automatic API documentation and support for asynchronous requests, ideal for scalable applications.
- **TensorFlow Serving**: Designed for deep learning models (for example, autoencoders), it supports versioning and high-throughput inference, integrating well with cloud platforms.

These tools streamline the process of exposing models, with the choice depending on the application's complexity and performance needs.

Implementation with FastAPI

FastAPI (https://fastapi.tiangolo.com/) is a modern, high-performance Python framework for building REST APIs to deploy machine learning models.

Figure 10.2 shows the Python code to use create a **`FastAPI`** endpoint for a clustering model. We are using the model from the pickle file (**`kmeans_model.pkl`**) we serialized in the code shown in *Figure* 10.1. This code is placed in a Python script known as **`app_predictkmeans.py`**. You will need to install Python libraries **`fastapi`** and **`uvicorn`** to run this code. You can install it using the commands **pip install fastapi** and **pip install uvicorn** at your Anaconda prompt.

```
from fastapi import FastAPI, Body
import joblib
import numpy as np

app = FastAPI()
model = joblib.load('kmeans_model.pkl')

@app.post("/predict")
async def predict(data: list[float] = Body(..., embed=True)):
    arr = np.array(data).reshape(1, -1)
    cluster = model.predict(arr)
    return {"cluster": int(cluster[0])}
```

Figure 10.2: *Python App to Host Our Trained Kmeans Model Using FastAPI*

Once you have saved above code in a file called **app_predictkmeans.py**, run this script using the following command at your Anaconda prompt as shown in *Figure* 10.3:

```
uvicorn app_predictkmeans:app --reload
```

```
Anaconda Prompt (Anaconda  X   +  ⌄

(base) C:\Users\Nimrita Koul>conda activate pytorch_cuda

(pytorch_cuda) C:\Users\Nimrita Koul>uvicorn app_predictkmeans:app --reload
INFO:     Will watch for changes in these directories: ['C:\\Users\\Nimrita Koul']
INFO:     Uvicorn running on http://127.0.0.1:8000 (Press CTRL+C to quit)
INFO:     Started reloader process [21060] using WatchFiles
INFO:     Started server process [11160]
INFO:     Waiting for application startup.
INFO:     Application startup complete.
INFO:     127.0.0.1:49915 - "GET /docs HTTP/1.1" 200 OK
INFO:     127.0.0.1:49915 - "GET /openapi.json HTTP/1.1" 200 OK
INFO:     127.0.0.1:49916 - "POST /predict HTTP/1.1" 200 OK
```

Figure 10.3: *Running the FastAPI to Deploy Your K-Means Model Using Uvicorn*

Running this command deploys your model using Swagger UI of FastAPI at the URL: http://127.0.0.1:8000/docs. You can use your model for inference by entering a test data corresponding to the values of features in the iris dataset on which our K-means model was trained as shown in *Figure* 10.1. *Figure* 10.4 shows the hosted model in Swagger UI:

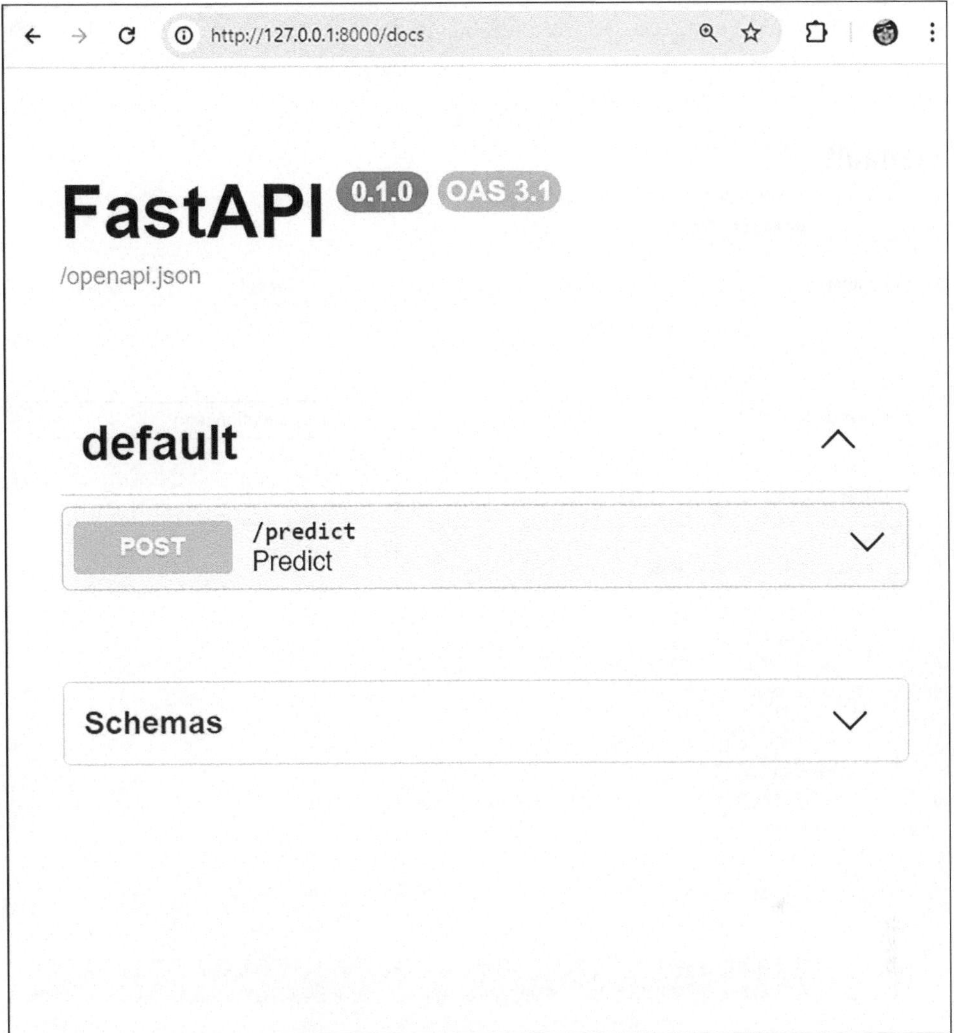

Figure 10.4: *Hosted K-Means Model*

To interact with your model, click the downward arrow next to **`Predict`** in **`POST`** area (shown in Green color), then click Try it out. You will see Request body and an editable JSON file. Enter the values in the form of a list here. Then click on **`Execute`**. The Fast API passes these values as input to your K-means model and returns the cluster number as the result in the browser as shown in *Figure* 10.5.

Figure 10.5: *Enter the Input Values for your K-means Model in the Request Body in the Form of a JSON List*

Figure 10.6 shows the results (the Cluster ID) to which your model assigned the input you gave.

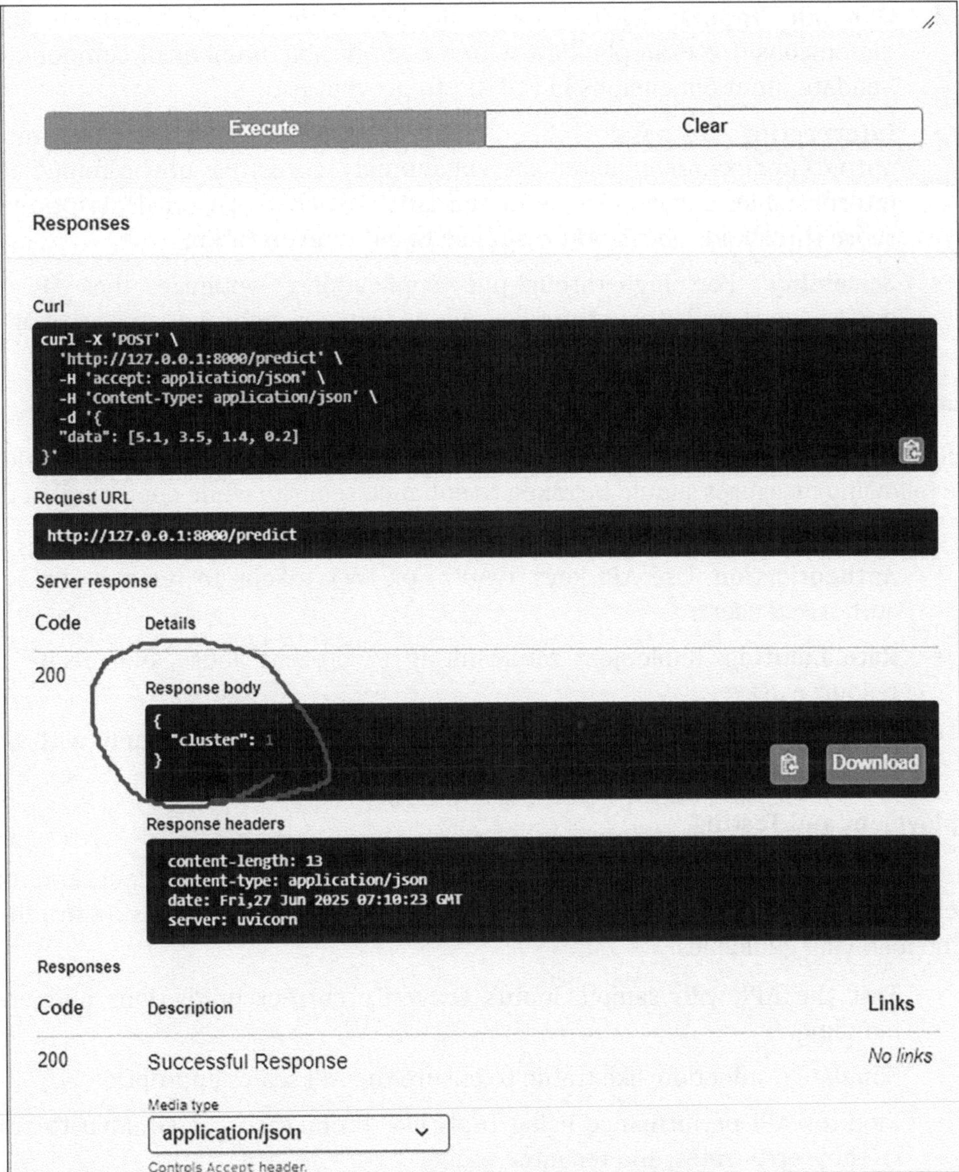

***Figure 10.6:** The Data is Assigned to Cluster 1*

Considerations for Unsupervised Models Deployed via REST APIs:

Unsupervised learning models introduce specific challenges when exposed via REST APIs:

- **Preprocessing Consistency**: Ensure that the same preprocessing steps (for example, scaling, normalization) applied during training are used in the API. Serializing and loading preprocessors, as shown in the example, is critical.

- **Dynamic Inputs**: Unsupervised models often handle variable input dimensions (for example, PCA with a configurable number of components). Validate input dimensions in the API to prevent errors.
- **Interpreting Outputs**: Unlike supervised models, unsupervised model outputs (for example, cluster labels or anomaly scores) may not be immediately interpretable. Consider including metadata, such as cluster descriptions or score thresholds, in the API response to aid interpretation.
- **Scalability**: For high-throughput applications, optimize the API for performance by batching predictions or using asynchronous processing, as supported by FastAPI's async functions.

Securing the API

Security is of utmost importance when exposing models to external applications. The following measures should be taken to enhance security while deploying models via APIs:

- **Authentication**: Use API keys, OAuth, or JWT tokens to restrict access to authorized users.
- **Rate Limiting**: Implement rate limiting to prevent abuse and ensure fair resource usage.
- **Data Privacy**: If handling sensitive data, use HTTPS and comply with data protection regulations (for example, GDPR, CCPA).

Deployment and Testing

You can deploy the API using a platform like AWS Lambda, Google Cloud Run, or a Docker container orchestrated by Kubernetes. Before going live, makes sure to adhere to the following guidelines:

- Test the API with sample inputs to verify correct predictions and error handling.
- Simulate production-like traffic to ensure the API scales appropriately.
- Monitor API performance using tools like Prometheus or Grafana to track latency, error rates, and resource usage.

By exposing unsupervised learning models via REST APIs, you can enable seamless integration with business applications. The next subsection will explore containerization for scalable and portable model deployment.

Deploying Models Using gRPC APIs

gRPC (Google's implementation of Remote Procedure Call) (https://grpc.io/) offers a high-performance alternative to REST API for deploying unsupervised learning models, especially in scenarios that require low latency, high throughput, or complex data interactions. gRPC thus enables efficient communication between services using protocol buffers (protobuf) for defining service contracts.

Advantages of gRPC for Model Deployment

gRPC provides several advantages over REST for deploying machine learning models:

- **Performance**: gRPC uses HTTP/2 and binary serialization (via protocol buffers), resulting in lower latency and smaller message sizes compared to JSON-based REST APIs.
- **Strong Typing**: Protocol buffers enforce strict data schemas, reducing the risk of invalid inputs and simplifying input validation for unsupervised models.
- **Streaming Support**: gRPC supports bidirectional streaming, which is useful for real-time applications like anomaly detection or clustering of streaming data.
- **Cross-Language Support**: gRPC generates client and server code in multiple languages, making it ideal for integrating models into diverse production environments.

However, gRPC has a steeper learning curve than REST and requires client applications to use gRPC-compatible libraries, which sometimes limits its use in a few web-based scenarios.

To expose an unsupervised learning model via gRPC, you first have to define the service and message structures in a `.proto` file.

Securing the gRPC API

To secure the gRPC API, you can use the following measures:

- **TLS/SSL**: Enable TLS to encrypt communication between clients and the server.
- **Authentication**: Implement token-based authentication using gRPC interceptors to restrict access to authorized clients.
- **Monitoring**: Use tools like Prometheus to monitor gRPC server metrics such as request latency and error rates.

Deployment and Testing of gRPC Server

One can deploy the gRPC server using a platform like Kubernetes for scalability, or a serverless platform like Google Cloud Run for simplicity. Before deployment, make sure to:

- Test the service with a variety of inputs to ensure correct predictions and error handling.
- Simulate production traffic to verify performance under load.

- Monitor server logs to detect issues with input data or model predictions.

Through gRPC APIs, you can deploy unsupervised learning models with high performance and reliability, thus making them suitable for latency-sensitive applications like real-time customer segmentation or anomaly detection. The next subsection will discuss strategies for containerizing these deployments to ensure portability and scalability.

By carefully selecting a deployment platform, leveraging containerization with Docker and Kubernetes and developing efficient APIs, you create a robust infrastructure for deploying unsupervised learning models. These components ensure that models are scalable, reliable, and accessible, which sets the stage for integration into production systems, as discussed in the next section.

Integrating Models into Production Systems

Once an unsupervised learning model is deployed, integrating it into production systems is critical to deliver actionable insights to end users or applications. This process involves connecting the model to data pipelines, ensuring scalability and performance, and embedding outputs into business applications. Unsupervised learning models such as those used for clustering, anomaly detection, or dimensionality reduction present unique challenges due to their reliance on evolving data patterns and lack of labeled outputs. We will explore three key aspects of integration: data pipeline integration, scalability and performance, and interfacing with applications.

Data Pipeline Integration

Integrating unsupervised learning models into production requires a robust data pipeline to deliver input data consistently and handle evolving patterns effectively. This involves connecting models to real-time or batch data pipelines, managing data drift and concept drift, and automating preprocessing steps.

Connecting Models to Real-Time or Batch Data Pipelines

Unsupervised learning models can be integrated with either real-time or batch data pipelines, depending on the use case:

- **Real-Time Pipelines**: Real-time pipelines are essential for applications like anomaly detection in IoT sensors or customer segmentation in live e-commerce platforms. Tools like Apache Kafka, AWS Kinesis, or Google Cloud Pub/Sub can stream data to the model's API or edge deployment. For example, a streaming pipeline might send sensor readings to an isolation forest model for immediate anomaly detection.

- **Batch Pipelines**: Batch pipelines suit applications like periodic customer segmentation or market basket analysis, where data is processed in large volumes at scheduled intervals. Tools like Apache Airflow or AWS Glue can orchestrate batch processing, pulling data from databases or data lakes (for example, PostgreSQL, AWS S3) and feeding it to the model.

You must ensure the pipeline matches the model's input requirements (for example, feature format, data types). Real-time pipelines prioritize low latency, while batch pipelines prioritize throughput and reliability.

Handling Data Drift and Concept Drift

Unsupervised learning models are sensitive to data drift (changes in the statistical properties of input data) and concept drift (changes in the underlying patterns the model was trained on). For example, a clustering model trained on historical customer data may produce irrelevant clusters if purchasing behavior shifts.

- **Detection**: Monitor statistical metrics like feature distributions (for example, mean, variance) or model outputs (for example, silhouette score for clustering, anomaly rates for isolation forests). Tools like Evidently AI or custom scripts can track data drift.
- **Mitigation**: Implement retraining triggers based on drift detection (for example, when silhouette score drops below a threshold). Use online learning techniques for models like incremental K-means to adapt to new data without full retraining. Maintain a feedback loop to log model outputs and retrain periodically.

Automating Data Preprocessing

Preprocessing steps like scaling, encoding, or dimensionality reduction must be consistent between training and production. You should automate these steps to ensure reliability:

- **Serialization**: Save preprocessors (for example, StandardScaler, OneHotEncoder) alongside the model using joblib or pickle.
- **Pipeline Integration**: Use libraries like scikit-learn's Pipeline to bundle preprocessing and model inference into a single object, reducing errors.
- **Automation Tools**: Integrate preprocessing into data pipelines using tools like Apache Airflow for batch jobs or Apache Spark for large-scale preprocessing. Ensure versioning of preprocessors to align with model versions.

Scalability and Performance

To ensure unsupervised learning models perform efficiently in production, you must optimize for low latency, high throughput, and scalability, especially for real-time applications.

Optimizing for Low Latency and High Throughput

- **Model Optimization**: Use lightweight models or optimization techniques like quantization (for example, TensorFlow Lite for edge deployment) to reduce inference time. For instance, a K-means model can be optimized by precomputing centroids for faster lookups.
- **Batching**: For batch pipelines, process data in batches to improve throughput. For real-time APIs, batch multiple requests when possible, to reduce overhead.
- **Hardware Acceleration**: Use GPUs or TPUs for computationally intensive models like deep autoencoders, especially in cloud or on-premises deployments.

Load Balancing and Horizontal Scaling

Load balancing and horizontal scaling are important for performance and are explained as follows:

- **Load Balancing**: Distribute inference requests across multiple model instances using load balancers (for example, AWS Elastic Load Balancer, Kubernetes Ingress). This ensures high availability and prevents bottlenecks.
- **Horizontal Scaling**: Deploy multiple containers or serverless functions to handle increased demand. Kubernetes can automatically scale pods based on CPU or request volume, while serverless platforms like AWS Lambda scale natively.

Caching Strategies for Frequent Queries

Caching can reduce latency for frequent or repetitive queries, such as clustering similar customer profiles.

There are several types of caching such as:

- **In-Memory Caching**: Use Redis or Memcached to store recent model outputs. For example, cache cluster assignments for frequently queried customer IDs.
- **Precomputed Results**: For static datasets, precompute outputs (for example, cluster assignments) and store them in a database to avoid redundant inference.

You should balance cache size with memory constraints and invalidate caches when the model is retrained to avoid stale results.

Interfacing with Applications

Embedding model outputs into business applications ensures that insights from unsupervised learning models are actionable. This involves designing interfaces to deliver results to end users or systems such as dashboards, APIs, or embedded analytics.

Embedding Model Outputs into Business Applications

- **APIs**: Expose model outputs via REST or gRPC APIs to integrate with web or mobile applications. For example, a clustering model's API can return customer segments to a CRM system.
- **Dashboards**: Use visualization tools like Tableau, Power BI, or custom web interfaces (for example, built with React) to display model outputs such as cluster visualizations or anomaly alerts.
- **Embedded Analytics**: Integrate outputs directly into application workflows such as displaying recommended products in an e-commerce platform or flagging anomalies in a monitoring system.

For example, an e-commerce platform might use a K-means model to segment customers and recommend products based on their cluster. Or an isolation forest model can flag anomalies in real-time data, such as network traffic and outputs can be visualized in a dashboard using a framework like React.

Considerations while Interfacing Deployed Models with Applications

When interfacing your models with applications, keep following considerations in mind:

- **User Experience**: Ensure outputs are interpretable, such as mapping cluster IDs to meaningful labels (for example, "High-Value Customers") or providing anomaly score thresholds.
- **Latency**: Optimize API or dashboard response times to meet application requirements, using caching or edge deployment for real-time use cases.
- **Feedback Loops**: Allow users to provide feedback on model outputs (for example, incorrect recommendations) to inform retraining or model refinement.

Hence, by integrating unsupervised learning models into production systems through robust data pipelines, scalable infrastructure, and user-friendly interfaces, organizations can unlock their full potential for various applications.

Monitoring and Maintenance of Deployed Models

Once an unsupervised learning model is deployed, ongoing monitoring and maintenance are essential to ensure that it continues to deliver reliable and meaningful results. Unlike supervised models, unsupervised models lack explicit ground truth, which makes it challenging to assess performance in production. We will explore four key aspects of monitoring and maintenance: monitoring model performance, handling data drift, logging and auditing, and model retraining and updates. These aspects help maintain model effectiveness, adapt to changing data patterns, and ensure compliance and traceability.

Monitoring Model Performance

Monitoring the performance of unsupervised learning models in production involves tracking relevant metrics and setting up alerts to detect degradation. Since these models often produce outputs like cluster assignments or anomaly scores without labeled data, monitoring focuses on statistical properties and achieving consistency in results.

Tracking Metrics in Production

It is important to track the metrics to evaluate model performance in production. Key metrics depend on the model type and use case:

- **Clustering Models**: For models like K-means or DBSCAN, track metrics such as:
    - **Silhouette Score**: Measures how well-separated clusters are, with values closer to 1 indicating better clustering. A drop in silhouette score may indicate deteriorating cluster quality.
    - **Within-Cluster Sum of Squares (WCSS)**: Measures compactness of clusters, useful for K-means. Increasing WCSS may suggest clusters are becoming less cohesive.
    - **Cluster Stability**: Tracks consistency of cluster assignments over time for similar inputs, using metrics like the Adjusted Rand Index (if some labeled data is available) or cluster overlap.
- **Anomaly Detection Models**: For models like isolation forests or autoencoders, remember to monitor:
    - **Anomaly Rate**: The proportion of data points flagged as anomalies. A sudden increase or decrease may indicate data drift or model issues.
    - **Score Distribution**: Track the distribution of anomaly scores to detect shifts in data behavior.
    - **False Positive Rate**: If labeled data becomes available (for example, via user feedback), estimate false positives to assess model reliability.
- **Dimensionality Reduction Models**: For PCA or autoencoders, monitor:
    - **Reconstruction Error**: For autoencoders, high reconstruction errors may indicate that the model is failing to capture data patterns.

- **Explained Variance Ratio**: For PCA, ensure that the model retains sufficient variance in production data.

Setting Up Alerts for Performance Degradation

Setting up automated alerts helps in detection of performance issues promptly. Alerts can be set up in several ways such as:

- **Threshold-Based Alerts**: Set thresholds for key metrics (for example, silhouette score < 0.3, anomaly rate > 10%) and trigger alerts via tools like Prometheus with Alertmanager or AWS CloudWatch.
- **Visualization Dashboards**: Use Grafana or Kibana to visualize metrics over time, thereby enabling teams to spot trends or anomalies in model performance.
- **Notification Channels**: Integrate alerts with communication platforms like Slack or email to notify data scientists or engineers of issues.

You should balance alert sensitivity to avoid false positives while timely detecting real issues. Regularly review thresholds based on production data.

Handling Data Drift

Data drift, where the statistical properties of input data change; and concept drift, where the underlying patterns the model was trained on shift, are critical challenges for unsupervised learning models. These shifts can degrade performance, such as producing irrelevant clusters or misidentifying anomalies. Therefore, it is important to detect drifts in data distributions.

Detecting Shifts in Data Distributions

Effective drift detection involves comparing production data to training data:

- **Statistical Tests**: Use tests like the Kolmogorov-Smirnov (KS) test or chi-squared test to compare feature distributions.
- **Model-Based Detection**: Monitor model-specific metrics (for example, silhouette score, anomaly rate) as proxies for drift. A sudden change in these metrics often indicates a shift in data distribution.
- **Tools**: Use libraries like Evidently AI or Alibi Detect to automate drift detection, providing visualizations and statistical reports.
- **Frequency**: Perform drift checks on a schedule (for example, daily for real-time pipelines, weekly for batch pipelines) or after significant events (for example, new product launches affecting customer behavior).

Strategies for Retraining or Updating Models

When drift is detected, retraining or updating the model is necessary. The following are the types of retraining of the model:

- **Full Retraining:** Retrain the model on recent data to capture new patterns. This is suitable for batch pipelines with sufficient computational resources.
- **Incremental Learning:** For dynamic datasets, use models that support incremental updates, such as IncrementalPCA or online clustering algorithms (for example, MiniBatchKMeans).
- **Retraining Triggers:** Automate retraining based on drift metrics (for example, KS test p-value < 0.05) or performance thresholds (for example, silhouette score < 0.3). Use orchestration tools like Apache Airflow to schedule retraining.

Versioning of models, that is, maintaining model versions to enable rollback if a new model underperforms is important. Store models and metadata (for example, training data stats) in a model registry like MLflow.

Model Retraining and Updates

Regular retraining and updates ensure that unsupervised learning models remain relevant as data evolves. This involves scheduling periodic retraining and leveraging incremental learning for dynamic datasets.

Scheduling Periodic Retraining

- **Frequency**: Schedule retraining based on data volatility and application needs (for example, weekly for customer segmentation, monthly for market basket analysis). You can use orchestration tools like Apache Airflow.
- **Validation**: Before deploying a retrained model, validate its performance using metrics like silhouette score or reconstruction error. Use A/B testing to compare the new model against the current one.
- **Deployment**: Automate model deployment using CI/CD pipelines or tools like Kubernetes to minimize downtime.

Incremental Learning for Dynamic Datasets

For datasets that evolve rapidly, incremental learning allows models to adapt without full retraining, saving computational resources. Use models like MiniBatchKMeans, IncrementalPCA, or online variants of isolation forests for incremental learning. Incremental learning reduces retraining time and supports real-time applications like streaming anomaly detection. However, incremental updates may accumulate errors or drift, if not carefully monitored. Regularly validate model performance against a baseline. This hybrid approach combines periodic full retraining with incremental updates to balance adaptability and stability of your deployed models.

Logging and Auditing

Logging predictions and model decisions is crucial for debugging, compliance, and improving model performance. Auditing ensures traceability, especially in regulated industries like finance or healthcare.

You should log input data, model outputs (for example, cluster labels, anomaly scores), inference timestamps, and system metrics (for example, latency, CPU usage). Store the logs in a centralized system such as Elasticsearch, AWS CloudWatch Logs or a database for easy querying and analysis. Use appropriate log levels such as INFO for predictions, ERROR for failures to prioritize critical events. While maintaining logs it is important to balance log verbosity with storage costs and performance impact. Anonymize sensitive data to comply with privacy regulations.

Ensuring Traceability for Compliance and Debugging

- **Traceability**: Assign unique identifiers to each prediction to trace inputs to outputs. This is critical for auditing in regulated environments.
- **Audit Trails**: Maintain audit trails linking predictions to model versions, preprocessing steps, and training data. Use tools like MLflow to track model metadata.
- **Compliance**: Ensure that logs comply with regulations (for example, GDPR, HIPAA) by encrypting sensitive data and implementing retention policies.
- **Debugging**: Use logs to diagnose issues, such as unexpected cluster assignments or high anomaly rates, by correlating inputs with outputs and system metrics.

Considerations in Monitoring Model Performance

When monitoring the performance of your deployed model, keep following considerations in mind:

- **Resource Management**: Balance retraining frequency with computational costs, especially for resource-intensive models because retraining a model is often computationally expensive.
- **Model Registry**: Use tools like MLflow or AWS SageMaker Model Registry to manage model versions and metadata.
- **Rollback Plans**: Maintain previous model versions to revert if a new model underperforms or introduces errors.

By implementing robust monitoring, drift detection, logging, and retraining strategies, unsupervised learning models can maintain high performance and reliability in production.

Tools and Frameworks for Deployment

Deploying unsupervised learning models requires robust tools and frameworks to streamline the process, ensure scalability, and support monitoring and maintenance. These tools help automate tasks like model serialization, pipeline orchestration, and performance tracking, which are critical for unsupervised models due to their sensitivity to data drift and lack of explicit ground truth. In this section, we will cover an overview of popular tools (MLflow, Kubeflow, and Seldon), and compare the frameworks for deploying unsupervised learning models. We will also evaluate open source versus commercial solutions for various deployment scenarios.

Several tools and frameworks are widely used for deploying machine learning models, including unsupervised ones. We will explore three popular options–MLflow, Kubeflow, and Seldon–with their features, use cases, and relevance to unsupervised learning.

MLflow

MLflow (https://mlflow.org/) is an open-source platform for managing the machine learning lifecycle, including experimentation, reproducibility, and deployment. It is particularly well-suited to manage unsupervised learning models due to its flexibility and integration capabilities.

Features

- **Model Registry**: Stores and versions models, which makes it easy to track and deploy different versions of unsupervised models like K-means or autoencoders
- **Model Serving**: Supports deployment to REST APIs, Docker containers, or cloud platforms like AWS SageMaker and Azure ML
- **Tracking**: Logs metrics (for example, silhouette score, anomaly rate), parameters, and artifacts, enabling performance monitoring
- **Projects**: Ensures reproducible environments by packaging code and dependencies

MLflow is ideal for teams needing a lightweight, flexible tool for model management and deployment, especially for batch or near-real-time applications like customer segmentation. MLflow's logging capabilities support tracking metrics like silhouette score or reconstruction error, which are crucial for monitoring unsupervised models. Its model registry simplifies versioning for retraining scenarios.

Kubeflow

Kubeflow (https://www.kubeflow.org/) is an open-source platform designed for deploying, scaling, and managing machine learning workflows on Kubernetes. It is well-suited for complex, scalable deployments of unsupervised models.

Features:

- **Pipeline Orchestration**: Automates data preprocessing, model training, and deployment; ideal for managing end-to-end workflows for unsupervised models
- **Scalability**: Leverages Kubernetes for horizontal scaling, load balancing, and fault tolerance, thereby supporting high-throughput applications
- **Model Serving**: Integrates with tools such as Seldon Core or KFServing for deploying models as APIs or gRPC services
- **Monitoring**: Supports integration with Prometheus and Grafana for tracking performance metrics

Kubeflow is best for organizations with Kubernetes expertise, deploying complex workflows, or requiring high scalability for real-time applications like anomaly detection in IoT. Kubeflow's pipeline automation is ideal for handling data drift through scheduled retraining, and its scalability supports high-volume inference for clustering or dimensionality reduction.

Seldon

Seldon (https://www.seldon.io/) is an open-source framework focused on model serving and offers flexible deployment options for machine learning models, including unsupervised ones.

Features

- **Model Serving**: Deploys models as REST or gRPC APIs, supporting frameworks like scikit-learn, TensorFlow, and PyTorch
- **Advanced Inference**: Supports complex inference graphs, such as combining a PCA model for dimensionality reduction with a clustering model
- **Monitoring and Logging**: Integrates with Prometheus and Grafana for real-time monitoring and logging of predictions
- **Scalability**: Runs on Kubernetes, enabling auto-scaling and load balancing

Seldon is suitable for teams needing flexible model serving with advanced inference capabilities, such as combining unsupervised models for real-time applications like fraud detection. Seldon's support for custom inference graphs is valuable for chaining unsupervised tasks (for example, dimensionality reduction followed by clustering), and its monitoring tools help track metrics like anomaly rates.

Comparison of Frameworks for Unsupervised Model Deployment

Table 10.1 shows the comparison of popular frameworks for deployment of unsupervised models. We cover the frameworks – Mlflow, Kubeflow, Seldon, TensorFlow Serving and BentoML:

Criteria	MLflow	Kubeflow	Seldon	TensorFlow Serving	BentoML
Ease of Use	High: Simple API, minimal setup	Moderate: Requires Kubernetes expertise	Moderate: Kubernetes-based, but simpler than Kubeflow	Moderate: TensorFlow-focused, steep learning curve	High: User-friendly, supports multiple frameworks
Scalability	Moderate: Relies on external platforms (for example, cloud)	High: Native Kubernetes scaling	High: Kubernetes-based scaling	High: Optimized for TensorFlow models	Moderate: Supports containerization, cloud
Unsupervised Model Support	Strong: Flexible for scikit-learn, custom models	Strong: Supports any model via pipelines	Strong: Custom inference graphs for unsupervised tasks	Moderate: Best for TensorFlow-based models (for example, autoencoders)	Strong: Supports scikit-learn, PyTorch, and so on.
Monitoring	Good: Logs metrics, integrates with external tools	Excellent: Prometheus/ Grafana integration	Excellent: Built-in monitoring with Prometheus	Good: Requires custom monitoring setup	Good: Built-in logging, external integrations
Pipeline Automation	Limited: Manual pipeline setup	Excellent: Kubeflow Pipelines for end-to-end automation	Moderate: Focus on serving, not pipelines	Limited: Focus on serving, not pipelines	Good: Supports batch and real-time pipelines
Real-Time Inference	Good: REST API support	Excellent: Kubernetes-based low-latency serving	Excellent: REST/gRPC, low-latency support	Excellent: Optimized for high-throughput	Good: REST/gRPC APIs, batch support

Cost	Low: Open-source, cloud costs apply	Moderate: Kubernetes infrastructure costs	Moderate: Kubernetes infrastructure costs	Low: Open-source, infrastructure costs	Low: Open-source, cloud costs apply
Community and Support	Strong: Large community, active development	Strong: Active community, enterprise adoption	Strong: Growing community, enterprise focus	Strong: Backed by Google, TensorFlow ecosystem	Moderate: Growing community, newer framework

Table 10.1: *Comparison of Popular Open-Source Frameworks for Model Deployment*

MLflow is best for teams seeking simplicity and flexibility, especially for batch or near-real-time deployments of unsupervised models like clustering or anomaly detection. It excels in model management but requires external tools for advanced scalability. Kubeflow is best for complex, scalable deployments with end-to-end automation, suitable for real-time applications like streaming anomaly detection. Its Kubernetes dependency makes it complex for smaller teams. Seldon is best for advanced inference scenarios, such as combining multiple unsupervised models (for example, PCA and clustering), and offers robust monitoring for production environments. TensorFlow Serving is best for TensorFlow-based models like autoencoders, but less flexible for scikit-learn or other frameworks common in unsupervised learning. BentoML is a versatile option for teams needing easy-to-use serving with support for multiple frameworks, suitable for both batch and real-time unsupervised model deployments.

Open-Source vs. Commercial Solutions

The choice between open-source and commercial solutions depends on budget, customization needs, and team expertise. Both have trade-offs for deploying unsupervised learning models.

Open-Source Solutions

Open-source solutions such as MLflow, Kubeflow, Seldon, TensorFlow Serving, BentoML, Apache Airflow (for pipelines), Prometheus/Grafana (for monitoring) has the following benefits and challenges:

- **Benefits**
    - **Cost**: Free to use, with costs limited to infrastructure (for example, cloud or on-premises servers)
    - **Customization**: Full access to source code allows tailoring to specific needs, such as custom drift detection for unsupervised models.
    - **Community Support**: Large communities provide updates, plugins, and forums for troubleshooting.

  - **Flexibility**: Supports a wide range of models and frameworks, ideal for diverse unsupervised learning tasks (for example, scikit-learn for K-means, PyTorch for autoencoders)
- **Challenges**
  - **Expertise**: Requires in-house expertise for setup, maintenance, and integration, especially for complex tools like Kubeflow
  - **Maintenance**: Teams are responsible for updates, security patches, and infrastructure management
  - **Integration Effort**: May require custom integrations for monitoring, logging, or pipeline automation

Open-source solutions are best for organizations with strong technical teams, custom requirements, or budget constraints. For example, a startup deploying a clustering model for customer segmentation might use MLflow for its simplicity and low cost.

Commercial Solutions

Commercial solutions such as AWS SageMaker, Google Cloud AI Platform, Microsoft Azure Machine Learning, Databricks have the following benefits and challenges:

- **Benefits**
  - **Managed Services**: Fully managed infrastructure reduces setup and maintenance effort, including auto-scaling, monitoring, and security.
  - **Integrated Tools**: Built-in features for drift detection, retraining pipelines, and monitoring simplify deployment of unsupervised models.
  - **Support**: Enterprise-grade support and SLAs ensure reliability for critical applications like real-time anomaly detection.
  - **Ease of Use**: User-friendly interfaces and prebuilt integrations lower the barrier for teams with limited DevOps expertise.
- **Challenges**
  - **Cost**: Usage-based pricing can be expensive for high-throughput or GPU-based models.
  - **Vendor Lock-in**: Proprietary tools may limit portability to other platforms.
  - **Limited Customization**: It has less flexibility for highly specialized unsupervised learning workflows, compared to open-source tools.

Commercial solutions are best for the organizations with budget flexibility, limited in-house expertise, or need for rapid deployment. For example, a financial institution deploying an anomaly detection model might use AWS SageMaker for its managed monitoring and compliance features. *Table* 10.2 shows a tabular comparison of open-source and commercial solutions:

Aspect	**Open-Source**	**Commercial**
Cost	Low (infrastructure costs only)	High (usage-based pricing)
Customization	High: Full control over code	Moderate: Limited by platform
Ease of Use	Moderate: Requires expertise	High: Managed services, user-friendly
Scalability	High: Depends on infrastructure	High: Built-in auto-scaling
Support	Community-driven, variable	Enterprise-grade, reliable
Unsupervised Learning Fit	Flexible for custom metrics, workflows	Strong for managed monitoring, drift detection

Table 10.2: *Comparison of Open-Source and Commercial Solutions for Model Deployment*

Recommendations about Frameworks for Unsupervised Learning

Based on several factors such as team size, complexity of your workflows and so on, we have listed the following recommendations for tools and frameworks you may use to deploy your unsupervised models:

- **Small Teams or Startups**: Use MLflow or BentoML for simplicity and low cost and to deploy on cloud platforms like AWS or Google Cloud for scalability.
- **Complex Workflows**: Choose Kubeflow for end-to-end automation, especially for real-time applications with frequent retraining due to data drift.
- **Advanced Inference Needs**: Use Seldon for custom inference graphs, such as combining PCA and clustering for customer analytics.
- **Regulated Industries**: Opt for commercial solutions like AWS SageMaker or Azure ML for managed compliance and monitoring, supplemented with open-source tools like Evidently AI for drift detection.
- **Edge Deployments**: Pair lightweight frameworks like BentoML with TensorFlow Lite for deploying unsupervised models on resource-constrained devices.

Through appropriate tools and frameworks, teams can streamline the deployment of unsupervised learning models and ensure scalability, reliability, and adaptability to evolving data patterns.

Ethical and Practical Considerations in Model Deployment

Deploying unsupervised learning models in production involves not only technical challenges but also ethical and practical considerations. These models, used for tasks like clustering or anomaly detection, can impact stakeholders and require careful handling to ensure fairness, compliance, and trust. In this section, we explore ethical implications, regulatory compliance, and effective communication with stakeholders to address these concerns.

Ethical Implications

Unsupervised learning models can inadvertently perpetuate biases or lack transparency, affecting their reliability and trustworthiness.

- **Bias in Unsupervised Learning Outputs**: Since unsupervised models rely on patterns in data without labeled ground truth, they may amplify biases present in the input data. For example, a clustering model for customer segmentation might group individuals based on biased features (for example, purchase history skewed by socioeconomic factors), leading to unfair treatment. To mitigate this, audit input data for biases using statistical tests (for example, checking feature distributions across demographic groups) and apply fairness-aware techniques such as reweighting or feature selection before training.
- **Transparency and Explainability**: Unsupervised model outputs, like cluster assignments or anomaly scores, can be difficult to interpret. Use explainability tools like SHAP (SHapley Additive exPlanations) for feature importance, or visualization techniques (for example, t-SNE for cluster visualization) to make results understandable to stakeholders. For instance, a t-SNE plot can illustrate customer clusters to business teams, enhancing trust and usability.

Regulatory Compliance

Deployed models must adhere to legal and ethical standards, particularly in regulated industries like finance or healthcare.

- **Adhering to Data Privacy Regulations**: Compliance with regulations like GDPR (General Data Protection Regulation) or CCPA (California Consumer Privacy Act) is critical when handling personal data. Implement data anonymization, encryption, and access controls in data pipelines and logging systems. For example, pseudonymize customer IDs in logs used for clustering to protect privacy.
- **Ensuring Model Fairness**: Regularly audit model outputs for fairness, especially in applications like anomaly detection for fraud, where false positives could disproportionately affect certain groups. Use fairness metrics (for example, demographic parity) and retrain models if unfair patterns are detected. Tools like Fairlearn can help assess and mitigate bias in production.

Stakeholder Communication

Effectively communicating model results to non-technical stakeholders is essential for adoption and trust. This effective communication involves:

- **Presenting Model Results**: Translate technical outputs into business-relevant insights. For example, instead of presenting raw cluster labels, describe clusters as "`High-Value Customers`" or "`At-Risk Accounts`" in dashboards or reports. Use visualizations like bar charts or heatmaps to make results accessible.
- **Managing Expectations**: Unsupervised learning outcomes are inherently exploratory and may not provide definitive answers. Educate stakeholders about limitations, such as the potential for clusters to shift with new data and set realistic expectations for accuracy and interpretability. For instance, explain that anomaly detection models may require manual validation to refine thresholds.

By addressing ethical implications, ensuring regulatory compliance, and communicating effectively, teams can deploy unsupervised learning models responsibly, foster trust and maximize impact.

Conclusion

In this chapter, we learned how deploying unsupervised learning models into production is a multifaceted process that transforms theoretical algorithms into practical solutions driving real-world impact. By carefully addressing model serialization, deployment platforms, data pipeline integration, scalability, monitoring, and ethical considerations, organizations can ensure that these models deliver reliable and actionable insights. Tools like MLflow, Kubeflow, and Seldon streamline deployment, while robust monitoring and maintenance strategies mitigate challenges like data drift and bias. Ethical practices and clear stakeholder communication further enhance trust and compliance.

In the next chapter, we will cover several case studies that implement unsupervised learning in various scenarios, and we will learn about the best practices in unsupervised learning.

Key Terms

- **Model Deployment**: The process of integrating a trained unsupervised learning model into a production environment to make predictions or process data in real-time or batch settings

- **Model Serialization**: The technique of converting a trained model into a format that can be saved, stored, and loaded across different platforms or environments for inference
- **REST API**: A web-based interface that allows client applications to communicate with a deployed unsupervised learning model using standard HTTP methods, enabling easy integration
- **gRPC**: A high-performance, open-source framework for remote procedure calls that supports low-latency communication, often used for deploying models requiring fast inference
- **Containerization**: The practice of packaging a model and its dependencies into a portable container (for example, Docker) to ensure consistent execution across development and production environments
- **Scalability**: The ability of a deployed unsupervised learning model to handle increasing workloads or data volumes efficiently without compromising performance
- **Prediction Drift**: A phenomenon where the statistical properties of incoming data change over time, potentially degrading the performance of an unsupervised learning model in production
- **Latency**: The time taken for a deployed model to process an input and return a prediction, a critical metric for real-time applications
- **Preprocessing Pipeline**: A series of data transformation steps, such as normalization or feature extraction, applied to input data before feeding it into a deployed model
- **Monitoring**: The ongoing process of tracking a deployed model's performance metrics, such as accuracy, latency, and drift, to ensure reliability and detect issues in production

Questions

1. Explain the key steps involved in preparing an unsupervised learning model for deployment to ensure scalability and performance in a production environment.
2. Describe the role of model serialization in deploying unsupervised learning models and why it is critical for cross-platform compatibility.
3. Discuss the advantages and disadvantages of using REST APIs versus gRPC for deploying unsupervised learning models in real-time applications.
4. How does containerization, such as using Docker, facilitate the deployment of unsupervised learning models, and what specific benefits does it provide?

5. What factors should be considered when selecting a deployment platform for an unsupervised learning model, and how do they impact the deployment process?
6. Explain the importance of monitoring prediction drift and latency after deploying an unsupervised learning model. Describe how these metrics can be tracked.
7. Describe the process of validating an unsupervised learning model before deployment, including the role of test datasets and evaluation metrics.
8. Discuss the benefits of deploying unsupervised learning models on cloud-based platforms compared to on-premises solutions, focusing on scalability and maintenance.
9. How can preprocessing steps, such as data normalization or feature engineering, be effectively integrated into the deployment pipeline of an unsupervised learning model?
10. Explain the role of logging and error handling in maintaining the reliability of an unsupervised learning model in a production environment.

Multiple Choice Questions

1. What is a primary consideration when preparing an unsupervised learning model for deployment?
   a. Ensuring model scalability and performance
   b. Increasing model complexity
   c. Reducing the dataset size
   d. Ignoring monitoring mechanisms
2. Which deployment platform is best suited for real-time inference with low latency?
   a. Batch processing systems
   b. Local desktop applications
   c. Cloud-based API services
   d. Manual script execution

3. What is a key benefit of using REST APIs for deploying unsupervised learning models?
    a. High computational overhead
    b. Complex authentication protocols
    c. Limited scalability
    d. Simplified integration with web applications
4. Why is model serialization important in the deployment process?
    a. It reduces model accuracy.
    b. It enables model storage and loading across platforms.
    c. It increases inference time.
    d. It eliminates the need for monitoring.
5. Which factor is critical when choosing a deployment platform for unsupervised models?
    a. Compatibility with the model's framework
    b. Number of features in the dataset
    c. Color scheme of the platform's interface
    d. Size of the training dataset
6. What does containerization (for example, using Docker) provide in model deployment?
    a. Increased dependency conflicts
    b. Consistent environments across development and production
    c. Slower deployment processes
    d. Reduced model accuracy
7. What is a key advantage of using gRPC over REST for model deployment?
    a. Simpler implementation
    b. Reduced security features
    c. Better support for streaming and low-latency communication
    d. Limited compatibility with cloud platforms

8. What should be monitored post-deployment to ensure model performance?
    a. Model's training dataset size
    b. Prediction drift and latency
    c. Number of model parameters
    d. Development environment settings
9. Which step is essential before deploying an unsupervised learning model to production?
    a. Retraining the model daily
    b. Disabling logging mechanisms
    c. Removing all preprocessing steps
    d. Validating the model on a test dataset
10. Why might a cloud-based deployment be preferred for unsupervised learning models?
    a. It eliminates the need for model updates.
    b. It offers scalability and managed infrastructure.
    c. It restricts access to APIs.
    d. It requires manual server maintenance.

Answers

1. a
2. c
3. d
4. b
5. a
6. b
7. c
8. b
9. d
10. b

CHAPTER 11
Case Studies and Best Practices in Unsupervised Learning

Introduction

In this final chapter, we will discuss real-world case studies showcasing how data scientists and industry practitioners apply unsupervised learning to solve real-world challenges across diverse domains. These case studies highlight common themes, such as aligning models with business goals, overcoming deployment challenges, and addressing ethical considerations, while building on concepts like preprocessing and deployment. By illustrating how data scientists and ML engineers tackle real-world problems, these examples provide practical insights you can adapt to your own projects. We will also explore ethical considerations and emerging trends, equipping you to apply unsupervised learning effectively in your own projects.

Structure

In this chapter, we will discuss the following topics:

- Case Study 1: Customer Segmentation in Retail for Strategic Marketing
- Case Study 2: Anomaly Detection in Cybersecurity for Threat Detection
- Case Study 3: Market Basket Analysis in E-commerce for Recommendations
- Case Study 4: Supply Chain Optimization in Manufacturing
- Case Study 5: Patient Clustering for Personalized Treatment Plans in Healthcare
- Best Practices for Unsupervised Learning Projects

- Common Pitfalls in Real-World Applications and Mitigation Strategies
- Ethical Considerations in Unsupervised Learning
- Integrating Unsupervised Learning with Broader AI Systems
- Future Trends and Emerging Applications

Case Study 1: Customer Segmentation in Retail for Strategic Marketing

A global retailer, Earthmart Ltd., aimed to boost sales by delivering personalized marketing campaigns to a diverse customer base of millions. With vast transaction data but no predefined customer categories, the retailer leveraged unsupervised learning to uncover hidden patterns in purchasing behavior. The objective was to segment customers into meaningful groups to tailor promotions, optimize inventory, and enhance loyalty. *Figure 11.1* shows a possible customer categorization for Earthmart Ltd.

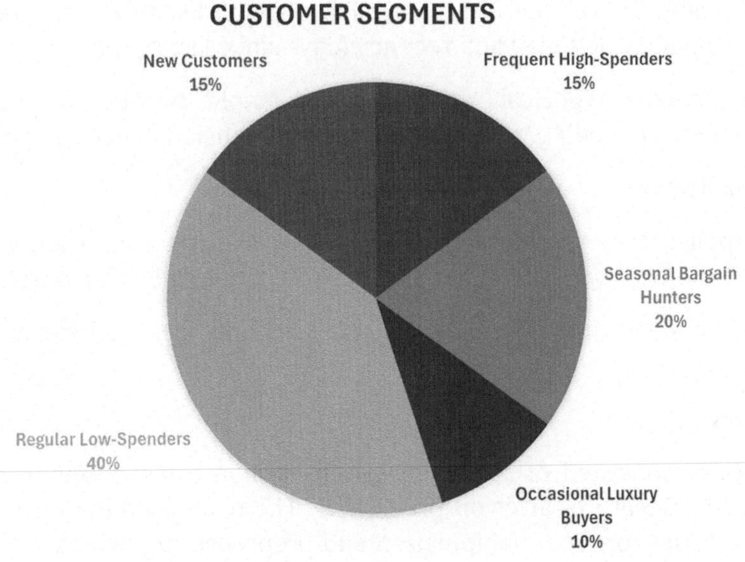

Figure 11.1: *Customer Segmentation Based on Spending Habits*

Data Collection and Preprocessing

The data science team aggregated customer transaction data from multiple sources, including point-of-sale systems and online purchases, spanning two years. The dataset included features such as:

- **Purchase Frequency**: Number of transactions per customer over time

- **Product Categories**: Types of products purchased (for example, electronics, apparel, groceries)
- **Spending Amounts**: Total and average spend per transaction
- **Transaction Timestamps**: Dates and times to capture temporal patterns
- **Customer Demographics**: Limited to anonymized features such as region and age group, where available

Preprocessing Steps:

1. Data Cleaning:
   a. Handled missing values by imputing median spend for numerical features and mode for categorical features (for example, product category)
   b. Removed outliers using the Inter-Quartile Range (IQR) method and filtered transactions with spending amounts beyond 1.5 * IQR to reduce noise from erroneous entries
2. Feature Engineering:
   a. Created derived features such as average basket size (total spend divided by number of items) and recency (days since last purchase)
   b. Encoded categorical variables (for example, product categories) using one-hot encoding, resulting in a high-dimensional feature space
3. Normalization:
   a. Applied Min-Max scaling to numerical features (for example, spending amounts, purchase frequency) to ensure equal weighting during clustering
   b. Used log-transformation for skewed features like total spend to stabilize variance

Data Summary

The final dataset consisted of approximately 10 million transactions from 2 million customers, with 25 features after preprocessing. The team used Python's pandas and scikit-learn libraries for data manipulation and preprocessing, which were executed on a distributed Spark cluster for scalability.

Model Selection and Training

The team selected k-means clustering for its simplicity, scalability, and interpretability, suitable for the large dataset. Alternative algorithms like DBSCAN were considered, but discarded due to computational complexity and sensitivity to parameter tuning on noisy retail data.

Clustering Process

1. Feature Selection:
    a. Applied Principal Component Analysis (PCA) to reduce dimensionality from 25 features to 10 principal components and retained 85% of the variance to balance interpretability and information loss
    b. Visualized feature correlations using a heatmap to ensure selected features were not redundant
2. Choosing the Number of Clusters:
    a. Used the elbow method by plotting the Within-Cluster Sum of Squares (WCSS) against the number of clusters (k from 2 to 10)
    b. Computed silhouette scores to assess cluster cohesion and separation, while identifying k=5 as optimal, balancing granularity and interpretability
3. Model Training:
    a. Implemented k-means using scikit-learn with k=5, initialized with the k-means++ algorithm for better centroid placement
    b. Ran 10 iterations with different random seeds to ensure stability and selected the model with the lowest WCSS

Segment Interpretation

The k-means model identified five distinct customer segments as shown in *Table 11.1*:

Segment	Characteristics	Business Strategy
Frequent High-Spenders	High purchase frequency, large basket sizes, prefer electronics and premium goods	Exclusive loyalty discounts, premium product offers
Seasonal Bargain Hunters	Shop during sales events, focus on discounted items	Targeted promotions during sales seasons
Occasional Luxury Buyers	Infrequent purchases, high spend on luxury apparel and accessories	Personalized luxury product recommendations
Regular Low-Spenders	Consistent but low-value purchases, mainly groceries	Bundle offers to increase the basket size
New Customers	Recent sign-ups, low transaction history	Welcome discounts, onboarding campaigns

Table 11.1: *Identified Retail Customer Segments*

The team visualized segments using t-SNE for 2D projections, highlighting cluster separation, and created bar charts to compare average spend and frequency across segments. These visualizations were shared with the marketing team to align clusters with business strategies.

Model Deployment

The clustering model was integrated into the retailer's Customer Relationship Management (CRM) system for real-time segment assignment:

- Pipeline Design
  - Built a REST API using Flask to serve the k-means model, which was hosted on a Kubernetes cluster for scalability
  - Used Docker containers to ensure consistent environments across development and production
- Real-Time Processing
  - New customer transactions were preprocessed (normalized, PCA-transformed) and assigned to clusters using the trained model
  - Processed up to 1 million transactions daily with sub-second latency
- Handling Data Drift
  - Monitored cluster stability using silhouette scores on new data monthly
  - Retrained the model quarterly to account for shifts in customer behavior (for example, holiday seasons), using an automated pipeline with Airflow

Challenges and Solutions

The team faced the following challenges during and after the deployment of the model. They addressed the challenges effectively:

- **Stakeholder Skepticism**: Marketing teams were initially wary of unsupervised methods due to the lack of labeled data. The team addressed this by presenting t-SNE visualizations and conducting A/B tests, showing a 12% higher click-through rate for segment-targeted campaigns.
- **Scalability**: High transaction volumes require distributed computing. The team used Spark for preprocessing and Kubernetes for deployment to handle scale.
- **Data Drift**: Seasonal shifts caused cluster misalignment. The team implemented a monitoring dashboard to track feature distributions and retrained the model as needed.

Business Impact

The primary business impact of the use of the customer segmentation model included the following factors:

- **Sales Uplift**: Personalized campaigns based on segments increased sales by 10% within six months

- **Customer Retention**: High-spender retention improved by 15% due to targeted loyalty programs
- **Operational Efficiency**: Optimized inventory allocation for seasonal bargain hunters, reducing stockouts by 8%

Key Lessons

The key lessons learned during the model training and deployment included:

- **Cross-Functional Collaboration**: It is important to ensure cross-functional collaboration. It can be done through regular workshops with marketing to ensure segment interpretability and alignment with business goals.
- **Robust Deployment**: Containerization and automated retraining pipelines are critical for scalability and adaptability of the deployed solutions.
- **Iterative Validation**: Continuous monitoring and A/B testing are important to build trust in unsupervised methods and ensure sustained performance.

This case study demonstrates how k-means clustering transformed raw transaction data into actionable insights, highlighting the importance of preprocessing, visualization, and deployment strategies in real-world unsupervised learning applications.

Case Study 2: Anomaly Detection in Cybersecurity for Threat Detection

A major financial institution, ABC Ltd., aimed to safeguard its extensive network of transactions and customer data from sophisticated cyber threats. As it processed millions of daily network events, such as login attempts, financial transfers, and API calls, the institution needed to detect potential intrusions in real-time without relying on predefined attack signatures. Unsupervised learning, specifically anomaly detection, was employed to identify unusual patterns in network traffic that could indicate threats, addressing the challenge of scarce or outdated labeled attack data in a dynamic threat landscape. *Figure* 11.2 shows anomalies in red color and the normal data in blue:

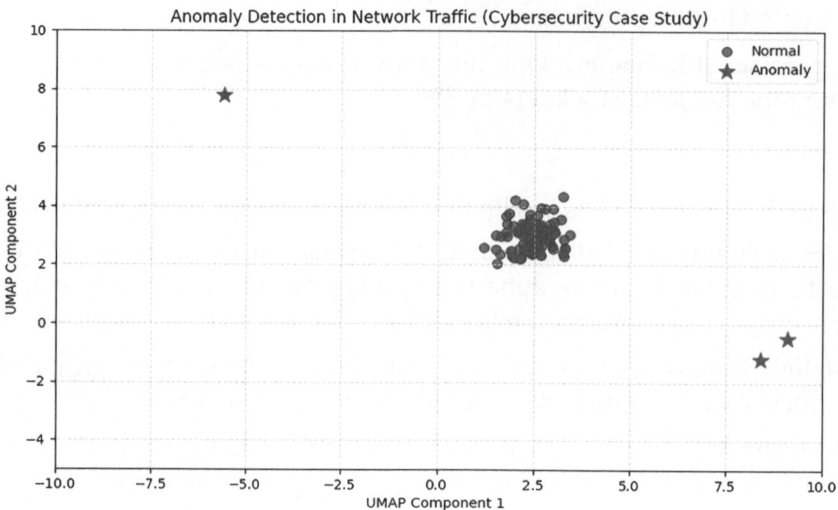

Figure 11.2: *Anomaly Detection in Cybersecurity for Threat Detection*

Data Collection and Preprocessing

The data science team aggregated network logs from multiple sources, including firewalls, intrusion detection systems, and application servers, covering a six-month period. The dataset included features such as:

- **Timestamps**: Date and time of each event to capture temporal patterns
- **IP Addresses**: Source and destination IPs for tracking communication origins
- **Packet Sizes**: Byte counts for data transfers to detect unusual payloads
- **User Activity Metrics**: Login frequency, session duration, and transaction volume
- **Protocol Types**: HTTP, HTTPS, or FTP to identify protocol-specific anomalies

Preprocessing Steps

1. Data Cleaning:
    a. Filtered out irrelevant events (for example, routine system logs) using rule-based exclusions to reduce noise
    b. Handled missing values by imputing median packet sizes for numerical features and dropping events with incomplete IP data (less than 2% of the dataset)
    c. Removed duplicate logs caused by redundant logging systems, ensuring unique event records

2. Feature Engineering:

    a. Created derived features like average packets per session, time between login attempts, and entropy of IP address distributions to capture behavioral patterns

    b. Encoded categorical features (for example, protocol types) using target encoding to reduce dimensionality compared to one-hot encoding

3. Normalization and Scaling:

    a. Applied StandardScaler to numerical features (for example, packet sizes, session durations) to standardize distributions, since isolation forests are sensitive to scale

    b. Log-transformed highly skewed features (for example, transaction volumes) to mitigate the impact of extreme values

4. Dimensionality Reduction:

    a. Used Uniform Manifold Approximation and Projection (UMAP) to reduce the feature space from 30 to 12 dimensions, thereby preserving non-linear relationships and retaining 90% of the variance for efficient processing

Data Summary

The final dataset comprised approximately 50 million network events from 1 million unique users, with 12 features after preprocessing. The team utilized Python's pandas, scikit-learn, and UMAP libraries on a distributed Databricks cluster to handle large-scale data efficiently.

Model Selection and Training

The team selected **Isolation Forests** for anomaly detection due to their efficiency in high-dimensional datasets, ability to scale for real-time processing, and robustness to noise in network logs. Alternatives like One-Class SVM were considered but rejected due to computational overhead on large datasets and sensitivity to parameter tuning.

Model Training Process:

1. Feature Selection:

    a. Evaluated feature importance using tree-based feature scores from a preliminary isolation forest model and prioritized features such as IP entropy and packet size variance

    b. Visualized feature correlations using a covariance matrix heatmap to identify redundant features, thereby ensuring model efficiency

2. Hyperparameter Tuning:
    a. Tuned the contamination parameter (fraction of anomalies) between 0.01 and 0.1, settling on 0.05 after evaluating false positive rates on a validation set of known benign and simulated attack data
    b. Set the number of trees to 100 and max samples to 256 per tree to balance speed and accuracy, hence optimizing for real-time performance
3. Model Validation:
    a. Used silhouette scores adapted for anomaly detection to assess the separation between normal and anomalous events
    b. Conducted stress tests with synthetic anomalies (for example, simulated DDoS attacks) to ensure the model detected rare events without excessive false positives

Anomaly Interpretation

The isolation forest model flagged anomalies as shown in *Table 11.2*:

Anomaly Type	Characteristics	Action Taken
Unusual Login Patterns	Multiple login attempts from new IPs in short timeframes	Triggered multi-factor authentication (MFA)
Unexpected Data Transfers	Large packet sizes from unknown destinations at odd hours	Flagged for SOC investigation
Traffic Spikes	Sudden increases in request volume from a single IP	Blocked IP and initiated DDoS mitigation
Protocol Anomalies	Rare use of FTP in a predominantly HTTPS environment	Isolated for forensic analysis

Table 11.2: *Anomalies Identified in Network Traffic*

The team visualized anomalies using a 2D UMAP projection, highlighting outliers in a scatter plot, and created time-series plots of traffic volume to contextualize spikes. These visualizations were integrated into a dashboard for SOC analysts, providing real-time insights alongside anomaly scores.

Model Deployment

The anomaly detection model was integrated into the institution's Security Operations Center (SOC) for real-time threat monitoring through the following steps:

1. Pipeline Design:
    a. Deployed the model using a gRPC API for low-latency communication, which was hosted on a Kubernetes cluster with auto-scaling to handle peak traffic

   b. Used Docker containers to ensure consistency across development, testing, and production environments

2. Real-Time Processing:

   a. Processed incoming network events in batches of 10,000, applying preprocessing (normalization, UMAP transformation) and anomaly scoring with sub-second latency

   b. Integrated with the SOC's Splunk platform, sending high-priority alerts for anomalies with scores above the 95th percentile

3. Handling Data Drift:

   a. Monitored feature distributions (for example, packet size, login frequency) weekly using Kolmogorov-Smirnov tests to detect shifts in network behavior

   b. Retrained the model monthly using an automated pipeline with MLflow and incorporated new data to adapt to evolving user patterns and attack methods

Challenges and Solutions

The model deployment effort faced the following solutions, which were effectively handled by the team:

- **Stakeholder Skepticism**: SOC analysts were initially skeptical of unsupervised methods due to the lack of labeled outcomes. The team mitigated this by providing UMAP visualizations, anomaly score histograms, and workshops explaining the probabilistic nature of isolation forests.
- **Alert Fatigue**: Early iterations flagged too many false positives, overwhelming analysts. The team reduced false positives by 20% through iterative tuning of the contamination parameter and prioritizing high-confidence anomalies for alerts.
- **Regulatory Compliance**: Network logs contained sensitive customer data, requiring compliance with GDPR and PCI-DSS. The team anonymized IPs and user IDs during preprocessing using SHA-256 hashing and conducted quarterly audits to ensure compliance.

Business Impact

Major business impact of the use of anomaly detection models included the following features:

- **Threat Detection**: Within nine months, the model identified several novel intrusions, including a zero-day malware attack, preventing estimated losses of $2 million.

- **Operational Efficiency**: False positive reduction improved analyst efficiency, thereby reducing alert triage time by 25%.
- **Compliance**: Anonymization and audits ensured adherence to data privacy regulations, hence avoiding potential fines.

Key Lessons

The important lessons learned during this deployment included:

- **Balancing Sensitivity**: Tuning the contamination parameter was critical to minimize false positives while detecting genuine threats.
- **Stakeholder Communication**: Clear visualizations and workshops bridged the gap between technical outputs and operational needs.
- **Hybrid Integration**: Combining unsupervised anomaly detection with supervised classifiers created a robust defense strategy.
- **Regulatory Alignment**: Proactive anonymization and audits ensured compliance in a sensitive domain.

This case study illustrates how isolation forests enabled real-time threat detection in a high-stakes cybersecurity environment, highlighting the importance of preprocessing, visualization, and integration with existing systems to deliver actionable insights.

Case Study 3: Market Basket Analysis in E-Commerce for Recommendations

A leading e-commerce platform, XYZ.com, aimed to enhance customer experience and increase sales by delivering personalized product recommendations. Processing millions of daily transactions, the platform sought to uncover patterns in customer purchasing behavior to suggest complementary products, such as batteries with electronics or socks with running shoes. Market basket analysis, an unsupervised learning technique, was employed to identify frequent item associations in transaction data, thus resulting in tailored recommendations without requiring labeled data in a dynamic retail environment.

Figure 11.3 shows the frequently bought together items–bread, butter, and eggs in a supermarket aisle:

Figure 11.3: *Supermarket aisles often Display Items Based on Market Basket Analysis*

Data Collection and Preprocessing

The data science team aggregated transaction data from the platform's databases, spanning one year and covering online purchases across multiple regions. The dataset included:

- **Transaction Items**: Products purchased in each order, identified by unique SKUs
- **Purchase Timestamps**: Date and time of transactions to capture temporal trends
- **Product Categories**: Hierarchical classifications (for example, electronics, apparel, home goods)
- **Customer Metadata**: Anonymized features such as region and purchase frequency, where available
- **Order IDs**: Unique identifiers linking items bought together in a single transaction

Preprocessing Steps

1. Data Cleaning:
    a. Removed incomplete transactions (less than 1% of the dataset), missing order IDs/ item details to ensure data integrity
    b. Filtered out low-frequency items (SKUs appearing in less than 0.01% of transactions) to reduce sparsity and computational load, thus retaining 50,000 high-demand products
    c. Handled missing product category data by imputing the most frequent category for the respective SKU based on historical patterns
2. Feature Engineering:
    a. Transformed transaction data into a binary item matrix, where rows represented orders and columns indicated the presence (1) or absence (0) of each product
    b. Created aggregated features, such as average items per order and category diversity (number of unique categories per transaction), to inform rule prioritization
3. Data Reduction:
    a. Grouped similar products (for example, different colors of the same shoe model) into parent SKUs to reduce dimensionality while preserving meaningful associations
    b. Applied stratified sampling by region to balance representation across markets, ensuring rules were not biased toward high-traffic areas

Data Summary

The final dataset comprised 100 million transactions involving 50,000 unique products from 10 million customers, with a sparse binary matrix of 50,000 columns. The team used Python's pandas and MLxtend libraries, which were executed on a distributed Apache Spark cluster, to handle the large-scale data efficiently.

Model Selection and Training

The team selected the **Apriori algorithm** for market basket analysis due to its interpretability, ability to generate actionable association rules, and compatibility with sparse transaction data. Alternatives like FP-Growth were considered but deemed less interpretable for business stakeholders, despite faster computation.

Model Training Process:

1. Parameter Tuning:

    a. Set a minimum support threshold of 0.001 (items appearing in at least 0.1% of transactions) to focus on frequent itemsets while managing computational complexity

    b. Configured a minimum confidence threshold of 0.5 to ensure rules were reliable, later adjusted to 0.6 for high-value product categories like electronics

    c. Applied a lift threshold of 1.5 to prioritize rules with stronger-than-expected associations, while filtering out trivial co-occurrences

2. Rule Generation:

    a. Generated frequent itemsets using Apriori, producing 10,000 itemsets with support above the threshold

    b. Derived 5,000 association rules (for example, **`{laptop} → {laptop bag}`**) after applying confidence and lift filters, ranked by lift for business relevance

3. Validation:

    a. Evaluated rule quality using metrics like conviction and leverage to assess rule strength beyond lift

    b. Conducted manual reviews with product managers to ensure rules aligned with domain knowledge, discarding rules involving unrelated items (for example, diapers and power tools)

Rule Interpretation

The Apriori algorithm produced actionable association rules as shown in *Table 11.3*:

Rule	Support	Confidence	Lift	Business Action
`{Laptop} → {Laptop Bag}`	0.005	0.65	2.1	Recommend laptop bags on laptop product pages
`{Running Shoes}→ {Athletic Socks}`	0.003	0.70	1.8	Bundle socks with running shoe purchases
`{Camera} → {Memory Card}`	0.002	0.60	2.5	Suggest memory cards during camera checkout
`{Coffee Maker} → {Coffee Filters}`	0.004	0.55	1.9	Cross-promote filters on coffee maker pages

Table 11.3: *Apriori Algorithm for Actionable Association Rules*

The team visualized rules using a network graph, with nodes representing products and edges indicating rule strength (weighted by lift) and created heatmaps of item co-occurrences to highlight popular itemsets. These visualizations were shared via a web-based dashboard to facilitate discussions with product managers.

Model Deployment

The following association rules were integrated into the platform's recommendation engine for real-time product suggestions:

1. Pipeline Design:
    a. Deployed rules via a REST API using FastAPI, hosted on an AWS ECS cluster with auto-scaling to handle peak traffic (for example, Black Friday)
    b. Used Docker containers to ensure consistency across development and production environments
    c. Cached frequent rules in Redis to reduce latency, enabling sub-100ms response times for recommendation queries
2. Real-Time Processing:
    a. Processed incoming transactions in micro-batches (10,000 orders per second), mapped items to rules, and served recommendations on product pages and checkout flows
    b. Personalized recommendations by filtering rules based on customer metadata (for example, region, purchase history, and so on)
3. Handling Rule Redundancy:
    a. Applied post-processing filters to eliminate redundant rules (for example, `{laptop, mouse} → {laptop bag}` if `{laptop} → {laptop bag}` had higher lift)
    b. Monitored rule performance using Click-Through Rates (CTR), while pruning low-performing rules weekly

Challenges and Solutions

Important challenges faced by the deployment team and the solutions used by them to overcome those challenges included:

- **Stakeholder Buy-in**: Product managers initially favored explicit feedback over unsupervised rules. The team addressed this with A/B tests, showing a 15% higher CTR for rule-based recommendations and visualizations demonstrating rule relevance.
- **Scalability**: High transaction volumes during peak periods strained

computational resources. The team optimized performance using Spark for rule generation and Redis for caching, achieving 99.99% uptime.

- **Dynamic Catalogs**: New products and seasonal trends caused rule obsolescence. The team scheduled monthly rule updates and monitored support metrics to detect shifts, retraining on new data as needed.
- **Ethical Concerns**: Aggressive recommendations led to customer fatigue or perceived manipulation. The team limited suggestions to three per page, disclosed "Recommended based on popular purchases," and allowed opt-out options.

Business Impact

The primary business impact of using market basket analysis included:

- **Sales Growth**: Rule-based recommendations increased average basket sizes by 10% and boosted overall sales by 8% within six months.
- **Customer Engagement**: Personalized suggestions improved CTR by 12% and reduced cart abandonment rates by 5%.
- **Operational Efficiency**: Automated rule updates and caching reduced computational costs by 30% compared to initial prototypes.

Key Lessons

Important lessons learnt during the model deployment included:

- **Business Alignment**: Collaboration with product teams ensured that rules translated into actionable strategies.
- **Scalability Optimization**: Distributed computing and caching were critical for handling high-traffic environments.
- **Ethical Balance**: Limiting suggestion frequency and ensuring transparency were critical to maintain customer trust.
- **Hybrid Approach**: Integrating association rules with collaborative filtering enhanced recommendation robustness.

This case study demonstrates how market basket analysis, powered by the Apriori algorithm, transformed transaction data into personalized recommendations, thus highlighting the importance of preprocessing, scalability, and ethical considerations in driving e-commerce growth.

Case Study 4: Supply Chain Optimization in Manufacturing

A global automotive manufacturer, ToToTa Ltd, aimed to optimize its supply chain to reduce inventory costs and enhance delivery efficiency across a network of over

500 suppliers. Facing fluctuating demand, varying lead times, and diverse product requirements, the company sought to identify patterns in supplier performance and demand to streamline operations. Unsupervised learning, specifically clustering, was employed to group suppliers and parts based on shared characteristics, enabling data-driven inventory management and logistics planning without predefined categories in a complex industrial environment.

Figure 11.4 shows the typical steps in the supply chain in a typical industry, and which steps can be optimized using clustering techniques:

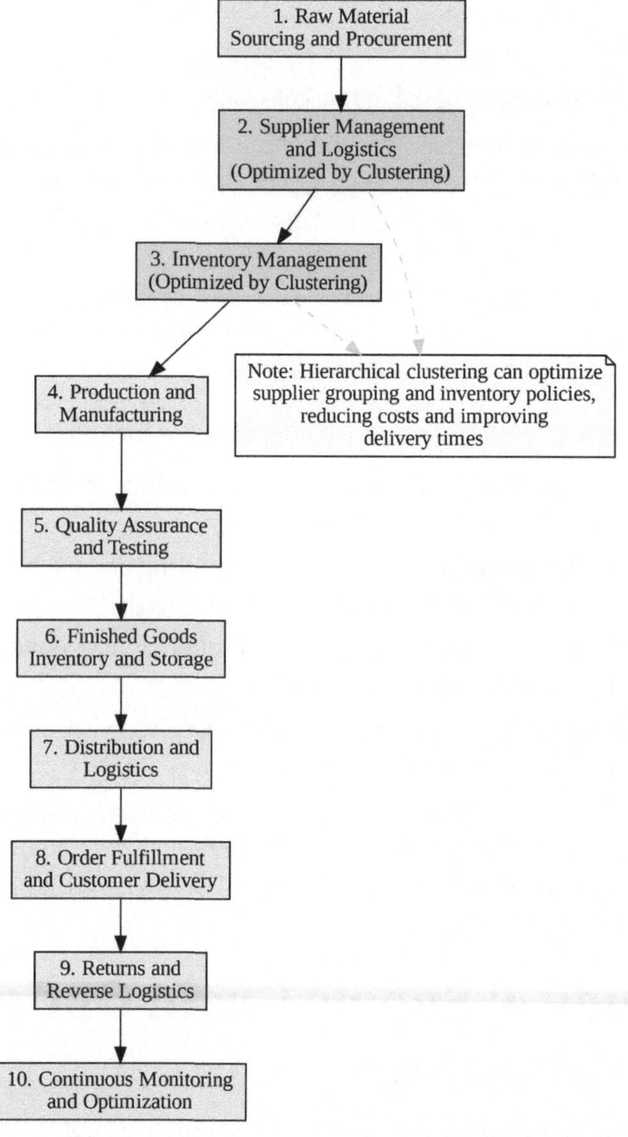

Figure 11.4: *Typical Steps in Supply Chain Management*

Data Collection and Preprocessing

The data science team aggregated supply chain data from multiple sources, including supplier contracts, logistics records, and demand forecasts, spanning two years. The dataset included:

- **Supplier Delivery Times**: Lead times and delivery reliability scores
- **Order Volumes**: Quantities ordered per part and supplier
- **Part Types**: Categories such as critical (for example, engines), standard (for example, bolts), or specialty (for example, custom electronics)
- **Historical Demand Patterns**: Monthly demand for each part, capturing seasonality and trends
- **Supplier Metadata**: Geographic location, contract duration, and quality ratings

Preprocessing Steps

1. Data Cleaning:
   a. Standardized inconsistent formats (for example, date formats, unit measurements) across regional systems to ensure uniformity
   b. Imputed missing delivery times (5% of records) using the median lead time for each supplier, which was validated against historical trends
   c. Removed outliers, such as erroneous delivery times exceeding 365 days, using the interquartile range (IQR) method
2. Feature Engineering:
   a. Created derived features, including demand volatility (standard deviation of monthly demand), delivery consistency (percentage of on-time deliveries), and part criticality score (based on production impact)
   b. Encoded categorical variables like part types using target encoding to reduce dimensionality while preserving relationships
3. Normalization and Scaling:
   a. Applied StandardScaler to numerical features (for example, order volumes, lead times) to ensure equal weighting in clustering
   b. Log-transformed skewed features like demand volumes to stabilize variance and improve cluster separation
4. Dimensionality Reduction:
   a. Used Principal Component Analysis (PCA) to reduce the feature space from 20 to 8 principal components, retaining 88% of variance to balance computational efficiency and information preservation

Data Summary

The final dataset comprised 2 million supply chain records for 10,000 unique parts from 500 suppliers, with 8 features after preprocessing. The team used Python's pandas, scikit-learn, and PySpark libraries on a cloud-based Databricks cluster to process the large-scale data efficiently.

Model Selection and Training

The team selected **hierarchical clustering** for its ability to reveal nested supplier relationships, handle mixed data types (numerical and categorical), and provide interpretable dendrograms for stakeholder communication. Alternatives like k-means were considered but discarded due to their assumption of spherical clusters, unsuitable for the complex, hierarchical nature of supply chain data.

Model Training Process

1. Distance Metric Selection:
    a. Chose the Ward linkage method with Euclidean distance for numerical features, combined with Gower's distance for mixed data types, to capture both minimize within-cluster variance and accommodating categorical variables.
    b. Experimented with Manhattan and cosine distances, but found Ward's method provided the best cluster cohesion based on silhouette scores
2. Cluster Determination:
    a. Generated a dendrogram to visualize hierarchical relationships and cut it at a height yielding five clusters after consultation with supply chain managers
    b. Validated cluster quality using silhouette scores (average 0.62) and Calinski-Harabasz index to ensure meaningful separation
3. Validation:
    a. Cross-referenced clusters with operational data (for example, supplier spend reports) to ensure alignment with known performance trends
    b. Conducted a sensitivity analysis to assess cluster stability by perturbing input features and confirming consistent groupings

Cluster Interpretation

The hierarchical clustering model identified five supplier groups as shown in *Table 11.4*:

Cluster	Characteristics	Actionable Strategy
High-Frequency Critical Parts Suppliers	High delivery reliability, low demand volatility, supply critical components (for example, engines)	Maintain high safety stock, prioritize premium logistics
Seasonal Bulk Suppliers	High-volume, seasonal orders, moderate reliability (for example, tires)	Use demand forecasts for just-in-time inventory
Low-Volume Specialty Suppliers	Low order frequency, high part cost, niche parts (for example, custom electronics)	Negotiate long-term contracts, minimal stock
Unreliable Late Deliverers	High lead time variance, frequent delays (for example, low-quality fasteners)	Supplier improvement plans, diversify sourcing
Stable Mid-Tier Suppliers	Consistent delivery, moderate volumes, standard parts (for example, bolts)	Standard inventory policies, bulk discounts

***Table 11.4**: Hierarchical Clustering to Identify Supplier Groups*

The team visualized clusters using a dendrogram to illustrate hierarchical relationships and a 2D PCA scatter plot to show cluster separation. Bar charts comparing delivery reliability and demand volatility across clusters were shared via a Power BI dashboard to facilitate discussions with supply chain managers.

Model Deployment

The clustering model was integrated into the company's Enterprise Resource Planning (ERP) system to support real-time supplier classification through the following steps:

1. Pipeline Design:

    a. Deployed the model via a REST API using Flask, which was hosted on an Azure Kubernetes Service (AKS) cluster with auto-scaling to handle global operations

    b. Used Docker containers to ensure consistency across development, testing, and production environments

    c. Stored cluster assignments in a PostgreSQL database, accessible to the ERP system for inventory and procurement decisions

2. Real-Time Processing:

    a. Processed new supplier data (for example, delivery records) in batches of 1,000, applying preprocessing (normalization, PCA transformation) and assigning clusters with sub-second latency

   b. Enabled dynamic supplier onboarding by classifying new suppliers based on initial metrics

3. Handling Dynamic Patterns:
   a. Monitored cluster stability using silhouette scores and feature distribution shifts (for example, lead time variance) biweekly via automated dashboards
   b. Retrained the model quarterly using an Airflow-orchestrated pipeline, incorporating updated demand and supplier data to adapt to market changes

Challenges and Solutions

The team faced the following challenges and handled them effectively:

- **Stakeholder Resistance**: Supply chain managers, who were accustomed to manual planning, initially distrusted automated clusters. The team conducted training sessions with dendrogram and profile visualizations, and ended up achieving 80% manager adoption after three months.
- **Dynamic Demand**: Market shifts (for example, semiconductor shortages) outdated clusters. The team implemented automated monitoring and retraining, and reduced misalignment by 90%.
- **Ethical Concerns**: Clustering exposed unreliable suppliers, risking contract terminations. The team used clusters to design improvement plans (for example, delivery schedule adjustments), thus preserving relationships and avoiding job losses.
- **Data Integration**: Legacy ERP systems had compatibility issues. The team used middleware to translate API outputs, ensuring seamless integration.

Business Impact

Important business impact of this supplier segmentation included:

- **Cost Savings**: Optimized inventory reduced holding costs by 15%, thus saving $5 million annually
- **Efficiency Gains**: Improved delivery times by 12%, thereby enhancing production schedules
- **Supplier Relations**: Improvement plans for unreliable suppliers increased delivery reliability by 20% within six months.

Key Lessons

Key lessons learnt during the deployment of the models were:

- **Operational Alignment**: Collaboration with managers ensured that clusters supported business objectives.

- **Continuous Maintenance**: Automated monitoring and retraining were critical for dynamic environments.
- **Stakeholder Engagement**: Clear visualizations and training bridged the gap between technical and operational teams.
- **Ethical Responsibility**: Using clusters for supplier improvement rather than penalties fostered collaboration.

This case study illustrates how hierarchical clustering transformed supply chain data into actionable insights, highlighting the importance of preprocessing, visualization, and ethical considerations in optimizing complex manufacturing operations.

Case Study 5: Patient Clustering for Personalized Treatment Plans in Healthcare

A leading healthcare provider, Care Clinik, sought to enhance patient outcomes by developing personalized treatment plans tailored to diverse medical profiles. Managing thousands of patients with complex datasets from Electronic Health Records (EHRs), lab results, and demographic information, the provider aimed to identify groups with similar health characteristics to guide customized care. Unsupervised learning, specifically clustering, was employed to uncover hidden patterns in patient data, enabling data-driven treatment strategies without relying on predefined disease categories in a sensitive healthcare environment. *Figure* 11.5 shows a possible set of patient categories with specific treatment needs.

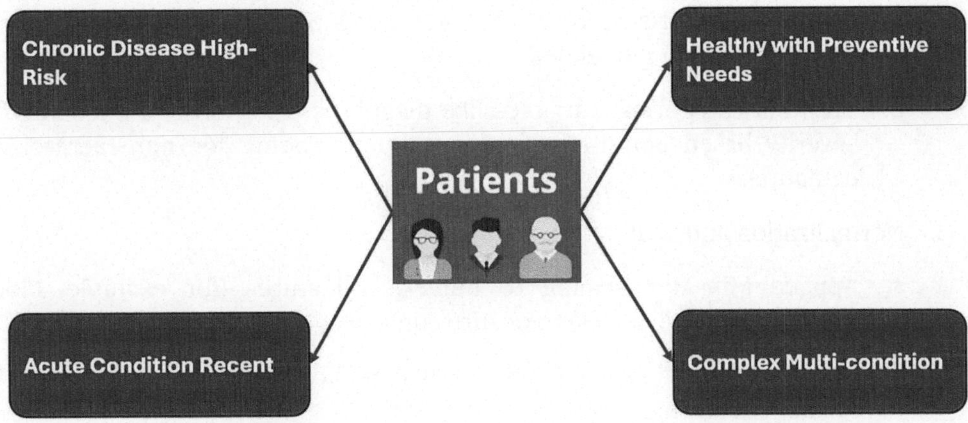

Figure 11.5: *Patient Segments with Specific Treatment Needs*

Data Collection and Preprocessing

The data science team aggregated EHR data spanning three years from the provider's centralized database, covering inpatient and outpatient records. The dataset included:

- **Vital Signs**: Blood pressure, heart rate, and Body Mass Index (BMI)
- **Diagnoses**: ICD-10 codes for conditions such as diabetes, hypertension, or asthma
- **Medication Histories**: Prescribed drugs, dosages, and adherence rates
- **Lab Results**: Blood glucose, cholesterol levels, and other biomarkers
- **Lifestyle and Demographic Factors**: Age, gender, smoking status, and anonymized socioeconomic indicators

Preprocessing Steps

1. Data Cleaning:
    a. Addressed missing lab results (10% of records) by imputing median values for numerical biomarkers (for example, cholesterol) within similar age and diagnosis groups, as validated by clinical experts
    b. Standardized ICD-10 codes to resolve inconsistencies across regional clinics, ensuring uniform diagnosis representation
    c. Removed outliers (for example, implausible heart rates above 200 bpm) using z-score thresholding (`z > 3`)
2. Feature Engineering:
    a. Created derived features, such as comorbidity count (number of concurrent diagnoses) and risk scores (weighted sums of vital signs and lab results based on clinical guidelines)
    b. Encoded categorical variables like diagnoses using ordinal encoding for severity-based conditions and one-hot encoding for non-hierarchical categories
3. Normalization and Scaling:
    a. Applied Min-Max scaling to numerical features (for example, blood pressure, glucose levels) to ensure equal weighting during clustering
    b. Log-transformed skewed features, like medication dosages to reduce the impact of extreme values

4. Dimensionality Reduction:
    a. Used Recursive Feature Elimination (RFE) with a random forest classifier to select the top 15 features from an initial set of 50, prioritizing those with high clinical relevance (for example, BMI, comorbidity count)
    b. Applied t-Distributed Stochastic Neighbor Embedding (t-SNE) to project data into two dimensions for visualization, preserving local structure

Data Summary

The final dataset comprised 500,000 patient records with 15 features after preprocessing, representing 100,000 unique patients. The team utilized Python's pandas, scikit-learn, and TensorFlow libraries on a HIPAA-compliant AWS cloud environment to process the sensitive data securely.

Model Selection and Training

The team selected **k-means clustering** for its scalability, interpretability, and ability to handle large patient datasets. Alternatives like DBSCAN were considered but rejected due to their sensitivity to noise in high-dimensional EHR data and computational complexity.

Model Training Process

1. Feature Selection:
    a. Prioritized features such as comorbidity count, blood glucose, and smoking status based on RFE results and clinical input to ensure medical relevance
    b. Visualized feature correlations using a heatmap to identify redundancies (for example, blood pressure and hypertension diagnosis), removing redundant features
2. Cluster Determination:
    a. Used the elbow method to plot Within-Cluster Sum of Squares (WCSS) against cluster counts (k from 2 to 10), identifying k=4 as optimal
    b. Validated cluster quality with silhouette scores (average 0.68) and clinical reviews to ensure groupings aligned with medical expectations
3. Validation:
    a. Conducted cross-validation by splitting the dataset into training and test sets, confirming stable cluster assignments across subsets

b. Collaborated with clinicians to map clusters to known patient archetypes, ensuring interpretability (for example, high-risk patients with multiple chronic conditions)

Cluster Interpretation

The k-means model identified four patient clusters as shown in *Table 11.5*:

Cluster	Characteristics	Treatment Strategy
Chronic Disease High-Risk	Multiple comorbidities (for example, diabetes, hypertension), elevated biomarkers	Intensive monitoring, multidisciplinary care
Acute Condition Recent	Recent diagnoses (for example, pneumonia), short-term medication use	Short-term treatment plans, follow-up care
Healthy with Preventive Needs	Normal vitals, minimal diagnoses, lifestyle risk factors (for example, smoking)	Preventive screenings, lifestyle interventions
Complex Multi-condition	Diverse diagnoses, inconsistent medication adherence	Coordinated care, adherence support programs

Table 11.5: *Patient Clusters for Effective Treatments*

The team visualized clusters using a t-SNE scatter plot to highlight separation and created parallel coordinate plots to compare feature distributions (for example, BMI, glucose levels) across clusters. These visualizations were integrated into a Tableau dashboard for clinician access, facilitating treatment planning.

Model Deployment

The clustering model was embedded into the hospital's EHR system for real-time patient classification:

1. Pipeline Design:

   a. Deployed the model via a REST API using FastAPI, which was hosted on a HIPAA-compliant AWS ECS cluster with encryption for data security

   b. Used Docker containers to ensure consistent performance across development and production environments

   c. Stored cluster assignments in a secure MongoDB database, integrated with the EHR system for seamless access

2. Real-Time Processing:

   a. Processed new patient records (for example, updated vitals, diagnoses) in batches of 1,000, applying preprocessing (normalization, feature selection) and assigning clusters with sub-200ms latency

   b. Enabled real-time classification for incoming patients during admissions or outpatient visits

3. Handling Dynamic Data:

   a. Monitored cluster stability using silhouette scores and feature distribution shifts (for example, glucose trends) weekly via automated dashboards

   b. Retrained the model quarterly using an MLflow-orchestrated pipeline, incorporating new patient data to adapt to evolving health profiles

Challenges and Solutions

The team faced critical challenges during the deployment and came out with effective solutions:

- **Clinician Resistance**: Physicians were skeptical of automated clusters due to their unsupervised nature. The team conducted training sessions with t-SNE visualizations and case studies, achieving 85% clinician adoption after six months.
- **Data Privacy**: HIPAA compliance requires strict data handling. The team anonymized patient IDs using UUID hashing, encrypted data in transit and at rest, and conducted monthly audits.
- **Bias Mitigation**: Initial clusters underrepresented minority groups due to imbalanced data. The team applied stratified sampling by demographics and audited cluster fairness using demographic parity metrics.
- **Dynamic Profiles**: New diagnoses and seasonal health trends (for example, flu season), outdated clusters. Automated monitoring and retraining reduced misalignment by 95%.

Business Impact

The overall business impact of this deployment included the following important factors:

- **Reduced Readmissions**: Personalized treatment plans decreased hospital readmissions by 10%, saving $3 million annually.
- **Improved Satisfaction**: Patient satisfaction scores rose by 15% due to tailored care and preventive interventions.
- **Operational Efficiency**: Streamlined care coordination for complex patients reduced consultation times by 20%.

Key Lessons

Key lessons learnt during this deployment included:

- **Clinical Alignment**: Collaboration with physicians ensured clusters supported actionable treatment plans.
- **Privacy and Fairness**: Robust anonymization and bias audits were critical for regulatory compliance and equitable care.
- **Stakeholder Trust**: Visualizations and training bridged the gap between technical outputs and clinical adoption.
- **Continuous Adaptation**: Automated monitoring and retraining maintained model relevance in dynamic healthcare settings.

This case study demonstrates how k-means clustering transformed complex patient data into personalized treatment strategies, highlighting the importance of preprocessing, privacy, and stakeholder engagement in delivering impactful healthcare solutions.

Best Practices for Unsupervised Learning Projects

Unsupervised learning projects require careful planning and execution to translate complex data patterns into meaningful business outcomes. Whether segmenting customers in retail, detecting anomalies in cybersecurity, or optimizing supply chains in manufacturing, success hinges on aligning technical efforts with practical goals. Drawing on lessons from the real-world applications and concepts we learned in this book, we next outline best practices for managing unsupervised learning projects effectively. These strategies focus on defining objectives, collaborating with stakeholders, and ensuring iterative improvement, which will equip you to navigate the unique challenges of unsupervised learning in diverse domains.

- **Define Clear Business Objectives**: Begin by anchoring the project in a well-defined business problem. Engage stakeholders to clarify goals, such as improving sales, reducing costs, or enhancing customer satisfaction. Translate these into measurable outcomes (for example, percentage increase in revenue or reduced downtime) to guide model development and evaluation. Avoid vague objectives like "find patterns," as they can lead to misaligned results.
- **Collaborate with Domain Experts and Stakeholders**: Unsupervised learning outputs, such as clusters or anomalies, often require interpretation to be actionable. The retail case study showed how data scientists worked with marketing teams to translate customer segments into campaigns. Involve domain experts early to validate data assumptions and interpret results. Conduct workshops or use visualizations (for example, scatter plots, word

clouds) to bridge technical and non-technical perspectives, fostering trust and alignment.

- **Prioritize Data Quality and Preprocessing**: High-quality data is critical, as poor inputs can lead to misleading patterns. Apply techniques like handling missing values or standardizing features, but tailor them to the project's context. Regularly audit data for biases to ensure ethical and reliable outcomes.
- **Choose Models with Business Context in Mind**: Select algorithms based on project requirements, not just technical performance. The cybersecurity case study chose isolation forests for real-time scalability, while the manufacturing case study used hierarchical clustering for interpretable supplier relationships. Balance complexity with practicality and steer clear of overly sophisticated models that stakeholders may not trust. Validate model choices with pilot tests to ensure alignment with operational needs.
- **Design Scalable and Robust Deployment Pipelines**: Deployment is critical for real-world impact. Use containerization (for example, Docker) for consistency and implement monitoring to detect data drift. Plan for scalability to handle large or dynamic datasets.
- **Iterate and Validate Continuously**: Unsupervised learning models require ongoing refinement, as static patterns may become outdated. Use business metrics (for example, sales uplift, cost savings) and stakeholder feedback to validate results. Iterate based on real-world performance, ensuring that models remain relevant and effective.
- **Communicate Results Effectively**: Clear communication is essential to overcome skepticism about unsupervised methods. Present results in intuitive formats like visualizations or dashboards. Tailor outputs to stakeholder needs and avoid jargon to ensure accessibility.
- **Address Ethical Considerations**: Unsupervised learning can inadvertently amplify biases or raise privacy concerns. Incorporate fairness checks and comply with regulations (for example, GDPR, HIPAA. Engage stakeholders to balance business goals with ethical responsibilities.

These best practices form a framework for success: start with clear objectives, collaborate across teams, ensure data quality, choose appropriate models, deploy robustly, iterate continuously, communicate clearly, and prioritize ethics. By applying these strategies, you can transform unsupervised learning from an exploratory tool into a strategic asset and drive considerable impact in retail, healthcare, energy, and beyond.

Common Pitfalls in Real-World Applications and Mitigation Strategies

Unsupervised learning is a powerful tool for uncovering hidden patterns, but it comes with unique challenges that can derail success if not addressed promptly. From misinterpreting clusters to neglecting data drift, these pitfalls can undermine the effectiveness of models in real-world settings. Drawing on lessons from various industries and domains such as retail, cybersecurity, e-commerce, manufacturing, healthcare, energy, and NLP applications, this section highlights common pitfalls and provides practical strategies to avoid them, further ensuring that your unsupervised learning projects deliver meaningful impact.

- **Misinterpreting Model Outputs:** Unsupervised learning results like clusters or anomalies lack explicit labels, which often leads to misinterpretation. Involve domain experts early on to validate outputs, as seen in the healthcare case study, where clinicians guided patient cluster interpretations. Use visualizations such as scatter plots or word clouds and conduct iterative feedback sessions to align results with business needs.
- **Poor Data Quality:** Low-quality or biased data can produce misleading patterns. Apply robust preprocessing techniques such as handling missing values and auditing for bias. Regularly validate data with stakeholders to ensure reliability and fairness.
- **Over-Reliance on Automation:** Treating unsupervised models as "set-and-forget" solutions can lead to outdated results. Implement continuous monitoring and periodic retraining to address data drift. Schedule regular model updates to maintain relevance.
- **Stakeholder Skepticism:** Non-technical stakeholders may distrust unsupervised outputs due to their probabilistic nature. Mitigate this by presenting clear, intuitive outputs, such as dashboards or summaries. Conduct workshops and pilot tests to demonstrate value and build trust.
- **Ignoring Scalability and Deployment Challenges**: Failing to plan for production environments can hinder impact. Design scalable pipelines using tools such as containerization or APIs. Test deployment under realistic conditions to ensure performance.
- **Neglecting Ethical Considerations:** Unsupervised learning can amplify biases or raise privacy concerns. Conduct fairness audits, as in the retail case study's bias checks, and comply with regulations such as GDPR or HIPAA. Engage stakeholders to balance business goals with ethical responsibilities.

Thus, by anticipating pitfalls like misinterpretation, poor data quality, over-automation, stakeholder skepticism, deployment issues, and ethical concerns, you can steer unsupervised learning projects toward success. These case study-grounded strategies emphasize collaboration, robust design, and ethical awareness to ensure that your models deliver reliable, impactful results in real-world scenarios.

Ethical Considerations in Unsupervised Learning

The ability of unsupervised learning to uncover hidden patterns in data brings powerful opportunities, but also significant ethical responsibilities. Without predefined labels, models can inadvertently amplify biases, compromise privacy, or produce opaque results that erode stakeholder trust. From biased customer segments in retail to sensitive data handling in healthcare, ethical challenges are pervasive in real-world applications. In this section, we discuss important ethical considerations and offer strategies to ensure your unsupervised learning projects are fair, responsible, and trustworthy.

- **Mitigating Bias in Model Outputs:** Unsupervised learning models can reflect or amplify biases present in data, leading to unfair outcomes. Involve diverse stakeholders to validate outputs, use metrics like demographic parity to assess fairness and ensure equitable results.
- **Protecting Data Privacy:** Unsupervised learning often involves sensitive data, raising privacy concerns. Implement robust data anonymization techniques and secure data pipelines. Regularly audit compliance with regulations and limit data access to authorized personnel to safeguard privacy.
- **Ensuring Transparency and Interpretability:** Unsupervised models can appear as "black boxes," reducing trust among stakeholders. Provide interpretable outputs like visualizations, document model assumptions and limitations, and engage stakeholders through workshops to build trust and clarity.
- **Balancing Business Goals with Ethical Responsibility:** Aggressive use of unsupervised learning can prioritize business outcomes over ethical concerns. Adopt a balanced approach by setting ethical boundaries, such as limiting recommendation frequency in e-commerce or using supplier clusters for improvement plans, rather than terminations in manufacturing. Engage stakeholders to align models with ethical priorities, ensuring outcomes benefit both businesses and users.
- **Continuous Ethical Monitoring:** Ethical challenges evolve as data and contexts change. Implement ongoing audits to detect emerging biases or privacy risks. Establish feedback loops with stakeholders to address ethical concerns iteratively and ensure that models remain responsible throughout their lifecycle.

Hence, by addressing bias, privacy, transparency, and ethical balance, unsupervised learning projects can deliver impactful results while upholding responsibility. These strategies empower you to navigate ethical complexities, while ensuring that your models are not only effective, but are also fair and trustworthy in real-world scenarios.

Integrating Unsupervised Learning with Broader AI Systems

Unsupervised learning excels at uncovering hidden patterns in data, but its true power emerges when it is integrated with broader AI systems like supervised learning, rule-based systems or recommendation engines. From enhancing cybersecurity defenses to refining e-commerce recommendations, combining unsupervised learning with other AI tools creates robust, hybrid solutions that address complex real-world problems. In this section, we will explore strategies for effective integration and provide practical guidance to ensure seamless collaboration between systems, maximizing business impact.

- **Combining Unsupervised and Supervised Learning:** Unsupervised learning can enhance supervised models by providing initial insights or features. To integrate them effectively, use unsupervised outputs (for example, clusters, anomalies) as features or triggers for supervised models and ensure that data pipelines align formats and scales.
- **Integrating with Rule-Based Systems:** Unsupervised learning can augment traditional rule-based systems by identifying patterns beyond predefined rules. Ensure compatibility by mapping unsupervised outputs to rule-based triggers, using clear thresholds or mappings, and validating with stakeholders.
- **Enhancing Recommendation Engines:** Unsupervised learning can enrich recommendation systems. To integrate, blend unsupervised outputs (for example, association rules, text clusters) with user behavior data, ensuring real-time compatibility via APIs. Test hybrid recommendations through A/B testing to validate impact.
- **Addressing Integration Challenges:** Integrating unsupervised learning with other systems often faces challenges like data incompatibility or performance bottlenecks. Use standardized data formats, optimized inference. Use modular architectures (for example, containerization) and robust APIs to ensure seamless data flow and conduct pilot tests to identify bottlenecks early on.
- **Ensuring Stakeholder Alignment:** Successful integration requires collaboration with teams managing other AI systems. Engage stakeholders early to define integration requirements and provide clear documentation and visualizations to facilitate adoption.

- **Monitoring and Iterating Hybrid Systems:** Integrated systems require ongoing maintenance to remain effective. Implement monitoring pipelines to track system performance and data drift and schedule regular updates to maintain alignment between unsupervised and other AI components.

By integrating unsupervised learning with broader AI systems, you can create powerful, hybrid solutions that amplify impact. These strategies like combining with supervised models, enhancing rule-based systems, enriching recommendations, addressing technical challenges, aligning with stakeholders, and continuous monitoring, ensure that unsupervised learning complements existing tools, delivering robust outcomes in diverse applications.

Future Trends and Emerging Applications

As unsupervised learning continues to evolve, new techniques and applications are reshaping industries, building on the real-world successes seen in our case studies. From retail segmentation to healthcare clustering, unsupervised learning has proven its value in uncovering hidden patterns, and emerging trends promise to expand its impact further. In this section, we will discuss the key developments in unsupervised learning, like self-supervised learning, multimodal generative models, and applications in IoT and personalized medicine, while highlighting their potential and the skills you should develop to stay ahead.

- **Self-Supervised Learning:** Self-supervised learning, which leverages unlabeled data to create supervisory signals, is gaining traction for its ability to reduce reliance on labeled datasets. Self-supervised approaches generate embeddings from raw data, as seen in recent advancements in natural language models. These techniques enhance applications by improving feature extraction from data. You should learn self-supervised learning by developing skills in frameworks such as PyTorch or TensorFlow, and exploring self-supervised methods like contrastive learning.
- **Multimodal Generative Models:** Multimodal models, combining text, images, or other data types, are emerging as powerful tools for unsupervised learning. For example, clustering user posts with both text and visuals could uncover nuanced consumer preferences. These models build on dimensionality reduction techniques but require handling complex data interactions. Gain expertise in multimodal architectures like variational autoencoders to leverage these opportunities of working with multimodal generative AI models.
- **IoT and Real-Time Applications:** The Internet of Things (IoT) is driving demand for unsupervised learning in real-time settings. Future applications include clustering IoT sensor data for smart city traffic management or detecting anomalies in manufacturing equipment beyond the supply chain case study's scope. These require scalable, edge-based deployments. Master

edge computing and real-time data processing to capitalize on IoT's growth, focusing on lightweight models for resource-constrained environments.

- **Personalized Medicine and Healthcare:** Unsupervised learning is advancing personalized medicine by identifying novel disease patterns or treatment responses. For instance, clustering genomic and clinical data could uncover new patient subgroups. These applications demand robust data privacy measures. Develop skills in bioinformatics and privacy-preserving techniques, like federated learning, to contribute to this field.
- **Hybrid AI Systems:** Future trends point to tighter integration of ML approaches such as combining clustering with reinforcement learning for dynamic pricing in retail. These hybrid systems require seamless data pipelines and stakeholder collaboration.

Conclusion

In this final chapter, we covered the case studies illustrating the power of unsupervised learning through diverse case studies in retail, cybersecurity, e-commerce, manufacturing, and healthcare, demonstrating its ability to uncover hidden patterns in complex, unlabeled datasets. From customer segmentation to anomaly detection, market basket analysis, supply chain optimization, and patient clustering, these applications highlight the versatility of unsupervised techniques in driving strategic outcomes. The discussed best practices emphasize robust preprocessing, thoughtful model selection, and scalable deployment, while addressing common pitfalls such as data drift and stakeholder skepticism through continuous monitoring and clear communication. Ethical considerations, such as mitigating bias and ensuring data privacy, underscore the need for responsible AI practices. Therefore, by integrating unsupervised learning with broader AI systems, organizations can enhance decision-making, as seen in hybrid approaches combining clustering with supervised models. Looking ahead, emerging trends like automated feature discovery and real-time adaptive learning promise to further expand the impact of unsupervised learning, positioning it as a vital tool for innovative, data-driven solutions in an ever-evolving landscape.

As we conclude *Kickstart Unsupervised Machine Learning Fundamentals*, this book has well-equipped you with the foundational knowledge, practical tools, and forward-thinking insights to harness unsupervised learning's potential, empowering you to transform raw data into innovative solutions in an ever-evolving, data-driven world.

Key Terms

- **K-Means Clustering:** A partitioning algorithm that groups data points into a predefined number of clusters (k) by minimizing the within-cluster variance;

used in customer segmentation and healthcare case studies to identify distinct customer or patient groups

- **Isolation Forests:** An anomaly detection algorithm that isolates outliers by constructing random decision trees; applied in the cybersecurity case study to detect unusual network traffic patterns efficiently in high-dimensional data
- **Customer Segmentation:** The process of dividing customers into distinct groups based on shared characteristics, such as purchasing behavior, using unsupervised learning techniques like k-means clustering, as demonstrated in the retail case study, to enable personalized marketing
- **Hierarchical Clustering:** A clustering method that builds a hierarchy of clusters using a bottom-up (agglomerative) or top-down (divisive) approach; employed in the supply chain case study to group suppliers based on nested relationships
- **Data Drift:** The phenomenon where the statistical properties of input data change over time, posing a challenge in case studies such as customer segmentation and cybersecurity, mitigated through periodic model retraining and monitoring
- **Self-Supervised Learning:** An emerging unsupervised learning approach where models generate their own supervisory signals from unlabeled data; is a method to enhance feature discovery and adaptability in applications
- **Personalized Treatment:** Tailoring medical care plans to individual patient profiles based on clustered health characteristics, achieved in the healthcare case study through k-means clustering to improve outcomes and reduce hospital readmissions
- **Ethical Bias:** The risk of unfair outcomes in unsupervised learning models due to imbalanced or skewed data, addressed in the healthcare case study by auditing clusters for fairness and ensuring equitable representation
- **Hybrid AI Systems:** The integration of unsupervised learning with other AI techniques, such as combining anomaly detection with supervised classifiers in cybersecurity or market basket analysis with collaborative filtering in e-commerce, to enhance performance
- **Automated Feature Discovery:** An emerging trend in unsupervised learning that leverages deep learning to automatically identify relevant features from raw data

Questions

1. Describe how the global retailer in the customer segmentation case study used k-means clustering to enhance personalized marketing campaigns, including

the preprocessing steps, model deployment challenges, and the resulting business impact.

2. Explain the role of isolation forests in the cybersecurity case study for detecting anomalies in network traffic. Discuss how the data science team addressed stakeholder skepticism and ensured compliance with data privacy regulations.

3. In the e-commerce market basket analysis case study, discuss how the Apriori algorithm was applied to generate actionable product recommendation rules. Highlight the strategies used to manage rule redundancy and maintain customer trust.

4. Elaborate on the application of hierarchical clustering in the supply chain optimization case study for grouping suppliers. Describe how the team validated the clusters and translated them into actionable inventory strategies.

5. In the healthcare patient clustering case study, discuss how k-means clustering was used to develop personalized treatment plans. Explain the measures taken to address HIPAA compliance and mitigate potential biases in the clusters.

6. Outline the key best practices for unsupervised learning projects, focusing on preprocessing, model selection, and stakeholder collaboration. Provide examples from the case studies to illustrate these practices.

7. Identify and describe two common pitfalls in real-world unsupervised learning applications. Explain the mitigation strategies used in the case studies to overcome these challenges.

8. Discuss the ethical considerations for unsupervised learning, particularly in sensitive domains such as healthcare and supply chain management. Provide specific examples of how these concerns were addressed in the case studies.

9. Explain how unsupervised learning was integrated with broader AI systems in the case studies, such as combining anomaly detection with supervised classifiers in cybersecurity or market basket analysis with collaborative filtering in e-commerce.

10. Describe the future trends and emerging applications of unsupervised learning. Discuss how technologies such as automated feature discovery or real-time adaptive learning could enhance the impact of unsupervised learning in domains like those covered in the case studies.

Multiple Choice Questions

1. In the customer segmentation case study for a global retailer, what was the primary goal of using k-means clustering?
   a. Predict customer churn rates
   b. Identify patterns in purchasing behavior for personalized marketing
   c. Detect fraudulent transactions in real-time
   d. Optimize product pricing strategies
2. Which algorithm was chosen for anomaly detection in the cybersecurity case study due to its efficiency in high-dimensional data and scalability?
   a. K-means clustering
   b. Apriori algorithm
   c. Isolation forests
   d. Hierarchical clustering
3. In the e-commerce market basket analysis case study, what was a key challenge faced during model deployment?
   a. Lack of sufficient transaction data
   b. Managing rule redundancy in recommendations
   c. Inability to integrate with the ERP system
   d. High false positive rates in product suggestions
4. Which clustering algorithm was used in the supply chain optimization case study for its ability to reveal nested supplier relationships?
   a. K-means clustering
   b. DBSCAN
   c. Hierarchical clustering
   d. Gaussian mixture models

5. In the healthcare patient clustering case study, which regulatory compliance challenge was addressed to protect patient data?
   a. GDPR compliance for European customers
   b. HIPAA compliance for EHR data
   c. PCI-DSS compliance for payment data
   d. CCPA compliance for consumer privacy
6. According to the best practices, what is a critical step in preprocessing for unsupervised learning projects?
   a. Normalizing features to ensure equal weighting
   b. Labeling data with predefined categories
   c. Using raw data without cleaning to preserve information
   d. Reducing dataset size by random sampling
7. What is a common pitfall in unsupervised learning applications, as discussed in the case study, and how was it mitigated in the case study?
   a. Overfitting: Using cross-validation techniques
   b. Stakeholder skepticism: Providing clear visualizations and A/B testing
   c. Insufficient computational power: Relying on edge devices
   d. Data scarcity: Collecting more labeled data
8. Which ethical consideration was emphasized in the healthcare case study to ensure fairness?
   a. Ensuring high model accuracy for all predictions
   b. Maximizing hospital revenue through clustering
   c. Auditing clusters for potential bias against minority groups
   d. Reducing the number of features to simplify models
9. How was unsupervised learning integrated with broader AI systems in the cybersecurity case study?
   a. By replacing all supervised models with unsupervised ones
   b. By using anomalies to trigger deeper analysis by rule-based systems
   c. By eliminating the need for real-time monitoring
   d. By focusing only on static network configurations

10. What future trend in unsupervised learning is expected to enhance its applicability?

    a. Increased reliance on manual feature engineering

    b. Exclusive use of labeled data for validation

    c. Decreased focus on real-time applications

    d. Automated feature discovery through deep learning

Answers

1. b
2. c
3. b
4. c
5. b
6. a
7. b
8. c
9. b
10. d

Index

B

F

G

H

M

N

O

P

T

U

V

W